D1226931

MATERIALS
IN
INDUSTRY

Hot cells and remote control manipulators for handling radioactive materials at the Whiteshell Nuclear Research Establishment, Pinawa, Canada. The chemical apparatus on the left analyzes the gaseous products of nuclear fission.

Prentice-Hall, Inc.   Englewood Cliffs, New Jersey

W. J. PATTON

Department of Mechanical Technology
Manitoba Institute of Technology

MATERIALS
IN
INDUSTRY   [1968]

*TA403
.P32

Cover photograph shows a spot weld joining two sheets of
24-gauge mild steel

All rights reserved. No part of this
book may be reproduced in any
form or by any means without permis-
sion in writing from the publisher.

Library of Congress Catalog
Card Number 68—11939
Printed in the United States of America
Current printing (last digit):
10 9 8 7 6 5 4 3 2 1

PRENTICE-HALL INTERNATIONAL, INC., *London*
PRENTICE-HALL OF AUSTRALIA, PTY. LTD., *Sydney*
PRENTICE-HALL OF CANADA, LTD., *Toronto*
PRENTICE-HALL OF INDIA PRIVATE LTD., *New Delhi*
PRENTICE-HALL OF JAPAN, INC., *Tokyo*

© 1968 by Prentice-Hall, Inc., Englewood Cliffs, New Jersey

This Book is Dedicated to
The Lowly Firebrick,
unglamorous and expendable,
containing the fires where the basic materials are born;

and to
The Tool Steels,
the aristocrats among materials,
which give other materials their shape.

The Eskimo civilization, now largely defunct, suffered from a dearth of raw materials but showed a remarkable ability in the application of what they had. Western culture can match the Eskimo in his creativeness in materials technology, even if allowance is made for our much wider range of materials. Such inventions as tonnage steel, paper from wood, the rubber O-ring, pressure-sensitive tape, polyethylene, the transistor, the laser, and even the modern automobile, are towering achievements in materials science. The automobile may seem inappropriate to this list, yet in fact all the resources of materials science and its most sophisticated laboratory methods are applied to the selection of materials for automobile components—the automobile cannot be denied its place among these great achievements.

While materials engineering has increased greatly in stature in recent years, there still seem to be many contrasting points of view regarding its usefulness. For some mechanical engineers, materials science is often viewed as metallurgy, too narrow a view for the vast field of mechanical engineering. A few electronics engineers believe that materials science has little bearing on their specialty, an opinion greatly at variance with the requirements of their own industry. But in the industries with which the author is associated, an exhaustive knowledge of all types of materials is a prerequisite to successful problem-solving and decision-making.

A scientist's function is the generation of fundamental knowledge under certain traditional restraints of methodology preeminently suited to the physical sciences. The function of the engineer or technologist is to put knowledge to economic use, and the successful execution of this function

AUTHOR'S
REMARKS

demands ability both in fundamental science and in creative application or "art". The author hopes that in this book he has conveyed some intimation of how fundamental science is converted into engineering practice in materials. Successfully or unsuccessfully, he has tried to write a thorough book on materials, suited to the requirements of the undergraduate engineer and technologist and spanning both the science and the application of materials. The book is not written for any engineering specialty. The field of materials is so vast that it was thought best to present certain points of view to the reader that will enable him to assess the limitations, importance, and potential of materials. Materials dictate the very nature of our technical culture, just as they did for that of the Eskimo's. To know how the inevitable limitations of materials are either overcome or simply tolerated; to know the critical dependence of materials manufacture and use on both the refractory materials and the many tooling materials; and to know how properties of materials influence their conversion into finished products—these are all important. And it is especially important for the young engineer that he refrain from categorizing a material or a material property as, for example, nuclear, electronic, or mechanical. Electrical and electronic properties of materials are vital in mechanical applications; mechanical properties are equally vital to electrical and electronic applications. The nuclear, X-ray, ultrasonic, and photoelectric properties are too fundamental to be dismissed as of specialized interest only.

A perusal of the Contents will suggest the structure of this book. Some of the basic concepts of materials science are presented first. The second section of the book has for its subject air, water, and the ceramic materials, which are designated "natural materials", and perhaps most of them may be so viewed. The place of the ceramic materials in our technology seems generally not to be well understood. It is hoped that the treatment here overcomes any such deficiencies. Metals occupy the third section, and most of the metals are at least mentioned. The number of pure metals is fixed: students of materials science should be made aware of all of them.

Part Four presents the organic materials, which are a problem in a materials book such as this one. The carbon atom is too versatile, and organic materials multiply like rabbits. Finally, Part Five examines the testing and processing of materials. Emphasis is given primarily to the more modern and sophisticated testing and analytical methods. For the more routine testing methods, there are the several volumes of the American Society for Testing and Materials (ASTM) standards to consult. In dealing with the processing of materials, only scant attention is paid to processing methods; instead, the influence of material characteristics on the processing method is examined.

Today materials constitute much more than a mighty technology. They are a culture and a history. It would surely be a matter of regret if their wonderful culture and history were completely ignored. Therefore the reader will find occasional reference to, for example, the pottery of the Sung dynasty, the significance of materials problems in World War II, and opinions of architects on the employment of materials.

Acknowledgments are a difficulty. Most of what any man knows has been given to him by others. But a special indebtedness must be expressed to the American Society for Metals and its members, and those experts in materials, the personnel of Bristol Aerospace Limited, of Winnipeg. The author recognizes his continuing debt to his best teachers, who have been his subordinates and students through the years. These people have taught him much while slowly burying him in materials data, much of which has been included in this book.

W. J. P.

CONTENTS

350 *ADHESIVES AND SURFACE FINISHES* **15**

376 *FUELS AND RADIOACTIVE MATERIALS* **16**

Part **V** **THE PROCESSING OF MATERIALS**

17 **ANALYSIS AND TESTING 397**

18 **ECONOMIC CHARACTERISTICS OF MATERIALS 420**

19 **SEMIFINISHED PRODUCTS 424**

MATERIALS
SCIENCE

Part █

Sometime within the next thirty or forty million years, the Earth, the planet that is mankind's present habitation, will celebrate its four billionth birthday. The method of determining the age of the earth (see Chapter 2) is an outstanding example of the techniques of Materials Technology. But the method was discovered late in the age of the earth, actually in the twentieth century.

The earth was created with a bountiful supply and range of raw materials to serve the needs of the human race that was to inhabit it so late in its history. Until about a hundred years ago, man used the earth's materials as he found them: either rock or clay dug from the earth's crust, or wood products from the earth's forested regions, or simply the water and air around him. A few more fortunate civilizations used a restricted range of metals in small quantities. But within the last hundred years, men have begun to synthesize and formulate secondary materials based on the primary resources of the earth. These synthetic materials grow rapidly more numerous as our materials technology and our solid state physics advance in knowledge and techniques, and include such indispensable materials as:

> beryllium copper for remarkable fatigue resistance
> stainless steels for vacuum chambers
> polyurethane rubber for press-forming of metals and for the tires of fork-lift trucks
> synthetic fire-resistant oils for the hydraulic fluid power systems of warships and hydraulic presses
> silicon carbide for grinding wheels
> hydrazine for rocket propellants
> plastics for packaging

MATERIALS
FOR A
TECHNICAL CIVILIZATION

1

semiconductor materials for transistors
epoxies for high-strength cements and repairs to concrete floors
zirconium alloys for nuclear fuel rods
leaded steels for fast machining
very low carbon steels for porcelain enamelling.

The materials in this list may appear to be special materials for special purposes. This is true, but our civilization has largely abandoned general-purpose materials and replaced them with special-purpose materials formulated exactly for the purpose intended. This statement is true even for supposedly general-purpose materials such as wood, portland cement, concrete, and structural steel — there are, for example, not less than 250 alloys of structural steel for buildings and structural work. Not even water is exempt from exact formulation. The use of raw water is a rarity: water is treated with chemicals, or deoxidized, or deionized, or desalted.

The rapid increase in the number and variety of industrial materials is explained in part by the increasing demands made upon these materials. A hundred years ago, metals were required to have only the properties of reasonable tensile strength, reasonable ductility, and sufficient softness for such machining operations as punching and drilling. Nowadays, if a new metal is offered to the market, a wider range of requirements is imposed, including such qualities as weldability, machinability, corrosion resistance, controlled grain size, close tolerance on dimensions, fatigue resistance, hot strength, suitability for low temperature operation, plasticity, vibrational damping capacity, suitable electrical and magnetic characteristics, low neutron absorption for nuclear work, low vapor pressure for aerospace applications, impact and wear resistance, and many more.

Fig. 1 A projection microscope for the microscopic examination and photography of materials. Material specimens are placed on the platform and their bottom surfaces examined in the viewer on the right-hand side.

The starting point for the synthesis of present-day materials is the supply of materials in the earth's crust, plus water and the earth's atmosphere. The following table gives the percentages of the principal elements in the earth's crust.

ELEMENTS OF THE EARTH'S CRUST

oxygen	46.5%	rubidium	0.03%
silicon	27.6%	strontium	0.03%
aluminum	8.13%	chromium	0.02%
iron	5.00%	carbon	0.009%
calcium	3.64%	nickel	0.008%
sodium	2.83%	copper	0.007%
potassium	2.59%	tin	0.004%
magnesium	2.09%	lead	0.0016%
titanium	0.44%	uranium	0.0004%
hydrogen	0.14%	silver	0.00001%
manganese	0.10%		

It is interesting to note that the first metals used by mankind were the rare metals — copper, tin, and lead. Iron, the second most abundant metal, on which our steel civilization is based, did not assume its dominant position until about 100 years ago. Aluminum, which is one-twelfth of every shovelful of clay, is really a twentieth-century metal. Magnesium, also a common metal, again is a metal of this century, and titanium, one two-hundredth of the earth's crust, is not yet twenty years old in its industrial applications. By and large, the most abundant metals were the last ones used, and this unusual twist of fate is explained by the difficulties of extracting these metals from their ores and refining them.

Special attention must be given to silicon (27.6 percent) and carbon (0.009 percent). These two nonmetallic elements lie in the same column of the Periodic Table, and therefore have similarities in their chemical behavior. Both elements may be used to synthesize very large molecules. Silicon is the basic element in such ceramic materials as quartz, mineral ores, glass, portland cement, silicon carbide, firebrick, building brick, and sand. Carbon is the basic element for a million organic materials, including automobile tires, antifreeze for engine radiators, fuels (including solid rocket fuels), anesthetics, drugs, dyes, soaps and detergents, paints and finishes, solvents, refrigerants, plastics, nylon, textiles, and graphite electrodes for welding and melting of metals.

The next table presents the elements in the Earth's atmosphere, expressed as volume percentages. Water vapor is omitted, since the amount of water vapor varies.

materials for a technical civilization

ELEMENTS IN THE EARTH'S ATMOSPHERE

nitrogen	78.03%	neon	0.00123%
oxygen	20.99%	helium	0.0004%
argon	0.94%	krypton	0.00005%
carbon dioxide	0.03%	xenon	0.000006%
hydrogen	0.01%		

On a weight basis, air analyzes 75.5 percent nitrogen, 23.2 percent oxygen, 1.33 percent argon. All the gases in the table have a variety of interesting and critically important uses in industry, especially in the fields of metal melting, welding, refrigeration, and gas-filled discharge tubes. These uses are discussed in Chapter 5.

Finally, it must be remarked that the salt water of the oceans is a prolific source of minerals and metals, as yet unexploited to any considerable degree. The major solid constituents of salt water are listed in the following table. Minor constituents, such as nickel and gold, are not given.

MAJOR SOLID CONSTITUENTS OF SEA WATER

NaCl	2.71%	$MgSO_4$	0.12%
$MgCl_2$	0.54%	$CaSO_4$	0.08%
KCl	0.04%	$CaCO_3$	0.01%
$MgBr_2$	0.01%		

Sodium chloride is occasionally extracted from sea water, though underground brines are a richer source of supply. The most important industrial products extracted from sea water, aside from animal products, are magnesium oxide for firebrick and the metal magnesium. A great many other materials will in the future be drawn from the vast storehouse represented by the oceanic areas of the earth.

Each of the 92 elements of the earth has its special characteristics, and all these characteristics have a use in industry. Tungsten is valued for its unusually high melting point, while bismuth is equally useful for its low melting point. Beryllium offers the advantage of low density, while lead is used for its high density. Hydrogen gas is a useful coolant because of its remarkably high specific heat. Oxygen is a magnetic gas. Nickel is magnetostrictive, that is, its dimensions change if its magnetic field strength is changed. Cesium has one electron in its outer electron shell and is therefore a suitable material for photocell cathodes. Argon does not dissolve in metals, an unusual characteristic for a gas. Whatever the special properties of an element or compound, our technical civilization can find a use for them.

materials for a technical civilization

But in the brilliant catalogue of successes produced by the men and women whose vocation is solid state physics and materials technology, there are of course a few failures to record — two important failures in particular. After much recent effort and cost, we find ourselves unable to produce a ductile ceramic material, and this is a major defeat. Perhaps an even more serious frustration is our inability to produce materials capable of extended operation at temperatures above 2000°F. This is one of our greatest technical handicaps. We can make materials with sufficiently high melting points — hafnium carbide, for example, melts at 7500°F — but for one reason or another, such as oxidation or loss of strength, none of these materials can be used at temperatures near their melting points. There is at the moment no prospect of overcoming these two technical deficiencies in the near future.

1.1 a convenient classification of solid materials

It is impossible to be conversant with the thousands of industrial materials unless one can be guided by some broad and simple generalizations. Such general rules will be set out in this book as they arise. Some of them will have no scientific validity, such as the division of all gases into ideal and imperfect gases in Chapter 5, where an ideal gas is one that obeys a simple formula while an imperfect gas is one that does not. All such general rules, too, will have their exceptions. Nothing more than convenience is argued for such generalizations.

Most of the industrial materials are solids. Here we can set out the first of our broad and somewhat unscientific generalizations: almost all solids are either *metals, ceramics,* or *organics.*

A *metal* is an elemental substance (not a chemical compound) which readily conducts both heat and electric current. All the 80 or so metals share these two characteristics, but almost no other characteristics, though most metals are hard, lustrous, and have a high modulus of elasticity (stiffness). Most metals also are ductile. Among the solid materials, metals predominate because of their useful characteristics of hardness, strength, rigidity, formability, machinability, conductivity, and dimensional stability.

Ceramic materials are rock or clay mineral materials. Familiar examples of ceramic materials are sand, glass, brick, cement, concrete, minerals, clay, grinding wheels, plaster, fiberglass insulation, spark plug bodies. Most ceramics occur naturally and are simply dug out of the ground with or without further processing. Such natural ceramic materials include the ores from which we extract all our metals. Besides these natural ceramics, an increasing number of synthetic ceramics are in use, such as silicon carbide, tungsten carbide, boron nitride. In general, the ceramic materials are silicates, oxides, carbides, nitrides, or borides. Though an interesting group of materials, the ordinary person views them as devoid of the glamor that surrounds the metals and the plastics. Their dominant characteristics are these:

1. they are rock-like in appearance
2. they are brittle
3. they are hard materials, and most may be used as abrasives
4. they are resistant to high temperatures
5. they do not conduct electric currents
6. they are not easily corroded
7. they are opaque to light

Archeologists designate the first ages of man as Stone Ages, that is, ceramic ages. The first use of metals, thousands of years before Christ, initiated the Metal Ages, which carry us historically to the present day. However, a materials engineer would probably incline to the view that the Metals Age effectively began either with the invention of the blast furnace about 600 years ago, or with the widespread use of steel, beginning in 1864 when the Bessemer converter first made steel in large quantities.

The *organic* materials are in general a development of the twentieth century. These are the countless synthetic or manufactured materials based chemically on carbon, and including the following:

plastics	textiles
rubbers	lubricants
paper	detergents
refrigerants	paints and finishes
fuels	foods, vitamins, and medicines
adhesives	explosives

The structural organic materials, which include the rubbers, plastics, and wood, have the following characteristics:

1. light weight: specific gravity approximately 1.0
2. poor conductors of heat and electric current
3. combustible
4. soft and ductile
5. not dimensionally stable
6. poor temperature resistance

The selection of a material for a specific application is invariably a thorough, lengthy, and expensive investigation. Almost always more than one material is suited to the application, and the final selection is a compromise that weighs the relative advantages and disadvantages. The varied requirements demanded of any material may however be reduced to three broad demands:

1. service requirements
2. fabrication requirements
3. economic requirements

The service requirements of course are paramount. The material *must* stand up to service demands. Such demands commonly include dimensional stability, corrosion resistance, adequate strength, hardness, toughness, heat resistance. In addition to any such basic requirements, other properties may be required, such as low electrical resistance, high or low heat conductivity, fatigue resistance, or others.

Fabrication requirements have tended to grow in importance. It must be possible to shape the material, and to join it to other materials. Primary shaping methods include casting or sintering: those materials which cannot be cast, such as tungsten, must be sintered to shape from powders. The cast or sintered shapes are then usually formed into semifinished shapes such as bars or sheets by processes such as rolling, extruding, or wire-drawing. Secondary industries, often called fabricators or converters, then modify these semifinished shapes by either of two methods: machining or forming. In machining, metal is removed by cutting it out as chips on such machines as machine tools, and grinders. This is an inefficient method of producing the final shape, so that wherever possible, machining is replaced by forming methods such as pressing, forging, swaging, or hot and cold heading. The final operation is joining: this may be done by fasteners, such as bolts, studs, and pins, or by welding, brazing, soldering, or cementing methods. Extra fabrication operations such as heat treatment may also be required. By and large, then, the assessment of fabrication requirements concerns questions of machinability, hardenability, heat-treatability, ductility, castability, and weldability, qualities which are sometimes quite difficult to assess.

Finally, there are the economic requirements. The standard of living of any nation can only be improved by producing goods at lower cost, and whether a country's economy be capitalist, socialist, or communist, cost factors are microscopically scrutinized. The objective is the *minimum overall cost* of the component to be made, and this objective is sometimes attained only by increasing one or more of the cost components. For exam-

Fig. 2   The terminal operation in materials technology: the disposal
of wastes. In order to design this incinerator furnace, the physical
properties of the refuse must be determined.

ple, a more expensive free-machining metal may be substituted for a standard
metal, since the savings in machining cost may overweigh the increased cost
of the more expensive metal.   Again, the substitution of a light metal, such
as aluminum, for a heavier metal such as steel, increases the raw material
cost but may result in substantial freight savings to the customer.

In a capitalist economy, a less tangible economic requirement is that
the product must sell under competitive market conditions.   To improve
the sales of the product, expensive stainless steel may be substituted for
cheaper painted steel, or vinyl-coated steel may be substituted for plain
steel — changes made to improve the market for the product, and which
at first thought may appear to be economically unwarranted.   This may be
a false conclusion, however.   The most important variable affecting costs
is not a technical one at all, but the marketing variable of volume.   Anything that cannot be sold in volume simply cannot be economically produced, and the materials man who feels that marketing problems are not
his concern is certainly unwise, knowledgeable though he may be in his
field.

materials for a technical civilization

2.1   the structure of the atom

The thirty or more fundamental particles of physics that explain matter and energy are distinguished by two types of electric charge: positive and negative. In addition, a number of particles, such as the neutron and the photon, have no electric charge associated with them. The fundamental unit of electric charge is the charge associated with an electron (or a proton). This small unit of charge may be explained in macroscopic terms by noting that the passage of 6.28×10^{18} electrons per second through an electric circuit would register exactly 1 ampere on an ammeter.

An atom of any element has the structure of a small nucleus of closely bound heavy particles, collectively called "nucleons", surrounded by a "cloud" of electrons. The nucleons are a mixture of uncharged neutrons and positively charged protons. The total mass of the nucleons is substantially the mass of the atom, since the electrons have little mass. However, the volume occupied by the atom is determined by the volume of the cloud of electrons surrounding the nucleus. The radius of a nucleus is of the order of 10^{-14} meters; the radius of an atom is about $1-2 \times 10^{-10}$ m.

In the nuclei of the lighter elements, the number of neutrons is generally equal to the number of protons. But in the heavier elements, lead, uranium, or thorium, for instance, this equal proportion of nuclear particles is not possible if the nucleus is to be stable: the presence of too many protons in the nucleus would produce repulsive forces due to like charges,

THE SCIENCE
OF
MATERIALS

2

such that the binding energy holding the nucleus together would be over-come. Therefore in the larger nuclei the number of neutral neutrons exceeds the number of protons, perhaps by as much as fifty percent.

The structure or arrangement of electrons in any atom is a highly complex subject which cannot be properly explained except in terms of the mathematical concepts of quantum mechanics. Since the purpose of this book is the broad subject of the selection ↑ ˙ service requirements of industrial materials, we can apply certain simplified concepts to this matter of electronic structure. Such concepts will not be scientifically exact, but we can take comfort in the thought that not even research physicists have worked out entirely satisfactory theories.

The energy quantities applicable to atomic energy levels are of course extremely minute when compared to the standard industrial energy units of Btu, horsepower, or watt. A more suitable energy unit for atomic purposes is the *electron-volt*, a unit with the additional virtue of being much easier to understand and use in computation than the larger units. The electron-volt, abbreviated "ev", is the energy acquired by an electron when accelerated across a 1-v drop. Thus if 300 v is applied between the cathode and the anode of a vacuum tube, an electron leaving the cathode will arrive at the positive anode with an energy of 300 ev. Similarly an electron traversing an 18-v welding arc will acquire 18 ev of energy in doing so. Half-way across the arc its energy will be 9 ev. Note that this energy in the two examples cited is kinetic energy. A voltage is a force, and therefore will accelerate the electron throughout the voltage drop. The electron-volt is related to the watt through the following conversion factors:

$$1 \text{ electron-volt} = 1.602 \times 10^{-19} \text{ joules}$$

$$1 \text{ watt} = 1 \text{ joule per second}$$

The electron-volt is of course not restricted to kinetic energy. The electrostatic attraction between an electron and an atomic nucleus is measured as potential energy in electron-volts.

2.2   electron energy levels

The electrons of an atom are in orbit about the nucleus. For the case of the earth's orbiting path about the sun, it is known that equilibrium arises because the earth traverses a path such that the gravitational attraction of the sun for the earth is balanced by the opposing centrifugal force of the earth's motion. Suppose now that this concept is applied to the case of a negatively charged electron orbiting about its nucleus. The attraction of the positively charged protons in the nucleus for the electron would be balanced by the centrifugal force arising from the circular motion of the electron. This is not the end of the matter, however. It can be shown from simple mechanics and Newton's laws of motion that the electron, like the earth, is accelerating, simply because its motion is circular instead of

Fig. 3   Energy levels of the hydrogen atom (Bohr model of the hydrogen atom).

straight-line, the centrifugal force implying an acceleration (force = mass × acceleration). But an electron is electrically charged, and an accelerating electric charge must radiate energy. For example, the acceleration of electric charges in a transmitting antenna causes the radiation of radio waves to the atmosphere. The orbiting electron would thus continuously radiate energy as it circled the nucleus. This continuous loss of energy would result in the collapse of the electron into the nucleus in a remarkably short period of time.

But except for nuclear radioactivity, atoms are normally stable. The reasoning given above is wrong because it assumed that the energy of the atom was continuously variable. It is not. The energy state of any atom has only a certain set of permitted values, which will be different for different elements. This quantized set of energy values is infinite in number. In order to make a somewhat difficult subject simple, we will deal with this matter of atomic energy levels by discussing what is called "The Bohr Model of the Hydrogen Atom", which is a somewhat simplified description of the simplest of the atoms.

The hydrogen atom has a single electron, and according to the simpler concepts of quantum mechanics, this electron will be found only in certain permitted orbits in relation to the nucleus, and in no other positions. In these permitted positions the electron does not radiate or otherwise lose energy. Figure 3 sketches these orbits. Rather than refer to these positions as orbits, it is preferable to describe them as energy levels, since there will be a definite value of potential energy associated with each orbit. There are an infinite number of these distinct energy levels. The infinitieth level is that level farthest from the atom. In this level, mutual electrostatic attraction of the negative electron for the positive nucleus is zero, and this level is therefore assigned an energy of zero electron-volts. In this condition the nucleus has of course lost its electron, and is in the ionized condition. In any energy level closer to the nucleus than the ionized condition, the electron energy is assigned a minus value.

In the energy level closest to the nucleus, the K level, where the electron would normally be found, the hydrogen electron has an energy of -13.6 ev. If then the electron is bound to the nucleus by an energy of 13.6 ev in the K level, then a minimum energy of 13.6 ev will be required to ionize the atom by pulling the electron off the nucleus. For a practical case, suppose single atoms of hydrogen (i.e., not hydrogen molecules, H_2) were used as shielding gas in a welding arc. Then this gas would ionize if the arc voltage reached 13.6. It should be noted that these statements do not apply to the diatomic molecule of hydrogen, but only to single atoms. In the case of the molecule there are two nuclei to attract the electron, an entirely different configuration.

The K level of -13.6 ev has a nominal diameter of 1.06 A. An Angstrom, abbreviated "A", is 10^{-8} centimeters, or 10^{-10} meters. The electron moves around this orbit at about 1 percent of the speed of light.

The electron may be moved out of the K level to a more remote level by providing energy to the atom from heat, a voltage, a collision with another particle, or by other means. The energy of the electron in any energy level of the hydrogen atom is given by the simple relationship

$$E = -\frac{13.6}{n^2}$$

where E = energy in electron-volts

n = number of the energy level: K = 1, L = 2, M = 3, etc.

Thus in the K level, $E = -13.6/1^2 = -13.6$ ev

in the L level, $E = -13.6/2^2 = -3.35$ ev

in the M level, $E = -13.6/3^2 = -1.5$ ev

The energy differences between the outer electron levels become very small. The minimum energy that will be required to move the electron out of the K shell is $(13.6 - 3.35)$ or 10.25 ev, this being the difference in energy between the K and L levels. An energy less than this amount cannot change the energy level. If the electron should be displaced to a more remote energy level, it would be expected to drop back to the K level at a later time. To do so, it must release energy. Such energy is carried away as a photon (particle or wave) of electromagnetic radiation. The characteristics of such radiation will be dealt with presently.

To be more exact in our concepts, we should note that it is not possible to locate an electron precisely in space and time. Any experiment which attempts to fix the position of the electron must necessarily disturb the electron and ruin the precision of the experiment. Physicists therefore speak of a *probability distribution* for the electron in its energy level. The probability of finding the electron at the nucleus is of course zero. The maximum probability for the location of the electron is at a radius of 0.53 Angstroms, and there is less probability of finding the electron closer or farther from the nucleus. This position of maximum probability is made the position of the K level.

The hydrogen atom is of course the simplest atom, and presents the simplest possible case. However, the basic concepts set out here hold for any atom:

1. The total energy of the atom electron system is quantized in a restricted range of permitted values.
2. The precise positions of the electrons at any instant cannot be determined, and only the probability of finding an electron at any position can be specified. The position of highest probability sets the size (and the shape, which is not discussed here) of the atom.

2.3 more complex atoms than hydrogen

The fundamental particles in the atom are specified by two numbers. One number is the atomic number Z. This is the number of protons in the nucleus, and also the number of electrons if the atom is not ionized. The other number is the mass number A, which is the number of nucleons (protons plus neutrons). The mass and density of the atom are determined largely by A: most of the chemical properties of the atom are determined by Z. *The element is identified exclusively by the number of protons.* Thus any atom containing 53 protons is iodine and only iodine. Any atom containing 8 protons is oxygen and only oxygen. The number of electrons may vary due to ionization; the number of neutrons in the nucleus may vary also. But if the number of protons should vary, then the element is no longer the original element. To cite an example, let us take the case of the most frequently used radioactive element in industry and medicine: cobalt. Natural cobalt has a nucleus of 27 protons and a total of 59 nucleons (32 neutrons). This atom is made radioactive by adding 1 more neutron to the nucleus, for a total of 60 nucleons. The radioactive atom is still a cobalt atom, since the number of protons is unchanged. Radioactive cobalt serves its functions, such as whole-body radiation of a patient in a hospital or photography of a thick weld, by means of certain nuclear transformations which will be discussed later in this chapter. As a result of these transformations, the end condition of the atom is 28 protons and 32 neutrons. The change in the proton count to 28 indicates that the atom is now a nickel atom.

Fig. 4   Periodic table of the elements.

METALS — Transition Metals — Metalloids and Non-metals

I	II												III	IV	V	VI	VII	VIII
1 H Hydrogen																		2 He Helium
3 Li Lithium	4 Be Beryllium												5 B Boron	6 C Carbon	7 N Nitrogen	8 O Oxygen	9 F Fluorine	10 Ne Neon
11 Na Sodium	12 Mg Magnesium												13 Al Aluminum	14 Si Silicon	15 P Phosphorus	16 S Sulfur	17 Cl Chlorine	18 Ar Argon
19 K Potassium	20 Ca Calcium	21 Sc Scandium	22 Ti Titanium	23 V Vanadium	24 Cr Chromium	25 Mn Manganese	26 Fe Iron	27 Co Cobalt	28 Ni Nickel	29 Cu Copper	30 Zn Zinc		31 Ga Gallium	32 Ge Germanium	33 As Arsenic	34 Se Selenium	35 Br Bromine	36 Kr Krypton
37 Rb Rubidium	38 Sr Strontium	39 Y Yttrium	40 Zr Zirconium	41 Nb Niobium	42 Mo Molybdenum	43 Tc Technetium	44 Ru Ruthenium	45 Rh Rhodium	46 Pd Palladium	47 Ag Silver	48 Cd Cadmium		49 In Indium	50 Sn Tin	51 Sb Antimony	52 Te Tellurium	53 I Iodine	54 Xe Xenon
55 Cs Cesium	56 Ba Barium	57 La Lanthanum	72 Hf Hafnium	73 Ta Tantalum	74 W Tungsten	75 Re Rhenium	76 Os Osmium	77 Ir Iridium	78 Pt Platinum	79 Au Gold	80 Hg Mercury		81 Tl Thallium	82 Pb Lead	83 Bi Bismuth	84 Po Polonium	85 At Astatine	86 Rn Radon
87 Fr Francium	88 Ra Radium	89 Ac Actinium																

Lanthanides (Rare Earth Metals)

58 Ce Cerium	59 Pr Praseodymium	60 Nd Neodymium	61 Pm Promethium	62 Sm Samarium	63 Eu Europium	64 Gd Gadolinium	65 Tb Terbium	66 Dy Dysprosium	67 Ho Holmium	68 Er Erbium	69 Tm Thulium	70 Yb Ytterbium	71 Lu Lutetium

Actinides

90 Th Thorium	91 Pa Protoactinium	92 U Uranium	93 Np Neptunium	94 Pu Plutonium	95 Am Americium	96 Cm Curium	97 Bk Berkelium	98 Cf Californium	99 Es Einsteinium	100 Fm Fermium	101 Md Mendelevium	102 No Nobelium	103 Lw Lawrencium

Atoms of any element with varying numbers of neutrons are termed *isotopes*. Oxygen, for example, has three principal isotopes, $_8O^{16}$, $_8O^{17}$, $_8O^{18}$. Hydrogen has 3 isotopes also, $_1H^1$, $_1H^2$ (called deuterium and sometimes given as $_1D^2$), and $_1H^3$ (called tritium, used in dials of watches which can be read in the dark). The number of protons Z is the subscript, and mass number or atomic weight A, is the superscript. Frequently in industry only the atomic weight is given, thus Iridium-192, or Cobalt-60.

An atom of atomic number Z has a nuclear charge of $+Ze$, where e is the fundamental electric charge, and has Z electrons. The electron energy levels are quantized, but determination of these energy levels is complicated by the repulsion of the orbiting electrons from each other.

The Periodic Table of the Elements is an arrangement of the 102 or more known elements in the order of their atomic numbers Z, beginning with hydrogen, $Z = 1$, so that elements with similar properties fall in vertical groups in the table. Figure 4 is one arrangement of the Periodic Table, with several subgroups between Groups II and III.

The famous inert gases, helium, neon, argon, etc., form a group with certain industrially important characteristics:

(a) All are gases at ambient temperatures.
(b) All are chemically inert.
(c) They do not dissolve in metals.

Although they share a number of common properties, the inert gases have their individual characteristics, too, such as differences in their ionization potential (helium supplies a hotter welding arc than argon because of its higher ionization potential), and differences in their radiation characteristics (an electric discharge through a neon-filled tube produces a reddish light, while xenon gives a white light). All these elements, except helium, contain 8 electrons in their outermost filled electron energy level. Helium has only 2 electrons, both in the K level.

The maximum number of electrons that can be contained in any energy level of an atom follows this simple principle:

The K level can hold a maximum of $2 \times 1^2 = $ 2 electrons
L   " $2 \times 2^2 = $ 8 electrons
M   " $2 \times 3^2 = $ 18 electrons
N   " $2 \times 4^2 = $ 32 electrons, etc.

The inert gases, having a complete population of 8 electrons in the outermost filled level, do not normally engage in chemical activity, such activity being occasioned by incompletely filled shells of less than 8 electrons. Again, actual electron configurations are more complex than this simplified presentation would suggest: every level above the K level is subdivided into two or more sublevels.

Hydrogen has 1 electron. Helium has two. The second electron of helium completely fills the K level, giving the quality of inertness to helium. The next element in the Periodic Table, the metal lithium, has 3 electrons, the third being in the L level. Lithium is in Group I of the table. This group comprises the alkali metals, all of which have 1 electron in the outermost populated level. This single electron is the distinguishing characteristic of the group, just as was 8 electrons for the inert gases. The single outermost electron of the alkali metal group is not closely bound to the nucleus because of the masking effect of electrons in levels closer to the nucleus. As a result the ionization potential for these elements is only 4–5 electron volts. Such low levels of energy are obtainable from ultraviolet radiation, and accounts for the use of these metals in the cathodes of photoelectric cells.

Group II elements are also metals, with 2 electrons in the outermost populated level. Beryllium and magnesium crystallize in a hexagonal crystal pattern of atoms: so do the metals of the subgroup titanium, zirconium, and hafnium, a subgroup also characterized by two outermost electrons.

The two subgroups vanadium, columbium (also called niobium by scientists and nuclear industry personnel), tantalum, and chromium, molybdenum, tungsten, are important metals in metallurgical practice. These are the "refractory" or high melting-point metals, with the following common characteristics:

(a) Their crystal structure is body-centered cubic.
(b) All are used as alloying elements in steels.
(c) All readily form carbides, especially within the internal structure of steels (the preceding subgroup, titanium, zirconium, and hafnium, have an even stronger tendency to form carbides).

The subgroup copper, silver, gold, is again an industrially significant group, their common characteristics being these:

(a) Their conductivity for both heat and electric current is outstanding.
(b) They are exceedingly ductile, and can readily be beaten out to very fine foils.
(c) Their crystal structure is face-centered cubic.

Group III metals have 3 electrons in the outer populated level. Note that the group number in the Periodic Table is the number of outer electrons. There are no metals to the right of Group III in the table, so that a metal might be defined as an element with no more than 3 electrons in the outer populated level.

Group IV contains the semiconductor materials silicon and germanium, used in transistors and semiconductor rectifiers. Silicon is also the base element for the cements used in the construction industry. The group also includes the important element carbon. The presence of 4 outer electrons gives silicon and carbon their remarkable chemical versatility.

We need not address any general remarks to Groups V and VI. These include elements with a variety of special uses in materials technology, such as the formulation of low melting-point alloys. Group VII is the "halogen" group. Since the halogens have 7 electrons in the outer level, they combine readily with the alkali metals of Group I to produce a closed configuration of 8 electrons.

2.4   aspects of relativity theory

The theory of relativity, like quantum mechanics and solid state physics, is one of the powerful scientific developments of the twentieth century which has greatly extended the applications of materials technology. The theory of relativity is concerned with the speed of light. Here we are concerned only with that aspect of the theory relating energy and mass.

Mass can be converted into energy and energy can be converted into mass. To convert from mass to energy, the famous equation of Einstein is used:

$$E = mc^2$$

where E = the energy produced by the disappearance of mass

   m = mass

   c = speed of light

Because c^2 is an enormous figure, the equation indicates that a small amount of mass will produce a large quantity of energy.

The Einstein equation may also be written

$$E = mc^2 = \frac{m_0 c^2}{\sqrt{1 - (v/c)^2}} = m_0 c^2 + \tfrac{1}{2} m v^2$$

where v = velocity of the body
   m_0 = the rest mass of the body, i.e., its mass when at rest.

This form of the equation shows that the total energy of a moving body is the sum of its mass energy and its kinetic energy. Suitable units for numerical work with the Einstein equation are:

   E = joules

   m = kilograms

   c = meters per second

As an example, we will calculate the amount of energy in joules produced by the conversion of 1 atomic mass unit to energy. This is almost equivalent to converting 1 neutron (1.00898 atomic mass units) or 1 proton to equivalent energy.

$$1 \text{ amu} = 1.660 \times 10^{-27} \text{ kilograms}$$

$$E = 1.660 \times 10^{-27} \times (3 \times 10^8)^2 = 1.494 \times 10^{-10} \text{ joules}$$

In terms of electron-volts, this is 931 Mev (million electron-volts) or almost 1 billion ev. The conversion from joules to electron-volts is made by way of the conversion factor 1 ev $= 1.602 \times 10^{-19}$ joules.

The reverse process of converting energy to mass occurs in certain cosmic ray processes, in nuclear operations, and in linear accelerator operations. The linear accelerator is a modification of the X-ray tube which is used to photograph heavy thicknesses of steel. Typically in such processes, a negative and a positive electron are created from a gamma ray. The process is called *pair production*, and is discussed in a later section of this book.

The mass of a body, measured at zero velocity, is termed its *rest-mass*. If the body is in motion, then its mass becomes greater:

$$m = \frac{m_0}{\sqrt{1 - (v/c)^2}}$$

The faster the body, the greater its mass. However the increase is negligible until the velocity approaches about one-sixth the speed of light, or about 30,000 miles per second. Such velocities are found in industry, principally in high-voltage equipment. Thus an electron accelerated across a 100,000-volt X-ray tube or electron-beam welding machine will acquire a terminal velocity of about one-half the speed of light. The above equation suggests that if a body can be accelerated to the speed of light it would have infinite mass, but it can be shown that no mass can be accelerated to this velocity. The only particles that can, and do, travel at the speed of light are those that have no rest mass, such as the photon, now to be discussed.

2.5 electromagnetic radiation

Any wave energy which can be radiated through space as a voltage wave accompanied by a magnetic field is termed electromagnetic radiation. The radiation of radio and television signals from a transmitting antenna, and received by a receiving antenna, is perhaps the most familiar example to cite.

Fig. 5 Electromagnetic radiation.

Figure 5 is a composite diagram of information on all the types of electromagnetic radiation. Actually, all the various types — radio, infrared, visible light, ultraviolet, and gamma ray — are identical in nature and differ only in frequency. There is no clear-cut distinction between any two types. But since certain frequency ranges of radiation are transmitted or received by special devices, such ranges are given special names. Thus if the radiation can be detected by the human eye, it is called *visible light*. If it comes from an X-ray tube, it is called *X-radiation*. If it has a heating effect, it is called *infrared* or *radiant heat*. It is rather interesting to note that the prominent natural types of radiation in the world around us are infrared to ultraviolet, especially from the sun, and that the human eye is sensitive to a narrow band of radiation in the middle of this broad range of "natural" radiation.

All electromagnetic radiation travels at the velocity of light through vacuum space. Such radiation includes both an alternating electric field and an alternating magnetic field normal to the electric field, as in Fig. 6.

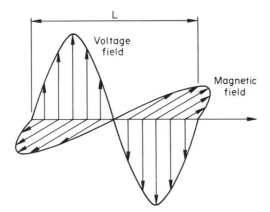

Fig. 6 Relationship of electric and magnetic fields in radiation.

One positive and one negative half-wave of the alternating wave are together termed one wavelength, as for 60-cycle alternating current. The frequency is the number of wavelengths that pass any fixed point in one second. As with most types of wave motion, the product of the frequency times the wavelength is equal to the velocity c:

$$fL = c$$

Thus to determine the wavelength of 60-cycle alternating current,

$$60 \times L = 186,000 \text{ mps}$$

$$L = 3100 \text{ miles}$$

Each a-c wave of radiation may also be considered as an energetic particle of zero rest mass, called a *photon*. Indeed, for the very high energy radiation in the gamma ray range, it is not usual to use the concept of a wave, this being less useful than the notion of a particle. The photon, being the wave, contains all the energy of the wave. It necessarily travels at the speed of light; indeed it exists only when traveling at this velocity. On colliding with another body, the photon transfers all its energy to the body. Being then without either mass or energy, it ceases to exist. The energy which is the photon varies directly with the frequency:

$E = hf$, where h is some constant

In industrial uses of high-frequency radiation beyond the radio range, a variant of this formula is used, based on the wavelength of the energy in Angstroms (1 A $= 10^{-8}$ cm). If the photon energy is proportional to the frequency, then it is proportional also to the reciprocal of the wavelength, since $fL = c$. The formula used in industry for determining photon energy is the following:

$$\text{photon energy in ev} = \frac{12430}{\text{wavelength in Angstroms}}$$

The constant 12430 is often made 12345 to make it easier to remember. The error is about 1 percent, which for industrial purposes is unimportant.

Example. Determine the wavelength of X-radiation if the X-ray tube uses an impressed voltage of 300,000.

$$300,000 \text{ ev} = 12345/L_A \quad \text{and} \quad L_A = 0.04 \text{ A}$$

Figure 5 shows the photon energy ranges of the high-frequency types of radiation.

2.6 biological and photographic effects of electromagnetic radiation

A practical understanding of photon energy, its implications, and its uses, is best gained in a brief review of its biological and photographic effects.

Radio, television, and radar waves are of very low energy, measured in electron-volts, because of their low frequency. The human body is ordinarily insensitive to them. Infrared radiation is more powerful, with energies ranging up to a maximum of about 1.3 ev. This radiation we can sense as radiant heat. Still farther up the scale of radiation is visible light, with maximum energy of 3 ev in the violet range. Such radiation is sufficiently powerful to make the retina of the eye respond.

Damaging radiation begins at ultraviolet energy levels, 3 ev or more. The ultraviolet components of the sun's spectrum can produce sunburn. The more powerful ultraviolet radiation from a welding arc can produce a variety of reactions in the human skin and eye. Both the retina, the light-receiving portion of the eye, and the cornea, the lens of the eye, are especially sensitive to the high energy of ultraviolet radiation, and if exposed, the result can be retinitis, conjunctivitis (the conjunctiva is the inner lining of the eyelid), or keratitis (thickening of the cornea). Serious reactions of the skin to radiation of the welding arc are not common, but cases of dermatitis and even carcinoma have been found or suspected.

Ultraviolet radiation is also powerful enough to depolymerize the long molecules of such organic materials as polyethylenes and rubbers. Carbon black is added to polyethylene pipe and automobile tires to absorb such radiation and thus protect the material.

Radiation energies above approximately 10 Kev (10,000 electron-volts) are termed X-ray and gamma ray radiation. Gamma and X-radiation are actually identical except for their source: X-radiation is produced by vacuum tubes and gamma radiation from radioisotopes, otherwise there is no difference whatever between them. This radiation is powerful enough to penetrate solid matter, and its penetrating power increases with its photon energy. Gamma ray or X-ray radiation above 1 Mev can penetrate 6 in. of steel without excessive attenuation: even at 100 Kev it is possible to radiograph steel 0.375 in. thick. Physiological damage to the human body results from the ionization produced by high-energy photons. This damage is more severe in the heavier and therefore more absorbing types of tissue, such as bone.

All types of electromagnetic radiation which are above the general radio range are used in photography. That is, it requires a minimum energy of about 1 electron-volt, which is infrared, to develop photographic emulsions, although special film is required for infrared photography. Visible light, 1.5 to 3 ev, is used for ordinary camera film, which therefore will also be sensitive to the shorter wavelengths of ultraviolet and X-radiation. Because X-radiation actually penetrates the film, X-ray film carries an emulsion on both sides.

2.7   electron-photon interaction

The hydrogen electron can be displaced to an outer energy level from the K level by acquiring energy. It can jump back to a lower energy level also (if there is an available hole or electron position for it to fill), but it must lose energy to do so. This energy is removed by a photon. A large jump will release a photon in the ultraviolet range, while a small jump will release a photon of radio or infrared energy.

Suppose this hydrogen atom to be part of an acetylene molecule which is being oxidized in an oxyacetylene flame. The heat of the flame causes the electron to jump from the K shell to an outer shell, let us say the M shell of energy 1.5 ev. As the acetylene molecule travels out of the flame and cools, it loses energy, causing the electron to fall back to the L or K shell from the M shell. Presumably the hydrogen atom is attached to an H_2O molecule after combustion, but we are ignoring any effect on energy levels due to the molecular configuration. Let us suppose the electron falls back to the L shell. To do so, it must lose 1.85 electron-volts, this being the energy difference between M and L. This lost energy of 1.85 ev becomes a single photon of radiation. The wavelength of the radiation is 6700 Angstroms. This is red visible light. If the electron had jumped back to the K shell, the photon would have an energy of 12.1 ev, which is ultraviolet.

Figure 5 indicates that about 10 Kev is the minimum photon energy for X-radiation. Since the maximum electron jump in the hydrogen atom is 13.6, it is not possible to produce X rays by means of electron jumps in hydrogen atoms.

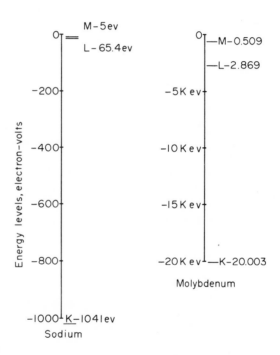

Fig. 7 Energy levels in sodium and molybdenum atoms.

Figure 7 shows the approximate K, L, and M energy levels of sodium and molybdenum. Sodium has 2 electrons in the K level, 8 in the L level, and 1 in the M level. The maximum electron jump in this atom is 1041 ev, from the K shell to the infinitieth level of ionization. Such a jump would produce a photon of ultraviolet. Molybdenum, which has 42 electrons, can produce a maximum photon energy of 20,000 ev, which is in the long-wave X-ray range.

A photoelectric cell is a simple application of these quantum concepts. This device is a vacuum tube diode, a diode being a two-electrode device, one electrode being an electron emitter and the other an electron collector and therefore having a voltage positive with respect to the electron emitter. The photocell can create a small electric current of a few microamps if exposed to radiation with a certain minimum photon energy, which is in the range of visible light to ultraviolet. The current arises from a flow of electrons from a radiation-sensitive cathode, not a heated cathode in the case of a photocell, to the collecting anode. The cathode material is some metal which is easily ionized by the loss of one electron. Suitable metals are Group I metals such as cesium and rubidium, with a single electron in the outermost populated level. Such electrons can be separated from their atoms by photon energies of a few electron-volts. The released electrons are attracted to the anode by a positive voltage, thus creating a small current.

2.8 the laser and fluorescence

Electromagnetic radiation is energy. Every small boy has tried the stunt of using a magnifying glass to concentrate the heat of the sun in order to char a piece of paper. The laser is a more sophisticated substitute for the small boy's magnifying glass, using the concepts of quantum mechanics.

Before discussing the laser, we ought first to discuss the case of a heating element in an electric stove. When current is switched to the heating element, it radiates a certain amount of infrared. As the temperature of the element rises, greater electron jumps become possible, and the element radiates a spectrum of infrared and visible light. Photons of red light are produced when an electron jumps back toward the nucleus through an energy difference of about 1 electron-volt. Those electrons which return toward the nucleus through smaller energy differences emit photons of infrared radiation. The radiation occurs over a very broad band of wavelengths, and it is not very intense.

The laser radiates in the same frequency range as the electric element, but with greater intensity and with closer control over the characteristics of the radiation. A great many solids, liquids, and gases will "lase"; here we will consider only the solid-state laser.

Suppose that in the laser crystal there are two characteristic energy levels which the electrons typically inhabit: a higher energy level when the electrons receive photon energy, and a lower energy level when they release photon energy. Three processes are possible:

1. When radiation interacts with electrons in the lower energy level, a photon is absorbed and the electron is raised to the upper level.

2. An electron can spontaneously emit a photon by dropping back to the lower level.
3. Radiation can interact with an electron in the upper level, causing it to emit a photon of radiation. In this case the photon emitted will travel in the same direction and be in phase (reinforce) with the stimulating photon. The radiation will then be twice as powerful, that is, it will be amplified. This third case is the laser process.

The laser solves the problem of producing huge amounts of power from radiation by two characteristics: the electron jumps all produce the same photon energy, and all the electrons make the jump at the same instant. Despite the publicity it has received, the high-power solid-state laser is hardly an impressive piece of equipment. High-power lasers consist of a ruby (aluminum oxide) crystal which has been doped with a few billion chromium atoms. Another type of laser crystal is made of certain types of glass doped with the rare earth metal, neodymium. The back end of the crystal is heavily silvered to reflect any internal radiation: the front end face is partially silvered. The intense beam of radiation is emitted from this front end. The crystal end faces must be ground smooth and flat to about a millionth of an inch. A xenon-filled flash tube is used to excite the electrons of the laser crystal. Figure 8 is a diagram of such a laser.

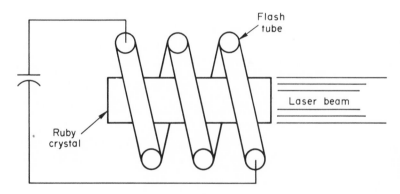

Fig. 8   Ruby laser.

The laser is fired by discharging the capacitor through the xenon tube, which then puts out a powerful pulse of white light. The chromium atoms in the ruby crystal absorb the yellow and green fraction of this visible radiation. This absorption pumps vast numbers of electrons from a lower energy level 1 to a higher energy level 3. The more powerful the flash, the greater the number of electrons excited to the higher level. From level 3 the electrons rapidly fall back to an intermediate level 2. This is a small energy drop, which appears as heat in the crystal. A few electrons fall back to energy level 1, producing photons of red light. This light is reflected back and forth between the ends of the crystal, stimulating the electrons in level 2 to fall in unison back to level 1, thus producing a pulse of red light of remarkable power.

Laser action is an example of *fluorescence*, which means the emission of radiation of longer wavelength during exposure to radiation of shorter wavelength. When the laser crystal is irradiated with shorter-wave green and yellow radiation, it delivers longer-wave red radiation. Virtually all materials can be made to fluoresce, not necessarily in the visible range, though they may require powerful radiation such as X rays to do so. If the emission of radiation from the substance persists after exposure to the primary radiation is discontinued, this is called *phosphorescence*.

Phosphors are materials which emit visible light when irradiated at high photon energies, such as ultraviolet. In parts of our country phosphorescent wood can be found which glows green in the dark. Such wood has been caused to phosphoresce by ultraviolet radiation from the sun, the phosphor material being certain salts in the wood. Fluorescent light bulbs have a phosphor painted on the glass bulb which fluoresces in the visible light range when irradiated by the ultraviolet discharge through the mercury vapor of the lamp. Similarly, cathode-ray tubes, such as television picture tubes, are coated with a phosphor surface.

2.9 energy bands in solids

The preceding sections make it obvious that there are many more allowable energy levels in an atom than there are electrons to fill them. So far, however, the discussion has been concerned with individual atoms. The more usual case of an aggregation of atoms such as might be found in a crystal must next be considered.

In the case of an isolated atom, the energy levels are determined by the forces within the atom, such as the attraction of the nucleus for the electron, and the repulsion between electrons. If we next concern ourselves with a crystal of iron, zirconium, or other element, any electron will be under the influence of the many nuclei and electrons that surround it on all sides. The influence of these neighboring atoms will change the energy levels within the atom. Taking the case of a system of two atoms only, in close proximity to each other — the usual interatomic distance in metal crystals is about 2–5 A — the energy levels shift slightly, and each energy level of the single atom is split into two levels separated by an extremely small energy interval of very much less than 1 electron-volt.

In any solid, enormous numbers of atoms are packed into a small volume, so that interaction between the atoms causes the splitting of energy levels. Each energy level now becomes a multitude of very closely spaced energy levels. These closely-packed ranges of energy levels, which in the single atom were one energy level, are now called *energy* bands, because the difference between energy levels within any permitted band may be of the order of only 10^{-19} ev, which is a negligible energy difference. The energy band appears to be continuous over its range, although the actual number of energy levels within the energy band is actually finite, and not infinite. We no longer have permitted and forbidden energy levels, but permitted and forbidden energy bands. Inner energy bands such as the K band corresponding to the K shell of a single atom are narrow-range energy bands with only a narrow interval of energy across the band. Higher energy levels, such as the M band, are broadened into wide energy bands.

The single hydrogen atom could radiate energy only in a relatively few permitted monochromatic frequencies, corresponding to the energy differences between levels K to L, K to M, M to N, etc. Because of the multitude of energy levels within an energy band, solids can absorb and emit radiation over a continuous range of frequencies, and thus give a continuous spectrum of radiation, as in the case of a hot plate of an electric stove. All solids show essentially the same spectrum when heated, and there is no characteristic spectrum by which the solid may be identified. All solids, metal, ceramic, or other, begin to produce visible radiation when heated above 1100°F.

In all solids the very lowest energy bands are completely filled by electrons. The highest normally filled energy band is called the *valence band* or *filled band*. The next higher band is called the *conduction band* or the *empty band*. At any temperature above absolute zero there are some electrons excited from the valence (filled) band to the lowest normally empty (conduction) band, and therefore some holes in the valence band. For silicon at room temperature the energy gap between the empty conduction band and the highest normally filled band is 1.09 ev, and for germanium it is 0.72 ev.

Fig. 9   Energy bands in solids.

No electric current can be carried by electrons in a filled band. If a solid has a partially filled band, then it is a good conductor of electricity. That is, a partially filled band (conduction band) conducts. Now it is a familiar fact that all good electrical conductors (chiefly metals and carbides) are opaque to heat and visible light. Such radiation has low photon energy. When such radiation falls on a conductor, the photon energy is absorbed as excitation energy to lift electrons in the conduction band to other energy levels within the same band. The energy interval between levels in the conduction band is small, corresponding to the small photon energy. Hence a good conductor should be opaque to light and heat.

Most nonmetals are insulators. In the case of an insulator the highest occupied energy band is completely filled. Although it might seem that such a case would be rare, it is actually the most common. In the case of an insulator, not only is the highest occupied band filled but also the unoccupied forbidden energy band just above the filled band is wide, that is, several electron-volts, and thermal excitation does not provide enough energy to jump electrons from the filled band to the next higher permitted band. The electrons then are more or less restricted to the occupied band, and the material is an insulator for both heat and electricity.

In addition to electrical conductors and insulators, there is a third type of material, the semiconductors, with a conductivity between that of conductors and insulators. This class includes silicon and germanium. A semiconductor has a narrow forbidden band between the filled and the conduction band. Heat energy at room temperature is sufficient to raise some electrons into the higher conduction band, where they can carry electric current. The number of electrons raised to the conduction band will increase with temperature.

Many good insulators are transparent to heat and light, glass and certain plastics, for example. Since the low-energy heat and light photons cannot excite the electrons in a filled band to the conduction band, the light must pass through unabsorbed in such materials. It has been found that, as the wavelength of the radiation shortens to the ultraviolet region, these solids begin to absorb the radiation, as is true for glass. This would be expected for those insulators in which the energy gap of the forbidden region corresponds to the energies of ultraviolet photons. Semiconductors, having narrow forbidden zones of about 1 electron-volt, are opaque to visible light but transparent in the infrared.

To illustrate, we may compare the behavior of three elements, each containing 4 electrons in the outermost electron occupied level. These are diamond (carbon), germanium, and lead. Diamond is an insulator, germanium is a semiconductor, and lead is a conductor. In the case of diamond, the filled and the conduction band are widely separated by a large forbidden band, so that a considerable amount of energy is required to excite an electron into the conduction band. Hence the insulating characteristic of diamond. The two energy bands in germanium are close enough, 0.72 ev, for a considerable number of electrons to make the jump into the conduction band. Finally, in the case of lead, the two bands actually overlap one another, and the valence electrons are free to move in the conduction band as free electrons in a conductor.

The energy released by electronic rearrangements within the atom is of the order of a relatively few electron-volts, although in atoms of higher atomic number, several thousand electron-volts are possible. The electron is an active and volatile particle because it can be removed from its atom by the expenditure of a relatively few electron-volts of work. By means of such small energy expenditures we can produce electric currents, operate electronic tubes and transistors, and produce such chemical reactions as the combustion of carbon to carbon dioxide. Previous sections of this chapter have centered interest on the electron, leaving by implication a picture of the nucleus as a tight, dense, and inert cluster of protons and neutrons serving only as a datum for electron energy levels. It is now well known that such a picture is false, for even a stable and quiescent nucleus is a sleeping giant and a Promethean source of energy. The great difference between nuclear and electronic sources of energy is indicated in the following little table of the particle energies employed by the human race:

PARTICLE ENERGIES IN ELECTRON-VOLTS

1 water molecule falling over Niagara Falls	0.00015 ev
1 visible photon of red light	1 ev
1 carbon atom burned to CO_2	4 ev
fission of 1 uranium nucleus	200,000,000 ev
(1 ev = 1.602 $\times$ 10^{-19} joules; 1 watt = 1 joule per second)	

The great disparity between nuclear and electronic energy releases is explained by their relative binding energies. For example, the ionization potential binding the hydrogen electron to the nucleus is 13.6 ev, but the binding energy per nucleon in the nucleus of deuterium is closely 1 Mev. For most nuclei, particularly heavier elements, the binding energy per nucleon holding the nucleus together is in the range of 6 to 9 million electron-volts, or about one hundred times the maximum energy levels that hold the electron to the nucleus.

For the release of nuclear energy, the nucleus must be made unstable, that is, the binding energy holding the nucleus together must be disrupted. Figure 10 is a stability diagram of the known isotopes of the light elements. Proton number (i.e., atomic number) Z is the abscissa and neutron number is the ordinate. Stable isotopes are designated by circles: unstable or radioactive isotopes are designated by solid circles. It is apparent from this figure that only isotopes with a ratio (neutrons)/(protons) = 1, approximately, are stable, for the case of the light nuclei. A line of stability corresponding to the stable neutron-proton ratio is drawn through the figure.

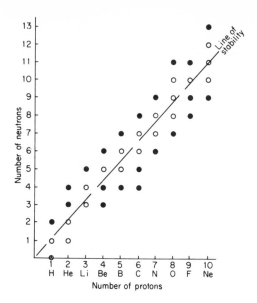

Fig. 10 Stability diagram for isotopes of the light elements. Those isotopes are stable which have a neutron-to-proton ratio of approximately one.

With increasing atomic number the line of stability leans increasingly toward a higher count of neutrons, that is, $N/Z > 1$. The greater fraction of neutrons in the heavier nuclei is explained by the greater electrostatic repulsion forces as the number of protons increase: the protons must be increasingly "diluted" with neutrons in order to hold the nucleus together. The heaviest stable nucleus is $_{83}Bi^{209}$ with $N/Z = 126/83$, or about 1.5. All nuclei heavier than this are radioactive.

The further that the N/Z ratio of a nucleus is from the line of stability, the more unstable the nucleus will be. Some isotopes, lying above the line of stability, have a high count of neutrons. Others, below the line, have a high count of protons. The radioactive decay process, for both conditions, will be such as to bring the N/Z ratio toward the line of stability. Isotopes lying above the line of stability will emit negative beta particles, actually electrons, thus changing neutrons into protons. The neutron thus involved will decay into a proton, an electron, and a neutrino (uncharged). Note that no electrons or neutrinos reside in the nucleus, but are created during radioactive decay in a fashion somewhat analogous to the creation of a photon. On the other hand, those isotopes lying below the line of stability have an excess of protons. This condition is adjusted either by release of a positron (positively charged electron) or by acquiring a neutralizing electron from the surrounding electron cloud about the nucleus. This second method of reducing the proton count in effect converts a proton to a neutron. The emission of a gamma photon accompanies all such types of radioactivity. In all these radioactive processes, neutrons are changed into protons or protons into neutrons, but since the proton count is altered, the original element, after radioactivity, becomes a different element.

A number of radioactive isotopes, or radioisotopes as they are usually termed, are found in nature, such as Carbon-14, tritium or Hydrogen-3, uranium, radium, thorium, polonium, radon, and others. A few of these were used in industry before the invention of the nuclear reactor, but their use now is in general not common. Instead, industry uses artificial radioisotopes manufactured in nuclear reactors. The most important by far of the industrial and medical radioisotopes is Cobalt-60; the next most important is Iridium-192. The powerful gamma radiation of Cobalt-60, with photon energies exceeding 1 Mev, is used in the radiography of steel thicker than about $2\frac{1}{2}$ in. Iridium-192, with gamma radiation in the range of about 0.5 Mev, is used to radiograph thinner sections of steel and the light metals such as aluminum and titanium.

The production of artificial radioisotopes is simple in principle, and will be explained in terms of Co-60. For the production of Co-60, natural cobalt, which is Co-59, is encased in an aluminum capsule. The capsule is pushed into one of the irradiation channels in a nuclear reactor, where it is bombarded with neutrons. The capsule must remain in the reactor for a considerable period of time. With the passage of time, more and more Cobalt-59 nuclei capture an extra neutron, thus converting to Co-60. The quantity of Co-59 cannot be left in the reactor until every atom of cobalt captures an extra neutron, for two reasons. First, to convert every atom of cobalt would require an infinite time. Second, while waiting for the last million nuclei to acquire an extra neutron, the first million to be converted would be already radioactive and would be decaying to a nonradioactive stability, so that the net result would be that nothing would be gained. Note that all artificial radioisotopes are made unstable by an increase in neutron count, thus placing the nucleus above the line of stability.

Fig. 11 Gamma camera. By means of the remote control crank shown, the radioactive source can be cranked out of the shielded container into the source tube at the bottom of the illustration.

the science of materials

33

For the gamma-ray photography of welds and castings, the isotope is enclosed in a container made of lead or spent uranium, called a *gamma camera*. Such a gamma camera is shown in Fig. 11. To photograph a weld, a sheet of X-ray film is placed against one side of the weld and the weld is irradiated from the other side by pushing the isotope out of its shielding container into the source tube attached to the camera.

2.11   half-life

The radioisotopes decay by emission of alpha and beta particles and gamma rays to an ultimately stable condition, in the case of the artificial isotopes, by beta and gamma emission. It is not possible to predict when any specific nucleus will disintegrate. But for any large number of nuclei, the *half-life* is the time period in which half the radioactive nuclei will decay.

The mathematical equation for radioactive decay is one of the most important in engineering science and characterizes a great many processes, such as the loss of voltage or charge on a capacitor.

Let N_0 = the number of unstable nuclei at time $t = 0$
    N = the number of unstable nuclei at time t. N is equal to or less than N_0.

Let k = the decay constant and
    e = 2.718 = base of the natural logarithms.

It has been determined that the rate at which nuclei decay is proportional to the number of remaining undecayed nuclei. Mathematically this is expressed as

$$\frac{dN}{dt} = -kN$$

By separation of variables N and t and integration, the mathematical law of decay is obtained:

$$N = N_0 e^{-kt}$$

In a time interval $1/k$ the number of unstable nuclei always decreases by a factor of $1/e$, where $1/e = 0.368$. In electrical work, the time constant of an induction coil or capacitor circuit is the time interval required for the voltage to fall to 36.8 percent of the initial voltage. Similarly, the time constant for an isotope would be the time interval required to reduce the number of unstable nuclei to 36.8 percent of their original number. However, the time constant concept is not employed in radioactivity: the half-life is substituted. This is the time interval in which the number of unstable nuclei is reduced by one-half. The half-life = $0.693/k$.

Fig. 12 Decay curve for Iridium-192.

The half-life of isotopes may vary from microseconds to years. For Co-60 the half-life is 5.3 years, and for Ir-192 it is 74 days. Thus if one were to purchase 100 active atoms of Ir-192, in 74 days only 50 would still be active, in 148 days only 25 would be active, and in 222 days only 12 would be active.

The only useful characteristic of an isotope is its nuclear activity. This radioactivity is measured in *curies*, abbreviated "c". The curie is therefore the unit in which radioactive sources are purchased, instead of pounds, ounces, or grams. A curie is that quantity of isotope in which 3.7×10^{10} atoms are decaying every second. The reason for the use of this unusual unit of activity is explained by the fact that prior to the invention of the nuclear reactor radium was the radioactive material used by industry and medicine, and in 1 gram of radium there are 3.7×10^{10} atomic disintegrations every second. Since radium has a half-life of 1520 years, its activity is almost constant. But for a short-lived isotope such as Ir-192, the 1 curie initially purchased will have decayed to 0.5 curie in 74 days.

The number of curies used for industrial processes depends on the use to which the isotope is put. For the radiography of welds, castings, and forgings, from 10 to 100 curies would be employed, but for such purposes as leak testing, a few microcuries or millicuries might be sufficient.

2.12 cross-section

An atom acquires energy, and thus becomes excited, at the moment of impact with another particle having the requisite amount of energy. The incident energetic particle may be a neutron, an atom, a photon, or any other particle, and the energy of the incident particle may be its kinetic energy of velocity, or internal energy as in the case of an excited atom.

the science of materials
35

Fig. 13   Collision cross-section.

The probability of a collision between two particles is expressed in the concept of a collision *cross-section*. In this concept, we imagine the bullet particle to be a hard spherical particle of radius r_1, and the target particle also to be hard and spherical, with radius r_2. A collision will occur whenever the separation of the centers of the two particles becomes not greater than the sum of the radii, $r_1 + r_2$, as in Fig. 13. It does not matter whether the bullet particle is small, and the target particle large, or conversely: the possibility of collision is based only on the sum of the radii.

Now it is convenient to consider the bullet particle as having zero radius, and to assign to the target particle a radius $(r_1 + r_2)$. The target area that each such equivalent target particle presents is called its *cross-section*. The symbol for cross-section is σ.

$$\sigma = \pi (r_1 + r_2)^2$$

The particles have been assumed to be hard spheres with a definite boundary at radius r. The actual particles must of course not be imagined to have any particular shape, and certainly do not have well-defined boundaries. In addition, the cross-section for an electron or other charged particle must take account of electrostatic forces. To adjust for these actual characteristics instead of the assumed ones, values of the radii r_1 and r_2 are those which hard spheres would require in order to produce the same collision effects as the actual particles. Thus the cross-section for interaction between a proton and an atom will not be the same as that for an electron and an atom, because the interactions are different in the two cases. Hence in quoting the collision cross-section of a particle, the type of interaction must be stated. Cross-sections are usually measured in *barns*, a barn being 10^{-24} square centimeters. The barn unit arose from the flippant idea that it is easier to hit the side of a barn than to hit an atomic nucleus.

An important factor influencing the cross-section is the kinetic energy or velocity of a particle. Increased energy gives to a bullet particle the capacity to penetrate more deeply into the electrostatic force field of the target particle before being deflected away again. In the case of a neutron approaching a uranium nucteus in a nuclear reactor, the collision cross-section is increased by reducing the velocity of the neutrons. The neutrons produced by fission of the uranium nucleus have high energies in the millions of electron-volts. If decelerated they spend more time in the neighborhood of a uranium nucleus, and the probability of neutron capture by the uranium nucleus is thus increased. This deceleration process is performed by substances called *moderators*.

A moderator is a suitable material dispersed through a reactor and which moderates (decelerates) the neutrons by allowing them to collide with the nuclei of the moderating substance, without being captured by such nuclei. The neutrons thus are "scattered" but not absorbed. These must be "elastic" collisions, meaning that energy is lost from the neutron to the target nucleus because of the collision, but no energy is lost by radio-activity or other type of nuclear reaction. The neutrons lose only kinetic energy in being moderated. Moderating materials must have a high cross-section for neutron scattering (high σ_S), and a small cross-section for neutron absorption (σ_A); this is the opposite of what is desired of the uranium nucleus.

The best moderators are most of the light elements, such as hydrogen, deuterium, helium, beryllium, carbon, nitrogen, oxygen. Like moderators, the metals used in the fuel rods of nuclear reactors must have high scattering cross-section for neutrons and low cross-section for absorption: aluminum and zirconium are principally used for this purpose.

To slow down the nuclear process in a reactor, control rods made of materials of high absorption cross-section are inserted into the reactor. Suitable absorbing materials are cadmium, boron, hafnium, and the rare earth metals.

NEUTRON CROSS-SECTIONS, barns

Element	σ_A	σ_S
$_1H^1$	0.33	38.0
$_1H^2$	0.0005	7
He	0.000	0.8
Be	0.010	7
B	755	4
C	0.0032	4.8
O	0.0002	4.2
Mg	0.063	3.6
Al	0.230	1.4
Ti	5.6	4
Cr	2.9	3.0
Fe	2.53	11
Zr	0.180	8
Cd	2550	7
Gd	46,000	?
Hf	105	8.2
Ta	21.3	5
U	2.7	8.3

2.13 absorption, transmission, and reflection

A highly important part of the information needed for the selection of materials concerns the effect of the surface or body of the material upon incident radiant and acoustic energy. Consider the following examples:

(a) Photographic darkrooms must be painted with nonreflective paints.
(b) Ceiling tile must absorb acoustic energy without reflecting an excessive fraction of that energy.
(c) Beryllium "windows" are used on X-ray tubes because this light metal has a very low absorption for X-radiation.
(d) Lead is used as a shield against X- and gamma radiation because of its high absorptivity for such high energy radiation.
(e) Polished aluminum surfaces are used in automobile sealed-beam headlights.
(f) Photographic filters are used to absorb certain colors (frequencies) in photography.
(g) The dark glass used in arc welding helmets transmits less than one ten-thousandth of the incident light of the arc.
(h) Punched tape is commonly used in computer work and in numerically controlled machine tools. If the holes in the tape are to be read by photocells, then the paper tape must have a sufficiently high absorptivity for light, so that light can reach the photocell only through the holes in the tape.

Suppose that an infrared or a visible light wave falls upon a sheet of window glass. The glass will produce three effects on the incident radiation:

1. Most of the radiated energy will be passed or *transmitted* by the glass. We say that glass is transparent to heat and light. But if higher-energy radiation, such as ultraviolet or X-radiation, is incident on the glass, such energy is powerful enough to raise electrons to a higher energy level; such radiation is absorbed by the glass.
2. A lesser fraction of the incident radiation is *reflected* by the surface of the glass.
3. A fraction of the radiation will be *absorbed* by the glass. The absorbed fraction of the radiant energy will raise the temperature of the glass window.

Now the following simple relationship must hold (Fig. 14):

The energy incident on the glass
= transmitted energy + reflected energy + absorbed energy.

This of course is simply a special statement of the most fundamental of scientific theories, the law of conservation of energy. In other words,

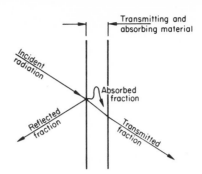

Fig. 14 Transmission, absorption, and reflection of incident radiation.

the sum of the fractions transmitted, reflected, and absorbed must equal 1. The decimal fraction transmitted is termed the *transmittance*, the decimal fraction reflected is termed the *reflectance*, and the fraction absorbed is termed the *absorptivity*.

$$T + R + A = 1$$

While the sum of these three fractions is always equal to 1 for any wavelength, the fractions themselves are dependent on wavelength. Thus the transmittance of beryllium metal for visible light is zero, but for X-radiation it is close to unity. Note also that while reflectivity is a surface characteristic, transmittance and absorptivity will depend on the thickness of the material. Thus a single sheet of white typewriter paper transmits 40 percent of visible light incident on it, but a pad of 100 sheets will transmit no measurable amount of light.

Suppose a surface to have a high absorptivity for radiation at a certain wavelength. The absorbed energy of radiation will raise the temperature of the absorbing body and therefore cause it to radiate heat. For any given wavelength, it is known that a good absorber is also a good radiator or emitter of energy (this is true also for X-radiation, subject to some qualifications), therefore for any body and any wavelength

absorptivity = emissivity

Rough-surfaced bodies absorb and emit heat well, while smooth-surfaced bodies are less efficient in these characteristics. A perfect absorber is a perfect emitter and is called a black body.

A rather interesting aspect of absorptivity concerns the color of metals. Most metals have distinctive colors, which experienced metals men use for identification. Stainless steels have a grayish cast, titanium is faintly blue, etc. Let us consider the familiar case of copper and silver. Figure 15 shows that the absorptivity of silver is quite low over the whole range of visible light. Silver therefore efficiently reflects all visible wavelengths to

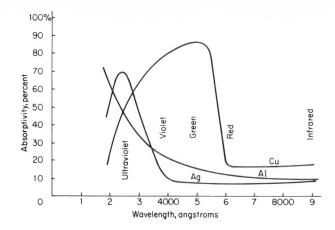

Fig. 15 Absorptivity of copper, silver, and aluminum. The curves are typical only, since actual values are markedly affected by the condition of the metal surface, and would be less for polished surfaces.

produce a white, silvery color. Aluminum has the same low absorption in the same frequency range, and thus produces a similar color. But copper absorbs the shorter wavelengths above red: the reflection of red frequencies accounts for its color.

The following table presents some typical absorptivities. The values are for broad-spectrum radiation, not for monochromatic radiation.

TYPICAL ABSORPTIVITIES (at room temperature)

aluminum sheet	0.03–0.055
aluminum paint	0.50
copper, polished	0.02
firebrick	0.70
concrete	0.9
paper	0.93
steel, polished	0.15–0.35
steel, oxidized	0.7
water	0.95

2.14 absorption coefficients for transmitted radiation

The word "transparent" should not be understood merely in terms of visible light. Thus all substances are transparent to X-radiation (gamma radiation). Absorption of radiation by transparent materials depends on the thickness of the material. The effect of thickness may be introduced

Fig. 16 Transmission of visible radiation by paper sheets. The thickness of the sheet is equivalent to a 40-percent value layer, if nonreflective conditions.

by means of a simple example. It was noted earlier that a sheet of type-writer paper transmits 0.4 of any visible light incident on one side of the paper. If then two sheets of this paper are used as a transmitting medium, the second sheet will transmit 0.4 of the light passed by the first sheet, or 0.4 × 0.4, which is 0.16 of the light incident on the first sheet. See Fig. 16. Three sheets of paper will transmit 0.4 × 0.4 × 0.4 or 0.064 of the light incident on the first sheet. And so on. Mathematically, the transmitted radiation follows the same equation as was used for radioactive decay:

$$I = I_0 e^{-\mu t}$$

where I = intensity of radiation after transmission

I_0 = intensity before transmission through the medium

t = thickness of the medium, in inches or centimeters

μ = linear absorption coefficient, or fractional decrease in intensity per unit thickness of material.

The equation assumes monochromatic (single wavelength) radiation.

In the case of X-radiation, the concept of the "half-value layer" is used, just as the half-life was used for radioactive decay. A *half-value layer* of any material is the thickness of that material required to reduce the intensity of the radiation to one-half. The half-value layer (HVL) = $0.693/\mu$. The more powerful the energy of the radiation in electron-volts, the larger the half-value layer will be: Co-60 (about 1.2 Mev) requires a HVL in steel of 0.87 inches, while Ir-192 (about 0.5 Mev) has a HVL of 0.44 inches of steel.

A "filter" must be understood to be a material with a controlled absorption characteristic. The colored glass filters used with visible light cameras reduce the range of wavelengths reaching the photographic film; such filters in effect make the radiation somewhat more monochromatic. Filters are used for the same purpose in X-ray photography, though the materials used for X-ray filters are metals such as copper, aluminum, and lead.

Fig. 17 Radiograph of an air-craft magnesium casting.

2.15 X-radiation

X-ray photography differs from visible light photography in that it photographs the *absorption effects*. Figure 17 is a radiograph of an aircraft magnesium casting. This radiograph was made by exposing the X-ray film on one side of the casting and irradiating the opposite side of the casting with an X-ray tube operated at about 70,000 v. Like all radiographs, it is a negative. The casting contains a steel insert and several blowholes. The blowholes show darker on the negative, since more radiation is transmitted through a hole than through the solid magnesium. In the opposite case, the film is underdeveloped in the region of the steel insert, because steel has about twenty times more absorption than magnesium at the X-ray voltage used to make this radiograph. In brief, a radiograph is a *shadowgraph*.

The subject of radiation absorption by materials is a lengthy and complex one. The easiest insights into the theory of absorption are provided by a brief summary of X-ray absorption effects for radiation in the range of 100 Kev to 30 Mev. This range covers the use of X- and gamma radiation in industry, though lower-energy X-radiation is used in laboratory work for the analysis of metal alloys, police work in crime detection, etc. This brief description will also serve well as a final review of that most basic scientific notion, the electron-photon interaction.

Three processes occur when radiation in the X-ray range is absorbed by a material:

1. photoelectric absorption
2. scattering
3. electron pair production

The absorption coefficient is the sum of these three effects:

μ = (photoelectric absorption fraction) + (scattering fraction)
   + (pair production fraction)

In *photoelectric absorption*, the energy of the incident photon is used to eject an electron from an atom. The electron thus ionized is termed a photoelectron. This is exactly the same process that occurs in the cathode of a photoelectric cell, hence the term photoelectric absorption. The probability of photoelectric absorption is greatest if the photon has enough energy to eject an electron from a K level (energy in the range of about 50–70 Kev). All the photon energy is absorbed by the electron, any energy remaining after ionization being used as kinetic energy by the electron.

Fig. 18 Relative absorption of gamma rays by lead.

The vacancy thus created in the K level will be filled by an electron moving into it from an outer shell. This will result in the emission of a photon of lower electron-volt energy than that which caused the vacancy. The process then is another example of fluorescence, though not in the visible light range. Photoelectric absorption is the predominant effect for X-radiation up to about 300 Kev.

Compton scattering results from collisions between photons and electrons such that the photon is deflected in direction. The photon also loses energy to the electron, so that the wavelength of the photon becomes longer. Compton scattering is the predominant absorption effect in the middle range of radiation energies, that is, below about one million electron volts.

Electron pair production is an interesting case of the conversion of energy to mass. The mass of an electron is the equivalent of 0.51 Mev. Now a photon with an energy of 0.51 Mev cannot create an electron, even though it has the required amount of energy, for the photon has no charge, and a negative charge is required for an electron. But a photon with an energy of at least 2×0.51 Mev, or 1.02 Mev, can be converted into mass in the following process, which is pair production. Two electrons will be produced by annihilation of the photon, one being a negative electron and the other a positive electron or positron. The sum of 1 negative charge and 1 positive charge equals the charge on the photon, which is zero. However the positron very quickly disappears by combining with a negative electron, the two particles being annihilated to produce two photons of 0.51 million electron-volts. The cross-section for pair production is approximately proportional to $(E - 1.02)$, where E is given in Mev. Thus pair production becomes more probable at energy levels of 5 Mev or higher.

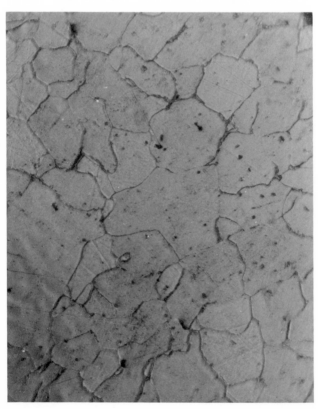

Fig. 19 Micrograph of commercial iron.

Most solid materials are aggregations of crystals, such as the metallic solid of Fig. 19, the individual crystals usually being referred to as *grains*. Each such crystal or grain is actually a single molecule with its atoms arranged in a regular repeating pattern called a space lattice. While a total of fourteen space lattices is possible, only five will be described here.

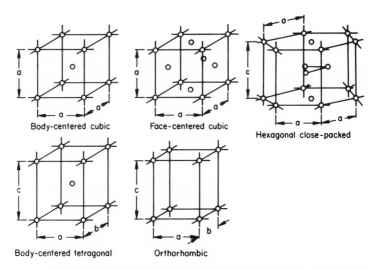

Body-centered cubic   Face-centered cubic

Hexagonal close-packed

Body-centered tetragonal   Orthorhombic

Fig. 20 Crystal structures. The small circles representing the positions of atoms are not drawn to the full scale of the atom. Interatomic distances are in the range of 2-5 Angstroms for metals.

These space lattices form three-dimensional coordinate systems, the unit distances of the coordinate system being the locations of the atoms in the space lattice. Figure 20 shows unit cells of the space lattices to which most of the metals conform. The unit distances between atoms are designated *a, b,* and *c* in three-dimensional space.

Body-centered cubic (bcc) — a cubic cell, with all three sides of length *a*, and all angles right angles. One atom in the center of the cell.
Face-centered cubic (fcc) — a cubic cell, with all three sides of length *a*, and all angles right angles. One atom in the center of each of the six faces of the unit cell.
Hexagonal close-packed (hcp) — three coplanar axes at 120° apart, all at right angles to the fourth axis. $a \neq c$.
Body-centered tetragonal (bct) — similar to bcc, except that $a = b \neq c$.
Orthorhombic — all angles right angles, but $a \neq b \neq c$.

Neglecting a few exceptions, most metals at room temperature adopt the bcc, fcc, or hcp crystal structure. The distance between atom centers in metal crystals is between 2 and 5 Angstroms. The following is a list of typical interatomic distances at room temperature, in Angstroms:

aluminum	4.0490 A
chromium	2.8845
copper	3.6153
iron	2.8664
nickel	3.5238

CRYSTAL STRUCTURES AT ROOM TEMPERATURE

bcc	fcc	hcp
iron	some stainless steels	titanium
most steels	aluminum	zinc
chromium	copper	zirconium
columbium	gold	hafnium
molybdenum	lead	rhenium
tantalum	nickel	magnesium
tungsten	platinum	beryllium
vanadium	silver	cadmium

The bcc group of metals includes only metals with high melting points. The fcc group is distinguished by the great ductility of its metals; all commercially available metal foils are made from metals of this group. The fcc group also does not become brittle at low temperatures, which explains the use of these metals for refrigeration and cryogenic equipment. (Cryogenics is the technology of low temperatures below $-250°F$.)

2.17 X-ray diffraction

The interatomic distance in metal crystals ranges from 2 to 5 A. These distances correspond roughly to the wavelength of low-energy X rays. Indeed, interatomic distances and crystal structures are determined by X rays in the following fashion, which is simple in principle though not always so simple in practice. The method is called X-ray diffraction.

Figure 21 shows two crystal planes containing rows of atoms, the interatomic distance between planes being d. A monochromatic beam of X rays is incident on, and reflected from, these planes at an angle θ. The atomic planes can be considered to act as reflecting planes, at least at low angles of incidence.

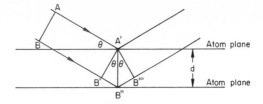

Fig. 21   Diagram for the Bragg
equation.

Suppose *AB* is the advancing wavefront of the X-ray beam, with wavelength *L*. When the wavefront has advanced to *A′B′*, the part of the wavefront reaching the top plane reflects radiation of the same wavelength as the incident radiation. This radiation propagates in all directions. The wavefront continues on from *B′* to *B″*. On reaching *B″* radiation is again emitted in all directions.

Suppose that the distance *B′B″B‴* is an integral number of wavelengths. Then the two waves from the two atomic planes will reinforce each other. But if this distance is not an integral number of wavelengths, then the two waves are out of phase, and there will be a degree of mutual cancellation between them. For the case of reinforcement

$$B'B''B''' = nL$$

where *n* represents the number of wavelengths' difference between the two reflected waves.

But $B'B'' = B''B''' = d \sin \theta$
and $B'B''B''' = 2d \sin \theta$

Then $nL = 2d \sin \theta$ — the Bragg Equation. Suppose $n = 1$, then $L = 2d \sin \theta$.

If the interatomic distance *d* is to be determined, then monochromatic radiation of known wavelength must be used. A Geiger-Muller counter or other radiation detector is rotated around the metal specimen to determine the angle θ at which the strongest X-ray reading is obtained. This gives angle θ, and the distance *d* is calculated from the Bragg equation.

2.18   *phases*

A *phase* is any recognizable state or condition of a substance. Most materials have at least three phases: solid, liquid, and gas. No material has fewer than two phases. Many materials, especially the radioactive metals plutonium and uranium, may have as many as six solid phases. The possession of more than one solid phase implies more than one crystal structure.

Carbon has five phases: gas, liquid, amorphous carbon, graphite, diamond. Iron has three solid phases, termed alpha (bcc), gamma (fcc), and delta (bcc) (there is no beta phase in iron). The reason there are two bcc phases in iron is simply that the two are separated by the fcc phase — alpha exists at room temperature, gamma at red heat, and delta close to the melting point. Each phase of any material exists within a definite temperature range. Thus the ice phase of water cannot exist above 32°F.

Now if heat energy is supplied to a material, one of two possible changes will occur:

1. The temperature of the material will be raised.
2. The temperature will remain fixed, but the phase will change.

But if the temperature is changing, the phase will not change, and conversely. This is familiar from the fact that the phase change from water to steam is isothermal, like all other phase changes. Heat may change the temperature or the phase, but not both at the same time. If the temperature is changing, the heat supplied is termed "sensible heat", since the heat effect can be sensed by means of a thermometer. If the phase is changing, the heat is termed "latent heat" ("latent" meaning hidden, since a thermometer is of no help).

Suppose a crystalline material with a single solid phase, such as beryllium, is to be heated. The heat energy introduced into the material will have several effects. One effect will be to expand the interatomic distance between atoms, resulting in an increase in dimensions of the body (the delta phase of plutonium is an exception; it contracts when heated to a higher temperature). Another effect may be changes in electron energy levels, which will be ignored here. A third effect is to set up increased vibrational motion of the atoms about their regular position in the space lattice. It is these vibrational motions of the atoms that give a metal its electrical resistance: if a metal is heated, the amplitude of vibration increases, making more difficult the passage of the electrons of the electric current and thus increasing the resistance.

If the heat energy supplied to the material is continually increased, the vibrational amplitude will increase to the point where some of the interatomic bonding of the space lattice is broken. When this occurs, some of the atoms are freed from the lattice and acquire a degree of mobility. We then say that melting has begun. The phase is being changed to the liquid phase.

A liquid phase however is not completely disordered in its atomic groupings. Small groups of atoms continually form into a space lattice, break up again, and reform. These groupings are short both in space and time, and it is common to refer to such groupings as *crystallites*.

There are a number of materials, such as glass and polyethylene, which, though apparently solid at room temperature, possess only the short-order crystallite groups instead of the long-range space lattice. This non-crystalline condition in a presumably solid phase is termed the *amorphous* condition. Such materials, when heated, do not exhibit a sharp and definite melting point, but instead grow continually less viscous as the temperature is raised. Since such materials behave like liquids or have liquid-like structures, the question arises: Are they actually liquids? The answer is yes. Glass must be considered a stiff liquid. So is firebrick, though it is harder than steel. These and other amorphous ceramic materials are often referred to as *glasses*.

2.19 solid solutions and equilibrium diagrams

An *alloy* is a mixture of two or more metals, or metal and nonmetallic elements. The most important by far of the alloy groups is the carbon-iron alloy group called "steels", which includes perhaps 25,000 different alloy mixtures. The use of alloys is more usual than pure or nearly pure metals. The pure metals do not provide highest strengths, but are employed when the highest possible electrical and thermal conductivity, or the highest resistance to corrosion, is required. Alloying is employed where strength is the paramount requirement, but always at a sacrifice in corrosion resistance. The steels, being alloys, have little corrosion resistance, while pure iron is considerably better in this respect.

The pure metals, being crystalline, have definite melting points. But alloys of two or more metals, although they also are invariably crystalline, do not usually have definite melting points, but melt over a range of temperatures.

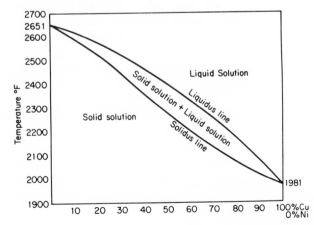

Fig. 22 Copper-nickel equilibrium diagram.

The melting and phase characteristics of metal alloys and of ceramic mixtures are displayed by means of *equilibrium diagrams*, also called constitution diagrams, of which Fig. 22 is an example. This is an equilibrium diagram for copper-nickel alloys. On such a diagram, the alloy composition is the abscissa, and temperature is the ordinate.

For pure nickel, the melting point is 2651°F, while the melting point of pure copper is 1981°F. These two melting temperatures are the end points of the curves on the diagram. Connecting these two points across all possible alloys of the two metals are two lines. The upper line is called the *liquidus* line. Above the liquidus line the alloy mixture is in the liquid phase. The lower line is called the *solidus* line. Below the solidus line the alloy mixture is in the solid phase. Between the solidus and the liquidus any alloy is partially solid and partially liquid, that is, the alloy mixture freezes or melts in the range of temperatures between the solidus and liquidus lines. For copper-nickel alloys, this melting range is about 100°. The solidus line, the liquidus line, and any other such line appearing on an equilibrium diaaram, are boundary lines separating phases.

Fig. 23   Typical space lattice of a substitutional solid solution.

Copper and nickel dissolve each other in any and all proportions, producing an infinite range of solid solutions. Since both metals are fcc, it is reasonable to expect that a solid solution of the two metals will likewise crystallize as face-centered cubic. The two types of metal atoms will be interspersed in the fcc lattice at random, as suggested by Fig. 23. The interatomic distances are altered from those of the pure metals, producing a degree of distortion in the lattice structure. It is this lattice distortion that creates the additional strength of an alloy.

A different type of equilibrium diagram is shown in Fig. 24. This is the diagram for the familiar lead-tin solders. In addition to liquidus and solidus lines, there are two other boundary lines, due to the presence of two alloy phases labelled alpha and beta.

Consider an alloy of 10 percent Sn — 90 percent Pb, which happens to be a low-cost solder with a high liquidus temperature and with too much lead to "wet out" well — lead does not readily wet other materials, hence the addition of tin to the solder. Suppose this alloy to be deposited in the liquid phase in a soldered joint at 650°F. When it cools to 570°F, the liquidus line is reached, and the alloy begins to freeze. Freezing continues as the temperature falls, until at 515°F solidification is complete. The

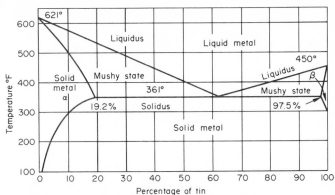

Fig. 24 Lead-tin equilibrium diagram.

freezing range is thus 55°F. The frozen alloy is in the alpha solid phase. But when the alloy is cooled to 300°F it crosses another phase line, indicating a phase transformation. Below 300°F the alloy will be not a solid solution but a mixture of two phases, alpha plus beta.

For a mixture of 61.9 percent Sn — 38.1 percent Pb, notice that the solidus and liquidus temperatures are the same. This alloy has a definite melting point, like pure lead and pure tin. Its composition is called the *eutectic* composition of the alloy. The eutectic mixture is always the alloy mixture with the lowest melting temperature and also the one with a definite melting point. Referring back to the copper-nickel equilibrium diagram, no eutectic is indicated for mixtures of these two metals. This is always true for any pair of metals which are soluble in each other in all proportions and at all temperatures.

Equilibrium diagrams are as useful in ceramic engineering as in metallurgy. Figure 25 is an equilibrium diagram for mixtures of silica and alumina. The eutectic composition is about 5 percent SiO_2 — 95 percent Al_2O_3. To show the practical application of this equilibrium diagram, we

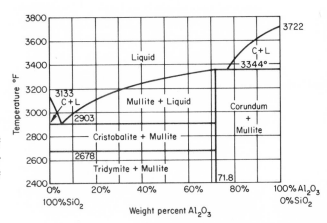

Fig. 25 Equilibrium diagram of silica-alumina. Tridymite and cristobalite are phases of silica; mullite is $3Al_2O_3 \cdot 2SiO_2$.

may consider the case of a standard firebrick, which has a composition of about 40 percent alumina and 60 percent silica. Such a firebrick cannot resist furnace temperatures higher than the solidus temperature of 2813°F. By increasing the alumina content we can produce a firebrick with improved resistance to the corrosion of molten slags, but notice that the increase in alumina does not alter the solidus temperature until the alumina content reaches 72 percent. Above 72 percent alumina, a new phase appears, called mullite, with a solidus temperature of 3290°F. Mullite brick then must be used for the linings of furnaces where firebrick requirements are exceedingly severe. (There are a rather large number of silica-high alumina phases, not shown here, including — besides mullite — andalusite, kyanite, sillimanite, and corundum. Not all are used in firebrick.)

The ceramic oxides have very high melting points, with the exception of a few such as iron oxide and borax. A high melting point or solidus temperature is an advantage in a firebrick, but in other circumstances a high melting point in an oxide may produce serious difficulties. Consider the problem of welding aluminum. Aluminum has a melting point of about 1200°F, but the metal always has a very thin surface of aluminum oxide. If the aluminum metal is to be melted during welding, this cannot be done without first melting the surface oxide. Unfortunately aluminum oxide melts at 3722°F. If a welding temperature sufficient to melt the oxide is employed, an enormous hole will be burned in the aluminum metal. The difficulty is circumvented by the practical employment of the eutectic concept. An oxide "flux" is added to the surface of the aluminum. The flux mixes with the alumina to produce a low-melting eutectic composition which makes the welding of the low-melting metal possible. Typical fluxes for reducing the softening points of oxides and silicates are borax, iron oxide, and others. Unfortunately the word "flux" has many meanings, but in general it means a ceramic additive, usually for the purpose of reducing a softening or melting point. Fluxes are employed in the melting and welding of most metals and in the manufacture of portland cement.

2.20 defects and interstitials in crystal lattices

The case of the substitutional solid solution, typified by copper-nickel solid solutions, was briefly discussed in the previous section. In such substitutional solid solutions, one metal atom can substitute for another metal atom in the space lattice. The effect is to produce some distortion in the space lattice, leading to variations of interatomic bonding, and the macroscopic effect being a stronger metal. If a metal is strong, this statement simply means that the interatomic bonding of the space lattice is strong.

Sometimes alloying results in vacancies in the atomic positions in the space lattice. Where this occurs, a *defect structure* is produced, again with lattice distortion in the region of the defect. Vacancy defects can also be produced by high energy radiation, as when a high-velocity particle removes an atom from the space lattice.

A more important type of space lattice variation is the *interstitial solid solution*. The most important practical uses of the interstitial solid solution occur in the case of the space lattice of iron, which therefore will be used as an example of this effect.

Iron has three solid phases. The delta phase is of no practical significance, and need not be mentioned. For pure iron the phase change from bcc to the fcc condition occurs at 1666°F, fcc being the structure at the higher temperature. Both fcc and bcc iron can deposit carbon atoms between iron atoms in the space lattice in what is termed an interstitial solid solution. Figure 26 shows the interstitial positions in the iron lattice which a carbon atom may occupy. These positions are the largest gaps between positions in the lattice. In the case of bcc iron the holes have a radius of 0.36 A, while for fcc iron, the interstitial hole measures 0.52 A.

bcc Iron   fcc Iron

Fig. 26   Interstitial positions in bcc and fcc iron. The largest sphere that can be inserted between iron atoms in a bcc crystal is 0.36A; in an fcc crystal 0.52A. A larger interstitial atom will produce distortion of the space lattice.

The carbon atom however measures 0.70 A. Therefore, when dissolved interstitially, the carbon atom will produce some distortion in the space lattice. This distortion will be less in the case of fcc iron, because the space gap is larger. As a result, fcc iron can dissolve more carbon than bcc iron. Fcc iron can dissolve a maximum of 2 percent by weight of carbon; this amount of carbon would fill about 10 percent of the interstitial holes. The solubility of carbon in bcc iron increases from 0.008 percent at room temperature to a maximum of 0.025 percent at 1333°F.

One last type of crystal defect remains to be described. This is the dislocation.

2.21 dislocations

The theoretical tensile strength of a metal bar can be calculated as the force required to rupture the interatomic bonding forces within the crystal. If, however, the bar is tested in a tension testing machine, it will fail at a load of perhaps one-hundredth of its theoretical capacity. This is true of any metal. The explanation for the disappointing performance is the presence of *dislocations* in the lattice structure.

Fig. 27 A dislocation.

A dislocation is a disregistry such as the one shown in Fig. 27. Suppose two bricklayers work each on one end of a wall, and one mason completes the wall height with one less brick course than the other. The result will be a "dislocation" where their work joins, except that the bricklayers would call the disregistry a "hog". The presence of dislocations in large amounts results in great weaknesses in the metal crystal, and it is unfortunately not possible to cast and freeze metals in such a way as to avoid the development of innumerable dislocations. However, dislocation-free metal whiskers have been produced in research laboratories. Since there is an extra half-sheet of atoms above the line of dislocation in Fig. 27, the upper half of the crystal is in compression, while the lower half is in tension. A shear stress exists along the line of dislocation.

2.22 polymerization

If the interatomic distance in a metal crystal or grain is 3 A, and the crystal measures 0.0025 millimeters in each of its three dimensions, the space lattice then is a single molecule containing about 500×10^9 metal atoms. The chemical formula, assuming an iron crystal, would be $(Fe)_{500 \times 10^9}$. The molecular grain is built up of simple unit patterns which are repeated throughout the volume of the grain.

Silicate minerals, such as glass and clays, have a similar repeating molecular structure, illustrated by Fig. 28. Here the unit pattern is a basic chemical group SiO_4 or Si_2O_7, which, like the case of the metal grain, is repeated in three dimensions.

Fig. 28   Silicate molecule.

In the case of organic materials, the unit pattern is called a *monomer*, and the large molecule which is made up of repeated strings of monomers, is termed a *polymer*. Figure 29 shows the monomer ethylene and the corresponding polymer polyethylene, a well-known plastic. The plastics, rubbers, drugs, foods, wood, and many other types of organic materials have a polymer structure. The chemical engineer can control the length of these long-chain polymers, just as the metallurgist or the heat-treater can control the size of the metal grains by control of the heat-treating time and temperature as the metal is heated in a furnace.

Fig. 29   Ethylene and polyethylene.

2.23   inclusions and composites

Most metals will contain foreign particles, usually ceramic materials. If such particles are undesirable, they are called *inclusions*. If however they belong in the metal, they do not seem to be honored with a generic name. Figure 30 is a micrograph of cast copper showing lenticular inclusions of copper oxide. Such inclusions may enter the metal by a wide variety of methods. The oxide inclusions in the figure are of course the result of chemical combination of copper with oxygen during furnace melting. When "tapping" molten metal from a melting furnace, the metal must run out through a firebrick-lined trough. The flow of metal will wash particles out of the firebrick; these will appear in the metal. Ceramic particles also can fall or drip from the roof of a melting furnace into the molten bath. Silicon and aluminum are added to steel to combine with dissolved oxygen, and manganese is likewise added to take up sulfur. The end result is the appearance of SiO_2, Al_2O_3, and MnS as inclusions in the steel. Still another source of inclusions is welding slag which has been trapped in the molten metal during welding operations.

The harmful effects of inclusions are many. In the case of forming operations employed in the production of automobile bodies, the presence of inclusions may cause the sheet metal to tear while being formed between

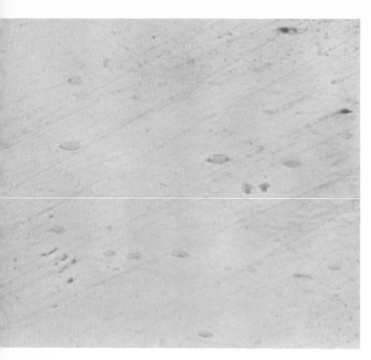

Fig. 30   Cast copper with Cu_2O inclusions.

dies. The same inclusions will cause cracks to initiate in forgings, or will lead to eventual failure of such machine parts as the balls in ball bearings and engine exhaust valve stems.

In other cases, inclusions may serve useful purposes and may be purposely added to a metal or other material. Carbon black is added to some plastics and rubbers for protection against ultraviolet radiation. Lead is added to metal bars to make them more machinable. High speed steels obtain their hardness from the addition of carbides to the steel. Gray cast iron derives many of its useful characteristics from the flakes of graphite distributed throughout its structure.

The ultimate in inclusions is the blending of two or more dissimilar materials in such a way as to produce a new material with the characteristics of both materials — a blend termed a *composite*. Perhaps the most familiar composite is the group of reinforced plastics, reinforced with fiberglass, asbestos, or other filaments. Pairs of highly incongruous materials have been blended to make such useful composites as lead and polyethylene.

A highly useful type of composite is the ceramic-metal mixture, sometimes called a "cermet". One example is the carbide cutter bit used for machining metals. This is a mixture of finely ground carbides of tantalum and tungsten bonded together with cobalt metal. The structure of such a material is therefore a continuous phase of metal with a discontinuous ceramic phase. The strength and ductility characteristics of the composite material are primarily those of the continuous phase. Often, too, in a standard metal alloy there will be a distinct phase deposited at the grain boundaries of the metal, so that in effect each grain appears to be embedded in the grain boundary phase. Again, the strength characteristics of the metal will be those of the continuous phase. In general, though, such a continuous phase is undesirable in a metal, and will be removed by a suitable heat-treating operation.

PROBLEMS

1 (a) Using the American Society for Metals *Metals Handbook* or other reference, decide which of the three crystal structures, bcc, fcc, or hcp, is generally associated with high tensile strength in metals.
(b) Which of the three crystal structures appears to be associated with high melting point?

2 What is the number of protons and of neutrons in each of the following isotopes: $_3Li^7$, $_{11}Na^{25}$, $_{16}S^{36}$?

3 Determine the wavelength of radiation corresponding to photon energies of 0.5 and 6000 electron-volts, and state the type of radiation in each case.

4 Name devices in use for the detection of the following types of radiation: radio, infrared, visible light, ultraviolet, gamma ray.

5 Could the radiation from an X-ray tube activate the photocell on an elevator door? Why?

6 Explain why elements of Group I of the Periodic Table are suitable cathode materials for photocells.

7 The forbidden energy band between allowed energy bands in germanium is 0.72 ev wide. What photon wavelength corresponds to this bandwidth?

8 What is the general effect of a filter on the spectrum of a broad-band radiation?

9 If a metal is used as a filter for broad-band X-radiation, will such a filter suppress long-wave or short-wave radiation in general? Why?

10 Explain why in fluorescence the stimulated radiation has a longer wavelength than the exciting radiation.

11 Explain why many electrical insulating materials, such as window glass, are transparent to visible radiation.

12 What is the half-life of an element with a stable nucleus?

13 Why are radioactive sources bought by the curie instead of the pound or kilogram?

14 Suppose radioactive Iridium-192 costs $20 a curie. If shipped by airfreight, the cost of freight is $1 per curie higher than the rail rate. Airfreight, however, saves 7.5 days' delivery time. Explain the argument for airfreight.

15 Determine the age of the earth, given the following information. Uranium-238, with a half-life of 4.5 billion years, decays to Pb-206, which is stable. U-238 always contains Pb-206 because the lead is the end element of uranium disintegration. For every 100 atoms in the lead-uranium mixture, 46 are lead and 54 are uranium.

16 A wooden ship, which turns out to be a remarkable historical discovery, is recovered from the sand dunes of Libya. The discovery party of historians must be certain of the age of the ship. Find its age, given the following information.

A small amount of carbon in CO_2 is converted from C-12 to C-14 due to cosmic radiation. This carbon is taken up by plants during photosynthesis. During the life of a plant, the ratio of C-14 to C-12 in the plant is constant, but decreases when CO_2 absorption ceases at the death of the plant. Assume the half-life of C-14 to be 5600 years. The radioactivity of a living tree is 255 disintegrations per kg per sec. The radioactivity of wood from the ship is 240 disintegrations per kg per sec.

17 Why is gamma radiation more dangerous to bone than to soft tissue in the human body?

18 The half-value thickness of aluminum is to be determined for a certain X-ray tube. A sheet of aluminum 0.10 in. thick is available. When used as an X-ray barrier, this sheet reduces the radiation to 20 percent of the incident radiation. What is the half-value thickness of aluminum for this radiation?

19 If bond paper 0.002 in. thick passes 40 percent of visible light incident on it, what is the half-value thickness of this bond paper for visible light?

20 An opaque material has a reflectance of 0.20. What fraction of the incident radiation is absorbed by the material?

21 Explain the mechanism of photoelectric absorption of high-energy radiation.

22 Explain why the electrical resistance of metals increases with temperature, while that of ceramic materials such as firebrick decreases with temperature.

23 The space lattice of a nickel specimen is to be determined using the Bragg equation. If $\sin \theta = 0.1445$, $n = 1$, and the photon energy of the radiation is 12.0 Kev, what is the space lattice dimension?

24 What is a eutectic temperature?

25 How is it possible for iron to have three solid phases, yet only two crystal structures?

26 What is the difference between an interstitial solid solution and a substitutional solid solution?

The technology of materials has acquired such a degree of sophistication that it is not possible to make a summary review of the significant characteristics of materials. In this book therefore, material characteristics are grouped into four sections: physical, electrical, mechanical, and economic. This grouping is of course arbitrary. By "physical characteristics" we mean those more or less fundamental characteristics which may be understood or explained from the basic concepts of physics. On the other hand, performance characteristics of an empirical or less fundamental nature, such as metal fatigue, coefficient of friction, or hardness, are classified here as mechanical characteristics.

Many of the physical properties of materials have already been discussed in the previous chapter, such properties including neutron cross-section, absorptivity, half-life, and others. These need not be further reviewed.

3.1   stress and strain

While the words "stress" and "strain" are often confused in ordinary conversation, they each have specific meanings. Consider the case of a towing cable connecting a tractor to a towed vehicle. There is some force, measured in pounds, at each end of the cable. The *stress* in the cable is the tension

PHYSICAL PROPERTIES
OF
MATERIALS

3

force divided by the cross-sectional area of the cable. Thus if the towing force applied to the cable is 150 lb, and the area of the cable 0.5 sq in., then the stress in the cable is 300 lb per sq in. (psi).

Accompanying any stress, there is always some deformation (change in dimension) of the stressed part. The cable elongates due to the tension force applied to it. This deformation, when expressed as elongation per unit length, is termed *unit strain*. If the cable is 120 in. long, and under the stress of 300 psi it elongates 0.3 in., the unit strain will be

$$\frac{0.3 \text{ in.}}{120 \text{ in.}} = 0.0025 \text{ in./in.}$$

There are only three possible types of stresses: *tension, compression,* and *shear*. These are illustrated in Fig. 31. A shear force or stress tends to cut through the material, as occurs in the shearing and punching of metal plates, or it may be a twisting force or stress such as shears the head from a bolt when the torque of a wrench is excessively high. The strength of materials is lower in shear than in tension, and for most materials, especially brittle materials, the strength in tension is lower than the compressive strength.

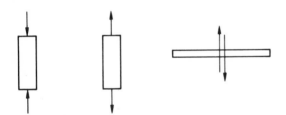

Fig. 31 Forces producing compression, tension, and shear stress.

If the load or stress is removed from a material, two types of behavior are possible:

1. The material may remain permanently deformed by the stress. This kind of strain behavior, in which the strain is permanent, is termed *plasticity*. Wet concrete or damp soil are plastic materials. When walked on, they retain the impression of the walker's shoe.
2. The material may return to its original shape and size. This behavior, in which the strain disappears with the stress, is called *elasticity*.

Many materials exhibit elasticity under limited conditions of stress. Only a few brittle materials, such as glass, are wholly elastic when loaded to their failure stress. In general, the word "brittle" suggests a material in which strain behavior will be elastic, since such a material is capable of only a limited amount of strain. Ductile materials are those materials capable of a considerable amount of plastic deformation.

Materials do not strain only because of applied stress. Expansion due to temperature rise is a strain, usually elastic. Vibrations are a type of cyclical elastic strain. Electric and magnetic fields likewise may strain certain materials elastically.

Both elastic and plastic strain are desirable characteristics. Dimensional stability is expected of manufactured industrial goods; such goods are designed so that any predictable stresses which they must carry will fall within the limited elastic range of the material. On the other hand, most forming operations during manufacture require plasticity for their execution. The raw material for an automobile fender is a flat sheet of steel. It must be deformed plastically to become a fender. But when installed on an automobile only elastic deformations are desirable (though rarely obtained in car accidents). Even hard firebrick and glass must be manufactured while they are in a plastic condition.

3.2   Poisson's ratio

Suppose a bar to be stretched by a tensile stress in its x-direction. If the volume of the bar is to remain constant, then it must experience a lateral *contraction* in the y- and z-directions. Within the elastic range, this lateral strain is proportional to the axial strain, and Poisson's ratio expresses the ratio of the two strains:

$$\text{Poisson's ratio} = \mu = \frac{\text{lateral strain}}{\text{axial strain}}$$

For metals, Poisson's ratio is in the range of 0.27 to 0.30 for elastic strains. Poisson's ratio for plastic strain is taken as 0.5.

3.3   modulus of elasticity

Most metals, rubbers, and a number of other materials, exhibit elastic behavior below a stress termed the elastic limit. In this elastic range the unit strain is usually found to be proportional to the stress. The modulus of elasticity, symbol E, is the ratio of stress to strain:

$$E = \frac{\text{stress}}{\text{strain}}$$

In conversation, E is commonly called the E-value of the material. A very rigid material will necessarily have a very high E-value, since a large stress

physical properties of materials

will be accompanied by only a small strain. If the stress and the strain are measured for a small rubber band, the E-value will be found to be about 200. The metals however have moduli of elasticity ranging from about 6.5×10^6 for magnesium to 80×10^6 for osmium. The units of E are psi.

MODULI OF ELASTICITY (psi)

glass	10×10^6 (varies)	steel	29×10^6
alumina	40×10^6	lead	2×10^6
graphite	1×10^6 (varies)	magnesium	6.5×10^6
wood	1.5×10^6 (varies)	molybdenum	47×10^6
concrete	3×10^6 (varies)	nickel	30×10^6
polyethylene	35,000	titanium	16.5×10^6
aluminum	10×10^6	tungsten	50×10^6
beryllium	44×10^6	zirconium	14×10^6
copper	16×10^6		

3.4   stress-strain diagrams

The *tension test* is the most commonly performed of the standard tests applied to materials. This test provides at least three basic items of information about a solid material:

1. tensile strength
2. ductility
3. modulus of elasticity

A typical sample of material used for a tension test specimen is shown in Fig. 32. Two center-punch marks are made in the test length of the speci-

Fig. 32 Typical tension test specimen with 2-inch gauge marks.

Fig. 33 Universal testing machine. The test load is indicated on the large dial.

men exactly 2.000 in. apart. The material between these gauge marks is the material analyzed under test, and the 2.000 in. length is termed the gauge length. A suitable strain gauge is mounted on the specimen to record the tensile strain in the gauge length under load. The specimen is then mounted in a tension testing machine such as the one shown in Fig. 33. This testing machine is actually a highly accurate, instrumented hydraulic press which can load materials in either tension or compression. The large dial indicates the load in pounds applied to the specimen, while the strain gauge indicates the elongation in the 2-in. gauge length. For any load, therefore, the stress is found by dividing the cross-sectional area of the specimen into the load, and the unit strain by dividing the elongation by 2. Suppose the results of the test are those given in the following table.

STRESS-STRAIN READINGS FOR A STEEL TEST SAMPLE

Load (lb)	Stress (psi)	Elongation in 2 in.	Unit Strain (in.)
1000	1000	0.000066	0.000033
2000	2000	0.000133	0.000066
4000	4000	0.000266	0.000133
6000	6000	0.000400	0.000200
10000	10000	0.000666	0.000333
20000	20000	0.001333	0.000666
30000	30000	0.002000	0.001000
42000	42000	0.0028	0.0014
42000	42000	0.040	0.020
44000	44000	0.060	0.030
50000	50000	0.170	0.085
60000	60000	0.264	0.132
63000	63000	0.280	0.140 *Rupture.*

Fig. 34 Stress-strain curve.

The graph of stress (ordinate) versus strain (abscissa) is given in Fig. 34. Examination of either the data or the graph discloses much information. The *ultimate tensile stress* (UTS) is 63,000 psi. The maximum elongation is 14 percent in 2 in. The reduction in area (R.A.) is often measured at the break and reported with the elongation as an additional indicator of ductility, since a very ductile material will neck down considerably before fracturing. The modulus of elasticity may be calculated from the readings at 30,000 lb:

$$E = \frac{30,000}{0.001} = 30 \times 10^6$$

The strain is linear up to 42,000 psi. The latter value of stress is the *proportional limit*. The material may exhibit some nonlinear elasticity above the proportional limit, however; the end of the elastic range is termed the *elastic limit*. More attention however is given to the *yield stress*. This is the stress corresponding to the intersection of the stress-strain curve with a line parallel to the linear part of the curve and intersecting the strain axis at 0.2 percent strain.

The meaning of the terms "brittle" and "ductile" is disclosed by this stress-strain curve. A brittle material shows little plastic strain or none whatever, while a ductile material has an extended plastic region. The stress-strain readings for the above steel sample indicate that while not brittle, the steel is not especially ductile, since the elongation is only 14 percent. A total strain of not less than 10 percent is demanded of most metals except cast irons, but a ductile metal might give 35–50 percent elongation.

Notice that at 42,000 lb the material yields plastically without an increase in load, but at 44,000 lb this yielding ceases, and the metal takes on more stress. The metal strengthens as a result of plastic deformation. This effect is called *work-hardening* or *strain-hardening*, and is found in all metals to some degree. Metals become harder and stronger when deformed plastically. If a wire must be cut, and no pliers are available, it is usual to flex the wire repeatedly in one place to cause it to break. This is strain-hardening. The repeated flexing makes the metal harder and thus more brittle.

3.5   strain mechanisms

Strains and stresses may be determined by the method of X-ray diffraction and Bragg's Law as explained in Chapter 2, but only for elastic strains. In elastic deformation, the interatomic spacing within the crystal lattice must increase or decrease, and the X-ray diffraction method uses the interatomic distance as a gauge length.

Plastic deformation however proceeds by mechanisms other than change of interatomic spacing. These mechanisms are *slip* and *twinning*.

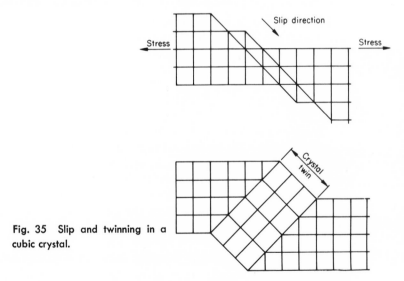

Fig. 35 Slip and twinning in a cubic crystal.

Slip is shown in Fig. 35. Here the atoms have moved over one integral interatomic distance along the slip plane, and when the stress is removed, there will be no interatomic force to return the atoms below the slip plane to their original positions. Slip occurs along planes of greatest atomic

Fig. 36   Slip planes in fcc, bcc, and hcp metals. These planes are those of greatest atomic density. In the fcc crystal lattice there are eight such planes, including the shaded one in the diagram, in the bcc lattice six. In an hcp lattice the base plane has the greatest atomic density.

density.   Such planes are shown for fcc, bcc, and hcp metals in Fig. 36. There are three such planes in the hcp lattice.   Since the face-centered cubic lattice has the greatest number of slip planes, eight in all, fcc metals are the most ductile.

Twinning, like slip, is a shear strain, in which there is a uniform tilting of the surface in the twinned region.   Figure 37 shows micrographs of slip and twinning.

Fig. 37 (a) The sets of parallel lines within the individual crystals are twins.

Fig. 37 (b) A series of twins with sliplines crossing the twinning planes. This micrograph is taken at a higher magnification than (a). Both specimens are brasses.

The brittleness of the ceramic materials is explained by the atomic structure of a ceramic crystal. Figure 38 represents the space lattice of magnesium oxide. Slip cannot occur, for a movement of one interatomic distance will align like atoms, thus destroying the molecular structure. A sufficiently large force to execute such distortion is not physically possible.

Fig. 38 Comparison of the cubic crystal structures of a metal and magnesium oxide.

Metal

Magnesium oxide

If a metal crystal were a perfect crystal, without dislocations (see Chapter 2), for slip to occur it would be necessary for the bonds between all atoms across the slip plane to break simultaneously. Such a crystal would be perhaps a hundred times stronger than any metals which any experimenter has tested in a tension test. The actual strengths of metals are explained by the presence of dislocations in the crystal. Slip occurs by movement of the dislocation, one atomic bond at a time, across the slip plane as in Fig. 39. If the plastic deformation is continued, then dislocations are gradually consumed, and the crystal becomes more perfect and therefore stronger. This is the explanation of strain-hardening. Finally a condition is reached where the stress required for slip to continue exceeds the stress required for rupture, and the metal finally breaks.

physical properties of materials

67

Fig. 39 Movement of a dislocation due to stress.

3.6 anisotropy

An isotropic material has identical physical properties in all three dimensions. Such a material is difficult to produce, though highly desirable.
Steel sheet used in deep-drawing operations, for example, must flow uniformly in all directions while it is being shaped in the die.

Since most metals are formed by rolling, extruding, and similar processes which give a marked directionality to the metal, it would be expected
that such materials would be anisotropic. The greatest strength of the
material occurs in the direction of rolling, and the degree of anisotropy
increases with the degree of reduction by rolling.

3.7 coefficient of linear thermal
expansion

This expansion coefficient is the amount of expansion in a one-foot or
one-inch length of a solid material as a result of a temperature rise of 1°.
The expansion coefficient is a pure number reported as inches per inch or
feet per foot per degree, and is of course a thermal strain. The convenient
assumption can usually be made that this coefficient is a constant, though
this assumption must be abandoned if thermal strains are to be calculated
over temperature ranges of hundreds of degrees. For most materials the
expansion coefficient increases slightly with temperature, and will change
with any phase change in the material.

COEFFICIENTS OF LINEAR EXPANSION

in./in. at 70°F.

carbon steel	0.000 006
copper, brass	0.000 009
aluminum	0.000 012

When laying up firebrick in industrial furnaces, an expansion allowance of $\frac{1}{4}$ in. every 4 ft is used. The silica brick used in the roofs of open-hearth furnaces for the melting of steel present a special problem. Silica brick has a very large expansion up to about 1000°F, but almost no expansion at higher temperatures. Damage to the furnace roof can be expected if the furnace temperature falls below 1000°F. Techniques have therefore been developed to repair such roofs while hot.

Dimensional stability being a highly desirable characteristic in finished goods, the lowest possible expansion coefficient is always sought. Aluminum having twice the coefficient of steels, it can be expected to show twice the warpage during welding operations. In other applications the coefficient of expansion must be formulated to suit the conditions of use, as in the case of vacuum tubes for the electronics industry. If these are not to lose their vacuum, the metal and glass components of the tube must have matching expansion coefficients. The alloys of nickel and iron can be blended to give a suitably wide range of expansion coefficients.

3.8 melting point and boiling point

These are temperatures of phase change from solid to liquid and liquid to gas. The heat required to melt or boil unit weight of a substance is termed its latent heat.

The evaporation of water at temperatures below the nominal boiling point is a familiar phenomenon. This phenomenon occurs with all substances. The evaporated gas exerts a pressure termed the *vapor pressure*. If the pressure on the substance is reduced, then its boiling point falls to a lower temperature and its vapor pressure is increased, indicating that evaporation occurs at a faster rate. If therefore metals with low boiling points are used in high vacua or in aerospace vehicles, there may be loss of the metal through evaporation. Thus iron boils at about 5500°F at atmospheric pressure, but in outer space its boiling point would be reduced to the region of about 1500°F. Cadmium and zinc cannot be used in space vehicles for this reason; both metals will boil away in outer space at a temperature in the range of 100°F.

It is generally true that the oxides of metals have higher melting points than the metals themselves. There are some exceptions. The oxides of iron melt at approximately the same temperature as iron, and this is the reason why steels can be cut with the oxyacetylene torch while other metals cannot.

MELTING POINTS OF THE METALS

mercury	−38°F	silicon	2570°F
gallium	85.5	nickel	2651
sodium	208	iron	2804
lithium	367	titanium	3074
tin	449	zirconium	3326
bismuth	520	thorium	3348
cadmium	609	vanadium	3452
lead	621	boron	3812
zinc	787	hafnium	3866
magnesium	1204	columbium	4379
aluminum	1224	molybdenum	4752
copper	1918	tantalum	5425
uranium	2071	tungsten	6152
beryllium	2343	carbon	6600

The material with the highest melting point so far produced is hafnium carbide.

MELTING POINTS OF CERAMIC MATERIALS

hafnium carbide	7520°F	silicon carbide	4890°F
tantalum carbide	7025	zirconia	4850
carbon	6600	calcium oxide	4660
zirconium carbide	6370	beryllia	4570
tantalum nitride	6050	titania	3870
titanium carbide	5660	alumina	3722
thoria	5630	nickel oxide	3560
zirconium boride	5530	silica	3110
magnesia	5070		

The specific heat of any material is the amount of heat energy, measured in Btu's, that will raise the temperature of 1 lb of the material 1°F. The specific heat is therefore a measure of the amount of heat that can be stored in a material. Although the specific heat is frequently assumed to be constant, for any material it varies somewhat with temperature, usually increasing with temperature. Therefore any specific heats quoted usually apply to temperature conditions of 70°F or 20°C. These are almost the same temperature.

The light elements of the periodic table have the highest specific heats, while the heavy elements have low specific heats.

TABLE OF SPECIFIC HEATS

Btu/lb/°F

hydrogen	3.4	air	0.24
helium	1.25	steel	0.11
water	1.00	cast iron	0.12
lithium	0.79	aluminum	0.22
boron	0.305	copper	0.09
beryllium	0.52	nickel	0.105
ice	0.5	zirconium	0.066
steam	0.5 (approx)	uranium	0.028

The specific heat of ceramic materials is frequently taken at the rough figure of 0.2. Since organic materials contain considerable hydrogen usually, their specific heats are in the range of 0.3 to 0.5.

3.10   *thermal conductivity*

The thermal conductivity of a material is also known as the *K*-factor. A low *K*-factor, below 1.0, indicates that the material is a heat insulator. Being highly conductive, the metals have *K*-factors in the range 100 to 2700 Btu/sq ft-in.-°F-hr.

Figure 40 shows a board foot of insulating material, say fiberglass, with a *K*-factor of 0.3. Suppose there is a temperature difference of 1°F between the two flat faces of the fiberglass. Then heat will flow through the fiberglass from the hot face to the cold face. The actual heat flow through the board foot of fiberglass with a 1° face difference of temperature

Fig. 40   Explanation of *K*-factor
or thermal conductivity.

will be 0.3 Btu/hr. The quantity of heat conducted by the material under these unit conditions is termed the thermal conductivity or *K*-factor, which for fiberglass will of course be 0.3 Btu per hr. Since *K*-factor is defined in terms of a board foot of material, the *K*-factor has mixed units of feet and inches.

Like the specific heat and the coefficient of expansion, the thermal conductivity is assumed to be constant over short ranges of temperature. But like these other physical "constants", the thermal conductivity increases with temperature. The *K*-factor for many insulating concretes used for lining industrial furnaces may increase by a factor of 5 between room temperature and 1000°.

TABLE OF THERMAL CONDUCTIVITIES

Btu/hr-sq ft-°F-in.

soils	4–12 (increased by moisture content)
ice	12
snow	5 (varies)
carbon steel (at 70°F)	310
stainless steel #304	105
copper (70°F)	2740
aluminum	1400

The thermal conductivity is one of the more significant properties of any material, with an influence in areas where the novice might least expect to find it. Figure 41 shows micrographs of two spot welds, one made on low carbon steel with a relatively high *K*-factor, and the other on stainless steel with a low *K*-factor. Because heat cannot readily flow from the area of the spot weld in stainless steel, the heat is retained in this area and the effect is an undesirable large grain growth. Such grain growth is absent in the higher conductivity carbon steel. By and large, a low thermal conductivity indicates a material which is easy to weld, since the welding heat

Fig. 41 (a) Spot weld joining two sheets of 24-gauge mild steel.

Fig. 41 (b) Spot weld joining two sheets of 24-gauge type 304 stainless steel.

is retained in the area of the weld. Stainless steel is easy to weld, despite unfavorable grain growth. Copper has such a high conductivity that it is virtually unweldable by many welding methods.

The following is the equation for one-dimensional heat flow:

$$Q = \frac{kA(t_1 - t_2)}{L}$$

where Q = heat transferred in Btu/hour
   K = thermal conductivity of the material, Btu/sq ft-hr-°F-in.
   t_1 = temperature of the hot side of the material
   t_2 = temperature of the cold side of the material
   L = thickness of the material in *inches*
   A = cross-sectional area of heat flow path, in square *feet*.

3.11 viscosity

Fluids have the characteristic that they can be pumped or otherwise made to flow. The term "fluids" therefore includes both liquids and gases. A shear stress is required to make a fluid flow. Thus if water is flowing through a pipe, the water at the axis of the pipe has the highest velocity, while a thin layer of fluid in contact with the pipe wall has zero velocity, and any layer of fluid must shear against the adjacent layer. In a solid material, shear stress is proportional to the *magnitude* of the deformation. In a fluid, the shear stress is proportional to the *time rate* of deformation. We are then led to a better definition of a fluid: a fluid is a substance that undergoes continuous deformation when subjected to a shearing stress.

One of the most important of fluid properties is *viscosity*, which may be defined as the resistance of the fluid to flow or to shear. Comparing molasses to water, molasses is a high-viscosity (viscous) fluid, while water has a low viscosity. Since fluids must be moved by pumps and fans which consume horsepower, the ideal fluid would have zero viscosity. The viscosity of most fluids does not change if the rate of deformation changes. Such fluids are termed *Newtonian fluids*.

Certain fluids however are non-Newtonian. A ductile metal will require a certain magnitude of shear stress before plastic flow occurs, and such behavior is non-Newtonian. A perfectly elastic solid must have an infinitely large viscosity. Still another and an important type of non-Newtonian fluid is a *thixotropic* fluid, of which the most familiar example is a non-sag house paint. If the paint will not sag when applied to a vertical wall, this would seem to imply an exceedingly high viscosity. But if this were the case, the paint could not be brushed out on the wall. Instead, a thixotropic fluid shows a decrease in viscosity when subject to a shear stress: the viscosity of the paint is higher when on the wall than when being brushed out. Other examples of thixotropic fluids are clay-water mixtures and firebrick mortars.

The viscosity of liquids (and solids) *decreases* with temperature; that of gases increases with temperature. The viscosity of liquids increases slightly with pressure up to about 1000 psi, but increases rapidly for higher pressures. Thus the viscosity of some hydraulic oils when used in hydraulic presses at pressure of 10,000 psi may be five times the viscosity at atmospheric pressure. To minimize leakage, higher viscosity fluids are used in high-pressure hydraulic systems, although the higher viscosity of the oil demands greater power consumption in the hydraulic pump.

It is unfortunate that the property of viscosity is measured in a bewildering variety of engineering units. Only the more commonly used units of viscosity will be mentioned here.

The fundamental equation for viscosity may be explained by reference to Fig. 42. Here two parallel plates are a distance b feet apart, one plate

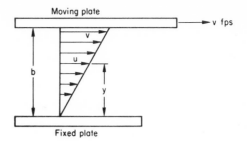

Fig. 42 Shear stress in a fluid between two plates.

being fixed and the other moving at velocity V in feet per second. The fluid adheres to each plate, so that the fluid velocity is zero at the fixed plate and V at the moving plate. At any point y above the fixed plate the velocity u is

$$u = \frac{V}{b} y$$

The shearing stress $= \lambda = \mu(V/b)$ where $\mu = $ viscosity. This equation defines viscosity. Therefore the viscosity $= \mu = \lambda(b/V)$.

The absolute viscosity then is a force acting on unit area of a plane surface moving at unit velocity relative to another surface at unit distance away from it. For the units of absolute viscosity, consider that

$$\mu = \lambda\frac{b}{V} = \text{stress}\left(\frac{\text{length}}{\text{velocity}}\right) = \frac{F}{L^2}\frac{L}{L/T}$$

where $F = $ force
   $L = $ length
   $T = $ time

giving units for absolute viscosity of pound-seconds per square foot, or in the metric system, dyne-seconds per square centimeter. The metric unit is called a *poise*.

$$1 \, \frac{\text{lb-sec}}{\text{ft}^2} = 478.8 \text{ poise}$$

The disadvantage of these absolute units of viscosity is the difficulty of setting up convenient apparatus for their measurement. The most widely used instrument for determining viscosity in this country is the Saybolt Universal Viscosimeter. Using this instrument, the time in seconds for 60 cu cm of liquid to flow vertically through a small orifice is measured. This time is called the viscosity, expressed as Saybolt seconds universal (SSU). Since viscosity varies with temperature, the temperature of the test must be specified. Temperatures of 100°F and 210°F are in common use.

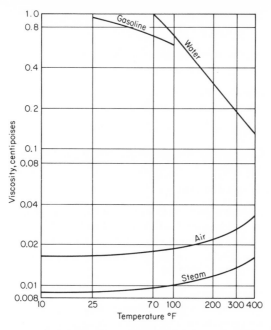

Fig. 43 Viscosities of common fluids.

In hydraulic systems, oils with viscosities in the range of 500–950 SSU at 100°F are used for higher pressures, 2500 psi or higher. For low-pressure systems, below 2500 psi, the viscosity is usually in the range of 150 to 300 SSU at 100°F. The latter range is approximately the viscosity of a #20 or #30 motor oil.

PROBLEMS

1 Plot the stress-strain curve for the steel sample of Sec. 3.4 and determine the 0.2 percent yield stress. Draw a line parallel to the elastic line of the material and passing through the 0.2 percent point on the abscissa axis. The intersection of this line with the stress-strain curve is the 0.2 percent yield stress.

2 Determine the 0.2 percent yield stress and the modulus of elasticity of the materials of Figs. 121 and 141 on pages 267 and 324, respectively.

3 A mine timber measuring 4 in. × 4 in. carries a compression load of 8000 lb and measures 50 in. in length. Its modulus of elasticity is 1.5×10^6. By how much does it shorten under this load?

4 Determine the strain (in./in.) if a magnesium bar is stressed in tension to 10,000 psi. The modulus of elasticity is 6.5×10^6.

5 What force is required to shear a ¼-in. steel plate in punching a 2-in. diameter hole? The ultimate shear strength of the plate is 40,000 psi.

6 Instrumentation based on the Bragg equation can be used to determine elastic strains in metals. Can this also be done for plastic strain due to slip?

7 Explain how both the elastic and the plastic behavior of steel have established its large market.

8 Suppose that a material is elastic in the solid phase under all possible conditions. What methods are available for forming it into useful products?

9 Should a sound-absorbing material be made of elastic or plastic material?

10 Explain why hydrogen is used as a coolant in large electric motors and generators.

11 Explain why copper is a difficult metal to weld.

12 A stainless steel pipe 6.625 in. in outside diameter is butt-welded to a zirconium pipe of the same diameter. This piping system is then heated to 1100°F from 100°F. At this high temperature the butt weld cracks. What is the difference in O.D.'s between the two pipes at 1100°? Expansion coefficient of the stainless steel is 0.000008, and of the zirconium is 0.000004.

13 A precision gauge block presumed to measure 0.75000 in. in length at 68°F is to be compared with a master block of the same length. The instructions given to the metrologist state that he must compare the two blocks while they are seated on an aluminum plate, and that they must remain on the aluminum plate for 20 min before comparison is undertaken. Explain the reason for the aluminum plate.

14 A furnace lining of 25,000 firebrick, each weighing 8 lb, has a specific heat of 0.2 Btu/lb/°F. The furnace is heated from cold (100°F) to an operating temperature of 2000°F. At operating temperature the hot face of the brick is at 2000°F and the cold end of the brick at 1000°F. How much heat must be stored in this firebrick lining before the furnace reaches operating temperature?

15 A 1000-gallon water tank is made of $\frac{1}{8}$ in. steel sheet and has a total surface area of 200 sq ft. The inside surface of the steel shell is at water temperature of 40°F and the outside surface of the shell at 39°F. What is the heat loss from the tank in Btuh? K-factor of the steel = 320 Btuh/in.-°F.

16 The tank in the previous question is next insulated with 1 in. of foamed polyurethane insulation with a K-factor of 0.25. The steel shell now supplies a negligible resistance to heat flow and can be ignored. The temperature drop across the insulation is 20°. What is the heat loss from the insulated tank?

NATURAL
MATERIALS

Part **II**

4.1 characteristics of water

The system ice-water-steam is the most familiar and one of the most important of the industrial materials. Both water and steam are used in enormous quantities by industry, though ice is less important. A steam power plant of moderate capacity may consume 20,000,000 gallons of water per hour, and produce perhaps 700,000 lb of steam per hr for the production of electric power from a steam turbine driving an electric generator.

The chemical H_2O is in a number of respects a most unusual one. Its most outstanding property is its unparalleled capacity for *heat storage*. The specific heats of ice, water, and steam, are all very large, and the latent heat of evaporation of water is about 1000 Btu per lb.

The human race makes generous use of this heat storage capacity. A small amount of water or steam can remove or transport a great amount of heat, hence the use of steam and water for heating of buildings, or water cooling in various industrial processes. The heat storage of water is also sometimes a disadvantage, as expressed in the time-honored saying "A watched pot never boils", or in its effect of depressing temperatures in the vicinity of large bodies of water such as Lake Superior.

A second unusual characteristic of water is its *availability*. Most of the earth's surface is covered by either salt water, fresh water, or ice (permafrost). While less than 1 percent of the earth's atmosphere is water vapor,

WATER
AND
STEAM

4

Fig. 44 Air view of a river during a snowstorm in early winter. The high heat storage of the water in the river produces a micro-climate in its vicinity which is mild enough to melt the snow, while the surrounding countryside is blanketed in snow.

this still represents a sizeable reservoir of water. The general availability of water gives it the economic advantage of cheapness.

Water was found to be adaptable even to the atomic age, by virtue of its low neutron absorption cross-section and its *high neutron scattering cross-section*. Both oxygen and hydrogen have these properties. Water therefore has uses in atomic reactors, although heavy water or deuterium oxide is even better.

A fourth characteristic of water is its general *corrosiveness*, although it is not one of the more aggressive chemicals. Ferrous metals can be afforded a good degree of protection from water corrosion by removing dissolved oxygen from the water in a deaeration process and increasing the alkalinity of the water. Both processes are usually necessary. High pressure steam is corrosive to ordinary glass.

A disadvantageous characteristic of water is its expansion as it is cooled from 39°F down to ice at 32°F. This volume expansion is about 10 percent (actually 9.3 percent), a considerable amount and the cause of much maintenance expense in colder countries.

Water has a relatively *low viscosity*. This is an advantage, since motors driving water pumps do not demand high horsepower to overcome pressure drops due to viscosity losses.

Another disadvantage of water is the high pressures required to cause water to boil at temperatures much above 212°F. This characteristic will be further discussed.

Fresh water has a specific gravity of 1.0 at 60°F and 160°F. A cubic foot of water at 60°F weighs 62.4 lb, and a gallon 8.3 lb.

The specific heats of hydrogen oxide are as follows:

ice	0.5 Btu/lb/°F
water	1.0 at low temperatures
steam	0.5 (approximately)

The latent heat of fusion of ice is 144 Btu per lb. This figure is the basis for the capacity rating of refrigeration equipment. One ton of refrigeration is the refrigeration capacity needed to remove sufficient heat to freeze 1 ton of water at 32°F, in 24 hours. This is a heat removal capacity of 2000 × 144 or 288,000 Btu per 24 hrs, 12,000 Btuh, or 200 Btu/min.

Knowledge of the properties of steam and water is necessary if a person is to work in such fields as operating engineering, heating, refrigeration, air-conditioning, and internal combustion engines. The properties of steam and water, including specific heat, specific volume, latent heat, and others, are tabulated in detail in the Steam Tables, from which extracts are given below. Before information can be extracted from such tables, certain definitions and symbols must be understood.

Sometimes we speak of steam, sometimes of water vapor. There is, however, no fundamental difference. If the steam is part of an atmospheric

Fig. 45 A utilidor. When building on permafrost (permanently frozen ground) in arctic areas, utilities such as sewer and water cannot be laid underground. Instead, a steam-heated and insulated trench, called a utilidor, carries sewer, water, steam heat, electric power and other utilities to all buildings of the town. The arctic is still waiting for some materials engineer to design a good utilidor, since existing installations have many defects.

mixture of air and steam, it is referred to as "water vapor". If the steam is contained in a piping system, boiler, or heat exchanger, it is referred to as "steam". Again, we may use the word "boiling" or the word "evaporation". There is no difference between boiling and evaporation: both represent a phase change between the liquid and the gas state of hydrogen oxide.

As the Steam Table shows, the liquid phase of hydrogen oxide cannot exist above a temperature of 705.4°F. This temperature is called the *critical temperature* of water. A pressure of at least 3206 psi (the critical pressure) is required to make water boil at 705.4°F. Under these conditions there is no latent heat, and water flashes into steam spontaneously. Because of the resulting savings in heat, a number of large boilers in the Eastern United States are operated under critical or supercritical boiling conditions.

THE STEAM TABLE

psi	Temp °F	v_f	v_g	h_f	h_{fg}	h_g
0.178	50	0.01602	1703.2	18.07	1065.6	1083.7
.2563	60	0.01603	1206.7	28.06	1059.9	1088.0
.3631	70	0.01605	867.9	38.04	1054.3	1092.3
.5069	80	0.01607	633.1	48.02	1048.6	1096.6
.6982	90	0.01610	468.0	57.99	1042.9	1100.9
1.0	101.74	0.01614	333.6	69.70	1036.3	1106.0
2.0	126.08	0.01623	173.73	93.99	1022.2	1116.2
3.0	141.48	.1630	118.71	109.37	1013.2	1122.6
4.0	152.97	.01636	90.63	120.86	1006.4	1127.3
5.0	162.24	.01640	73.52	130.13	1001.0	1131.1
10.0	193.21	.01659	38.42	161.17	982.1	1143.3
14.7	212.0	.01672	26.80	180.07	970.3	1150.4
20	227.96	.01683	20.089	196.06	960.4	1156.3
50	281.01	.01727	8.515	250.09	924.0	1174.1
100	327.81	.01774	4.432	298.40	888.8	1187.2
140	353.02	.01802	3.220	324.82	868.0	1193.0
200	381.79	0.01839	2.288	355.36	843.0	1198.4
250	400.95	0.01865	1.8438	376.00	825.1	1201.1
500	467.01	.0197	0.9278	448.4	775.0	1204.4
900	531.98	0.0212	0.5006	526.6	668.8	1191.8
1000	544.61	.0216	0.4456	542.4	649.4	1101.8
1500	596.23	.0235	0.2760	611.0	445.3	1167.9
2000	635.82	.0257	0.1878	671.7	463.4	1135.1
2400	662.12	.0280	0.1407	708.4	382.7	1101.1
2800	684.99	.0310	0.1035	720.01	234.7	1054.8
3000	695.36	.0346	0.0850	802.5	217.3	1020.3
3200	705.11	0.0444	0.0580	872.4	62.0	934.4
3206	705.4	.0503	.0503	902.7	0	902.7

The Steam Table tabulates the properties of pressure, temperature, specific volume, enthalpy, and entropy. Entropy will not be discussed here.

The reading of the Steam Table is not difficult, and is best explained in terms of the familiar boiling of water at atmospheric pressure and 212°F. If the psi column is consulted for 14.7 psi, the corresponding temperature in the second column is 212°F. The two columns give corresponding temperatures and pressures of evaporation.

The third and fourth columns are tables of specific volume. Specific volume, symbol v, simply means the number of cubic feet in 1 lb of material, and is the reciprocal of the pounds per cubic foot, which is the specific weight. The subscript f indicates the liquid phase; the subscript g signifies the gas phase. For 14.7 psi and 212°F, v_f is 0.01672 (cubic feet per pound of water at 212°F). The reciprocal of 0.01672 is 59.8 (pounds per cubic foot of water at 212°F). Similarly the number of cubic feet in one pound of steam at these conditions is 26.80.

The symbol h means enthalpy, and indicates the total heat content above 32°F. The enthalpy of water, h_f, at 212°F is 180.07. Note that 212°F is 180°F above 32°F, and the specific heat of water over this range is approximately 1.0. The latent heat of evaporation at these conditions is 970.3 Btu per lb, h_{fg}. The enthalpy of steam at 212°F is the sum of the sensible heat per pound above 32°F and the latent heat of evaporation: $h_g = h_f + h_{fg}$.

Suppose you are sitting in a room with a constant temperature of 70°F. The room air contains water vapor (steam). If the relative humidity in the room is 100 percent, then 70°F is the boiling point of this water vapor. The pressure of this water vapor is 0.36 psi. Atmospheric pressure is the sum of the water vapor pressure and the pressure of the other atmospheric gases. At 70°F, the latent heat of this water vapor is 1054.3 Btu/lb.

Notice that the latent heat of steam continuously decreases as the boiling pressure increases, finally decreasing to zero at the critical pressure of 3206 psi. At the critical pressure the specific weights of water and of steam are equal, 0.05 cu ft per lb for specific volume, or about 20 lb/cu ft. It is more economical in terms of heat to boil water at high pressures than at low, and this is the explanation for the very high steam pressures employed in steam power plants.

The specific heat of water may be found from the h_f column. Suppose we determine the specific heat of water between the temperatures of 50°F and 60°F. This is a temperature difference of 10°F. The corresponding enthalpies are 18.07 and 28.06 Btu/lb, a difference of nearly 10 Btu per lb. The specific heat of water within this temperature range is thus 1.0 Btu/lb/°F. The specific heat of water however becomes very large at higher evaporation temperatures.

The symbols v_f, h_{fg}, etc. as used in the Steam Table have the same meanings in other tables for air, refrigerants, welding gases, and similar tables.

4.3 water treatment

The solvent powers of water bring with them a host of problems that must be solved by complex and expensive water treatment processes. Water containing dissolved oxygen cannot be pumped into a boiler because the boiler tubes would be corroded by the combination of water and oxygen. Hard water cannot be used by soft drink manufacturers or breweries, nor by laundries, because of damage to clothing and reasons of soap consumption. Water containing very small amounts of dissolved iron will stain utensils, plumbing fixtures, and dishes red. Most water used for industry or domestic consumption therefore requires treatment to remove or reduce dissolved gases, liquids, and solids.

There is no general-purpose water treatment method. Before any particular water treatment can be specified, an analysis of the water must be made. A standard water analysis provides data on such matters as the *p*H of the water and the dissolved and suspended solids in parts per million by weight (ppm). Ten thousand parts per million is equal to 1 percent. The *p*H value of the water expresses its alkalinity or acidity. A distilled or neutral water sample has a *p*H of 7.0. Smaller values indicate an acid water. Thus beer or soft drinks may have a *p*H of about 4. Values higher than 7.0 indicate an alkaline water. Lime or other basic compounds are commonly added to water to increase the *p*H, since acid waters are highly corrosive to piping systems.

As a comparison, two water analyses are presented below, the first one for a western city with an excellent water supply, the second an analysis of well water so poor that the well was not used.

	City	Well
pH	6.9	7.8
calcium	25.2 ppm	1060 ppm
magnesium	8.1	648
sodium	–	3660
total cations	33.3	5368
bicarbonate	107.0 ppm	217 ppm
carbonate	nil	nil
chloride	2.1	3817
sulfate	9.5	1310
total anions	118.6	5344
iron oxide	nil	0.53 ppm
total solids	125 ppm	6874 ppm

These two water analyses may be compared with the water standards of the U.S. Department of Health & Public Welfare:

	Maximum Permissible	Suggested Limits
lead	0.1 ppm	
fluorine	1.5	
arsenic	0.05	
copper	2	
zinc		15.0 ppm
iron		0.3
total solids		500–1000 ppm
magnesium		125

The city water analysis exceeds the standard, although its low pH suggests that the water will be somewhat corrosive to piping and hot water tanks: experience confirms this. The pH of a water supply should be at least 8.0 to prevent corrosion. In the case of the well water, the pH is acceptable, but 6874 ppm of solids means that over $\frac{1}{2}$ of 1 percent of the supply is solid matter, or 1 gallon of solids in every 200 gallons of water. The water is also quite brackish, since the total of sodium and chloride is over 7500 ppm. Water begins to taste salty when the salt concentration exceeds 500 ppm.

The dissolved compounds that make a water "hard" are calcium bicarbonate, calcium carbonate, calcium sulfate, magnesium bicarbonate, magnesium carbonate, and magnesium sulfate. If the sum of these dissolved compounds is less than 60, the water is called soft, while in concentrations exceeding 180 the water is considered hard. "Hardness" is the quality in water that prevents a soap from forming a lather, though the hardness components listed have a variety of other harmful effects. They may leave deposits on pipe walls to form a hard scale, and instances are known where pipes were completely closed by scale. Again, if carbonates in water are heated in boilers or heat exchangers, they break down to release carbon dioxide. The combination of carbon dioxide and water forms carbonic acid, which is corrosive to iron and steel.

At 70°F and atmospheric pressure, water can dissolve 8 parts per million of oxygen. This small amount of oxygen is necessary in fresh water for the survival of fish and other animal life, but it presents another cause of corrosion in industrial equipment. This oxygen must be removed before water is fed into boilers. This is done in de-aerators which heat the water to release the dissolved oxygen.

water and steam

4.4 sewage and industrial wastes

Sewage is about 99.99 percent water, and it is unfortunate that so much water is used to transport so little sewage. As a result, sewage treatment plants must be designed to handle vast quantities of water.

Domestic sewage consists chiefly of bathroom, laundry, and kitchen wastes. Since the average family uses 50 to 100 gallons of water per person per day, this will be the quantity of sewage discharged from the usual household. Such sewage contains waste food, soap, dirt, and the wet and dry components of human wastes, the dry matter averaging about 75 grams per person per day. Sewage systems also collect rainwater, and industrial wastes from automotive service stations, meat packing plants, sugar beet factories, and the infinitude of other industrial operations which connect to municipal sewer systems.

The treatment of industrial wastes is a science in itself, and a difficult or intractable one sometimes. Domestic sewage, being organic in type, is treated by oxidizing it with air, either the 8 ppm of oxygen usually found in water, or by bubbling air through the wet sewage. Sewage treatment may be described as a "wet combustion" method. An exception is the septic tank, which does not have access to air. Sewage is commonly treated simply by dumping it into a large body of water, such as a lake or sea, leaving it to be oxidized by the oxygen in the water. But if the body of water is a river, the sewage discharge may exceed the combustion capacity of the limited amount of dissolved oxygen. Consumption of this dissolved oxygen results in the death of fish and other aquatic life, and the deposit of gray-colored semitreated sewage films on the banks of the river.

The broad spectrum of human and industrial wastes includes liquid sewage, garbage and other combustible or noncombustible solid wastes, and chimney gases vented to the atmosphere. The treatment of each of these three types of waste is a specialty in itself. Probably no boy or girl ever selected industrial wastes for a career. However, these are interesting engineering sciences which grow more interesting as they become better known. The quantities of these wastes that must be handled daily verge on the astronomical. Given the figure of 2 lb of garbage and solid refuse per capita per day, the reader may be interested in estimating the total amount of garbage generated each day in the United States.

PROBLEMS

1 What is the weight of a cubic foot of water (a) at 90°F; (b) at 532°?

2 How much heat is required to bring 1 lb of ice at 0°F to superheated steam at 14.7 psia and 250°?

3 What is the specific heat of water between the temperatures of 281° and 327.8°?

4 If a room measuring 40 × 30 × 10 ft is held at a temperature of 70°F and 100 percent relative humidity, how many pounds of water vapor does this room contain?

5 A fired pressure vessel producing steam at 3500 psi is not called a boiler but a steam generator. Why?

5.1 ideal and imperfect gases

The basic physical properties of gases are three: pressure, temperature, and volume, or specific volume. An absolute temperature scale is necessary for gas calculations, either the Kelvin or the Rankine scale, the latter being used in engineering in some of the English-speaking countries such as the USA and Canada. The Kelvin and Rankine scales are defined as follows:

$$°K = °C + 273$$
$$°R = °F + 460$$

The temperatures -273 and -460 are of course absolute temperatures for the Centigrade and Fahrenheit temperature scales, respectively.

Similarly, absolute pressures must be employed in gas calculations rather than gauge pressures. Gauge pressure means pressure above atmospheric pressure. Atmospheric pressure reads zero on a standard Bourdon pressure gauge, but is actually 14.7 psi absolute at sea level. Pressure in psi absolute (psia) is equal to gauge pressure (psig) plus 14.7.

In this country a variety of other pressure scales are in use in industry. Fuel gas pressures and air pressures in ventilating systems are often measured in inches of water. Gas burners for industrial furnaces may use ounces per square inch. In instrumentation work, inches of mercury may

INDUSTRIAL
GASES

5

be used for pressure readings. Finally, vacuum systems use the torr as the unit of pressure.

34 ft of water column (34 ft w.c.)	= 14.7 psi
2.3 ft w.c.	= 1 psi
1 ft of water	= 0.434 psi
30 in. Hg	= 14.7 psi
760 mm Hg	= 14.7 psi
specific gravity of mercury	= 13.6
1 in. Hg	= 0.491 psi
1 torr	= 1 mm Hg

Units of pressure, like most other engineering units in use in North America, are unnecessarily confusing, but practitioners seem to survive with few complaints. Consider the following example.

A centrifugal fan supplies air at a pressure of 1 in. w.c. What is the fan pressure expressed as psi?

34 ft w.c. = 14.7 psi.

$$1 \text{ in. w.c.} = 1/12 \text{ ft} = \frac{1}{12 \times 34} \times 14.7 = 0.036 \text{ psi.}$$

Certain gases follow simple mathematical relationships between their basic properties of temperature, pressure, and volume. These relationships are called Boyle's Law and Charles's Law:

If the gas pressure is held constant, the volume of a gas varies directly with its temperature.

If the temperature of the gas is held constant, the volume of the gas is inversely proportional to its pressure.

Scientific "laws", like the statutory kind, are honored both in the breach and the observance. Gases whose behavior is in close accord with these two relationships are called "ideal" or "perfect" gases. Gases which do not closely obey such rules are called "imperfect" gases. In practical terms, we might say that the pressure, volume, or temperature of an ideal gas may be determined by calculation, but that this procedure is not readily possible for an imperfect gas, for which gas tables similar to the Steam Tables must be used. Steam is an imperfect gas; therefore the properties of steam are obtained from steam tables, not from Boyle's or Charles's Law. Tables similar to those for steam are available for other imperfect gases, such as ammonia.

Ideal Gases	Imperfect Gases
oxygen	steam
nitrogen	carbon dioxide
air	ammonia
argon	sulfur dioxide
helium	freon refrigerants
hydrogen	methyl chloride
	methane, propane, butane

Boyle's and Charles's Laws are not especially useful for purposes of gas calculations, and are therefore combined into one formula for practical use. The most useful form of this relationship is the following:

$$PV = wRT$$

where T = temperature, °R

P = pressure, pounds per square *foot*, not psi, absolute

V = volume, cubic feet

w = weight of gas, pounds

R = gas constant for the gas in question

$$= \frac{1544}{\text{molecular weight}}$$

= 53.3 for air

= 85.7 for steam

= 772 for hydrogen

Example. A gas welding shop buys a standard cylinder of oxygen. The cylinder contains 244 cu ft of oxygen, measured at 14.7 psia and 70°F, cylinder pressure being 2200 psi. Determine the weight of oxygen in the cylinder.

$P = 14.7 \times 144$ psf

$V = 244$ cu ft

$T = 530°R$

$R = \dfrac{1544}{32} = 48.4$

Substituting these values in the equation

$$14.7 \times 144 \times 244 = w \times 48.4 \times 530$$

$$w = 20.1 \text{ lb oxygen}$$

The gas constituents of the earth's atmosphere were tabulated in the first chapter. The most important constituent, oxygen, is of course of critical importance to both life and industry. The oxygen however is heavily diluted with nitrogen; air is mostly nitrogen. The principal uses of air are the following:

1. oxygen supply for combustion processes
2. ventilation air for environmental control
3. automatic control systems operated by air, usually at 20 psig supply pressure
4. pneumatic power systems operated at pressures up to about 80 psig, as in reciprocating air cylinders
5. compressed air for the operation of paint spray guns, pneumatic rock drills, etc.
6. pneumatic tires for highway and off-the-road vehicles

The consumption of air for these purposes runs to large figures. Over 125 lb of air are inspirated into an engine's cylinders to burn a gallon of fuel, or about 20 times as much air as fuel by weight. A small ventilating fan may handle 500 lb of air every hour. A steam power station may consume 25,000 tons of air in an hour.

1 standard cubic foot of air (scf) at 70°F and 14.7 psia = 0.075 lb

13.4 scf air = 1 lb

These two constants are of basic importance in mechanical work, and must be memorized by practitioners who design with air. The specific heat of air at constant pressure at 70°F is 0.24, at 500°F 0.247, and at 1000°F 0.263. The viscosity of air at 70°F is 0.0000126 lb-sec/ft², increasing to 0.0000185 at 500°F.

Nitrogen The properties and constants of nitrogen must necessarily be nearly those of air. Nitrogen is a rather inert gas. It boils at −320.3°F at atmospheric pressure, and cannot be liquefied above −232° (critical temperature). It is available in standard gas cylinders and is chiefly used as liquid nitrogen for refrigeration of transport vehicles and as an inert or purging gas.

Oxygen Oxygen is a slightly magnetic gas, weighing 11 percent more than air. Its boiling point at atmospheric pressure is −297.3°F. It is probably the most dangerous of the industrial gases. Many hydrocarbons, such as greases, will explode in the presence of oxygen.

Oxygen is available both as therapy oxygen for hospital use and industrial oxygen in 2400 psi cylinders and in larger quantities. The two types of oxygen are supplied in cylinders with a different color coding, and a cylinder of oxygen for the one purpose is never permitted to be used for the other purpose, the reason being that industrial oxygen may become contaminated with other gases through the piping system to which a cylinder of industrial oxygen is attached.

Liquid oxygen, or lox, is consumed in tonnage quantities chiefly for the following uses:

1. rocket fuel
2. steel refining. Oxygen is used to burn excess carbon out of steel and to accelerate the operation of blast furnaces and open hearth furnaces
3. flame drilling of hard rock, using kerosene as fuel

In addition, oxygen is used as a welding gas for both gas welding and certain types of arc welding, and for torch cutting of steels.

Argon Argon is a monatomic inert gas which does not dissolve in liquid metals. These characteristics make it an especially useful gas. Its boiling point at atmospheric pressure is −302.4°F, and its specific gravity compared to air as 1.0 is 1.38. Argon serves a wide range of uses in incandescent and fluorescent lamps, Geiger-Muller counter tubes, and inert atmosphere heating furnaces. Its largest use is in the welding and thermal cutting of metals that must be protected from oxidation, such as zirconium, aluminum, and titanium.

Helium Helium is another monatomic inert gas which does not dissolve in liquid metals. It therefore competes with argon in its industrial applications. Like argon, helium may be extracted from air, but is also available from natural gas wells in the western states and western Canada. Its specific weight at 70°F and 14.7 psia is exactly 10 percent that of argon. Its boiling point is very close to absolute zero, −452.1°. The specific heat of helium is very high, 1.25 Btu/lb, second only to that of hydrogen.

Because of its small molecule, helium serves as a most sensitive leak detector. It is also used as a refrigerant in the attainment of temperatures near absolute zero.

Neon Neon is familiar from the characteristic red color of the electric discharge through such neon-filled tubes as are used in advertising signs and stroboscopes.

Xenon Xenon is also used in electric-discharge tubes. The visible spectrum from such a tube is very similar to that from the sun. Such tubes give remarkably high illumination intensity and are therefore used to activate lasers and for microscope illumination.

Krypton Krypton is another fill gas for tubes, and is added to fluorescent lamps to increase the lighting intensity. Krypton-85 is a radioisotope used for leak testing.

Fig. 46 Cylinders of welding and medical gases at a cylinder-filling plant of Liquid Carbonic Corp.

5.3 carbon dioxide

Carbon dioxide gas and its solid phase, popularly termed "dry ice", is one of the most versatile chemicals of industry, with the added virtue of cheapness. It is not recovered from air but is usually produced by burning carbon compounds. Carbon dioxide gas is 53 percent heavier than air. At atmospheric pressure the phase change from dry ice to CO_2 gas occurs at $-109.2°$. Some of the uses of dry ice are these:

1. general purpose refrigerant
2. shrink-fitting of mating parts by cooling the inserted part
3. branding of cattle with an iron cooled with dry ice

Gaseous carbon dioxide is used in the following and many other applications in food, drug, and chemical processing:

1. fire extinguishers
2. heat transfer medium in British nuclear reactors
3. soft drinks and beer
4. removal of heat during machining and grinding operations on plastics, soft rubber, and other heat-sensitive materials
5. inert atmosphere and purging gas for removing flammable vapors
6. pressure gas for aerosol spray cans
7. greenhouse atmosphere to increase yield of tomatoes and other plants
8. shielding gas for welding

THERMODYNAMIC PROPERTIES OF CARBON DIOXIDE

Temperature, °F	Pressure, psia	v_f	v_g	h_f	h_{fg}	h_g
−60	94.7	.0138	.927	−9.2	145.8	136.6
−40	145.8	.0143	.611	0.0	137.8	137.8
−20	214.9	.0149	.416	9.1	129.4	138.5
0	305.5	.0157	.290	18.8	120.1	138.9
+20	421.8	.0166	.205	29.4	108.9	138.3

This carbon dioxide table is read in exactly the same way as the Steam Table was read: h_{fg} means latent heat of boiling, and so on. In the case of the Steam Table, the datum for heat was taken at 32°, at which temperature h_f, the heat content of water, was arbitrarily taken as zero. In the case of the refrigerants, including carbon dioxide, the heat datum is arbitrarily taken at −40°F, as may be seen from the carbon dioxide table.

5.4   arc welding gases

The familiar tall, small-diameter, color-coded cylinders used for welding gas supply are usually rated for a maximum internal pressure of 2400 psi, except in the case of acetylene. Such cylinders are seamless deep-drawn tubes, with a wall thickness of about ¼ in., manufactured in the same presses as drawn artillery shells. The handling of such cylinders is subject to government regulation, and every cylinder must be hydrostatically tested every five years.

The use of oxygen and acetylene for torch welding of metals is about 60 years old. However, this type of gas welding is of small importance in production welding on the factory floor, where electric arc methods dominate the scene. The most important of the production welding processes is the MIG method (pronounced "mig", an abbreviation of metal-inert gas). In this welding method a continuous spooled wire is fed into the arc at a controlled rate and is protected from the atmosphere by a flow of shielding gas from the welding gun (see Fig. 193 on p. 447). The most commonly used gas for MIG welding is CO_2. Except for spot welding, the welding done on automobiles and trucks is performed by the MIG-CO_2 method. However, CO_2 is not an inert gas, since it can dissociate into carbon monoxide and oxygen. Carbon dioxide therefore cannot be used for welding such readily oxidizable metals as aluminum, copper, and titanium. For such metals, either argon or helium is employed to shield the arc.

Fig. 47 MIG welding of light angle iron frames using a shielding gas of 5 percent argon and 95 percent carbon dioxide. A spool of MIG wire can be seen on the right of the photograph. The extensive fine spatter of the MIG arc as seen here is characteristic of this welding method.

Helium, being only one tenth the weight of argon, does not provide quite as good shielding of the arc in the presence of drafts or air currents.

Helium has a higher ionization voltage than argon. At a MIG welding current of 200 amps the arc potential drop will be about 25 v with argon and 30 v with helium. These voltages are not the ionization voltages of the gases but the arc voltage drop. Since the heat generated by the arc is proportional to the product of amps times volts, more heat is produced by helium. Therefore helium is preferred for welding metals of high thermal conductivity to compensate for heat conduction losses through the metal. In particular it may be impossible to weld copper with argon because of the unusually high thermal conductivity of this metal.

5.5 fuel gases

The most commonly used fuel gases are hydrogen (H_2), acetylene (C_2H_2), natural gas (largely methane, CH_4), propane (C_3H_8), and butane (C_4H_{10}). These gases are burned either with oxygen or air, the chemical reaction being called *combustion*. Combustion is an *oxidation* process occurring at a sufficiently rapid rate to produce a high temperature, usually with the appearance of a flame. If the total amount of oxidizable material oxidizes at a more or less uncontrolled rate, the process is then called *explosion*.

Gas burners, sometimes called torches, are devices for mixing gas and air in the proper proportions for combustion. The actual combustion process occurs in the visible flame after the fuel gas and the oxygen are mixed. Since the gases issue from the burner ports at a constant velocity, the flame front must continually burn back toward the burner. Therefore the size of the burner ports must produce a forward velocity of the same order as the *flame propagation velocity*, the speed at which the flame propagates through the gas mixture. Different gases have different flame propagation velocities and different air-gas ratios; this is the reason that the burner or torch must be changed if the fuel gas is changed. The flame velocity is influenced by many variables and cannot be readily stated for any fuel gas. Methane is a typical slow-burning gas: its flame velocity is only a few feet per second. Hydrogen burns at a high velocity, of the order of 20 ft per sec.

For the design of gas piping and burners the *specific gravity* of the gas must be known. When the specific gravity of a gas is reported, it is compared to air as 1.0, not water as 1.0, as is done in the case of liquids. Thus natural gas has a specific gravity of 0.65 (it varies from city to city between the limits of 0.60 and 0.70), indicating that natural gas is two-thirds as heavy as air.

The *heating value* of the fuel gas is the amount of combustion heat released per cubic foot of fuel gas measured at standard temperature and pressure and with the products of combustion cooled back to the initial temperature. The gross heating value is usually stipulated: this includes the latent heat of condensable water vapor.

The *flame temperature* of a fuel gas cannot be accurately measured. Usually a theoretical flame temperature is referred to. This is the flame temperature assuming instantaneous and perfect combustion with no heat loss to the surroundings. For a theoretical flame temperature all the combustion heat is used to heat the products of combustion, that is,

$$Q = wc(t_2 - t_1)$$

where Q = Btu per pound liberated per pound of fuel

w = weight of combustion products, pounds

c = specific heat of combustion products

t_2 = flame temperature

t_1 = initial temperature

While this equation represents a simple specific heat calculation, it must be noted that the specific heat of the combustion products must be the mean specific heat of the mixture of product gases over the range $(t_2 - t_1)$. This is a somewhat uncertain figure. We may attempt an example, however. Suppose we find the theoretical flame temperature for natural gas burned with air, using approximations.

We will assume natural gas to be pure methane, t_1 to be zero, and the specific heat of the combustion products (CO_2, H_2O, and N_2) to be 0.33.

The heating value of methane nearly equals 24,000 Btu per pound. There are almost 18 lb of products yielded per pound of methane.

$$24,000 = 18 \times 0.33(t_2 - 0)$$

$$t_2 = 4000°F$$

This solution is a few hundred degrees too high.

A much higher flame temperature is produced in the absence of nitrogen, which forms a substantial fraction of the combustion products when air is used. The nitrogen contributes nothing to the combustion process but acts as a heating load on the heat produced.

PROPERTIES OF FUEL GASES

Gas	Sp Gr	Flame Temperature	Lbs Products per lb Gas	Gross Btu/lb	Heating Value Btu/cu ft
hydrogen in O_2	0.069	4000	8.94	61,000	
acetylene in O_2	0.90	6200	4.07	21,570	
natural gas in air	0.65	3600	18.2	23,900	1000
propane in air	1.52	3660	16.6	21,800	2510
butane in air	1.95	3640	16.3	214,000	3100

Hydrogen has a higher specific heat than any other substance, 3.4 Btu per lb. This explains its use as a cooling gas in large electric motors and generators. Hydrogen is also used as a rocket fuel and as a reducing agent in the manufacture of parts made from metal powders, such as carbide cutting tools and self-lubricated sintered bearings. Without hydrogen, the film of oxide on the surface of the metal grains would prevent them from sintering together.

Acetylene is well known for its use in oxyacetylene welding and thermal cutting of metals. For welding purposes it is commonly supplied in squat black cylinders fitted with left-hand threads. Its flame temperature is the highest obtainable from the fuel gases.

Acetylene explodes readily if compressed to pressures above 15 psig. The explosion requires no oxygen, the acetylene simply decomposing into carbon and hydrogen. Cylinders of acetylene therefore are filled by a unique method. The cylinder contains a porous plastic or other substance, and this filler is used to absorb acetone. The acetylene gas is then dissolved

Fig. 48 Oxyacetylene flame-cutting of steel plate with five cutting heads.

Fig. 49 A tank farm for liquefied petroleum gases. The horizontal tanks are for propane storage; the spherical tanks store butane.

industrial gases
100

in the acetone. Because of this special preparation, considerable time is required to fill an acetylene cylinder to the usual pressure of 250 psig.

Propane and *butane* are referred to as *liquefied petroleum gases* or LPG. These gases are obtained from both oil and gas wells. Figure 49 shows storage tanks for these gases at a tank farm. The stored gas may be identified by the shape of its storage vessel. The bullet-shaped tanks store propane, while the spherical tanks contain butane. Both gases are used for heating and for gas welding and cutting.

Natural gas is composed of 90 percent or more methane, together with small amounts of ethane, nitrogen, and carbon dioxide. Since natural gas is odorless, a small amount of a sulfur compound is added. The smell provides warning of gas leaks.

5.6 vacuum

A vacuum, as used in industry, must be considered as an atmosphere or gas with special inert properties. Vacua are increasingly employed for industrial processing, so that recent years have seen the development of a separate "vacuum technology".

Industrial vacua for process uses are almost always what are called "very high vacua", that is, in the range of 10^{-3} to 10^{-7} torr (10^{-3} to 10^{-7} mm Hg). At least two vacuum pumps in series are required to reach such low vacuum conditions. Vacua for such purposes as electron beam welding or the vacuum melting of steel are at the high pressure end of this range, but vacuum tubes, including X-ray tubes and oscilloscope tubes, must maintain a vacuum of at least 10^{-6} torr if they are to function properly. If the pressure is too high, there are too many gas molecules present, and the electrons of the tube current lose excessive energy in collisions with gas molecules.

A wide range of metals react rapidly with oxygen at temperatures above 1000°F and must be melted under vacuum conditions. Such metals include titanium, beryllium, zirconium, all the refractory metals, and the semiconductors such as silicon and germanium. Circumstances sometimes permit the heat-treating or welding of such metals under a protective atmosphere of argon or helium. However the welding of these metals by means of a beam of electrons under a vacuum of about 10^{-4} torr is perhaps more common.

The evaporation of low-melting metals under low vacua has been mentioned in an earlier chapter. Vacuum deposition of metal films has become a standard practice. The reflecting surfaces of sealed-beam headlights for automobiles are vacuum-deposited.

The vacuum degassing of steels will be examined when the manufacture of steel is examined later in this book.

The firebrick linings for vacuum melting furnaces present special problems. Under vacuum conditions the melted metal, which is a reducing agent, tends to attack the firebrick oxides more aggressively than it would under air-melting conditions. Thus a metal melted in an alumina or silica crucible will tend to combine with the oxygen in the crucible, releasing silicon or aluminum to dissolve in the melt. The resulting alloying effect is undesirable. Furnace linings therefore must be selected with some discrimination, and in any case have a reduced life, when used in vacuum-melting practice, of perhaps only 40–50 heats.

PROBLEMS

1   What is the weight in pounds per cubic foot of both liquid and gaseous carbon dioxide at −60°F and 94.7 psia?

2   As you drive through a strange town, you estimate the height of its overhead water tank to be 92 ft above grade. What then is the maximum water pressure available on the ground floor of a house in this town?

3   A large boiler water feed pump supplies a feedwater pressure of 2500 psi. How many feet of water column does this pump deliver?

4   Using the ideal gas equation, calculate the specific volume (cu ft per lb) of 1 lb of steam at 14.7 psia and 212°F. Compare your result with the Steam Tables.

5   Using the ideal gas equation, calculate the weight of air in a receiving tank of 20 cu ft capacity at 100 psig and 120°F.

6.1 mechanical and electrical equipment

Mechanical engineering and electrical engineering are two broad technical areas which, though nominally distinct, overlap in such a comprehensive fashion that it is often impossible to designate a problem or project as specifically "electrical" or "mechanical". A mechanical engineer simply cannot ply his trade without comprehensive knowledge of things electrical. Similarly, in time of trouble the electrical engineer may discover that the defects in his electrical equipment are mechanical defects.

Consider first some mechanical aspects of electrical equipment. If an electric motor is down for maintenance, the reason may be either bearings or a burnout, both mechanical failures. Breakage of electric power lines due to ice accumulation or wind vibration is mechanical failure. Fracture of the Bakelite parts of switchgear is mechanical failure. So is evaporation of the tungsten filament when an incandescent lamp fails. The dissipation of heat from electronic microcomponents is a mechanical design problem, as are the glass-to-metal seals required in all vacuum tubes.

More confusing are the electrical and electronic areas sometimes served by mechanical servicemen rather than electrical people. The serviceman who maintains electronic boiler controls is, to the author's knowledge, never an electronic serviceman but a boiler specialist. The crew which

ELECTRICAL PROPERTIES OF MATERIALS

6

installs electronic automation for a production process such as a steel rolling mill way well be made up predominantly of mechanical personnel. Despite its name, the General Electric Company is famous for its mechanical engineering, both in research and in products.

The uses of electrical equipment for nonelectrical applications are almost without number. Most welding equipment is electrical. Most of the non-destructive testing methods used in manufacturing operations are electrical methods — ultrasonic, X-ray, magnetic flaw detection, eddy-current testing. An electronic induction heater used for brazing and heat-treating of metals is similar in design and components to the frequency generator of a radio transmitting station. The electrical characteristics of materials, then, are not of peripheral importance, or of interest only to electrical specialists. Ignorance of these electrical properties may prove a severe occupational handicap. The following is a case in point.

A weld shop decided to install a common ground for ten 300-amp welding machines. Without making any electrical calculations, it was decided to use a $\frac{5}{8}$-in. diameter steel bar for the ground, simply because such a bar would be "plenty big enough". It wasn't, and had to be replaced immediately after it was installed, much to the embarrassment of the supervisor responsible.

6.2   electrical resistance

The one-dimensional flow of electricity through a resistance and the similar flow of heat by conduction are mathematically identical. For electric current

$$E = IR, \text{ Ohm's Law}, \quad \text{and} \quad R = \frac{\sigma L}{A}$$

where σ = the specific resistance of the resistor material in some suitable units;

$$L = \text{length of the conductor}$$

$$A = \text{cross-section of the conductor.}$$

For heat flow by one-dimensional conduction, $Q = (KA\Delta t)/L$. If the formula for heat flow is rearranged, it becomes identical mathematically with Ohm's Law:

$$\Delta t = Q\left(\frac{L}{KA}\right)$$

Here Δt, the temperature differential, is the potential causing heat flow and corresponding to E, Q Btu/hr is the flow, and L/KA is the heat-flow resistance R, where $1/K$ corresponds to the specific resistance.

For purposes of mechanical engineering, the most convenient unit for specific resistance is ohms per cubic inch, because the conductors involved in mechanical engineering may be of rectangular or irregular shape. On the other hand, most resistance calculations in electrical engineering are concerned with wire and cable of circular cross-section, for which the circular mil-foot is a convenient unit for specific resistance. Finally, for scientific work, the unit of ohm-centimeter is used.

If L is given in inches, and A in square inches, then the units of σ are ohm-inches (ohms per cubic inch). If the circular mil-foot is used, then L must be in feet, and A must be in circular mils. The area of a circle with diameter n mils (thousandths of an inch) is simply n^2 circular mils. This avoids the use of π in calculations. A square inch of wire contains 1,273,240 circular mils. The following examples are offered for clarification.

Example 1. A frozen steel pipe with a 2-in. nominal diameter is to be thawed by running current from a welding transformer through it. The two welding cables are connected to the pipe at points 200 ft apart. The cross-section of the pipe wall is 1.075 sq in. If the specific resistance of steel at 32°F is 5.0 microhm-inches, what is the resistance of the pipe in ohms?

Here $L = 200 \times 12$ in.

$A = 1.075$ sq in.

$\sigma = 0.000\ 005$ ohm-in.

and $R = 0.0111$ ohm.

Example 2. A nickel alloy resistance wire has a specific resistance of 800 ohms per circular mil-foot. What is the resistance of such a wire 0.1 in. in diameter and 5 ft long?

0.1 in. $= 100$ mils

$A \quad = 10,000$ circular mils

$L \quad = 5$ ft

and $R \quad = 0.4$ ohm.

Wire used as electrical conductor is usually identified either by gauge number or by circular mils. Electric wire uses the American Wire Gauge (AWG), while steel wire not for electrical conduction uses the Birmingham Wire Gauge (BWG).

electrical properties of materials
105

ELECTRIC WIRE TABLE

AWG	Diameter, mils	Cross-section, circ. mils	Cross-section, sq in.
0000	460	211,600	0.1662
000	409.6	167,800	0.1318
00	364.8	133,100	0.1045
0	324.9	105,500	0.0809
1	289.3	83,690	0.0657
2	257.6	66,370	0.0521
4	204.3	41,740	0.0328
6	162	26,250	0.0206
8	128.5	16,510	0.0130
10	101.9	10,380	0.0082

SPECIFIC RESISTANCE OF MATERIALS AT 20°C

Material	Microhm-inches	Ohms/circ. mil-foot
silver	0.6	9.6
copper	0.7	10.4
aluminum	1.12	17.1
mercury	3.8	–
nickel	2.7	41
iron	4.0	60
mild steel	5.0	–
302 stainless steel	29.0	–
tungsten	2.2	33.3
carbon	1300	–
silicon	450	–

In the above table of specific resistances, there are some uncertainties, since such factors as the purity of the material, the amount of cold-working, and the presence of alloying elements are not specified. Such factors may have a powerful influence on resistance.

Four methods are available for changing the properties of a material, including its electrical resistivity:

1. *Alloying*. Alloying increases both the strength of a metal and its electrical resistance, but reduces the electrical resistance of a semiconductor.
2. *Plastic deformation*. This increases the strength and resistivity of a metal, and decreases its ductility.
3. *Heat treatment*. Depending on the heat treatment, properties may be improved or harmed.
4. *Irradiation* by high energy particles.

electrical properties of materials
106

Fig. 50 Induction heating. The copper coil carries a high-frequency current of high amperage, inducing eddy currents in the bar inserted in it.

The effect of alloying on electrical resistance may be noted in the table of specific resistances by comparing resistance values for pure iron, mild steel, and stainless steel. Mild steel is iron alloyed with about 0.2 percent carbon and 0.3 percent of silicon and of manganese, or a total of less than 1 percent alloying additions. The effect, however, is a 20 percent increase in resistance. Type 302 stainless steel contains about 29 percent of alloying additions, chiefly chromium and nickel. As a result the resistance is increased by a factor of 7 over that of pure iron. For the same reasons, brasses have about 4 times the resistance of pure copper. About 0.1 percent of phosphorus in copper will double the electrical resistance of copper. Silicon and aluminum additions greatly increase the resistance of steel, and are used when high-resistance steels are desired, as in the steel cores of transformers. The effect of alloying elements on specific resistance is so powerful that the purity of metals and semiconductors is actually evaluated by means of resistance measurements.

The resistance of most pure metals increases by a factor of 0.4 percent per degree Centigrade, or 0.23 percent per degree Fahrenheit. This statement is not true of alloys, nor of magnesium, nickel, mercury, or the rare earth metals, all of which may have temperature coefficients of resistance greater or less than this value.

All substances conduct electrically charged particles. According to the Ohm's Law equation, $E = IR$, a nonconductor would ideally have an infinite resistance. No known material has this characteristic. However, three kinds of electrically conductive materials may be distinguished:

1. conductors
2. semiconductors
3. insulators

electrical properties of materials
107

Conductors are metals, and therefore have low impedance to the flow of electrons and increasing resistance to electron flow with increasing temperature. The specific resistance of conductors is in the range of 1×10^{-6} to about 1×10^{-14} ohm-cm. (Specific resistance in ohm-cm is about 2.4 times resistance expressed in ohm-inches.) A *semiconductor* is partially insulating and partially conducting, with a specific resistance in the range of about 10^{-2} to 10^6 ohm-cm. All semiconductors have less resistance at higher temperatures and in less pure states. An *insulator* or dielectric has a specific resistance in the range of 10^6 to 10^{20} ohm-cm. Of all the properties of materials, none has a wider range than specific resistance — roughly 10^{40}.

Germanium is a typical semiconductor. At room temperature it has a specific resistance of about 60 ohm-cm. When doped with 0.0001 percent of arsenic, its resistance falls drastically to about 0.1 microhm-cm. The decrease in resistance is explained by the valence electrons of the two materials: germanium has 4 and arsenic 5 valence electrons. The extra electron of arsenic becomes free for conduction, greatly increasing the conductivity. Other elements with 5 valence electrons would have the same effect on germanium, such as phosphorus. Such elements are called "donors", and their presence in a semiconductor produces what is called an *n-type* (for negative) semiconductor. On the other hand, germanium could be doped with an element such as aluminum, which has only three valence electrons. Such an element produces electron deficiencies called "holes", and is called an "acceptor". The resulting semiconductor is a *p-type* (for positive).

The *n*-type impurities contribute electrons that appear in the conduction band of the solid. Current in a semiconductor is carried by electrons in the conduction band and by holes in the valence band. The hole travels when an electron fills it, thus leaving a new hole which likewise is filled by an electron leaving another hole, and so on. Crystal imperfections such as grain boundaries promote the recombination of holes and electrons, and must be avoided. For this reason semiconductors are produced as single crystals.

In general, a *semiconductor* must possess the following characteristics:

1. a forbidden energy gap between the valence band and the conduction band of about 1 electron-volt
2. sensitivity of its resistance to minute amounts of impurities
3. decreasing resistance with increasing temperature

An *insulator* has the following characteristics:

1. a wide forbidden energy gap between valence band and the conduction band of several electron-volts
2. much higher resistance than a semiconductor
3. resistance less sensitive to impurities

Metals, which are electrical conductors, conduct as electrons move through the crystal lattice under the attraction of an applied voltage. As the electrons move along the conductor, they meet interference from ions in the space lattice: this impedance to flow is the ohmic resistance of the material. If the metal conductor is heated to a higher temperature, the ions of the space lattice vibrate over greater amplitudes, thus producing a greater collision cross-section for the moving electron. The effect is an increased resistance. In a perfect crystal without imperfections, at absolute zero, there should be no interference to electron flow, and no resistance. This condition is the superconducting condition, to be discussed presently.

The resistance of a conductor is expressed as ohms or microhms (millionths of an ohm). Conductivity is the reciprocal of resistance, with the units of mhos. Mhos = 1/ohms. In certain applications, such as water treatment and water analysis, the conductivity is measured instead of the resistance.

Figure 51 shows the approximate specific resistance of some refractory oxides. The resistance of these insulating materials decreases markedly at higher temperatures, as in the case of semiconductors. The specific resistance of any ceramic material is sensitive to the presence of impurities such as foreign oxides.

For the transport of heavy currents in welding and the process industries, carbon and graphite are commonly used. Of the three phases of carbon, diamond is an insulator, while carbon and graphite are semiconductors. Graphite has about one-quarter the resistance of carbon, and is the preferred material for electrodes in carbon arc welding and in arc-melting furnaces. The specific resistance of carbon ranges from about 0.0010 to 0.004 ohm-inches at 20°C, decreasing at higher temperatures.

The electrical resistance of the common plastics and rubbers ranges between 10^{15} and 10^{20} ohm-inches.

Fig. 51 Typical electrical resistance of refractories.

electrical properties of materials

6.3 applications of resistance materials

Resistance wire is special wire for the purpose of converting electric energy into heat. Most such wire is either nickel or nickel-chromium alloy, with the properties of oxidation resistance and high electrical resistance in the range of 200–800 ohms per circular mil-foot. One such alloy with the trade name Constantan has virtually a constant resistance in the temperature range of 0–900°F. For heavy-duty heating, as in the case of electrically heated industrial furnaces, rods or tubes of silicon carbide may be used as heating elements because of their great resistance to high temperature effects. Silicon carbide has only limited resistance change with temperature.

Incandescent lamps use a tungsten filament wire which may range in diameter from 0.001 to 0.060 in. Both tungsten and molybdenum resistors are employed as heating elements in very high temperature furnaces (3000°F and higher).

For *power transmission cables* aluminum has become competitive with copper. Although the resistivity of aluminum is higher, aluminum is only one-third the specific weight of copper. For equal resistance, the weight of aluminum is 54 percent that of copper. For short cables, such as welding cables, the rule of thumb is that an aluminum cable should be one gauge heavier than the required copper cable.

Thermistors are semiconductor crystals with a high negative temperature coefficient of resistance of perhaps 2–3 percent per degree Fahrenheit. Thermistors are used as thermal switches. For example, a thermistor may be used within an electric motor winding to operate a relay when the motor becomes too hot.

Electrical contacts present special problems. They must be constructed of low-resistance metals, but in addition they must meet the service conditions of arcing, wear, overheating, and tendency to weld. Copper, copper alloys, carbon, and the platinum metals are the most frequently used materials in these applications. Copper oxidizes readily, and its oxide is an insulator. Frequently silver is plated over the copper contact. The reason for doing so is that silver oxide is more readily reduced to metallic silver by arcing than the oxides of other metals. Platinum, palladium, and iridium are perhaps the best contactor materials for low-voltage, low-current conditions, and may provide a service life of more than a billion interruptions of current.

In the field of microelectronics, the most celebrated innovation perhaps is the *printed circuit*. This consists of an insulator backing plate, the substrate, carrying a pattern of conductors and resistors etched to the required pattern from a solid sheet of conducting foil. Printed circuits are not necessarily produced by printing methods. Usually a metal foil is bonded to the insulator substrate and subsequently etched. Figure 52 shows printed circuitry in a control panel.

Fig. 52   Rear view of a printed circuit module board. The leads of the many resistors, capacitors, and solid-state components shown all pass through the substrate board and connect to the printed circuit on the other side of the substrate. This module board is one of the many elements in the Bunker-Ramo control cabinet of the milling machine of Fig. 190.

6.4 superconductivity

The resistance of a single crystal of pure metal without imperfections in its space lattice should be zero at absolute zero. At temperatures below 10°K, the specific resistance of certain conductors falls off rapidly to zero. Such conductors are termed *superconductors*. Superconductivity is not yet well understood, but as a technology is about to come out of the laboratory to be turned over to the engineering groups. The best electrical conductors, gold, silver, and copper, are not superconductors, that is, their resistance does not reach zero at absolute zero.

The temperature below which the electrical resistance disappears is termed the *critical temperature*. But if the magnetic field about the conductor exceeds a certain critical value, superconductivity is lost. Diamagnetism (see below — a diamagnetic material is repelled by a magnetic field) accompanies the superconducting condition, and the thermal conductivity is very low, though not zero.

Technetium has the highest critical temperature, 11.2°K, followed by niobium (columbium) at 9.2° and lead at 7.2°. The critical temperature of the other superconducting metals is generally in the range of 0.35–5.0°K. In general, a superconducting metal will have 2 to 5 valence electrons outside the closed energy levels, will be a poor conductor at room temperature, and will not be ferromagnetic. Certain chemical compounds are also superconducting, with transition temperatures as high as 18°K. Superconductivity at considerably higher temperatures may be a development of the near future.

Applications of superconductivity have been considered in the following areas:

(a) lossless power distribution
(b) space satellites
(c) computers
(d) magnetohydrodynamic generation of electric power

The benefits of power transmission without I^2R loss are obvious, but present equally obvious difficulties in refrigerating a long transmission line. The development of magnetohydrodynamic (MHD) power generation is already well under way. The explanation of this process is not a proper topic for this book: suffice it to say that MHD is a brilliantly imaginative application of Fleming's rule for direction of magnetic and electric fields as discussed in any high school physics text. The use of superconductivity for switching circuits is found in *cryotrons* or cold switches. If a superconductor has a coil wound about it, a sufficiently high current passed through the coil will create a magnetic field which will destroy superconductivity in the conductor. This is an example of a simple cryotron switch.

The theory of magnetism is a rather complex subject which is still being unravelled by physicists, and only its simpler aspects can be discussed here. Three kinds of magnetism must be noted.

1. Ferromagnetism. This is the type of magnetism shown by materials which are strongly attracted to a magnet. Ferromagnetism is a property of iron, cobalt, nickel, Fe_3O_4, gadolinium, dysprosium, terbium, and certain metal alloys and ceramic alloys. Ferromagnetism, like superconductivity, is found only below a certain critical temperature, which in the case of ferromagnetism is called the *Curie temperature*. The Curie temperature of gadolinium and dysprosium is below room temperature, while that of iron is 1435°F. Above the Curie temperature ferromagnetic materials become paramagnetic. Unlike paramagnetism and diamagnetism, ferromagnetism is a property only of solids.

2. Paramagnetism. Paramagnetic materials, which may be solid, liquid, or gas (oxygen exhibits strong paramagnetism, for example) are weakly magnetic and orient themselves parallel to a strong magnetic field. Unlike ferromagnetism, paramagnetism is not limited by temperature.

3. Diamagnetism. This is a weakly negative type of magnetism, that is, diamagnetic materials are repelled from the strongest part of a magnetic field to the weakest. The rare gases and the metals bismuth, beryllium, copper and zinc are examples of diamagnetic materials.

An electron may be considered as a spinning negative electric charge. Since any such spinning charge is magnetic, an electron is in effect a minute magnet. There are two possible rotations of spin, clockwise and counterclockwise. In any completely filled energy level of the atom, each electron pairs with another electron of opposite spin. The electron pair is nonmagnetic, since the magnetism of one spin cancels that of the opposite spin. When all the electrons in an atom are thus paired, there can be no paramagnetism, and diamagnetism results. An unpaired electron will produce a paramagnetic condition. Thus any atom such as a silver atom (one atom in the outermost populated energy level) must be paramagnetic. There are other electron configurations which can produce paramagnetism, but these will not be discussed.

The three types of magnetism may also be defined in terms of *permeability*. Permeability measures the relative ease with which magnetic flux or magnetism may be developed in a material, or is the relative conductivity of a material for magnetic lines of force. A vacuum is assigned a permeability of 1. Diamagnetic materials have a permeability of less than 1, while paramagnetic materials have a permeability greater than 1. The maximum permeability of the common ferromagnetic steels ranges up to about 20,000, though special alloys may have permeabilities exceeding 1,000,000.

Suppose that a material is enclosed in a wire coil and that the coil carries an electric current. This will produce a magnetizing effect on the material within the magnetic field of the coil. The magnetizing effect will be proportional to the ampere-turns of the coil. The flux density B (lines of magnetic force per unit cross-sectional area) in the magnetized material will be some function of the amp-turns per unit length H:

$$B = f(H)$$

For both diamagnetic and paramagnetic materials, $B = \mu H$, where μ is the permeability. See Fig. 53.

As Fig. 53 shows, the relationship between B and H for a ferromagnetic material is nonlinear, and the permeability, B/H, is not a constant. There is a limit to the flux density of any ferromagnetic material; when this point is reached the material is said to be saturated. Magnetic amplifiers and saturable reactors use this phenomenon of saturation for their operation.

Soft steels are used in such electromagnetic equipment as motors, transformers, and relays. The steel is magnetized when current is switched to the magnetizing coil. Such steels instantly lose their magnetism when the current is switched off. Hard steels and nickel-steel alloys are used for permanent magnet applications.

The steel core of a transformer presents special problems which are solved by the use of laminations of so-called "electric" steels. The purpose of a transformer is the induction of a voltage or current in the secondary winding. Unfortunately the steel core is also a secondary, and a current is likewise induced in it. This current is termed an *eddy current*, and represents an I^2R loss of power, usually referred to as an iron loss, just as the I^2R losses

Fig. 53 Flux density and magnetizing force.

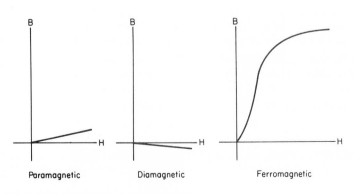

Paramagnetic   Diamagnetic   Ferromagnetic

electrical properties of materials

114

in the transformer windings are called copper losses. Soft steels have a relatively low specific resistance, and would produce large eddy currents and powerful heating effects in a transformer core. To reduce such eddy currents, the core is laminated to increase the resistance by reducing the cross-section carrying current, and the steel used is a silicon steel. Up to about 5 percent silicon is added. The silicon atoms replace iron atoms in the bcc space lattice. The effect is to produce distortions in the space lattice and thus to increase the specific resistance of the steel (by a factor of about 5 times for 3 percent silicon). Electric steels, however, have a lower saturation induction. Carbon and nitrogen reduce permeability in such steels and are therefore kept to as low values as possible; the permeability is improved if the steel is coarse-grained.

The following steels are not ferromagnetic:

1. type 300 stainless steels
2. steels containing about 12 percent manganese (Hadfield manganese steels)
3. any steel above its Curie temperature

The paramagnetic manganese and stainless steels are termed *austenitic*, and have pronounced work-hardening characteristics.

Certain nickel-iron alloys containing about 50 percent nickel, such as Perminvar, have a constant permeability. The most popular permanent magnet materials are the *Alnicos*. These are iron-nickel-aluminum alloys containing about one-quarter nickel. Like all permanent magnet materials, they are very hard.

Since World War II the *ferrites* have come into extensive use for electronic circuitry. These are complex ceramic oxides exhibiting strong paramagnetism. Typical ferrites are $NiO.Fe_2O_3$ or $MnO.Fe_2O_3$. Since such materials are insulators, no eddy current losses are involved in their use.

6.6   magnetostriction

The low-pitched hum of a 60-cycle transformer is a familiar sound. When the magnetic field of the steel transformer core builds up to the maximum in its positive or negative half-cycle, the core strains slightly under the influence of the magnetic field. This cyclical strain is the cause of the acoustic wave from the transformer. Since the steel core increases in length on both half-waves of alternating current, the sound wave is 120-cycle instead of 60-cycle. This strain that occurs when a ferromagnetic material is magnetized is called *magnetostriction*. The magnetostrictive effect is reversible: if a stress (and therefore a strain) is imposed on the material, the magnetization of the material will be altered.

Fig. 54 Ultrasonic transducers and amplifier-relay for such operations as counting packages on a conveyor belt, detecting pile-ups on a belt, etc. One transducer serves as ultrasonic transmitter and the other as receiver. (SONAC equipment of Delavan Manufacturing Company)

Magnetostriction produces a positive strain (elongation) in iron, and a negative strain (shortening) in cobalt and nickel. The effect is greatest in nickel, of the order of 30 millionths of an inch per inch maximum.

The famous antisubmarine Sonar was an early application of magnetostriction. Similar devices are now applied to ultrasonic inspection of welds and castings, ultrasonic detection and counting in automatic conveying, ultrasonic cleaning, ultrasonic welding, depth soundings in oceanography, phonograph pickups, and ultrasonic homogenization of milk, peanut butter, and other food products. Figure 54 shows an ultrasonic instrument for the detection of pile-ups on conveyor belts.

6.7   piezoelectricity

Piezoelectricity is analogous to magnetostriction. Certain ceramic materials such as quartz and titanates produce the piezoelectric effect. When a crystal of such material is compressed, a small voltage is generated across the opposite faces of the crystal, and conversely, a potential difference across the opposite faces will cause the crystal to expand or contract. Piezoelectricity is the preferred method of instrumentation for recording pressures in engine cylinders and gun barrels. For this purpose a small mounted crystal is screwed into the wall of the cylinder as a spark plug is, and the pressure read out as a voltage on an amplifier. While piezoelectricity as a method of instrumentation is competitive to magnetostriction in general, the piezoelectric effect is not capable of the high power that can be produced by the magnetostrictive effect. Ultrasonic cleaning, for example, requires considerable power in the hundreds of watts, and the transducers to supply such power must be magnetostrictive.

Figure 55 shows a piezoelectric transducer searching a material for flaws, which show as "pips" on an oscilloscope, also shown in the figure.

Fig. 55 Piezoelectric flaw detector. The detecting crystal under the operator's hand sends an ultrasonic wave into the workpiece underneath. Defects are disclosed by means of their ultrasonic echoes on an oscilloscope.

6.8 electron emission

Probably most people, particularly students of electrical, electronic, and mechanical engineering, are somewhat overwhelmed by the myriad types of electrical equipment in use in industry and science. This jungle of equipment can be reduced to intelligible order by reducing it to three basic types:

1. resistors — including wiring
2. inductors — including motors, generators, transformers, reactors, and solenoids
3. diodes

electrical properties of materials
117

A *diode* is any device composed of a negative electrode, called a *cathode*, which is a source of electrons, and a positive electrode, called an *anode*, which collects the supply of electrons released by the cathode. The commonly encountered diodes include vacuum tubes, gas-filled rectifiers such as the mercury-arc rectifier, X-ray tubes, photocells, and welding arcs.

Release of electrons from the material of the cathode is possible by the following methods:

1. heating, called thermionic emission
2. photon capture, called photoelectric emission
3. electron bombardment, called secondary emission
4. a high-voltage electric field, called field emission

The minimum energy required for an electron to escape from the metal cathode is called the *work function*. The work function is measured in electron-volts, and is analogous to an ionization potential, though the two are not the same thing. This work function may be supplied by any of the four methods enumerated above.

The work function of metals lies in the range of 1 to about 6 electron-volts. For electron emission efficiency the work function must of course be as low as possible. Metals such as cesium or rubidium, with a single outer electron, have work functions of about 2 ev. This low work function can be satisfied by photon energy in the visible light range, so that such one-electron metals are suitable cathodes for photocells. Platinum on the other hand has a work function of about $5\frac{1}{2}$ electron-volts, so that this metal might be used as an anode, but is unsuitable as a cathode material.

When heated to the usual operating temperature of 2500°K, tungsten is a copious source of electrons, with a work function of 4.5 ev. The work function of thorium is 3.4 ev. By adding 1–2 percent of thoria (the oxide of the metal) to the tungsten cathode, the work function is reduced to 2.7 ev. Thoriated tungsten electrodes are used both in vacuum tubes and in welding arcs for the tungsten inert gas (TIG) welding method used for much aerospace welding. Other oxides such as strontium oxide and barium oxide are also used to reduce work functions of cathode materials such as tungsten, tantalum, and nickel.

6.9   photoconductivity

The photoconductive effect occurs when a semiconductor is irradiated with a sufficiently high photon energy to cause a pronounced reduction in its electrical resistance. A semiconductor is distinguished by a relatively small energy gap between the valence band and the conduction band. The absorbed photon energy lifts an electron across this gap to the conduction condition. There are many photoconductive materials, but the more commonly used ones include selenium, silicon, cadmium sulfide, lead telluride, lead sulfide, and thallium sulfide. The photoconductive material is usually a deposited thin film on a substrate material Such materials may be used as detectors or switches to record the presence of visible light, ultraviolet, or X-radiation. Cadmium sulfide is preferred for X-ray detection.

6.10   the Hall effect

If a magnetic field is applied at right angles to a current in a conductor, the moving electric charges are deflected sideways and a potential difference occurs between the two sides of the conductor. The configuration is sketched in Fig. 56.

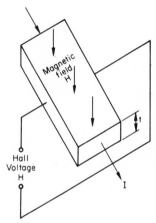

Fig. 56   The Hall effect.

The creation of the transverse electric field, perpendicular to both the current and the magnetic field, is called the *Hall effect* or *Hall voltage*. The Hall voltage $= V_{\mathrm{H}} = (KIH)/t$

where k = the Hall coefficient

I = current

H = magnetic field strength

t = conductor thickness

The Hall effect is small in metals, but considerable Hall voltages of 1 v or more can be developed in semiconductors such as germanium and silicon. Note that the Hall voltage is directly proportional to the magnetic field.

electrical properties of materials
119

This characteristic makes Hall devices very useful for electrical and electronic instrumentation. In mechanical engineering, Hall devices are becoming indispensable for such uses as measuring the large magnetic fields of resistance-welding machines, current-measuring devices, and eddy current testing of tubing and pipe for detection of flaws. (In eddy current testing a magnetic field is set up in the test specimen. If a flaw is present, the flaw distorts the magnetic field. This distortion can be read out on a Hall device.)

6.11 thermoelectricity

If two dissimilar metals are joined and this junction then heated, a small voltage in the millivolt range is produced, known as the *thermoelectric effect*. This is a method of producing direct-current electric power directly from heat. Currently the thermoelectric effect is being developed for a variety of uses.

There are actually three thermoelectric effects, but only the following two have industrial applications:

1. The Seebeck effect. If the two junctions of two dissimilar metals are held at different temperatures, a voltage is produced that is closely proportional to the temperature difference. This Seebeck arrangement of wiring is known as a thermocouple, and has been in use for the last hundred years as a temperature-measuring device.

2. The Peltier effect. If current flows through two junctions of two dissimilar metals, one junction will be heated and the other cooled. In terms of practical use, the Peltier effect indicates that one junction is a tiny furnace and the other a tiny refrigerator.

Since Seebeck's discovery there have been repeated attempts to produce electricity directly from heat by his method. So long as metal conductors were employed, these attempts failed because of the tiny currents produced and the abysmal efficiencies — less than 1 percent. But more recently, advances in solid state physics have led to the use of semiconductor thermoelectric devices with efficiencies closer to 10 percent. Bismuth telluride and lead telluride are the favored semiconductors for this purpose. Thermoelectric power generators with up to 5 kw capacity are now coming into use, and the thermoelectric refrigerator is nearing the end of its research and development stage. Figure 57 is a diagram of a semiconductor thermoelectric device, and operates in the following manner.

The heat energy applied at one end raises electrons from the valence band to the conduction band. For each electron thus transferred, a hole is left behind. The electrons travel to the cold junction through the *n*-type material, while the holes travel to the cold junction through the *p*-type material. The two unite at the cold junction, the electrons dropping into the holes and releasing energy to the cold junction. Since the charges carried by the holes and electrons are opposed to each other, there is a flow of electric current as indicated in the diagram. At the hot junction

Fig. 57 Semiconductor thermo-electric device.

both holes and electrons are moving away from the junction. To make up for the loss of these charges, electrons are raised from the valence band to the conduction band to create new pairs of electrons and holes. Since energy is required for this operation, heat is absorbed at the hot junction.

For temperature-indicating thermocouples, only four combinations are in common use, although other combinations must be used for very high temperature work:

1. copper-constantan, −300–700°F, 2% accuracy
2. iron-constantan, 0–1200°F, 4% accuracy
3. chromel-alumel, 1000–2200°F, 4% accuracy
4. platinum-platinum plus 4% rhodium, 2000–3000°F, 5% accuracy

The first metal in the pair is always the positive metal. The iron-constantan pair provides the highest electromotive force per degree. Chromel-alumel is the choice for oxidizing conditions, and platinum-platinum rhodium for reducing conditions. Chromel, alumel, and constantan are all very high nickel alloys.

For greater outputs, a number of thermocouples may be connected in series. Such a series is termed a *thermopile*. Many domestic gas furnaces contain a separate electric power system using a thermopile direct-current generator heated by the pilot gas flame of the furnace. If the pilot flame should go out, no thermopower is generated by the thermopile. The load on the little generator is a solenoid gas valve, and when the thermopile shuts down, the solenoid will cease to hold open the gas valve, which will then be shut by a spring. The house is thus protected against the possibility of an explosion due to raw gas flooding the furnace without being ignited by the pilot flame.

electrical properties of materials

6.12 dielectric strength

Since a dielectric is an insulator, dielectric strength means the insulating capacity of a material against high voltages. A sufficiently high voltage field across an insulator will cause it to break down and conduct. Dielectric strength is usually expressed as volts per mil thickness.

Dielectric strength of ceramic insulators such as the alumina of a spark plug body, or high voltage porcelain, ranges from 50 to 400 v per mil thickness. Refrigerants are required to have dielectric strengths of over 25 kv per in.; for most of the freons it is over 400 v per mil. Highest values of dielectric strength are given by such plastics as polyethylene and teflon, with values in the range of 1000–5000 v per mil.

6.13 dielectric constant

A capacitor is an electrical device for the temporary storage of electrons, and is essentially two parallel conducting plates with a dielectric between them. The electrons collect on either plate under the pressure of a voltage. The storage capacity of a capacitor is termed the capacitance. One of the variables determining capacitance is the *dielectric constant* of the dielectric material of the capacitor, the capacitance varying directly with the dielectric constant. A vacuum is assigned a dielectric constant of 1.0, just as the magnetic permeability of a vacuum is 1.0. Like most physical constants, the dielectric constant is a somewhat variable constant, generally decreasing at very high frequencies.

The dielectric constant for most plastics such as polyethylene is in the range of 2–3.0. For most ceramic materials, values lie between 4 and 10.

6.14 corrosion

Corrosion is any undesired chemical action that attacks industrial materials in such a way as to degrade their properties or reduce their economic value. The combustion of steel during oxyacetylene cutting is not corrosion, but the same chemical action during rusting of steel is corrosion. While discussion of corrosion is largely confined to metals, corrosion is an equally serious problem with firebrick linings of metal-melting furnaces. The chemical attack of a molten slag upon a firebrick may destroy the brick at a rate of an inch a day in an extreme case, necessitating replacement of the firebrick lining every week at great expense. Corrosion of concrete too is a common problem. Concrete may be corroded by sulfates in soils, by coal ash, or the concrete floor of a dairy may be corroded by the lactic acid in milk.

Corrosion then is one of the facts of life for industrial materials. Unfortunately, however, not all corrosion problems have textbook solutions; while extensive knowledge of materials and processes is certainly necessary, diagnostic skill and even intuition may often be required. Panacea solutions to corrosion problems are a snare for the unwary. People at large, engineers included, have great faith in the healing powers of the stainless steels for corrosion; unfortunately these expensive steels will solve only a restricted range of corrosion problems. Corrosion problems must be understood before they can be solved, although understanding may be hard to gain in some cases. It will not be our intention here to deal comprehensively with the whole field of corrosion, but merely to suggest some general approaches to the commoner kinds of corrosion in the commoner kinds of equipment and materials.

The beginning of wisdom in corrosion is to be convinced that no metallic, ceramic, or organic material is completely corrosion-resistant. So-called corrosion-resistant metals such as aluminum, stainless steels, and titanium, obtain their corrosion-resisting characteristics by the establishment of a thin adherent oxide surface film developed by an actual corrosion process with oxygen. This oxide film passivates the surface and prevents further corrosion — sometimes. Thus the surface of any sheet of aluminum is actually aluminum oxide. The oxides are perhaps the most stable of all chemical compounds, and of course chemical stability simply means corrosion resistance. In general it must be observed that metals tend to revert back to their ores by means of corrosion processes, or, in other words, an ore is a corroded metal.

Aluminum or stainless steel, being protected by surface oxides, will not normally be attacked by oxidizing chemicals. But a reducing chemical will attack them, since such a chemical can break down the protective surface oxide layer. Such metals therefore are readily attacked by chlorides, ferric chloride for example. Indeed, few chemicals are more corrosive than chlorides. The thought of using salts on icy roads, standard practice on this continent, is in principle a rather staggering metallurgical notion. Not even a stainless steel automobile would be proof against road salt.

One of the most frequently occurring types of corrosion is *galvanic* corrosion, the cause of which is electrical. In any wet battery or storage battery, there is an anode and a cathode connected by a liquid called an electrolyte. The electrolyte is partially ionized and thus can carry an electric current. The metal of the anode is corroded, and the process of corrosion in these circumstances is termed galvanic corrosion. In an electric storage battery or dry cell, galvanic corrosion is employed as a means of generating electric power.

electrical properties of materials
123

Now suppose a small rectangular water tank is welded together, using steel angle iron for the frame and sheet aluminum for the sides. Here we have the conditions for galvanic corrosion. The water in the tank will act as an electrolyte, one of the metals as an anode, and the other as a cathode. In this case, the aluminum will act as the anode and will corrode, probably in areas close to the angle iron. The corrosion proceeds by means of small electric currents circulating through the metal from the aluminum to the steel and back to the aluminum by way of the water. As in the case of a storage battery, there will be a difference in voltage between the anode and the cathode in the presence of the electrolyte. These electrode potentials are measured in the following fashion.

If a metal is placed in a solution containing ions of the same metal, metal ions will transfer either from the solution to the metal or vice versa. In the latter case, the metal becomes negative with respect to the electrolyte, and in the former case, positive. This follows from the fact that the metal ions are positive, and unlike charges attract. After a certain period of time an equilibrium condition will be reached, with the potential difference between metal and electrolyte equalizing the rate of transfer of ions back and forth, so that there will be no further transfer. This potential difference is known as the electrode potential, and depends on the nature of the metal, the temperature, and the concentration of the solution.

For a reference standard a so-called "hydrogen electrode" is used. This is actually a platinum electrode immersed in an acid solution through which is bubbled sufficient hydrogen gas to produce saturation. The potential between the electrode and electrolyte is defined to be zero when a normal acid solution is used. A normal solution is one which contains 1 gram per liter of hydrogen ions at 25°C.

The standard electrode potential of a metal is taken to be the potential difference between the hydrogen electrode and an electrode of the metal immersed in a normal solution of one of the metal's salts. For example, an aluminum electrode under these conditions will lose positive ions until the electrode reaches a steady negative potential of -1.70 v relative to the solution. Similarly a copper electrode will receive ions until it reaches a positive potential of $+0.34$ v relative to the solution.

These electrode potentials can be arranged in a series, known as a galvanic series, thus

Mg	-2.375
Al	-1.70
Zn	-0.762
Cr	-0.71
Fe	-0.44
Ni	-0.23
Pb	-0.126
H	0.00
Cu	$+0.34$

This series gives the relative corrodability of metals under conditions of galvanic corrosion. If two metals are coupled in a galvanic pair, the most anodic will be corroded. This will be the one with the highest negative electrode potential. Thus if zinc is plated on iron as galvanized iron, in the presence of rainwater as an electrolyte, the zinc will corrode. Corrosion is due to loss of ions to the electrolyte.

In any strict sense a galvanic series must be set up for different electrolytes, but the differences are rather minor. The following galvanic series for seawater is usually considered to be universal in application:

Anodic, or Corroded End	
magnesium	high copper brass
zinc	copper
aluminum	aluminum bronze
cadmium	nickel alloys
aluminum alloys	nickel
carbon and low alloy steels	stainless steel (passive)
cast iron	monel
stainless steel (active)	titanium
high zinc brass	*Cathodic, or Protected End*

Note that the position of the stainless steels is equivocal.

The usual methods of combating corrosion are these:

1. Use of high-purity metals. An alloy is always much more vulnerable to corrosion than a pure metal.
2. Proper design and fabrication. Examples are the avoidance of crevices into which an electrolyte can penetrate, or the use of aluminum rivets of the same alloy as the aluminum sheet joined by the rivets.
3. Cathodic protection, such as the insertion of a magnesium anode in a domestic hot water tank or the burying of a magnesium anode beside an underground gas pipeline.
4. Use of inhibitors, such as phosphate coatings on steel, chromate treatment of aluminum.
5. Surface coatings such as paints.

PROBLEMS

1 In many metal-working processes, the workpiece is heated by inducing eddy currents to flow in the workpiece itself. Pieces of tubing stock having a 3-in. length, 2-in. outside diameter, and a wall thickness of 0.06 in. are being induction-heated. The eddy currents circulate in the plane of the cross-section of the work. The specific resistance of the workpiece material is 6.0 microhm-inches, and the induced current 1000 amps. Calculate the resistance of the workpiece

electrical properties of materials
125

and the induced power in watts. The workpiece can be considered as a conductor with a cross-section 3.0×0.06 in.

2 300 amps of welding current is being carried through a #00 copper welding cable 50 ft long. For proper operation of the welding arc not more than a 2-v drop is allowed in this cable. Is the #00 cable size sufficiently large?

3 Corrosion occurs in an aluminum sheet around the rivets fastening the sheet due to condensation of water vapor. Can you diagnose the problem and suggest a cure?

By and large, the story of materials begins with the digging of a ceramic material, usually a mineral, out of the earth for processing in an industrial furnace. In the steel industry, for example, iron ore, a ceramic material, is extracted from open-pit mines and reduced to metal in a blast furnace. Cement, perhaps the most important manufactured ceramic product, also is manufactured in a type of industrial furnace called a rotary kiln, from the two ceramic raw materials clay and limestone.

These two instances illustrate the basic operations of the materials industries. The primary product is usually a ceramic material; the primary process requires an industrial furnace. Virtually all other industry is dependent on the massive and dirty primary processes of refining the basic ceramic materials.

Ceramic materials are unglamorous, and therefore their importance is little understood. But as finished products, they are indispensable throughout industry. Perhaps the most critically important ceramic products, are the refractories that confine the great process heats of the primary industries. But a full roster of everyday ceramic products includes the grinding wheel that puts the fine finish on ground steel shafting, the carbide bits used to machine metals, the piezoelectric crystal that reads the pressure in an engine cylinder, the mica spacer in a vacuum radio tube, the glass

CERAMIC
MATERIALS

7

envelope of a photocell, the ruby crystal in a laser, the titanium oxide in paints, the porcelain enamel on domestic appliances, the ferrites in the memory of a large digital computer, the clay and sodium sulfate in paper, and even the talc in baby powder and the calcium carbonate in toothpaste.

Ceramic materials did not phase out of technology when the Stone Ages of man (ceramic ages) ended. New uses are continually being found for these materials, and in recent years ceramic materials have even been used as lubricants (molybdenum disulfide) and fuels (uranium oxide for nuclear reactors and boron hydride for solid propellant rockets). Most of the ceramic materials are silicates, aluminates, oxides, carbides, borides, nitrides, or hydrides. A general classification of products is difficult because of the great versatility of these materials, but the following list includes the major groups:

1. abrasives
2. whiteware — toilet tanks, sinks, etc.
3. chemical stoneware
4. electrical porcelain
5. porcelain enamel
6. glass
7. brick and tile (such as clay sewer pipe)
8. cements and concretes
9. mineral ores
10. aggregates and grogs
11. refractories
12. slags and fluxes
13. insulations

The field of ceramics has a terminology of its own. Here are some of the more important definitions.

A *glass* is a ceramic or ceramic component which is amorphous. Thus most firebrick contains glass, but the term here obviously is not restricted to window glass.

A *slag* is a ceramic formulation used in the refining of molten metals. Slags usually serve two purposes:

1. They absorb undesired impurities from the metal, such as sulfur from steel.
2. They protect the metal from atmospheric gases.

A *flux* serves the same purpose in a ceramic mixture that an alloy serves in metals, that is, it lowers the melting or softening point of the mixture. Fluxes are usually necessary in the welding and brazing of metals in order to remove the oxide surface of the metal, because oxides usually have high melting points. Particularly in welding, it is often difficult to differentiate a flux from a slag, but this distinction is probably unimportant.

A *refractory* is a high-temperature ceramic used as a lining for a heating furnace.

A *frit* is a low-melting ceramic mixture, usually the raw material for porcelain enamel.

Refractories are subject to chemical action with metal-melting slags. Slags are either acid or base (alkaline), and refractories must be of the same type as the slag. Thus an acid refractory will be rapidly attacked by a basic slag made up of limestone. Silica is acid, magnesia is basic, and graphite and chromium oxide are neutral refractories.

7.2   pyrometric cone equivalent

Ceramic materials, like metals, are rarely used in pure form, and therefore do not have a definite melting point, particularly since most ceramic mixtures contain some amorphous glassy components.

A true melting point is the temperature at which solid and liquid phases of the same composition exist in equilibrium. Most of the commercially used ceramic materials soften progressively over a range of temperatures, and in this range both crystalline solid materials and glassy liquid coexist. To evaluate the high-temperature behavior of such materials, the usual method is to determine the "Pyrometric Cone Equivalent" or PCE. In this procedure, a ground sample of the material to be tested is molded into a test cone of slim pyramid shape, mounted with a series of standard pyrometric cones which have known softening values. The group is heated at a controlled rate until the test cones soften and bend. The number of the standard cone that softens at the same time as the test cone is reported as the PCE value of the material.

SELECTED PYROMETRIC CONE EQUIVALENTS

PCE	°F	PCE	°F	PCE	°F
6	2246	11	2417	20	2845
7	2282	12	2435	26	2950
8	2300	13	2462	28	2939
9	2345	14	2552	30	3002
10	2381	15	2605	32	3092
				40	3425

7.3 spalling

The term "spalling" is usually defined as the thermal cracking of ceramic materials. Most of these materials will crack if rapidly heated or cooled. Familiar examples of spalling are the cracking of concrete in barbecues and fireplaces. Spalling is an especially important problem in the case of firebrick.

Thermal expansion is a strain, and this strain is proportional to the thermal expansion coefficient. If the expansion is unimpeded, no stress accompanies this strain, according to Newton's third law. But frequently materials are not free to expand. Thus the hot face of a firebrick may be restrained from expansion by the cooler portion of the brick behind the hot face. Such restraint produces stress. The magnitude of these thermal stresses will be influenced by the thermal conductivity, the modulus of elasticity, and the expansion coefficient of the material. The stress will be proportional to the expansion coefficient, for a material with zero expansion will have zero thermal strain. Likewise the stress will be proportional to the modulus of elasticity, for a material with zero modulus of elasticity will not be stressed when it is strained. Now consider a material with an infinite thermal conductivity. There must be uniform temperature throughout the volume of such a material, and the bulk of the material, being at the same temperature as its heated surface, will not restrain the expansion of the heated surface.

Spalling of course will not occur in materials with considerable ductility. Nor, from the above argument, will it occur in materials with low expansion coefficients, low moduli of elasticity, and high thermal conductivity. This is borne out by experience. Metals rarely spall, because of their usual ductility and their high thermal conductivity. (Thermal stresses can be very high in stainless steels, however, because of the low thermal conductivity of these materials.) Graphite brick and crucibles cannot be spalled because of high thermal conductivity. Glass and silica brick will spall readily because of a very high expansion coefficient between room temperature and 600°F, though above this temperature range the thermal expansion is virtually zero and there is no risk of spalling. Pyrex

Cooled end

Heated end

Fig. 58 Spalling of refractory brick due to cooling (tension) and heating (shear).

glass, well known for its resistance to thermal cracking, contains boric oxide to provide a low expansion coefficient.

It is often possible to determine by inspection whether a ceramic material has spalled due to sudden heating or to sudden cooling. Sudden cooling produces failure by tensile stresses, shown by fracture lines at right angles to the edges of the material. See Fig. 58. Sudden heating results in shear failure, indicated by cracking at 45°F to the edges of the material.

7.4 general characteristics of the ceramic group

Before discussing individual members of the broad group of ceramic materials, we shall first summarize those characteristics generally shared by the whole group.

1. **Chemical composition.** The group consists chiefly of oxides, carbides, and silicates, though some borides, hydrides, and nitrides are in use in industry. In their chemical reactions with each other at high temperatures, such as reactions between slags and refractories, it has been noted that they may be acid, basic, or neutral. They are however chemically stable and generally uncorrodable at room temperature. In general these materials are somewhat impure, the commonest impurity being iron oxide. Most of the ceramic materials occur naturally, and are extracted by open-pit mining, quarrying, or excavating methods. But beginning in this century, an increasing number of these materials have been synthetically formulated. The synthetic ceramics include the carbides and most of the abrasives.

2. **Stress and strain.** The ceramic materials are brittle and therefore unworkable. When mixed with water in the unburned state, raw materials such as clays are plastic, however. All the ceramic materials become increasingly plastic or less viscous at high temperatures. The only applicable machining method for these materials is grinding.

3. **Joining methods.** The only joining method generally workable for ceramic materials is that of cementing with either inorganic mortars or organic cements. A few special solders are used with glass, and electron-beam welding will join ceramics to ceramics or ceramics to metals, although this method is little used.

4. **Cost.** The naturally occurring ceramics are inexpensive, with costs generally in the range of $\frac{1}{4}$ of a cent to 5 cents per pound. Synthetic ceramics

on the other hand are considerably more expensive than this, as anyone who has bought a carborundum sharpening stone knows. These materials being heavy and of low value, it is not usual to ship them over great distances.

5. Physical characteristics. Except at high temperatures, these materials are electrical insulators, though carbides will conduct at room temperature. Thermal conductivities are in the range of 5 to 100 Btu per in., making ceramics less thermally conductive than the metals, which have conductivities above 100 Btu per in. thickness. Most ceramics are good heat insulators when highly porous and are used as insulating materials. Specific heat is usually about 0.2 Btu per lb. Almost all are hard and abrasive, with very high melting or softening points.

7.5   the common oxides

Six common oxides are the basic materials for a wide range of industrial products:

silica	SiO_2
alumina	Al_2O_3
lime	CaO
magnesia	MgO
iron oxide	Fe_2O_3
rutile	TiO_2

Iron has two oxides. The red oxide of iron rust is Fe_2O_3, while the black oxide found on hot-rolled steel sheet is Fe_3O_4. Except as iron ore, iron oxide has few industrial uses, its chief one being as a flux in the manufacture of cement. It is an ever-present fluxing impurity in clays, minerals, and other deposits. White clays such as kaolin are white because of the absence of iron oxide, and this characteristic makes such clays valuable. The iron oxides are unusual in that they melt at approximately the same temperature as iron, 2800°F.

Lime and *magnesia* are basic (alkaline) in their chemical reactions. Lime is produced from limestone, $CaCO_3$, and magnesia from magnesite, $MgCO_3$. In addition the mineral dolomite is a solid solution of about half limestone and half magnesite. Magnesia is chiefly employed as a furnace refractory in metal-melting and cement-burning furnaces.

The chief uses of lime are these:

1. major ingredient in portland cement manufacture
2. component of window glass

3. metal-melting slag
4. chemical used in the manufacture of pulp and paper
5. chemical used in various water treatment processes and to raise the pH of water
6. manufacture of sand-lime brick
7. component of sand-lime-cement mortar
8. ingredient in masonry paints

This list by no means exhausts the manifold uses of lime.

Three simple chemical reactions are of great importance in the various uses of lime. Quicklime or hot lime is made by dissociation of calcium carbonate at 1830°F:

$$CaCO_3 \rightarrow CaO + CO_2$$

This process is called lime burning. Hydrated lime or slaked lime is produced by reacting hot lime with water:

$$CaO + H_2O \rightarrow Ca(OH)_2$$

Slaking produces considerable quantities of heat. Slaked lime hardens by a slow reaction with carbon dioxide in the air:

$$Ca(OH)_2 + CO_2 \rightarrow CaCO_3 + H_2O$$

Lime (CaO) has a cubic space lattice with alternating Ca and O atoms in the lattice.

Silica is found naturally in its quartz phase, most often encountered as quartz rock, quartz sand, or sandstone. At temperatures above 1600°F the phase changes to tridymite, and at 2678°F to cristobalite. The melting point of pure silica is 3130°F. Silica may be used at temperatures very close to its melting point, for like carbon, it has the unusual property of maintaining a very high strength almost to its melting point. Silica brick is used in the arched roofs of open-hearth steel-melting furnaces operated at temperatures of 3000°F. The high expansion and spalling characteristics of silica at low temperatures have already received mention.

When silica is melted and resolidified, a silica glass or quartz glass is formed (not the type of glass used as window glass) with two industrially significant properties:

1. transmission of ultraviolet radiation
2. low coefficient of expansion at low temperatures and remarkable spall resistance. Quartz glass is used in ultraviolet and infrared lamps.

Of these common oxides, *alumina* is the all-round best in its properties, and has a wide range of uses in ceramic technology such as nickel does in metals technology. The melting point of pure alumina is 3720°F. This material has good hot strength, reasonable spall resistance and good corrosion resistance against molten slags. Its many uses include spark-plug bodies, ceramic cutting tools for machining metals, grinding wheels, and firebrick. The equilibrium diagram for Al_2O_3–SiO_2 is given in Fig. 25 on page 51. A great many minerals and clays, many types of firebrick, and portland cement, are compounds of alumina and silica.

Rutile is one of the more common constituents of the earth's crust. It is a white oxide, used to provide opacity and whiteness to paints and porcelain enamels. Rutile and lime are the most useful flux coatings (so called; they are really slag coatings) on manual arc-welding rods.

7.6   ceramic insulating materials

Ceramic insulating materials give excellent service up to hot-face temperatures as high as 3000°F. The *K*-factor of these materials may be as low as 0.3 Btu per in. at room temperature, though at 1000°F it will be in the range of 1 Btu per in. thickness. Most of the foamed plastics, such as polyurethane and polystyrene, have lower *K*-factors but generally cannot be used at temperatures above 150°F.

Insulating materials are available in several forms: rigid board or block insulation, blankets or batts, formed insulation to fit piping, and granular loose fill in bags or bulk. Loose fill materials may also be used with cements to make insulating concretes or trowelled cements.

Asbestos is a fibrous mineral mined in Canada. Though its chief use is in porous insulating materials, it is also molded into hard asbestos millboard. Asbestos "shorts" are used for loose fill. Asbestos does not have unusually high temperature resistance, but tends to crumble at temperatures much above 1000°F.

Fiberglass is made of spun fibers of glass with a melamine or other plastic binder, and is used as pipe insulation as well as in insulation blankets. Its temperature limitations are even lower than those of asbestos. The binder burns out at about 600°F, indicated by a change of color from yellow to white.

Rockwool is another gray fibrous insulation made by blowing high-pressure steam at a stream of molten rock composition. Rockwool is usually supplied in blankets or rolls.

85-percent magnesia (with 15 percent asbestos) is a white powdery insulation usually formed into pipe insulation in three- or four-foot lengths for low-temperature applications.

Calcium silicate is white and powdery also, but has the higher temperature rating of about 1200°F.

Diatomaceous earth is the geological deposit of the skeletal remains of the marine alga known as diatoms. This material is almost pure silica, used as loose fill. Its fusion point is about 2450°F.

Vermiculite, often known by its trade name Zonolite, is a foliated aluminum-iron-magnesium silicate somewhat similar in appearance to fine mica. When heated at 2000°F it expands into accordion-like granules with excellent properties as an insulating material or a light-weight aggregate for concretes. The expansion may be as much as 30 times the original size. Vermiculite is supplied in bags of 4 cu ft, a bag weighing about 25 lb. It is possible to make a vermiculite concrete light enough to float on water.

Perlite is a white silica mineral which also can be expanded at a temperature of about 1600°F to provide a bulk material which is formed into wallboard and tile for sound insulation. Light-weight concretes made of perlite are not so tough or crack-resistant as vermiculite concretes.

Haydite. Certain types of clays when heated release gases which bloat the clay. This expanded clay is called haydite. Haydite is used as an aggregate in light-weight concrete blocks and in low-heat duty refractory concretes. However, a haydite concrete is heavier than concretes using perlite or vermiculite.

7.7   glass

In ceramic science, the word "glass" signifies any amorphous component of a ceramic mixture. More generally, glass is a transparent silica product which may be amorphous or crystalline, depending on heat treatment.

Glass has a remarkable range of uses. The architect Le Corbusier, a pioneer in the use of glass as an architectural material, once suggested that the story of architecture is simply the search for the window. Today the glass curtain wall on high-rise buildings is a part of the skyline of any large city. To the architect or the civil engineer, glass is a structural material. To the electrical engineer or the instrument engineer, glass is an electrical insulator or a tube envelope with transmission characteristics required for radiation. To the mechanical engineer, glass may be many things; he uses glass pipe, fiberglass insulation, and even glass springs. To the packaging engineer, glass is a container for such liquids as milk and beer.

Glass is a solid insofar as it has the rigidity and hardness customarily associated with solid bodies. However, it lacks a continuous space lattice. Any crystalline ordering is on a submicroscopic scale in glass, and in this respect, therefore, glass is a hard liquid. When molten glass is cooled, it tends to crystallize, but its high viscosity is a strong deterrent to crystal formation. As a result, the liquid state becomes "frozen in". Glass properties are unfavorably affected if crystals develop in the glass.

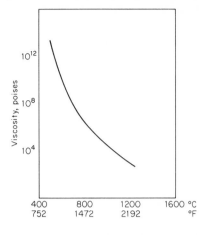

Fig. 59 Typical viscosity-temperature curve for a glass.

A convenient rule of thumb says that the "melting temperature" of glass (it does not possess such a characteristic) is that temperature at which glass has a viscosity of 10^2 poises. Although the many different grades of glass have considerable variation in their viscosity, Fig. 59 is a typical viscosity curve for glass.

A brittle material, glass at room temperature is completely elastic up to its ultimate tensile strength. It always fails in tension. See Fig. 60. The strength of glass depends to a very great extent on the residual stresses set

Fig. 60 A baseball may be used to prove that ceramics are brittle and have low tensile strength. The circle of fracture is a line of constant stress, the ultimate tensile strength of the glass.

ceramic materials

up in the glass as a result of cooling or other thermal treatments, the size and shape of the part, the surface condition, and the surrounding atmosphere. A network of microscopic cracks covers the surface of a glass, and these are a major factor in reducing the strength. Water and water vapor are mildly corrosive to glass when adsorbed within such cracks and assist in reducing the apparent strength. Maximum strength is found when a virgin surface exists on the test specimen. Freshly drawn glass fibers with extremely small diameters have given tensile strengths as high as 10^7 psi, while larger specimens break under stresses in the range of 10,000 to 20,000 psi.

The effect of water vapor on the strength of glass may be noted in the method that an experienced glass worker uses to break a glass rod. He scratches the glass with a cutter, then briefly exhales on it or wets it.

The modulus of elasticity of most glasses is in the range of 10,000,000 psi, about the same rigidity as aluminum.

Neglecting glasses tailored for special transmission characteristics, glass transmits visible light well, up to 90 percent, but is opaque to ultraviolet, and gives limited transmission in the infrared region.

7.8 types of glass

Four general classes of glass may be differentiated:

1. *Soda-lime glass.* This is the cheapest glass, used for windows and doors.
2. *Borosilicate glass* (Pyrex glass). This glass has a low expansion coefficient (about 20×10^{-7} in./in./°F), and therefore has good spall resistance.
3. *Fused silica.* Outstanding thermal shock resistance.
4. *Pyroceram.* A crystalline glass invented by Corning Glass Works.

The chief constituent of glass is of course silica, which is obtained from high-purity silica sand. Fused silica glass (quartz glass) has excellent spall resistance, good transmission of ultraviolet radiation, and the best resistance to chemical attack of any type of glass.

Quartz glass, however, has a high melting point and is difficult to work. To reduce the melting point and the viscosity, in most glass compositions the silica is fluxed with soda (Na_2O or K_2O), lime borax, phosphorous oxide (P_2O_5), and occasionally other oxides. Phosphate glasses will transmit in the ultraviolet range, while lead oxide provides shielding against X-radiation. Borosilicate glass contains about 80 percent silica, 10 percent borax, and 10 percent or less of alumina, soda, and other oxides. Lime-soda glasses may contain 70 percent silica, 20 percent soda, and 10 percent lime. If sufficient soda is added, the product becomes sodium silicate, which is water-soluble. In general the corrosion resistance of glass may be considered to be proportional to the silica content.

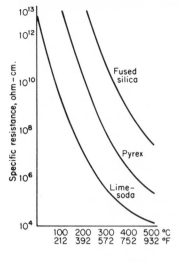

Fig. 61 Electrical resistance of glass.

Figure 61 shows typical electrical resistivities of glass. The electrical resistance is reduced by the addition of soda, potash, and alumina, particularly soda, while borax and lime increase resistance. Sodium ions in glass are carriers of electric charge. However lime-soda glass has sufficiently high resistance to be suitable for the envelopes of electron tubes, except for photocells, which may require transmission of ultraviolet radiation.

The pyrocerams are polycrystalline glasses with softening temperatures above 2000°F, low specific heat of about 0.1, thermal conductivity of about 30 Btu/°F/in., and a modulus of elasticity of $17–19 \times 10^6$. The thermal expansion can be formulated from slightly negative to 0.000003.

A very important detail in the construction of high vacuum electron tubes is the production of dependable glass-to-metal seals in the base of the tube which will preserve the high vacuum. A strong bond between the metal leads and the glass base of the tube is obtained by means of an oxide layer which is formed on the metal just before the seal is made. This oxide layer diffuses into the molten glass when the two are brought into contact. Such seals are not effective unless the thickness of the oxide layer is very closely controlled. Production of the seals is consequently a highly mechanized operation.

7.9 clays

Clays and soils have their origin in the mechanical and chemical disintegration of rock. Clays are complex aluminum silicates containing attached water molecules. If only alumina, silica, and water are present in the clay, the clay is white after firing. Most clays contain iron and manganese oxides. These fluxing ingredients give color to the clay and reduce the refractoriness or PCE of the clay.

A wide range of products is produced from clays. These include pottery, chemical stoneware, electrical porcelain, brick, tile, haydite, drilling mud for oil wells, filters, portland cement, and catalysts for the "cracking" of petroleum. Clay through the ages has appealed to the artistic impulses of men. Every civilization has produced beautiful pottery, perhaps the finest being the ceramic work of the Sung dynasty of China about a thousand years ago.

The civil engineer distinguishes three broad groups of soils:

1. granular or cohesionless soils, including sands and gravels
2. fine-grained soils, including silts and clays
3. organic soils, including peat, muskeg, and muck

The gravel component of a soil is that fraction with constituents larger than 2 mm (#10 U.S. standard sieve). The sand component is that fraction with constituents between 2 mm and 0.1 mm (#140 U.S. standard sieve). The individual particles of a fine-grained soil cannot be distinguished by the naked eye. Clays are plastic when blended with suitable water content, while silts cannot be thus plasticized. Silt particles are in the range of 0.05 to 0.005 mm, while clay particles are still smaller.

A large number of clay minerals have been distinguished, classified according to their silicate structure. The following clays are used as industrial raw materials:

1. Kaolin. A white clay, nearly pure kaolinite, $Al_2O_3.2SiO_2.2H_2O$. Kaolins are used for china, electrical porcelain bodies, sanitary ware, and in paper, rubber, and firebrick.

2. Montmorillonites. This is a large group of common clays. The group includes talc, which is used in the production of the electrical dielectric known as steatite, valued for high-frequency applications.

3. Aluminous clays. These are not widely distributed over the earth's surface; there are for example deposits in the United States but none in Canada. Bauxite, $Al_2O_3.3H_2O$, is found in the West Indies and the southern states and is the mineral from which aluminum is most cheaply extracted. Diaspore, $Al_2O_3.H_2O$, is a beautiful and highly refractory clay which is the basis of the remarkable fireclay industry of eastern Missouri.

4. Vermiculite. Found in Montana and elsewhere. This material was mentioned in Sec. 7.6.

5. Flint clays. These are hard clays almost devoid of plasticity, which are added to more plastic clays. The flint clay may be likened to the skeleton of the clay structure, with the plastic clay acting as cementing binder.

6. Feldspar. Feldspar is an alkali-aluminum silicate rock, not a clay. It is an ingredient of many industrial clay mixtures, however, serving as a flux.

7. Fireclays. These are plastic clays of high refractoriness, cone 27 (2920°) or higher. Deposits of fireclay are distributed over the United States and Canada.

8. Ball clays. These are fine-grained, highly plastic clays chiefly used in whiteware and electrical porcelain.

7.10 manufacture of clay products

Few clay products are made of a single type of clay. Electrical porcelain for example is a blend of feldspar, flint, ball, and china clay, all prepared to required sieve sizing. A vitreous sanitary ware, such as is used in sinks and bathtubs, may have the following composition:

flint clay	30%
feldspar	26
ball clay	18
kaolin	26

In order to process such clay mixtures into finished products, the mixture must be tempered with water. The several clay manufacturing methods may be classified in order of decreasing water content as follows:

1. slip casting	12–50% water (percent of weight of clay)
2. soft mud process	25–40% water
3. stiff mud process	15–30% water
4. dry press process	4–12% water

In *slip casting*, the water-clay mixture, called a slip, is poured into a mold of plaster of Paris, which takes up water and causes a solid shell to form. The slip in the center is then poured out and the mold removed after further drying.

The *soft mud process* is chiefly used in the manufacture of building brick, and the *stiff-mud process* chiefly for firebrick. These processes ex-

Fig. 62   A brick mural.

trude the clay products through an extrusion die in a continuous length, the long extrusion being cut into brick by means of wires pulled through the extrusion.

The *dry press process* forms the clay product in a steel mold. The stiff-mud extrusion process, because of the smearing action of the extrusion die on the product, produces a brick of lower porosity than the dry press method. Brick made by either method can be identified by surface appearance, the extruded brick showing longitudinal extrusion marks. The lower porosity of the stiff-mud process is often desirable for firebrick, which must resist the penetration and corrosive attack of metal-melting slags.

Building brick is either sand-lime brick or clay brick, in the grades of *common brick* and *face brick*. Face brick is darker, denser, stronger, and held to closer dimensional tolerances than common brick. The greater density of face brick implies lower porosity with better resistance to frost damage. Sand-lime brick contains about 10 percent hydrated lime in sand, the brick being cured in steam autoclaves to a monocalcium silicate.

Burning temperature for building brick may range from 1800–2200°F. Firebrick are burned at temperatures above 2400°F and as a result are considerably denser than building brick. A common brick weighs about 4 lb, as compared to 6 to 10 lb for firebrick. Standard size for a common brick is usually 8 × 4 × 2 in., while a standard firebrick, called a *nine-inch straight*, is 9 × 4½ × 2½. The reason for the difference in size is that often the two kinds of brick must be built into a wall, with the firebrick on the hot face and common brick on the outside of the wall.

ceramic materials
141

Firebrick does not use mortar joints in the usual meaning of the term. But building brick, because of their dimensional irregularities, require a thick bed of mortar. If building brick are laid with half-inch-thick mortar joints, and firebrick with joints of zero thickness, courses of common brick and firebrick can then be bonded together and the courses will match.

Certain clay products, such as chemical stoneware, must have zero porosity. This condition is obtained by burning the clay product in the *vitrification* range of temperature. This is the temperature range at which the most fusible or glassy ingredients of the product become suddenly less viscous, that is, they "melt". The liquid thus formed begins to dissolve the unfused material and flows into the pores to reduce porosity and increase density.

Radial chimney brick are made by the same methods as building brick. Such brick are segments of circles, used only in the construction of large radial brick chimneys.

Acid-proof brick and tile are used for building storage tanks which must contain acids (except hydrofluoric acid) and other corrosive chemicals used by such industries as pulp mills and water treatment plants. To resist chemical attack, such tile is very hard and has a smooth vitreous working face. Brick sizes correspond to those used in firebrick construction, and the mortar is a special acid-proof cement.

7.11 refractories

The ceramic products which line the nation's industrial furnaces are called refractories. These materials must be numbered among the most critically important of the materials that support an industrial civilization, for primary industries depend heavily on high-temperature processes. Such processes include the manufacture of abrasives, extraction of metals from their ores, heat-treating and forging of metals, generation of steam power, and the production of carbon products, glass, cement, brick and other materials.

Harbison-Walker Refractories Co., in the book *Modern Refractory Practice*, defines the place of refractories in the following quotation.

Refractories are defined as nonmetallic materials suitable for the construction or lining of furnaces operated at high temperatures. Stability at high temperatures — both physical and chemical — is the primary requirement for refractory materials. They may be called upon, while hot, to withstand pressures from the weight of furnace parts or contents, thermal shock resulting from rapid heating or cooling, other stresses induced by temperature change, mechanical wear resulting from movement of furnace contents, and chemical attack by heated solids, liquids, gases, or fumes.

Because of the severe operating conditions to which they are exposed, the life of refractory linings may be brief. In extreme cases a refractory lining may have to be replaced weekly.

The range of refractories employed in industry is literally enormous. Therefore only the more commonly used items can receive mention here. To reduce this complex range of products to simple order, we may first divide all refractories into three types:

1. Firebrick. These are modular burned refractory shapes, laid in an overlapping half bond with each other, and usually, but not always, bonding with thin refractory mortar.

2. Refractory castables. These are refractory concretes, poured in place.

3. Plastic refractories. These are unburned blocks of refractory in a plastic state. The soft slabs of plastic are piled up and pounded with a hammer into a monolithic wall, being burned in place when the furnace is lit. Certain types are referred to as ramming mixes, and these are installed with an air rammer.

Fig. 63   Refractory installation in a downdraft kiln. The burners are in the round turrets, and the exhaust flues are the holes in the floor brick being installed. A portion of the 40-foot diameter roof dome may be seen, dark-colored brick at the bottom of the dome and white brick at the top. The triangular patches on the white brick result from dipping the brick in the mortar.

Refractory castables are usually supplied in 100-lb sacks. Construction concretes are made by blending sacks of cement with sand, gravel, and water. A sack of refractory castables, however, includes all the required ingredients except the water. The castable is a mix of refractory cement, usually the high-alumina cement called lumnite cement (lumnite cement is discussed in the next chapter) and fireclay aggregate, called "grog". The grog may be crushed and burned firebrick. The use of sand and gravel, or of ordinary portland cement, is not possible in refractory concrete except for very low temperature applications.

Besides these differences in raw material mix, there are other differences between construction concrete and refractory castables:

1. Refractory castables are more expensive. A 100-lb sack of some special refractory castables may cost as much as a cubic yard of concrete, though this is an extreme case. On the other hand, castables are not poured in the large quantities that concrete is.
2. Refractory castables set very quickly and are frequently mixed only one sack at a time for this reason. Often they are simply mixed with water in a wheelbarrow.
3. Hardened castables weigh about 125 lb per cu ft. Concrete weighs 150 lb per cu ft.
4. Refractory castables are rarely trowelled. They are too rough to trowel well, and trowelling may promote spalling of the trowelled face at high temperatures.
5. Castables do not have the tensile or compressive strength of concrete. Castable strength is moderate at room temperature, decreases to low values at about 1000°F, then increases to a maximum above 2000°F due to the formation of a ceramic bond. See Fig. 64.

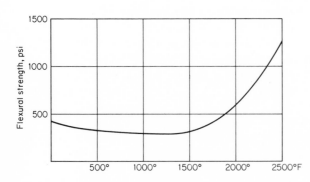

Fig. 64 Strength curve of a typical refractory castable. Strength is a minimum in the range of 1000–1500°F for all castables.

For light-duty applications, castables are sometimes made of ordinary portland cement, using for aggregate such materials as vermiculite, haydite, or perlite, but not sand, gravel, or crushed stone.

ceramic materials
144

Because of the varying demands of different types of industrial furnaces, firebrick shapes are available in many types of materials.

1. Fireclay brick. Except when special conditions dictate the use of special materials, fireclay brick are employed. There are however many applications that call for special materials. Fireclay brick are not generally suitable for metal melting, for slag and fume attack, nor for conditions of severe abrasion. Burned fireclay shapes are available in several grades of refractoriness: superduty, high heat duty, medium duty, and low duty. Such fireclay brick contains about 40 percent alumina and 60 percent silica. Both the stiff mud and the dry press process are used in their production.

2. High alumina brick. For more severe conditions such as in the manufacture of cement, high alumina brick is used, in grades of 50 percent, 60 percent, 70 percent, up to 99 percent alumina, or mullite brick, 72 percent alumina. Alumina is resistant to the attack of many slags and fumes and has higher strength than fireclay.

3. Silica. It has been noted that silica is an unusual material in that it maintains its strength at high temperatures. Silica brick therefore is used in applications where great strength is necessary, such as in the arched roofs of metal-melting furnaces. It is an acid brick, and therefore must be used in contact with acid slags in metal melting. Silica brick are rarely cooled below 1200°F. Below this temperature spalling is almost certain due to a high coefficient of expansion. Silica brick therefore cannot be used in intermittently operated furnaces.

4. Graphite. Because graphite oxidizes readily in the presence of air, graphite brick is used below the hearth line of metal-melting furnaces such as blast furnaces. Graphite is an excellent refractory since it cannot be spalled (because of high thermal conductivity) and its strength increases with temperature. If protected from oxidation it may be used at 6000°F. Few refractories are usable above 3000°F.

5. Silicon carbide. This versatile material, familiar as an abrasive, is also a remarkable refractory, Like graphite, it has a high thermal conductivity and great spall resistance. The thermal conductivity of firebrick is about 10 Btu/in., while that of silicon carbide is about 100 Btu/in. Silicon carbide is highly refractory, with a high strength and a high cost, and an outstanding performer under conditions of abrasion.

6. Zircon and zirconia. Zircon is zirconium silicate; zirconia is zirconium oxide. The latter is probably the most photogenic of the refractories, being a beautiful yellow color. Zircon is resistant to alkaline fluxes, which are generally ruinous to refractories, and therefore finds its chief applications in glass melting. Both zircon and zirconia are suitable for the vacuum-melting of metals.

7. Magnesite and chrome ore. Magnesite brick is magnesium oxide, the brick being a dark brown color. Chrome refractories, which are a rich green color and surprisingly heavy, are largely chromium oxide with liberal amounts of alumina and iron oxide. Large tonnages of magnesite refractories are made from the magnesium chloride in sea water. The principal products of the sea are fish and firebrick.

These are basic refractories and must be used to resist the attack of basic slags in metal melting. Actually most slags are basic, especially for steel, copper, and nickel; therefore the linings of melting furnaces are largely magnesite brick (this is not true of aluminum melting). Chrome is usually employed as a plastic refractory, being then referred to as "chrome ore". Both materials have poor hot strength and poor resistance to spalling.

The mortar for magnesite brick is a strange one indeed. For mortar a thin steel plate is used, and, surprisingly, it makes the strongest of all mortars. The magnesite brick are laid with thin steel plates between them, then the furnace is heated, and the steel oxidizes to ferric oxide which combines chemically with the magnesia. After this chemical reaction it is hardly possible to break the brick joint with anything less than a pneumatic hammer or explosives.

8. Insulating firebrick. These are light-weight porous refractories. While an ordinary firebrick may weigh from 6 to 10 pounds, an insulating firebrick may weigh $2\frac{1}{2}$ to 3 lb. Most insulating brick is made of fireclay. To obtain decreased density, fine coke or sawdust is added to the raw mix. The combustible additive burns out, producing a large amount of gases, which develops the required porosity in the firebrick.

Insulating firebrick offers little resistance to abrasion or slag attack. However, they are commonly employed in what are termed "reheat furnaces", which includes forge furnaces, heat-treating and brazing furnaces, etc. This brick is used simply to save on fuel costs. A large amount of heat is required to bring an industrial furnace up to temperature, if the furnace is lined with hard firebrick. Insulating brick has the same specific heat, but weighs only a third as much, so that only one-third the heat is required for warm-up.

The ingenious applications to which materials may be put are best illustrated by refractories. The use of steel plates with basic firebrick is one such example. Another is the use of ladle brick to line the holding ladles for molten steel. The molten steel may have a temperature of 2900°F or higher, and it would be expected that a highly refractory brick would be used for the ladle lining. On the contrary, the softening point of the ladle brick may be *lower* than the temperature of the steel. The reason is this. It is manifestly impossible to make a liquid-tight brick lining. Even if this were possible, the brick would probably crack. The molten steel will run into any small openings in the brick lining and may then melt through the steel ladle. The worst possible accident in a steel mill is a metal breakout in an area where men are working. The possibility of such a breakout is circumvented by using a low heat duty ladle brick. The skin of such a brick softens and runs, thus forming a closed glassy surface over the ladle to prevent a breakout. As an extra safeguard, ladle brick are formulated for a high coefficient of expansion.

7.13 firebrick shapes

Building brick is laid in thick joints of sand-cement-lime mortar. If such a mortar were to be used with firebrick, the mortar would spall out under the attack of heat, and the brick wall would collapse. This is occasionally proved by the rare masonry contractor who attempts to lay firebrick with the wrong mortar. Firebrick are bonded in the following fashion, except for basic brick and the linings of rotary kilns. The mortar used is a fireclay-base mortar. It is watered down to a soupy consistency. The brick is simply dipped into the mortar and laid on the wall. Note from this description that firebrick work is not a trowel trade.

Firebrick walls are given an expansion allowance of 1 in. every 16 ft, horizontally. Firebrick masons generally use pieces of corrugated cardboard for the expansion joint. The cardboard burns out when the furnace is fired.

A wide variety of shapes is required in firebrick construction. All these shapes are produced to a dimensional tolerance of ± 2 percent, since there is no thick mortar joint to compensate for variations in size from brick to brick. The standard $9 \times 4\frac{1}{2} \times 2\frac{1}{2}$ firebrick is referred to as a "9-inch straight". The standard series of 9-in. brick also includes the following:

1. 9" split — $9 \times 4\frac{1}{2} \times 1\frac{1}{4}$
2. 9" soap — $9 \times 2\frac{1}{4} \times 2\frac{1}{2}$
3. arch brick
4. wedge brick
5. key brick

The arch, wedge, and key shapes are used for building arches and for turning circles. These brick are illustrated in Fig. 65.

Fig. 65 Standard 9-inch firebrick shapes.

The soap and the split brick are exactly half the volume of the 9-inch straight, yet cost exactly the same. The identical prices make buyers suspicious. The explanation is one that is common to many ceramic products. The cost of most ceramic products is incurred in the manufacturing process, not in the raw material, which has a negligible cost. The manufacturing cost of a split brick is the same as that of a straight brick. In the same vein, a carborundum stone for sharpening hand tools costs several dollars, yet is actually manufactured from about one cent's worth of sand, sawdust, and coke.

Both building brick and firebrick are laid in several styles of courses. These are illustrated in Fig. 66. Header and stretcher courses are most commonly used. With both types of brick, a half-bond overlap is used with alternate courses. Sometimes in building construction using either brick or concrete block, no half bond is employed, and all courses are registered on the bottom one. This arrangement is known as *stack bond*. It is not used with firebrick.

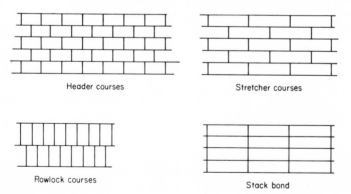

Header courses

Stretcher courses

Rowlock courses

Stack bond

Fig. 66 Brick courses.

ceramic materials
148

Fig. 67 Porcelain enamelled stoves.

7.14 porcelain enamels

These enamels are actually ceramic surface coatings applied to steel, iron, and aluminum for protection against corrosion and for decorative appearance. The enamel frit is a low-melting mixture of oxides resembling small particles of glass. Quartz and feldspar are blended with fluxes such as borax or soda ash (sodium oxide) and with materials such as titanium oxide or inorganic colors for color or opacity.

Enamel is applied after first cleaning the metal surface with an alkaline cleaner. The glassy frit is ground fine, mixed with water, and applied by dipping or spraying. The enamel coat is allowed to dry and is then "burned" or fired at temperatures in the range of 1000–1500°F.

Porcelain enamel is applied to a wide range of household appliances and equipment. It is also used for architectural purposes such as curtain wall sheets on high-rise buildings and automotive service stations, often with highly interesting effects.

A variant of the enamelling process is the application of *ceramic coatings* to parts requiring abrasion resistance or protection against high temperature or oxidation. Materials such as silica or tungsten carbide may be applied. Parts of aerospace vehicles, rocket motors, and gas turbines may require ceramic coatings.

7.15 ashes, slags, and fluxes

Ashes, slags, and cement are chemically similar. Most contain silica, alumina, lime, magnesia, and iron oxide, though in various amounts. Portland cement used in the making of concrete consists chiefly of silica and alumina and lime, with smaller amounts of the other oxides. Coal ash and furnace slags, which have nearly the same composition as cement, are often added to reduce the cost of the cement. An *ash* is the inorganic residue remaining after the combustion of some material such as coal, oil, or wood.

Slags are inorganic oxides necessary in the melting and extracting of metals. In steel melting, for example, phosphorus and sulfur, which are always present in steels, are undesirable and must be reduced to the lowest possible levels. Both substances oxidize during the melting of the steel. To extract them from the molten steel, a basic slag is made by charging lime into the melting furnace. The lime slag floats on the surface of the metal. In a manner of speaking, we may say that the oxidized impurities prefer the company of other oxides rather than the molten steel and are attracted into the slag, reacting chemically with it. The molten metal will oxidize too, but the slag is so formulated and controlled that metal losses to the slag are minimized. This, however, may be difficult to arrange in the case of metals that oxidize more readily. Such a metal is chromium. Stainless steels contain approximately 20 percent chromium, and in melting these steels there is some loss of chromium into the slag. Similar chromium loss occurs when welding stainless steel with flux-coated welding rods. In the case of metals that oxidize extensively at high temperatures, such as titanium or zirconium, air-melting under a slag blanket is quite out of the question, for such metals would be completely lost to the slag as oxides.

Fluxes are actually inorganic solvents used to dissolve and lower the fusion temperature of other oxides. A familiar example is a soldering flux. This is a substance which can dissolve and remove the surface oxide on the metal to be soldered. Soldering (brazing and welding also) is not possible until surface oxides have been removed. Chlorides and fluorides are the most powerful fluxes, but they are corrosive to metals and must be removed after application.

7.16 abrasives

With the exception of diamond, all the abrasives used in large volume in industry are synthetic. Natural abrasives still have minor uses: garnet and flint are used for sandpaper, emery paper is used for polishing metals, rottenstone and pumice for wood finishing, and walnut shells for cleaning aircraft engine parts.

An *abrasive* is a hard material used to wear away a softer material. The hardest materials are the ceramics; hence their selection for abrasive purposes.

Diamond, the only significant natural abrasive, is the hardest material known. It outlasts other abrasives by factors of 10 to 100 or more. Diamond therefore is used for those applications where the life of other abrasives is poor. Typical applications are in brick and concrete saws, wire-drawing dies, diamond drills for drilling hard rock (brass cores set with diamond grit), and cutters for machining hard metals. Like any abrasive, diamond is quickly ruined by impact.

Next to diamond, the hardest abrasive in common use is silicon carbide, SiC, perhaps better known by one of its trade names, carborundum. This highly versatile material, already mentioned for its uses as a refractory, also serves as a heating element in electrically heated industrial furnaces, as pipe, and is even formed into pumps for pumping sand. It is blue-black in color. Both beryllium carbide and boron carbide are harder than silicon carbide, but have not yet found extended use as abrasives.

Silicon carbide was discovered about 80 years ago as a result of un-successful attempts to make artificial diamond. The raw materials for silicon carbide are cheap, but the manufacturing process is not. Sand, coke, and sawdust are mixed, and a high-temperature (4500°F) electric arc is passed through the mixture for a considerable period of time. The saw-dust has the function of burning out to provide porosity for the escape of gases from the mass. At the conclusion of the process the center of the mixture is converted to silicon carbide, which is then crushed.

Aluminum oxide is known by various trade names, such as Aloxite. This material is easily distinguished from silicon carbide by its lighter color, which may be various shades of white or brown. It is made from bauxite, the ore of aluminum, by fusion of the bauxite and crushing.

Aluminum oxide is not quite so hard as silicon carbide, but is tougher and thus more resistant to impact. It is preferable to silicon carbide for such applications as floor sanding machines — wooden floors contain nails, which are damaging to the abrasive grit. Aluminum oxide is the preferred material for grinding the harder metals, since it wears away faster than silicon carbide, thus exposing new edges for cutting. Silicon carbide is selected for cast iron and the softer types of nonferrous metals.

In general, only these two abrasives are used in grinding wheels. The grit in the wheel is bonded either with a ceramic material such as sodium silicate, or an organic material such as a rubber or plastic cement.

7.17 carbides

The properties of silicon carbide are typical of other carbides: great hard-ness, high melting point, high compressive strength, and brittleness. The highest melting point so far discovered is that of hafnium carbide, 7520°F. Unfortunately these remarkably high temperatures cannot usually be exploited, because the carbides will oxidize above 2500°F in air, producing carbon dioxide and monoxide.

Fig. 68 Small melting crucibles for induction melting of metals. Graphite and clay crucible on the left, silicon carbide crucible on the right, sillimanite (alumina-silica) crucibles in the rear.

Aside from very special applications, only a few carbides are as yet in general use. Silicon carbide has abrasive and other applications. Tungsten carbide and tantalum carbide are used in cutting tool tips such as masonry drills and machining tips. The nuclear age has given birth to other carbides such as uranium carbide and boron carbide. Boron carbide, B_4C, 75–80 percent boron, is used as a shielding material against neutrons, deriving its effectiveness from the high neutron capture cross-section of boron. Though harder than silicon carbide, it is not used as an abrasive.

A most interesting employment of carbides, which is discussed in Chapter 10, is their use as a hard constituent in steel alloys such as tool steels for cutting other metals. Such carbides appear as microscopic constituents in steels as a result of suitable heat treatment, and are the ingredients that give tool steels their hardness, wear resistance, and cutting capacity.

The cemented carbide cutting tool materials consist of hard carbides, usually tungsten carbide, titanium carbide, and tantalum carbide embedded in a binder metal, usually cobalt. They are often given the name "carboloy" in conversation, though this is the trade name of only one of many manufacturers. Such carbide bits are supplied in two types: tungsten carbide, and complex carbide (WC + TaC + TiC). Though the tungsten carbide type is stronger for a given hardness, the machining chip tends to weld to this type if steels are cut. The complex carbides are therefore used for machining steels, and the tungsten carbide type is used when machining nonferrous metals, cast irons, and nonmetallic materials.

The carbide cutter bits contain about 90 percent carbides. A high speed tool steel will contain a maximum of 20 percent of carbide constituents. The carbide bits therefore considerably outwear high speed steels and other cutting steels, and retain their hardness much better at the high temperatures of metal cutting, which may exceed 1500°F.

The phases of carbon are included in this chapter because most of the uses of carbon are refractory uses, deriving from its high melting temperature. Like silicon carbide, the forms of carbon have a wide range of uses: graphite is used as a lubricant because of its softness, and diamond as a cutting tool because of its hardness.

Carbon and graphite offer the properties of chemical inertness (except against oxygen above 1000°F), absolute spall resistance, good electrical and thermal conductivity, low thermal expansion, low neutron absorption cross-section, and most important of all, *increasing* strength with increasing temperature. The carbon phases can be employed at temperatures as high as the sublimation point of the material, 6600°F. At atmospheric pressure, carbon does not melt but changes from solid to gas, that is, it sublimes, at 6600°F. But in metal-cleaning operations, as every housekeeper knows, carbon has the dubious honor of being the most difficult type of soil to remove from metal surfaces, since no standard metal cleaner will attack it chemically.

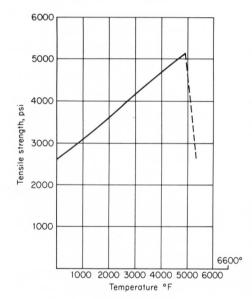

Fig. 69   Typical strength curve of graphite.

The tensile strength of carbon materials varies with the type, grade, and method of manufacture, but may range from 1000 to 3600 psi at room temperature. The tensile strength approximately doubles when the temperature is raised above 4000°F. The spall resistance of carbon materials is so outstanding that it is difficult to devise an experimental method of cracking them by thermal stresses only.

The various forms and grades of carbon embrace a wide range of products. *Carbon black* or amorphous carbon is a finely divided pigment produced by the thermal decomposition of oil or natural gas. Soot is a noncommercial example of carbon black. Such blacks are most familiar for their use in automobile tires and polyethylene water pipe. When carbon black is heated for a prolonged period at a high temperature, *graphite* is formed, a crystalline phase of carbon with properties markedly different from those of carbon black. Graphite is easily machined and has a relatively high thermal and electrical conductivity compared to other forms of carbon. Graphite is produced by heating carbon black to 5000°F approximately, but if instead the processing temperature is only 2750°F, *industrial carbon* is produced. Industrial carbon is extremely hard and has lower thermal and electrical conductivity than graphite. Both industrial carbon and graphite weigh approximately 100 lb per cu ft.

Graphite has a lower specific resistance (about 0.0004 ohms per in. cu), than other phases of carbon: it is therefore preferred as an electrical conductor, despite its higher cost. By far the greatest tonnage of carbon and graphite is used in the metallurgical and electrochemical industries as anodes in arc-melting furnaces, particularly in the steel and aluminum industries. Such anodes carry many thousands of amps, and range in diameter up to a maximum of about five feet. The arc-melting of steel, described in Chapter 10, requires electrodes with smaller diameters of 1 to 2 ft. The raw material for such products is usually *petroleum coke*, produced from crude oil at oil refineries. Other electrical uses for graphite and carbon include brushes for electric motors, and anodes for large electronic tubes such as rectifiers and ignitrons. These materials are not used as cathodes because they are poor emitters of thermal electrons.

Graphite as a refractory has already been discussed. The use of graphite or carbon in nuclear reactors is explained by the high scattering cross-section for neutrons. Carbon blocks are used to decelerate or "moderate" fast neutrons, since slow neutrons are more likely to be captured by a uranium nucleus.

7.19 ceramic lubricants

Ceramic materials are used as lubricants under conditions either of extreme high pressure or high temperature. Graphite is perhaps the best known of these lubricants. Lime is used as a lubricant in wire-drawing, and molten glass in the extrusion of steel shapes. Mica, soapstone, and talc are occasionally used as lubricants.

Molybdenum disulfide, MoS_2, is a more recent addition to the list of ceramic lubricants. This material is gray in color, with a high specific gravity of 4.9 and a melting point of 2200°F. Its coefficient of friction is very low, but it is capable of sustaining remarkably high bearing pressures.

The silicone oils, described in the next section, are lubricating oils with a silicon base instead of a carbon base. They are serviceable to 500–600°F, well beyond the useful range of petroleum oils, and at low temperatures do not congeal as the petroleum lubricants do.

7.20 silicones

Silicones are ceramic-organic polymers (see Sec. 2.22). These materials share some of the characteristics of both the ceramics and the organic materials. The unit monomer for a silicone polymer is the siloxane molecule shown in Fig. 70. A short-chain polymer results in a silicone liquid or oil, while longer molecules give solid silicones.

Monomer

Fig. 70 Silicone polymer chain.
$$- O - \overset{\displaystyle CH_3}{\underset{\displaystyle CH_3}{Si}} - O - \overset{\displaystyle CH_3}{\underset{\displaystyle CH_3}{Si}} - O - \overset{\displaystyle CH_3}{\underset{\displaystyle CH_3}{Si}} -$$

Silicone materials offer the characteristics of high temperature resistance, little change of viscosity with temperature, oxidation resistance, and fire resistance. They are, however, more expensive than the corresponding petroleum product. The chief uses of the silicones include:

1. high temperature oils and greases
2. protective coatings and sealers
3. mold release compound for plastics molding
4. silicone rubber
5. high temperature electric insulation for electric motors
6. liquid dielectrics
7. water repellent

PROBLEMS

1 Explain the influence of thermal conductivity on the spall resistance of ceramic materials.

2 Why is pure silica not used for window glass?

3 What is the difference between a silt and a clay?

4 Why does standard firebrick measure $9 \times 4\frac{1}{2} \times 2\frac{1}{2}$ in.?

5 Explain the meaning of vitrification. What clay products do you know that are vitrified?

6 What is a "glass"?

7 What is meant by the terms grog and castable?

8 Explain the purpose of a slag.

9 Why would crushed limestone not be used as aggregate in refractory castable?

10 How many 9-in. straight firebrick are required per square foot of furnace wall when laid in header courses?

11 Explain the reason for the following selections:
(a) silica brick for an arch roof on a high-temperature furnace
(b) graphite brick below the molten bath level in a metal-melting furnace
(c) magnesite brick at the slag line in a furnace using a lime slag.

The words "cement" and "concrete" are often confused in conversation, as in referring to a concrete sidewalk as a "cement sidewalk". Cements, whether organic such as rubber cements or inorganic such as the portland cement used in road and airport paving, are adhesive materials. In a concrete, the cement must coat the surface of all the particles of aggregate (bulk or filler material) in order to bind the whole into a monolithic mass.

Cements then are adhesives, as are brick mortars. Whether there is any difference in meaning between the words "cement" and "adhesive" is uncertain, though the word cement seems to imply a thicker adhesive joint than is used with an adhesive. An adhesive used to bond ceramic materials is almost always called a cement, but if the same adhesive material is used to bond metals or organic materials it may well be termed an adhesive.

The cement used in civil engineering construction is termed portland cement. This is a hydraulic silicate cement, and is produced in several types. Refractory castables and corrosion-resistant concretes commonly use an alumina-base cement called lumnite cement. Lumnite cement is more expensive than portland cement and is used only where its superior properties justify the additional cost.

Inorganic cements and mortars harden by taking up carbon dioxide or water in chemical reactions. The ancient Romans used a brick mortar resembling our own sand-lime-cement mortar by using quicklime, CaO,

CEMENTS
AND
CONCRETES

8

and burned clay in the form of crushed brick. Such mortars, ancient or modern, harden very slowly as the lime combines with carbon dioxide in the air to form rock-hard $CaCO_3$ or limestone. Portland cement is a more complex mixture of chemicals, and has a more complex chemistry of hardening. But compared to lime, portland cement hardens much more quickly and attains considerably higher strengths. This is chiefly due to the presence of tricalcium silicate, $3CaO.SiO_2$, which is not found in lime mixtures.

8.2 the raw materials for
portland cement

The method of manufacturing portland cement from its raw materials is largely determined by the fact that tricalcium silicate can only be produced within a restricted temperature range, and only in a solid-state chemical reaction. If tricalcium silicate is melted, it decomposes to lime and dicalcium silicate. The melting point is 4064°F; the temperature of manufacture must be in the range of 2300–3450°F.

The raw materials for portland cement are clay and limestone. The chemical composition of ordinary clay is such that its silica content is about twice its aluminum content, giving it the approximate chemical composition $Al_2O_3.2SiO_2.2H_2O$. The two basic ingredients, clay and limestone, must be blended in suitable proportions and "burned" together under conditions that produce an appreciable amount of tricalcium silicate. This solid-state reaction is promoted by including in the raw material mix a substance which serves chiefly as a flux: ferric oxide. Without the fluxing action of ferric oxide a much higher temperature of reaction between the clay and the limestone would be required.

Pure limestone, $CaCO_3$, without some dolomite, $MgCO_3$, is virtually unknown. Dolomitic limestones, which are about half limestone and half dolomite, are unsuitable for cement manufacture. Magnesia does not combine with the acid silica and remains as free magnesia in the finished product. If free magnesia, or even free lime, were present in the cement, it would "slake" or combine with water to produce $Mg(OH)_2$. This reaction produces an increase in volume, and the effect would be to crack and disintegrate the concrete. Expansion due to magnesia is more dangerous than expansion due to lime, because its rate of development is quite slow, and its first effects might not appear until the passage of a few years. For this reason most standard specifications for portland cement limit magnesia to a maximum of 5 percent. There are always limited amounts of magnesia in any cement, and it is this material which gives cement its gray-green color.

A typical raw feed by weight for a portland cement might be

SiO_2	15.5%
Al_2O_3	2.5
Fe_2O_3	2.0
CaO	42.0
MgO	2.5
CO_2	35.5
	100.0%

with CO_2 combined as $MgCO_3$ and $CaCO_3$. The raw materials are ground
to 200 mesh in a ball mill and burned in the cement kiln either dry or mixed
with water as a slurry.

Fig. 71 A cement kiln under repair. The large globules of clinker
adhering to the refractory lining are characteristic of kiln operation.
The steel shell of this kiln is 11 ft in diameter, ⅞ in. thick, and 400
ft long.

The rotary kiln in which the raw material is reacted is one of the big industrial furnaces which, like the blast furnace, plays an indispensable role in our industrial civilization. Rotary kilns are used to process a wide range of products, from alfalfa and alumina to brucite, chrome ore, dolomite, ferrochromium, garbage, haydite, iron ore, lime, and manganese ore, to pozzolans, pyrites, perlite, and plaster of Paris, to vermiculite and zinc oxide. The kiln is a cylinder made of steel. A small laboratory or pilot-plant kiln may have an inside diameter of 3 ft. A large cement kiln may be 16 ft or more in diameter, though the usual cement kiln is 11 or 12 ft in diameter. The length of the kiln shell may be from 400 to 600 ft. The steel plates of the kiln are not less than $\frac{7}{8}$ in. thick for a cement kiln. The kiln is inclined at an angle of a few degrees, so that raw material fed into the high end can travel slowly down toward the low end as the kiln rotates. The kiln is supported on large rollers and rotated at about 0.6 rpm by a large electric motor of 125 hp or more. A standby diesel engine is available in case of electric power failure, for if the kiln does not rotate it will warp due to its great weight and length. The kiln is driven through a geared bull-ring that encircles the kiln at the middle of its length. Expansion of the kiln is in both directions from this fixed point. Figure 71 shows an interior view of a cement kiln.

The discharge end of the kiln is enclosed in a housing called a firing hood. Figure 72 is a view of the inside of a firing hood with its refractory

Fig. 72 The firing hood at the end of the kiln shown in Fig. 71. The large gas burner may be seen in the middle of the hood.

lining of firebrick and plastic refractory. So that repair crews may have access to the interior of the kiln, the firing hood may be retracted on a set of railroad rails. A large gas burner about 12 in. in diameter supplies heat for the process through the end of the firing hood. The operating crew controls kiln operation from the firing end, on what is called the "burning floor"; here the panel of automatic control instruments is mounted.

The raw kiln feed is metered into the kiln at the high or feed end, and is slowly tumbled down to the discharge end in a journey that takes a few hours to complete. The tumbling action produces a product in pellet form. As the raw materials are heated, the following chemical actions occur in sequence along the kiln.

1. Water is driven out of the feed.
2. At 630°F, $MgCO_3$ decomposes to MgO and CO_2.
3. At 1632°F, $CaCO_3$ decomposes to CaO and CO_2.

One barrel of cement (or 4 sacks) weighs 376 lb. Due to loss of carbon dioxide, about 583 lb of solid feed are required to produce 376 lb of kiln product. The heat requirement is nearly 1,000,000 Btu per barrel of cement produced.

4. Finally in the "burning zone" of the kiln, which is about the last 70 ft, the components undergo a solid-state reaction at a temperature of about 2700°F to produce calcium silicates. This is an exothermic reaction, releasing heat. The reaction that is most difficult to complete is the combination of the last trace of lime with previously formed dicalcium silicate to form tricalcium silicate. The amount of lime remaining in the kiln product after burning is usually less than 1 percent.
5. The resulting product, a black slag in small globules, is dropped through the floor of the firing hood into a cooler below the kiln. This product is called "clinker".

Following the burning operation, the clinker is ground to about 325 mesh (44 microns), blended with about 3 percent gypsum, and bagged or stored in large cement silos.

An interior view of an 11-ft cement kiln shut down for repair is shown in Fig. 71. The kiln is lined with 9 in. of firebrick, and the clinker adhering to the firebrick can be seen in the figure. At the time the photograph was taken, the kiln had cooled for three days, yet the clinker, though relatively cool at its surface, was still red hot underneath. The two repair men in the kiln are drilling holes into the refractory lining to determine the extent to which the lining is worn away. Ordinarily the lining of the burning zone will last 8–9 months.

The operation of lining a cement kiln with firebrick is an interesting process that few persons have the fortune to witness. The lining is formed from segments of a circle, called kiln liners, with 35 brick liners to a circle for an 11-ft kiln. Each brick is 4 in. thick (in the direction of the axis of the kiln), which gives three courses per foot of kiln length. Since each kiln liner weighs 16 lb, the refractory lining weighs 1700 lb per ft of kiln, or almost a ton. About 8 ft of kiln are lined at a time, and the bricklaying is carried on continuously day and night until completed — this equipment is too expensive to be tied up with the casual effort of dayshifts only. The revenue loss for a kiln shut down is about $10,000 a day.

The firebrick are laid without mortar and stay in place simply by fitting tight together. The last brick in each circular course must be carefully cut to make a tight fit in closing the circle.

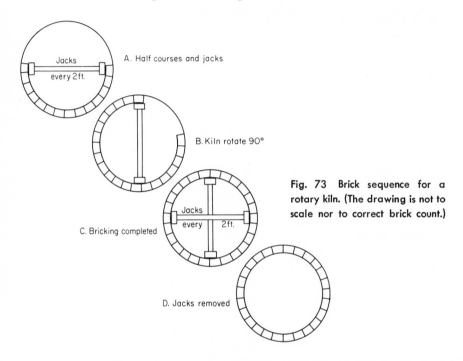

A. Half courses and jacks

Jacks every 2 ft.

B. Kiln rotate 90°

C. Bricking completed

Jacks every 2 ft.

D. Jacks removed

Fig. 73 Brick sequence for a rotary kiln. (The drawing is not to scale nor to correct brick count.)

The brick for about 8 lineal ft of kiln are laid in the bottom half of the kiln. Figure 73 shows the bricking sequence. A timber is run along the top of the courses on each side of the kiln, and trench jacks installed every 2 ft, jacking against these timbers with maximum pressure to prevent any movement of the brick. The kiln is then rotated a quarter turn. Another quadrant of the kiln wall is bricked, two more timbers set up, and another set of jacks installed, again at 2-ft intervals. There is now a jack every foot, making for crowded working conditions. The kiln is rotated another quarter turn, and the circular courses completed. The jacks are then carefully removed, the crew watching the bricks at the top of the kiln to see if they slip (since a kiln liner weighs 16 lb, the crew members wear hard hats). Occasionally the bricking is unsuccessful; if the bricks slip slightly, then the courses must be rebricked.

Portland cements are composed of four principal chemical compounds:

1. tricalcium silicate, $3CaO.SiO_2$, abbreviated C_3S.
2. dicalcium silicate, $2CaO.SiO_2$, abbreviated C_2S.
3. tricalcium aluminate, $3CaO.Al_2O_3$, abbreviated C_3A.
4. tetracalcium aluminoferrite, $4CaO.Al_2O_3.Fe_2O_3$, or C_4AF.

The strength of these cements is controlled by the content of the two calcium silicates, which together constitute at least 70 percent of the cement constituents.

Three types of portland cement are in common use, though certain industries and operations require special types such as oil-well cement. The three most used types are normal portland cement (Type I), high early strength cement (Type III), and sulfate-resistant cement (Type V). These cements have the following typical compositions:

Cement	% C_3S	% C_2S	% C_3A	% C_4AF
normal portland	45	27	11	8
high early strength	53	19	10	10
sulfate-resistant	38	43	4	8

High early strength cement is produced by employing a raw mix giving more tricalcium silicate at the expense of dicalcium silicate. Resistance to sulfates in soils results from reduction in tricalcium silicate.

All the four chemical constituents in portland cement take up water in different amounts and at different rates during the setting of the cement, and by adjusting the relative amounts of these constituents the properties of the cement may be altered appreciably.

The setting rate of both tricalcium and dicalcium silicate is slow, and if these two were the only constituents of cement, the cement would remain plastic for several hours after mixing with water. But the opposite happens with tricalcium aluminate. This constituent, when contacted with water, develops a "flash set" accompanied by the release of considerable heat. Although the proportion of C_3A in portland cement is not high, its presence would lead to flash setting of the whole cement mass. This explains the use of a small amount of gypsum, $CaSO_4$, in cement. Gypsum prevents such flash setting and regulates the setting time of the cement. It does this by quickly combining with C_3A to form a needle-like compound, calcium sulphoaluminate, which contains a considerable amount of chemically bound water or "water of crystallization".

8.5 hydration of portland cement

Portland cement, like any hydraulic cement, sets and hardens by taking up water in complex chemical reactions, a process called *hydration*. Provided that a source of water is constantly present (water vapor in the air is a suitable supply), portland cement may continue to harden over a period of months. The reaction completed first is the combination of gypsum with C_3A and water to form calcium sulfoaluminate. This chemical action is completed within 24 hours. The other compounds in cement will hydrate by taking up about 25 percent of their weight in water. The amount of water added to cement is not gauged from this relationship, however.

C_3S hydrates in the following reaction

$$2(3CaO.SiO_2) + 6H_2O \rightarrow 3CaO.2SiO_2.3H_2O + 3Ca(OH)_2$$

while C_2S hydrates thus

$$2(2CaO.SiO_2) + 4H_2O \rightarrow 3CaO.2SiO_2.3H_2O + Ca(OH)_2$$

Thus the final product of the hydration of both calcium silicates is $3CaO.2SiO_2.3H_2O$, a compound which is given the name *tobermorite*. But C_3S in its hydration releases three times as much calcium hydroxide to the concrete mix: this has a significance for the corrosion resistance of portland cements, which will be dealt with presently. C_3A hydrates without taking up or releasing any lime. Some of the lime set free by the hydration of the calcium silicates is taken up in the hydration of the C_4AF.

The workability of cement paste does not change for some time after water is mixed with it. In this apparently dormant period, however, there are rapid and complex chemical reactions, including the $CaSO_4$ and C_3S reactions just discussed. Setting of the cement is completed in a matter of hours, while hardening is not completed for months, although there is no fundamental difference between these two processes. Rapid setting, however, is not synonymous with rapid hardening. Gypsum retards setting; the use of hot water accelerates setting. The finer the cement powder is ground, the greater the surface exposed to water and the faster the set. Rapid setting and high early strength are provided by an increase in C_3S, as shown in the analysis of high early strength cement given earlier. Fast-setting cements, however, release considerable quantities of heat in their short setting times.

The ultimate compressive strength developed in a portland cement results from the hydration of the two calcium silicates. C_3A and C_4AF contribute little to strength of the concrete, although they reach their maximum strength levels in a comparatively short period of time.

The complex chemistry of cement setting just discussed occurs under atmospheric conditions of temperature and pressure. A variant of this method is used in the manufacture of sand-lime brick, and to a degree, in the manufacture of concrete blocks. These products are cured with steam under heat and pressure. Sand-lime brick uses a mixture of fine quartz sand and 5–7 percent hydrated lime. This is compacted, then cured for several hours at a steam pressure of 100 psi and a temperature of about 350°F. At this temperature the silica reacts readily with lime to form calcium silicate hydrates of high strength.

8.6 heat of hydration

When hot lime (quicklime) is slaked with water, the reaction with the water is exothermic, that is, heat is released. The generation of heat may be so pronounced that the water may boil. The lime in portland cement is eventually converted to calcium hydroxide also, through the formation of calcium silicate hydrates. The evolution of heat is therefore to be expected when cement sets. Most cements set at a sufficiently slow rate that this evolution of heat is not a source of trouble. However the heat of hydration in massive concrete structures such as dams could cause cracking due to expansion and subsequent contraction. Such pours may have to be re-frigerated. The cement manufactured for large pours is formulated for low heat of hydration. C_3S releases twice as much heat of hydration as C_2S, and C_3A three times as much.

8.7 corrosion of concrete

Water attacks concrete to a slight degree. Part of the hardened cement paste is free calcium hydroxide, a chemical that is fairly soluble in water and therefore can be leached out in the presence of water. This leaching action may produce the efflorescence occasionally observed on concrete and brick structures. Efflorescence is water-soluble matter such as salts or calcium carbonate which is deposited on the surface of the concrete through capillary action. Such efflorescence may be removed by wire-brushing or treatment with dilute hydrochloric acid.

Sulfates are often found in soils and water. Sulfates attack cement by reacting with calcium hydroxide in the cement to produce first gypsum and then water-rich calcium sulfoaluminate. This chemical action is harmful because of the volume expansion that accompanies it. Sulfate-resistant cement therefore is low in tricalcium aluminate. It may be noted here that sea water contains significant amounts of magnesium sulfate.

Occasionally damaging chemical reactions occur between the cement and the aggregate materials of the concrete. This is termed an *alkali-aggregate reaction*. The actual chemistry is complex and imperfectly understood, but in brief a high-alkali cement attacks susceptible aggregates containing silica (which is acid) and develops disruptive pressures in the concrete. Pozzolans are used to control this reaction.

8.8   pozzolans

Pozzolans are siliceous materials, not cements in themselves, which combine with lime in the presence of water to form compounds with cementing properties. Pozzolans are named from the fact that the ancient Romans used volcanic siliceous materials as pozzolans obtained from deposits at Pozzuoli near Naples. A wide range of materials offer possibilities as pozzolans: calcined clays and shales, pumicites, blast furnace slags, brick, and flyash from boilers. Pozzolans, like cement, must be finely ground.

As much as 40–50 percent of pozzolans may be added to cement, and generally produce the following effects on the concrete:

1. improved workability
2. lower heat of hydration
3. improved watertightness
4. improved resistance to sulfates
5. reduced alkali-aggregate reaction
6. better resistance to leaching
7. reduced cost

Weathering resistance however is lessened somewhat, and the modulus of elasticity of the concrete may be slightly reduced. Because of the lower heat of hydration, pozzolan additions are made to concrete used in large pours such as dams.

One of the most interesting of the pozzolanic materials is flyash. When pulverized coal is burned in a large steam generator, most of the ash is carried up the boiler toward the stack and collected in hoppers at the rear top of the boiler. This flyash is even finer than portland cement, and consists of small glassy spheres of rather complex chemistry. Most flyashes show about 30–50 percent silica, up to 10 percent carbon, 10–20 percent iron oxide, about 20 percent alumina, and lesser amounts of calcia, magnesia, and alkalis.

In the previous chapter we made some reference to the use of high-alumina cement in the blending of refractory concretes. Such aluminous cements are usually termed *lumnite cement*. Lumnite cement finds most of its applications in the field of mechanical engineering, just as most of the applications of portland siliceous cement are in civil engineering. Lumnite cement has additional uses in refractory castables, however. It was first produced in France in 1913, and its French name, Ciment Fondu, is sometimes used in this country. Compared to portland cement, it is more expensive, highly resistant to chemical attack (a characteristic of alumina), and fast-hardening, developing great strength in 24 hours.

Unlike portland cements, the chemical composition of a lumnite cement is somewhat variable, but approximates the following analysis:

SiO_2	3–11%
Al_2O_3	33–44%
CaO	35–44%
Fe_2O_3	4–12%
FeO	0–10%

The aluminates in this cement are chiefly monocalcium aluminate, CA, but include also CA_2 and $C_{12}A_7$. The silica may be combined as C_2S or in more complex compounds.

The limestone-clay raw materials used in the manufacture of portland cement are too low in alumina and too high in silica to be suitable for lumnite cement. Pure limestone and bauxite are employed. Bauxite, the usual ore of aluminum, is rather expensive owing to its relative scarcity. Lumnite cement cannot be produced by the clinkering of the raw mixture in a rotary kiln, as is the practice for portland cement. Instead, the mixture is melted, often in electric arc furnaces; hence the French name Ciment Fondu — molten cement.

The hydration of lumnite cement is virtually complete in 24 hours of curing. More water is used than in portland cement, and a higher-strength cement results. Hydration releases free alumina instead of free calcium hydroxide, and this in part explains the excellent corrosion resistance of this cement. Temperatures above 70°F in the curing process cause a significant drop in the strength of the concrete. Unfortunately the rapid hydration means a much more rapid release of heat than occurs in the case of portland cement. Concrete pours even as thin as two inches become noticeably hot to the touch. Sometimes water-cooled metal formwork is employed on lumnite concrete, and the forms are removed as soon as possible so that the concrete can be hosed with cold water.

Having no free calcium hydroxide, lumnite cement is resistant to sulfate attack.

Quick-setting cements for repair of water leaks are sometimes made by mixing lumnite cement and lime, or lumnite cement and portland cement. Such mixtures do not produce a strong cement, but serve the purpose intended, that is, flash-setting.

With the use of suitable aggregates such as burned fireclay materials, lumnite cement is used in refractory castables for use at temperatures as high as 2700°F. It is commonly employed in chimney linings, castable shapes, blast furnace foundations, furnace doors, rocket-launching pads, and taxi areas for jet aircraft. Finer aggregates are used in refractory castables than are customary in portland cement concretes. For high-temperature work, reinforcing rods must not be used in refractory concretes. Expansion of the rods can crack the concrete, and in any case there is no bond between the reinforcing material and the concrete, as there is in constructional reinforced concrete. As with portland cement, the lower the ratio of water to cement, the higher the strength of the concrete. Besides refractory uses, lumnite cement is used for floors which are subject to the attack of aggressive chemicals, such as acids in fertilizer plants, lactic acid in dairies, and organic acids in meat-packing plants.

Ordinary concrete should not be subjected to temperatures much higher than 500°F. Above this temperature, some type of spall and heat-resistant concrete should be used.

8.10 concrete mixtures

In a standard concrete about 75 percent of the volume of the mix is occupied by aggregates — crushed rock, gravel, and sand, with heavier pours using larger pieces of aggregate. Any cubic yard of concrete must be filled either with cement paste or with aggregate. Since the cement is the most expensive ingredient, the amount of cement must be minimized, consistent with the strength and other quality requirements of the concrete. The minimum cement requirement is met by suitably grading the aggregate particles so that small particles can fill the voids between the larger particles. Each aggregate particle, small or large, is completely embedded in cement paste, and all spaces not filled by aggregate must be filled by cement paste, except for entrained air in the concrete.

The hardened concrete will weigh about 150 lb per cu ft. Most concretes are batched to provide an ultimate compressive strength of 2500 to 4000 psi after 28 days, this being the standard curing interval before the strength of the concrete is tested. Figure 74 shows a typical strength curve

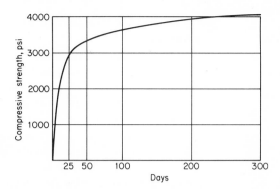

Fig. 74 Strength curve of a 3000 psi portland cement concrete cured in air. Strength after 28 days is 3050 psi.

of concrete with the passage of time. Higher strengths than 4000 psi are possible, but are not commonly required. The tensile strength of concrete is not high, but is proportional to the compressive strength. The modulus of elasticity of concrete is about 1000 times the ultimate compressive strength, though strain is not proportional to stress in concretes.

The strength of concrete depends chiefly on the water-cement ratio, with a low ratio producing a strong concrete. While only a small amount of water is required to complete the chemical reactions of setting concrete, more than this is used to make the concrete more workable.

A great many special admixtures have been developed for concrete. The use of accelerators such as calcium chloride has already been mentioned. Air-entraining mixtures are used to improve the resistance of concrete to frost action and salt corrosion. About 1 percent of the volume of air-entrained concrete will be minute voids from 10 to 1000 microns in diameter (1 micron = 1/25,000 in.). Hardeners are added to industrial concrete floors to improve the resistance of the floor to abrasion and dusting. Cast iron and emery particles are two of the many materials used as hardeners.

Light-weight concretes are made using perlite, haydite, vermiculite, or other expanded minerals as aggregates. In addition to the advantage of less weight, light-weight sections offer heat insulation and a degree of acoustic absorption. Light-weight concretes, however, have greater shrinkage on curing, and need more care in proportioning the required water. They require more water than standard aggregates because the expanded aggregates themselves absorb water.

Concrete is used as a biological shield for protection of personnel from radiation. Since all the elements in concrete, H, O, Al, Si, Ca, etc. are light elements, none has high absorption for gamma rays. Such absorption is provided by adding various materials to the concrete, including magnetite (iron ore), barite (containing barium, a heavy metal), or steel punchings.

cements and concretes
169

Fig. 75 Terrazzo floor in a clinic building.

Grout is a special concrete mix for seating machine bases, levelling base plates, and for closing up fissures in underground rock formations or dams. Since grouts must be thin, they are made up of nonshrinking mixes of cement and sand and occasionally other additives.

A terrazzo floor is shown in Fig. 75. Some remarkably beautiful floors are made in terrazzo, which is produced by laying mixtures of concrete containing colored marble chips, usually in black, white, red, yellow, or green. Terrazzo floors require special crews for their installation.

8.11 asphalt concrete

Asphalts, which are discussed more fully in Chapter 14, are residues from the distillation of crude oil. Although asphalts are also used for roofing and waterproofing, about three-quarters of all asphalt production is used for highway and airport paving. Asphalt refined to specifications for paving purposes is called asphalt cement.

Asphalt cements are produced in several grades. The relative hardness or "consistency" of asphalt cement is measured by the penetration of a weighted needle (100 grams) into the asphalt. The depth of penetration is measured in units of 0.1 mm at 77°F after 5 seconds. The test is similar to the types of hardness tests performed on rubber, plastics, and metals discussed in the following chapter. The deeper the penetration, the softer the material.

Asphalt makes a flexible pavement. Such pavements are mixtures of asphalt cement and aggregates. Although the pavement must be flexible, that is, elastic, it must be resistant to permanent displacement under traffic loads. The surface of the pavement must be sufficiently rough to provide traction under adverse weather conditions; otherwise the familiar "Slippery when wet" signs must be posted on the highway. With these requirements in mind, the function of the aggregate is to carry the traffic loads imposed on the pavement and to provide rough texture, while the asphalt cement binds the aggregate and provides waterproofing.

PROBLEMS

1 What purpose does iron oxide serve in the manufacture of portland cement?

2 What is the chief chemical compound in normal portland cement?

3 Why can magnesium oxide not be substituted for lime in portland cement?

4 What is the difference between rotary kiln clinker and finished portland cement?

5 Why is gypsum added to portland cement?

6 Why is mortar not used to bond the firebrick lining in a large rotary kiln?

7 Which of the several chemical compounds in portland cement is fast-setting?

8 What is a pozzolan?

9 Why are pozzolans added to the cements used in the heavy concrete pours of large dams?

10 Apart from the matter of cost, why would lumnite cement have few applications in the field of civil engineering?

METALS

Part **III**

The many mechanical characteristics of materials cover a wide range, chiefly empirical in nature, and few of them clearly and fundamentally understood. We shall deal first with the property of gettering, then particle size. Next we shall consider a group of characteristics which may be termed *serviceability* factors, including purity, brittle fracture, and others. Finally, we shall conclude the chapter with a discussion of *processability* factors such as machinability, formability, and weldability. In general it could be said rather ironically that the length of the word describing the characteristic is directly proportional to the depth of our ignorance surrounding it. Although we can put numerical values on the characteristic known as machinability, for example, we cannot really measure this factor, and the numerical values we have are the subject of some dispute and dissatisfaction.

9.1   gettering

Metals, like most substances, will readily adsorb gases on their surfaces, particularly water vapor. *Getters* are metals deliberately introduced into vacuum spaces for the purpose of adsorbing final traces of gases. Thus in the manufacture of small and inexpensive vacuum tubes, the tube may be pumped down to a vacuum of 10^{-4} torr (10^{-4} mm Hg), and a getter metal then used to reduce the vacuum pressure to about 10^{-6} torr. The getter

MECHANICAL CHARACTERISTICS
OF
MATERIALS

9

must of course have any adsorbed gases desorbed or baked out before it is inserted into the vacuum. The getter, in the form of a wire, a coating, or other shape, thus acts as an auxiliary pump or getter pump, though the gas thus "pumped" is not actually removed from the vacuum space.

Some of the materials used as getters are barium-aluminum alloys (for vacuum tube work), zirconium, titanium, tantalum, thorium, and molybdenum. Such metals can adsorb large amounts of residual gases. No getter however adsorbs all gases equally effectively; getters must be selected for the residual gas to be removed.

9.2 particle size

Small particle size is measured either in mesh or in microns. Mesh size refers to sieve sizes. Thus a 200-mesh sieve has 200 openings per lineal inch, or 40,000 per sq in. A micron is 1/1000 mm or 1/25,000 in. Portland cement is ground to an average of about 325 mesh, which is the same as 44 microns, while 200 mesh corresponds to 50 microns and 100 mesh to 149 microns.

Dusts consist of particles in size from 1 to 50 microns. Smoke is carbon particles smaller than 0.1 micron. Diameters of gas molecules range from 0.005 micron down.

It is not ordinarily desirable for particle size to be uniform in any aggregate of particles to be processed into finished materials. Just as in the blending of concrete aggregates, small particles are needed to fill the interstitial spaces between the larger particles. Particles for foundry sand or for sintered carbide cutting tools therefore must be graded over a range of sizes, with a proper proportion in each grade. Figure 76 shows a typical

Fig. 76 Fine aggregate grading for a concrete.

fine aggregate grading for a concrete. Notice that 100 percent of these fine particles will pass a #4 sieve (4 openings per inch) but virtually none will pass a #100 sieve (100 openings per inch).

In reducing bulk material to smaller size, usually several steps are required. The first reduction will be done by a primary crusher, such as a jaw crusher, gyratory crusher, or hammer mill, which may reduce the material to lump of about 4-in. size maximum. The next step may be a rod mill. This is a rotating heavy steel barrel which is loaded with the bulk material and long 2-in. diameter steel rods. As the material is tumbled the rods reduce the material perhaps to $\frac{1}{4}$-in. size. The rod mill makes a more uniform reduction of particles than other crushing or grinding methods because the grinding rods are supported by material all along their length. The final grinding stage will be a ball mill, using steel balls about 4-in. in diameter. The ball mill can grind to nonuniform powder sizes. The crushed and ground material will be finally sorted by screening.

Finer sizes require more power for their reduction. Horsepower requirements for reduction are approximately proportional to the surface area of the particles produced. This means that if 10 hp is required to reduce to 1-in. size, then 20 hp is required to reduce to $\frac{1}{2}$ in.

9.3 purity

At the same time as the number of alloys and composite materials increase, industry and science make ever more exacting demands for purity of materials. Standards of purity that were impossible twenty years ago are now routine in some types of manufacturing.

Transistor semiconductor materials such as germanium and silicon must be prepared to standards of almost absolute purity — a part or two per billion by weight. After purification by a remarkable vacuum melting method known as zone refining, the doping materials required to produce an n-type or a p-type transistor are added in amounts of a few parts per billion. Unless such purity standards are met, the characteristics of the transistor cannot be controlled within proper limits.

Steel technology can now control very closely the elements that dissolve interstitially in the iron space lattice, such as oxygen and nitrogen. These elements contribute to brittleness of various types in steel, and are held to maximums of a few thousandths of a percent by weight in air-melted steel, or less in vacuum-melted steel.

Small amounts of alloying impurities have a pronounced effect in increasing the electrical resistance of copper. About 0.02 percent arsenic or aluminum will reduce the conductivity of copper by 6 percent, though other alloying ingredients have less powerful effects on conductivity.

Nuclear fuels are frequently enclosed in zirconium tubes. Zirconium is selected for this application because of low neutron absorption, and therefore must be relatively free of impurities of high neutron absorption cross-section. Specifications for nuclear-grade zirconium therefore limit boron and cadmium to maximums of half a part per million by weight, because of their high absorption. Ores of zirconium contain about $2\frac{1}{2}$ percent hafnium, another neutron-absorbing element which must be limited to less than 50 parts per million in the finished zirconium. Even 50 ppm is only 0.005 percent.

Not even water escapes these stringent demands for purity, especially if it is used in the generation of high-pressure steam or in nuclear power generation. Since dissolved solids in water can absorb neutrons, cooling water for nuclear reactors may contain no more than about one part per million of dissolved solids.

Argon gas used for welding purposes is about 99.995 percent pure. Zinc for die-casting purposes must be at least 99.99 percent pure (four nines zinc) and sometimes is 99.999 percent pure (five nines). Without this rigorous purity, die castings develop various troubles, including dimensional instability and corrosion.

9.4 brittle fracture

The tension test described in Sec. 3.4 is a simple and reliable indication of the strength and ductility to be expected of a metal under many service conditions. However, this is true only when a metal exhibits ductile behavior in service. There are circumstances under which certain ductile metals behave in brittle fashion. Two important cases of brittle failure of ductile metals in service must be examined. These are called brittle fracture and fatigue. Fatigue will be examined in the next section.

Under the conditions of a standard tensile test the metal is subjected to stress in only one dimension. An inherently ductile metal, such as a structural steel, will elongate by slip along the planes in the crystal inhabited by the greatest number of atoms. The metal may also twin. These two mechanisms of ductile behavior were described in Sec. 3.5.

If now a saw cut is made in the specimen at right angles to the direction of stress, the metal will maintain its ductility during the tension test. It will not be sensitive to the presence of this notch. However, at the root of the saw cut stress conditions are complex and are no longer one-dimensional, but two-dimensional.

Under the impact conditions of the Charpy test, now to be discussed, it is possible for the ductile metal to lose its ductility and become remarkably brittle. The Charpy test uses a notch in the specimen to produce a complex stress concentration at the root of the notch, and therefore is a test of notch sensitivity.

The Charpy test is one of the most revealing of tests for disclosing low-temperature brittleness in otherwise ductile metals. While face-centered cubic metals such as copper, aluminum, and austenitic stainless steels remain ductile under all circumstances, the ductility of body-centered cubic and hexagonal metals is sensitive to the temperature of deformation, and the purpose of the Charpy test is to disclose such lack of ductility in the presence of a notch. In such brittle fracture the metal breaks in tension along the faces of the space lattice, but does not twin or slip in shear.

Fig. 77 Charpy impact specimen.

Fig. 78 Charpy impact testing machine with pendulum hammer raised to the 264 ft-lb position.

For a Charpy test of a metal, samples of the shape and size shown in Fig. 77 are prepared. The figure shows a vee-notch milled across the specimen, but other types of notches may be employed, such as a keyhole type. The specimen is supported horizontally at its ends in the impact testing machine and struck on the side opposite to the notch by a swinging hammer that begins its swing with 264 ft-lb of potential energy. When the hammer strikes the specimen at the bottom of its swing, it has 264 ft-lb of kinetic energy. This energy is partly dissipated by fracturing the specimen, the remaining energy carrying the hammer up on the backswing. The Charpy tester records on a scale the amount of energy in foot-pounds required for fracture — actually it measures the amount of backswing potential energy and subtracts this from the original 264 ft-lb to obtain the fracture energy. Figure 78 shows an impact tester with the pendulum hammer ready for release from the 264 ft-lb position.

Fig. 79 Charpy impact test results: (1) a notch-tough rimmed steel, (2) 2024 aluminum alloy in hard temper, (3) pure nickel, (4) a 0.35-percent carbon steel plate 2½ in. thick.

Suppose a number of Charpy specimens of a particular steel are tested over a range of temperatures from +200 to −100°F, and the results are plotted on a graph of foot-pounds against temperature. A typical S-curve results, similar to the curve 1 in Fig. 79, which is a plot of the results for a notch-tough rimmed steel. At the high end of the temperature range the steel offers great resistance to fracture, giving a torn appearance at the break in what is termed a *ductile failure*. The torn appearance of the break is due to shear failure along the slip planes within the grains of the metal. See Fig. 80. But as the temperature is dropped, a temperature range is reached in which the notch-toughness of the metal falls drastically, the fracture appearance changes to a bright crystalline break, and the steel has become brittle. Brittle fracture indicates a tension failure, as indicated in Fig. 80.

Ductile failure   Brittle failure

Fig. 80   Mechanics of Charpy impact failure. Above the transition temperature failure occurs by shear along the slip planes within the individual crystals. Below the transition temperature failure occurs by tension forces separating the interatomic planes.

The minimum impact strength allowed for many applications is 15 ft-lb per specimen. The temperature corresponding to this impact value is called, rather arbitrarily, the transition temperature between ductile and brittle failure. Other temperature values are sometimes called the transition temperature, and indeed any of the following temperatures might be termed the fracture transition temperature:

1. the temperature corresponding to 15 ft-lb
2. the average temperature between ductile and brittle failure
3. the inflection point on the S-curve (this would be almost the same as No. 2.)
4. the lowest temperature at which the specimens show 100% ductile failure
5. the temperature at which 50% of the area of the break is ductile and 50% brittle
6. the highest temperature for which none of the area of the break is ductile

Catastrophic failures of structures due to brittle fracture have been fairly common until recent years. Changes in steel specifications and more knowledgeable methods of fabrication have now greatly reduced the incidence of brittle fracture. But minor failures still occur, and are a source of mystery to many fabricators unacquainted with the brittle fracture phenomenon. The author has had reported to him a considerable number of brittle fractures of small steel parts used in cold storage rooms held at temperatures as high as +30°F. Brittle fracture has been especially evident in welded structures. The thermal strains of fusion welding build a great deal of residual stress into structures. "Big inch" gas pipelines have cracked over great lengths under very little stress, and even ships have split completely in two.

Such brittle failures occur only below the transition temperature of the steel, and are prevented by the simple expedient of using steel with a lower transition temperature than any service temperature likely to be met.

mechanical characteristics of materials
181

Some degree of prevention can also be exercised by good fabrication practice. Undercuts, notches, and arc burns due to welding operations, fillet welds, hammer marks, and other such defects can serve as fracture initiation points for a fulminating collapse, for these defects have the same influence as the notch in the Charpy specimen.

Several methods are available for lowering the transition temperature of a steel. Perhaps the cheapest method is that of killing the steel with aluminum or silicon. This killing operation is discussed in the following chapter. In brief, it removes oxygen from the steel, with the effect of lowering the transition temperature. An even more powerful method is to reduce the carbon content of the steel. Brittle fracture considerations are a part of the explanation why manual arc welding rods for mild steels do not contain more than 0.1 percent carbon. Both carbon and oxygen dissolve interstitially in the space lattice of iron: brittle fracture characteristics must therefore be affected by interstitial elements.

Fine-grained steels, other things being equal, will have lower transition temperatures than coarse-grained steels. Further, the thicker the plate, the higher the transition temperature, and this consideration often dictates adjustment of the chemistry of thicker plate.

Brittle fracture does not occur in face-centered cubic metals, such as nickel. Another method of lowering transition temperature in steels is to alloy the steel with nickel. A 3.5 percent nickel low carbon steel may be safely used at $-150°F$; for cryogenic vessels to store oxygen or nitrogen at $-320°F$, 9 percent nickel is required. Manganese is also beneficial, but does not have the powerful effect of nickel. The austenitic stainless steels, copper, and aluminum, all being fcc, are safely used in refrigeration and cryogenic equipment.

The nuclear age has disclosed new aspects of brittle fracture. The transition temperature of a bcc metal is raised if the metal is heavily irradiated.

9.5 fatigue of metals

Fatigue failure is another type of brittle failure in otherwise ductile metals, but unlike brittle fracture, is not influenced by crystal structure, that is, it cannot be prevented by selecting a face-centered cubic metal. Fatigue failures are produced by sufficient stress levels repeated thousands or millions of times, and therefore are found in shafts, gear teeth, hold-down bolts, vehicle frames, and other machine components. Fatigue failure is undoubtedly the most common type of failure in metals.

Fatigue failures in any metal occur at stress levels well below the yield stress of the metal. The failure begins as a slowly deepening crack at some region of stress concentration, such as the root of a gear tooth, a shoulder or keyway in a shaft, an impression stamped into a part (such as an identifying part number), a machining mark, or a change of section such as a fillet weld in a truck body or piece of farm machinery. With constantly repeated stress cycles the crack deepens, leaving progressively less metal to carry the load. Finally, without warning, fracture occurs.

The maximum repeated stress which can be applied indefinitely under fatigue conditions is called the *endurance limit* of the material. Obviously for one cycle only the fatigue strength of a material will be its elastic limit (since plastic deformation is usually not acceptable). As the number of cycles is increased, this allowable maximum fatigue stress decreases. Finally the endurance limit is reached, the stress at which no fatigue failure occurs at an indefinite number of stress cycles. Figure 81 shows a fatigue

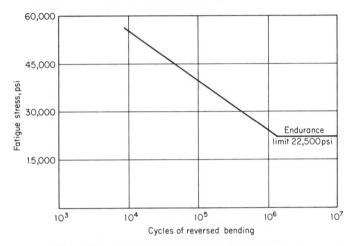

Fig. 81   Fatigue curve for a machinery steel with a sharp stress concentration machined into it. The reversed bending fatigue test was performed on the testing machine of Fig. 82.

curve for a steel. For steels, the endurance limit will be about 40 percent of the ultimate tensile stress, and will be reached at about 10,000,000 cycles of stress. These figures are based on the assumption of complete reversal of stress in each cycle. Note from Fig. 81 that a fatigue curve is plotted as linear stress against logarithmic cycles. Such a curve is really a plot of "fatigue elastic limit" against cycles.

Nonferrous metals in general do not exhibit an endurance limit (Fig. 117). The maximum allowable fatigue stress for such metals falls constantly, even to 1000×10^6 cycles. For nonferrous metals it is usual to determine the safe stress for a finite life of N cycles, which may be 10^8 cycles. Since fatigue stresses are a vital feature of aircraft operation, and since aircraft are built chiefly of nonferrous metals, great care is taken in the determination of allowable fatigue stresses in aircraft.

Figure 82 is an illustration of a fatigue testing machine. A small specimen of metal is flexed by the machine as it is rotated at 10,000 rpm. The machine has a revolution counter to indicate the number of cycles of stress reversal. When the specimen fails, the machine automatically stops.

Fig. 82 Fatigue testing machine. The fatigue sample is gripped by a collet at each end (a wrench is on one collet) and flexed as it is rotated at 10,000 rpm.

9.6 creep

Creep is long-term plastic deformation. It is a familiar effect in lead, wood, polyethylene, and paper, all of which will sag under relatively light loads if the loading period is sufficiently long. While only a few metals will creep at room temperature, creep is a cause of metal failures at elevated temperatures. Thus if the time of operation is sufficiently prolonged, or the combination of temperature and stress is sufficiently severe, the blades of a gas turbine engine may fail by striking the engine casing as they elongate from creep effects. Creep of course is accelerated by higher temperatures.

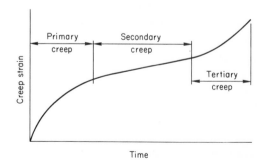

Fig. 83 Elongation due to creep.

Figure 83 shows the typical progress of creep in a metal. In the primary stage of creep, the metal elongates at a diminishing rate. This rate reaches a minimum which persists for a considerable period of time. A linear rate of creep thus is characteristic of the secondary stage of elongation. In the final or tertiary stage, the creep rate accelerates toward failure.

Large steam turbines are expected to last for 20 years while driven by steam at temperatures above 1000°F. For such machines the stress levels must confine creep to 1 percent elongation in 100,000 hours of operation.

9.7 high-temperature resistance

Throughout the twentieth century, and particularly since World War II, developments in the technology of materials have followed each other in rapid succession, accelerated by the relatively new science of solid state physics. This remarkable progress is nevertheless marked by a few failures. Competent researchers have been unable to produce a ductile ceramic, or a cutting tool bit which will meet the demands of machine tool operators. Perhaps the most notable failure is our inability to develop materials with an extended life under service conditions exceeding 2000°F.

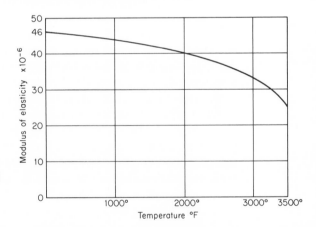

Fig. 84 Modulus of elasticity of molybdenum.

There is no serious lack of materials with high melting points. Refractory metals such as tungsten and molybdenum, natural oxides such as beryllia and thoria, and the element carbon, all have melting points in the range of 5000–6000°F or slightly higher. For still higher melting points we have developed such synthetic carbides as hafnium carbide. Unfortunately, all these refractory materials fail in some important property at temperatures far below their melting points. Carbon begins to oxidize rapidly above 1500°F. Moduli of elasticity of all the metals fall to lower values at several hundred degrees Fahrenheit (see Fig. 84), and so do yield strength, hardness, and ultimate strength. The highly refractory metals such as tungsten oxidize readily above 1000°F. A number of oxides such as beryllia are serviceable at temperatures of 3000°F, but such materials are too brittle to be used as structural components of equipment, and are confined in their applications to furnace linings and melting crucibles.

Since ductility as well as high-temperature resistance is a mandatory requirement for most materials in high-temperature applications, the only usable materials for high-temperature work are generally metal alloys. The most useful of the high-temperature metals is also the best low-temperature metal — nickel. This metal offers the best all-round combination of tensile strength, ductility, creep strength, and oxidation resistance, and many of the high-temperature alloys (the superalloys) are nickel-base. Some of these superalloys may be used at temperatures as high as 2200°F, though the useful life is rather short at such a temperature. Even the stainless steels with nickel contents from 8 to 35 percent have reasonably good high-temperature properties.

High-temperature resistance is of course not a property but a complex of highly demanding properties: strength, stiffness, hardness, ductility, dimensional stability, and oxidation resistance chiefly. An especially severe demand on materials at these temperatures is chemical inertness. Above 2000°F virtually all materials become chemically active, and it must be expected that the material will react with its environment.

One solution to the high-temperature problem is an obvious one, and is frequently used with a degree of success. That is to use a ceramic coating on a metal substrate. This solution may raise problems of its own, however. The coefficients of expansion of the two materials must be compatible, and at high temperatures the metal and the ceramic must not engage in chemical action or mutual diffusion into each other.

Aerospace vehicles require materials for short time exposure to temperatures as high as 15,000°F, in heat shields and rocket nozzles. Such a temperature is twice as high as the highest melting point known. Ironically, the low-melting plastic materials offer perhaps the best solution to this service problem due to certain other characteristics they possess. There are actually three possible methods of resisting such temperatures.

1. Heat sink method. A material of high thermal conductivity is used to distribute the heat developed throughout the entire mass of material. The material will of course reach a high temperature; therefore a metal must usually be employed. A metal such as beryllium has suitable properties: high specific heat, sufficiently high melting point, and low specific weight. Carbon also has these properties, and its high emissivity, almost 1.0, contributes to cooling the material.

2. Refractory metal method. The refractory metals such as tungsten, melting at 6152°F, have the properties of high melting point, rapid oxidation at higher temperatures, volatile oxides of low melting point, and high thermal conductivity. In use as a heat shield at ultrahigh temperature, the metal will oxidize. The oxide will melt or vaporize, and the latent heat can be used to cool the material.

3. Ablation method. This has been the most successful solution to the problem. The method relies on degradation and decomposition of a reinforced plastic material. Cooling action is produced by the following effects:

(a) high specific heat of the material
(b) high latent heat of the degradation products
(c) heat required for degradation
(d) radiation of heat
(e) loss of the decomposed and volatile materials, which flow into the adjacent air layer and keep the heat shield cool. The material ultimately chars to a porous carbon, and this acts as an insulating layer which also protects the heat shield

Both phenolic and epoxy reinforced plastics make excellent heat shields.

9.8   low-temperature resistance

Low-temperature resistance is as vague a term as high-temperature resistance. Here we shall interpret the term to mean suitability for use below −250°F, which is the cryogenic temperature range. The problems of creep, oxidation, low strength, and low E-value do not exist at low temperatures. Here the problem is largely that of notch brittleness.

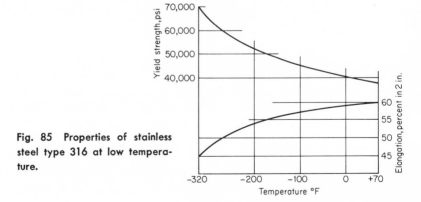

Fig. 85 Properties of stainless steel type 316 at low temperature.

Both strength and modulus of elasticity of metals increase somewhat at low temperatures, with sometimes some loss of ductility. In general face-centered cubic metals must be used for their notch toughness, such as the austenitic stainless steels or aluminum. Figure 85 shows the change in properties of type 316 stainless steel at low temperatures.

9.9   corrosion resistance

The subject of corrosion was briefly dealt with in Sec. 6.14. The subject of corrosion resistance of materials is too detailed to be dealt with in a single section of this book. Instead specific aspects of corrosion will be noted where they arise. Outstanding resistance to corrosion is given by such materials as tantalum, the plastic Teflon, and the ceramic alumina. However, all of these materials may be corroded by hydrofluoric acid. There is no panacean material which is resistant to all corrodents.

9.10   abrasion resistance and
impact resistance

Abrasion is a type of wear or loss of material caused by movement of an abrading material, such as sand, parallel to the surface of a machine component and causing scouring of the component. *Impact* is the type of wear that results from hammering effects perpendicular to the component. Wear by abrasion removes material by scratching; impact removes material by peening, mushrooming, cracking, chipping, or spalling.

These two types of wear call for different types of metal to resist them. Resistance to impact requires toughness, hardness, and strength, and often is best provided by some metal with pronounced work-hardening characteristics. Resistance to abrasion is provided by a very hard surface, such as is provided by carbides. An alternative method of providing abrasion resistance is the use of a suitable soft and elastic but tough material that will deform rather than score; rubber and nylon are two such materials which in many applications provide better wear resistance than harder materials. Pumps for pumping sand may be lined with silicon carbide; others may be lined with rubber.

The constant loss of metal caused by both abrasion and wear are corrected in the process industries by the use of hard-surfacing rods deposited by arc-welding methods. The selection of the best type of hard-surfacing material is a vexing problem that can sometimes be solved only by trial and error. Tungsten carbide and chromium carbide provide best resistance to abrasion, while austenitic stainless steels and austenitic manganese steel with 12 percent manganese offer best resistance to impact. Switch frogs on railroad lines must take the battering of train wheels, and are cast from 12 percent manganese steel.

9.11 surface roughness

Surface roughness determines how well many machine parts will execute their functions. Surface roughness is a factor determining fatigue strength. The surfaces of pins, bearings, lathe spindles, and interior walls of hydraulic cylinders must mate closely with other parts and require a high standard of smoothness to do so. While no doubt most surfaces would offer better performance if they were perfectly smooth, economics dictates the maximum roughness that may be tolerated, for a high degree of smoothness, like a high degree of accuracy, is expensive to obtain.

Surface roughness of machined parts is defined as the average deviation in millionths of an inch from the nominal surface of the part. So that this statement may be clearly understood, consider roughness specifications for the pins of the die set of Fig. 86, which are 5 microinches. This specification means that the total height of grinding scratches, measured from peak to valley, does not exceed 20 microinches. The maximum allowable

Fig. 86 A standard die set with a shearing die being set up in it. Bottom die shoe with the pins of the die set in the foreground; punch plate behind it.

deviation from the nominal surface of the pin is then ±10 microinches. The minimum conceivable deviation would be zero deviation, or the nominal surface itself. The average deviation, which is the surface roughness, must be 5 microinches. Such a finish is a mirror finish.

A surface roughness finer than about 50 microinches is almost impossible to obtain by standard machining methods. Finer finishes, down to about 15 microinches, are produced by grinding. Lapping, buffing, and superfinishing methods give the finest finishes currently in use, about 5 microinches.

Surface roughness is measured usually by a diamond needle pickup in a manner analogous to the operation of a phonograph needle pickup. The phonograph pickup and associated amplifier translate the movements of the needle into voltages which are finally transduced to the corresponding acoustic power of a loudspeaker. The surface roughness indicator operates in a somewhat similar manner, though with more sensitivity, translating vertical motion into voltages which move an indicator over a scale calibrated in microinches. The motion may be recorded on paper to give a permanent record of roughness. Figure 87 shows a Brush surface analyzer reading roughness on a short length of machined tubing, using a roughness recorder.

Fig. 87   Brush surface roughness recorder as set up to record surface roughness of a specimen of steel tubing.

9.12   hardness

There are a great many types of hardness tests currently in use. Among the reasons for this multiplicity of methods is that a single hardness method cannot span the great range of hardnesses from the soft plastics to the hard ceramics. Almost all hardness tests measure indentation hardness after the principle of asphalt testing outlined in Sec. 8.11. Some type of indentor is pressed into the specimen; a small indentation indicates high hardness, while a large indentation indicates low hardness. However, in an alternative method, the scleroscope test, a steel ball is bounced off the specimen to indicate the hardness by the height of the bounce.

Everyone early in life acquires the intuitive notion that hardness is related to strength. This of course is a generally correct idea. Metals are generally hard and strong, plastics usually soft and weak. Harder metals are stronger metals. Alloys are harder than their base metals. Hardness and strength may be increased by suitable heat treatments in the case of some metals and plastics, and in the case of plastics, by increasing molecular weight or length of polymer chain. Plastic straining (strain-hardening or work-hardening) increases the hardness of all metals, some to a greater degree than others. Figure 88 shows the effect of cold reduction of mild steel on its hardness.

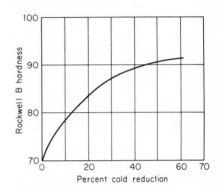

Fig. 88 Strain-hardening curve for a mild steel.

Since a standard tension test occupies considerable time in the operations of machining the specimen and then testing it, Brinell, a Swedish engineer, devised a hardness test which indicates ultimate tensile strength as well as hardness. This test is commonly used for metals, and provides a Brinell Hardness Number, or BHN.

The Brinell hardness tester is shown in Fig. 89. A hardened steel ball 10 mm in diameter is forced into the metal specimen under a 3000 kg load (500 kg for nonferrous metals). The average pressure on the spherical surface of the indentation is the BHN, or by formula

$$\text{BHN} = \frac{P}{\frac{\pi D}{2}[D - \sqrt{D^2 - d^2}]}$$

where P = load in kilograms

D = diameter of indentor ball

d = diameter of impression

Fig. 89 Brinell hardness tester.   Fig. 90 Rockwell hardness tester.

The diameter of the impression is determined by a low-power measuring microscope.

The ultimate tensile strength of a carbon steel is given closely by the simple formula

$$UTS = 500 \times BHN$$

This formula applies only to steels.

The Brinell test is not as quick or convenient a hardness test as the Rockwell test. Further, it leaves a rather large impression, which may be damaging to the part tested, and it cannot test material less than about $\frac{5}{16}$ in. thick nor small objects. However the large impression gives a good average reading over a considerable area and is relatively immune to the effect of scratches and machining marks.

The disadvantages of the Brinell hardness test led to the development of other indentation hardness methods. The Vickers Pyramid Hardness tester uses a very small four-sided pyramid indentor. The most popular indentation tester, however, is the Rockwell tester of Fig. 90. There are several Rockwell scales using different indentors and loads. These are summarized in the following table. Only the B and C tests are in widespread use.

mechanical characteristics of materials
192

Scale	Used for	Load, kg	Indentor	Hardness Read on
A	steel sheet	60	brale	black numbers on dial
B	standard test	100	$\frac{1}{16}''$ ball	red numbers on dial
C	standard test	150	brale	black numbers on dial
D		100	brale	black numbers on dial
E	soft metals	100	$\frac{1}{8}''$ ball	red numbers on dial
F	brass	60	$\frac{1}{16}''$ ball	red numbers on dial
G	phosphor bronze	150	$\frac{1}{16}''$ ball	red numbers on dial
H		60	$\frac{1}{8}''$ ball	red numbers on dial

The Rockwell C test is used for determining the hardness of hard steels. A conical diamond indentor is employed, called a Brale, under a 150-kg load. The Rockwell B test applies 100 kg to a $\frac{1}{16}$-in. diameter steel ball, and is used on mild steels. Both tests, and the other Rockwell tests in the table, can be executed on the same instrument. A 10-kg minor load is applied to the indentor to take up elastic deformation in the specimen. Then a major load, 150 kg for Rockwell C and 100 kg for Rockwell B, is applied. The depth of indentation due to the major load is measured and subtracted from a constant number. This is the Rockwell hardness, and is registered on the dial on the front of the instrument. Hardness is recorded as R_C 35, R_B 85, etc.

A Rockwell hardness test can be performed in seconds, and therefore this test is preferred for production testing. To obtain some notion of hardness ranges, the maximum hardness of any steel is about R_C 65; a steel is almost unmachinable when the hardness exceeds R_C 35.

The scleroscope test uses a steel weight dropped from a fixed height on to the surface of the specimen. The height of rebound measures the hardness. Although not as widely used, this instrument has the virtue of small size and portability. The explanation for this hardness method is simply that hard materials have high elastic limits and absorb little of the kinetic energy of the dropped weight. Softer materials will have lower elastic limits and thus deform plastically, absorbing more energy.

The hardness of plastics may be measured on the Rockwell scales R_R and R_M, which use larger ball indentors. The plastics, as their name implies, deform plastically, a basic requirement of the Rockwell method.

Hardness measurements on rubbers cannot be made with the Rockwell tester. Rubbers are elastic and not subject to plastic or permanent deformation. The hardness of rubber must therefore be measured during application of the load, as in the Shore durometer test. The Shore instrument is available in a number of styles, one of which is illustrated in Fig. 91. The instrument has a flat bottom surface with a projecting indentor.

Fig. 91 Shore durometer reading hardness of a block of polyurethane tooling rubber.

It is pressed against the surface of the rubber specimen and the relative movement of the indentor into the rubber is read out on the dial of the instrument immediately after the instrument is seated on the specimen. Rubber may creep, and the reading after 15 seconds may be lower than the initial reading. Hardness readings on rubber are sensitive to temperature changes of a relatively few degrees.

Very hard rubbers, harder than automobile tires, use the Shore D scale, and softer rubbers the Shore A. A rubber band has a hardness of about A20, and an automobile tire about A70. Figure 92 illustrates the two durometer scales.

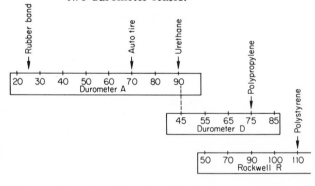

Fig. 92 Durometer scales. (From Du Pont, *Mechanical Properties of Adiprene*)

9.13 dimensional stability

The machinist who grinds a part to an accuracy of half a thousandth assumes that this accuracy will be preserved in the part. Such accuracy would not be sought if it could not be maintained. The assumption of dimensional stability similarly dictates that structural metals should not be loaded beyond their elastic limits or endurance limits. Nevertheless dimensional stability is not always easy to maintain, and many material properties work against it.

For dimensional stability, an ideal material would have the following properties:

1. coefficient of thermal expansion — zero
2. modulus of elasticity — infinite
3. no phase changes producing small changes in volume
4. no plasticity or creep
5. high tensile strength
6. absolute corrosion resistance
7. high hardness and wear resistance

The metals and ceramics most nearly approach the above properties, which accounts for the use of these materials in those components that require the best dimensional stability, such as measuring gauges. Of the basic groups of solid materials, the organics have the poorest dimensional stability, due to high expansion, low modulus of elasticity, plasticity, creep, low hardness, and in some cases, dimensional changes with changes in humidity.

Dimensional stability is most critical for the master standards of length used in metrology. The standard inch was formerly defined as 0.0254 times the length of the international meter, the latter measurement being the distance between two gauge marks on a platinum-iridium bar stored in France. A platinum-iridium alloy is an excellent choice for a dimensionally stable material. But a metal bar does not have *absolute* dimensional stability, and may be destroyed by fire or other accident.

Absolute dimensional stability is provided by photon wavelengths, however. The standard inch is now defined as 41,929.399 wavelengths of light from Krypton-86. Such a master dimension can be reproduced at any time and place as desired.

9.14 coefficient of friction

The coefficient of friction is both a processability factor and a serviceability factor. It is a ratio or pure number: the least force required to cause movement of one surface over another, divided by the force between the contacting surfaces. When such a coefficient is quoted, the usual assumption is that the mating surfaces are smooth and not lubricated.

A low coefficient of friction is required for sleeve bearings. In other cases a high coefficient is required, as with vehicle tires, brakes, tracked vehicles, and conveyor belts. The material offering lowest coefficients, as low as 0.04, is the plastic Teflon. Rubbers offer high coefficients, though the harder the rubber the lower the friction coefficient. Urethane rubbers in hard formulations offer coefficients as low as 0.20, and have occasional uses as bearings. Because of the slipperiness of lead, this metal is used in many bearing alloys and is added to metals to improve their machinability.

9.15   angle of repose

Angle of repose refers to the angle with the horizontal that a pile of bulk material will make. If a bulk material such as sand or coffee has a steep angle of repose, then more of it can be piled in a given area, on a truck, or on a conveyor belt. Angle of repose, therefore, is a significant characteristic for material handling purposes. For a high angle of repose, the particles must have a high friction coefficient against each other or must interlock.

9.16   machinability

Machinability has been defined as "a complex property of a material that controls the facility with which it can be cut to the size, shape, and surface finish required commercially". A brief definition is "relative ease of machining on machine tools", and a less reverent definition: "the ability of a material to go through a machine shop without irritating the machinist".

Machining with standard cutter bits is possible only within a restricted range of material hardness. Machining of materials with a hardness greater than R_C 35 is difficult and slow, and may require special tools and techniques. Harder materials must be ground with abrasive wheels. At the other extreme, soft plastics and rubbers may deform too readily to be machinable, or may require refrigeration in order to be machined. The softest steels are not readily machinable, nor is soft aluminum as machinable as its harder alloys.

The relative machinability of machinable materials, however, is subject to a host of variables besides hardness. The temperature at the point of contact between cutting tool and metal chip will be approximately 1500°F when machining steel at production rates (1500°F is a cherry red heat). The properties of the steel at this cutting temperature are therefore among the important variables, chiefly tensile strength and elongation. The velocity of the cut in surface feet per minute and the depth of cut are two more important variables. The angles of the cutting tool are other significant variables, complicated by the fact that these angles must be adjusted to suit various metals; sharper angles are needed for machining aluminum and rubber than for steel. The cutting oil used has an influence on friction and cooling effects. Other variables have more indirect effects. For example, stainless steel has a low thermal conductivity, and during machining, considerable heat builds up in the cutting area. Certain metals, such as soft steels and titanium, tend to gall or weld to the cutting tool. Finally the type of machining operation influences the machinability of the material; a metal may be easy to broach but difficult to turn.

The human race seems to associate brass with machinability. This relationship is borne out in practice: brass is an ingratiating metal to cut, and where machinability has a major bearing on cost, brass may be selected for the raw material.

Relative machinability ratings are given to metals based on steel alloy AISI B1112, which is discussed in the next chapter. This is a sulfurized low carbon steel, and is assigned the arbitrary machinability rating of 100. A metal with a machinability rating of 200 would be twice as machinable as B1112. When machined by methods appropriate to it, including suitable tool angles, presumably the more machinable metal could be machined at twice the speed of B1112. This is only partially true: machinability is too complex and insufficiently understood for such ratings to have dependable accuracy.

A great many steel, copper, and aluminum alloys are blended to provide a high machinability rating. These are called free-machining or free-cutting alloys. Copper is added to aluminum to promote hardness and therefore machinability. Lead is added to brasses, the lead inclusions serving to lubricate the tool. Selenium, lead, or sulfur are added to stainless steels, and lead, phosphorus, or sulfur to carbon, low alloy, or tool steels for improved machinability. Phosphorus is added to steels for its hardening effect on soft and stringy steels. Sulfur is added to produce manganese sulfide inclusions in the steel; like lead inclusions, these serve to lubricate the cutting tool. In addition to these alloying methods, steel bars specially prepared as machining stock are often cold-drawn, giving a surface hardening effect with improved machinability.

The selection of free-cutting grades of bar is of course a matter of economics. There is no purpose in paying a price premium for free-cutting quality throughout the cross-section of the bar if only a light skin cut will be made on the bar. Free-cutting grades are also uneconomic except in production machining on automatic lathes, numerically controlled machine tools, or other high-production equipment. As a rule of thumb, 10 percent of the bar must be removed as chips to justify the higher cost of free-machining stock.

In the case of beryllium, there may be an unusual limitation on machining speeds. Finely divided beryllium is exceedingly toxic, therefore machining chips must not be allowed to fly about at random as they are delivered from the cutting tool. The machining area is fitted with an exhaust hood, using a high air velocity to capture chips and carry them into the exhaust system. The machining speed will be limited by the capacity of the exhaust system to capture the chips, since too high a machining speed will throw the chips beyond the capture area of the exhaust hood. This case serves as one more example of the infinite variety of problems generated by the many materials now in use in industry.

Some of the more difficult alloys to machine are the high-nickel heat-resisting alloys used in aircraft gas turbines, such as the Inconels. These may have machinability ratings as low as 5. Such materials cannot be cut except with heavy and rigid machine tools equipped with large driving motors and sharp cutting tools. The following list is the approximate order of metals from least machinable to most machinable, assuming all metals to be in the soft or annealed condition:

Least machinable	mild steel
titanium	free-cutting mild steel
inconel	aluminum alloys
nickel	brass
stainless steels	zinc alloys
tool steels	free-cutting brass
copper	magnesium alloys
gray cast iron	*Most machinable*
high carbon steel	

9.17   formability

Broadly speaking, two methods are available for shaping materials: machining and forming. Machining removes metal or material in the form of chips, while forming shapes material in forms or dies. While machining is possible on either brittle or ductile materials (though it is easier to machine brittle materials, in general), forming is not possible on materials without a considerable degree of plasticity. This statement is subject to some exceptions, since brittle materials can be formed by such methods as casting or compacting of powders. In this section, however, we are concerned with the problem of forming sheet between male and female dies.

To form a sheet in brake dies or drawing dies, the stress in the metal must exceed the yield strength, but must not exceed the ultimate tensile strength. Should the yield strength of the material be very close to the ultimate strength, then the metal will have only a very limited plastic range.

Bending and drawing then must be carefully done, since slight overloading will fracture the material. Those metals are easiest to form which have yield strengths well below their ultimate strengths, such as pure aluminum and most stainless steels. Stainless steel alloy 301 will serve as an example. This metal is used in the hubcaps of automobiles. It has a yield strength of 40,000 psi and ultimate tensile strength of 110,000 psi, a ratio of almost 3 to 1. This ratio explains its suitability for the complex drawing operation involved in forming an automobile hubcap.

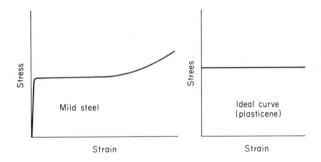

Fig. 93 Stress-strain curves. The curve for mild steel shows the elastic range, the cause of springback, and the work-hardening effect of plastic deformation. The ideal curve, which might be that for children's plasticene, has neither elastic deformation nor work-hardening.

The typical stress-strain curve of a drawing-quality metal sheet is shown in Fig. 93. Both the elastic and the plastic region present problems in forming operations. Let us suppose that the sheet is to be bent 90° in a braking die. As the sheet is bent between the mating dies, it is first stressed to the elastic limit. After bending is completed, and the dies are opened, this elastic strain is recovered. This *springback* in the metal must be compensated for by overbending. The higher the elastic limit of the material, the greater this springback will be. Next consider the plastic region. After yielding, the material can stretch with no rise in stress, but after considerable stretching the stress begins to increase. This is the strain-hardening effect possessed by all metals as the straining operation gradually uses up the dislocations in the space lattices of the metal. Such hardening reduces ductility. In severe drawing such as is required to make a welding gas cylinder or an artillery shell case, this strain-hardening effect will require the drawing to be done in graduated steps in a series of dies, the various stages of the drawing operation being separated by annealing operations (softening by heating) to remove the strain-hardening effects. This is especially true with most of the stainless steels, which though possessing considerable ductility will strain-harden rapidly. The ideal metal for forming would have a stress-strain curve like that of Fig. 93b, with no elastic springback and no strain-hardening.

Several methods are available for comparing the formability of metals. The standard tensile test will give data such as yield strength, which affects the amount of springback, modulus of elasticity, which determines the

Fig. 94 Olsen cup tester for assessing drawability of sheet metal. (Courtesy Tinius Olsen Co.)

force required for drawing, and elongation, which is a measure of the basic formability. An even simpler test is that of bending. If the material will bend 180° flat on itself, it has unusually good formability. More sophisticated tests are cup tests, such as the Erichsen or Olsen cup test. In these tests the metal sheet is clamped between ring-shaped dies, while a rounded punch is forced into one side of the sheet until fracture is initiated. The height of the dome produced is measured in millimeters and is taken as a measure of the formability of the sheet. The Olsen cup tester is illustrated in Fig. 94.

9.18   weldability and hardenability

Weldability does not mean the ability to be welded, just as machinability did not mean the ability to be machined. It must be presumed that there is a method of welding any material to itself, and even very dissimilar materials can be welded together, such as glass and metal. The term *weldability* means the relative ability of metals, usually steels, to be welded *without cracking*. In general, new structural steel alloys are formulated for good weldability, since this is a critical requirement in their use and assembly.

Weldability, like machinability and formability, can be rated on a rough numerical scale. The rating methods and tests are ingenious, but cannot be discussed at this point. Cracking of steels during welding operations results from the heat-treating effects of welding; these will be taken up in a later chapter.

Hardenability is a factor of concern in the processing of heat-treatable steels such as tool steels. Steels can be hardened only by rapid cooling, called quenching. If the cooling rate is not fast enough, the steel will not harden. If the hot steel is plunged into cold water, the exterior of the steel, in contact with the cold water, will harden by cooling at a sufficiently rapid rate. But in the interior of a thick section of steel, heat will be lost more slowly. The interior therefore may not harden. Hardenability is measured by the depth in the steel to which hardening occurs.

9.19 summing up

So far this book has attempted to discuss a rather wide range of the properties of materials, under the groupings of physical, electrical, and mechanical characteristics. A later chapter will deal with an equally important group of characteristics, the economic ones. All material properties are really economic properties, of course. Needless to say, only the more common and most universal of material characteristics have been considered. This wide range of characteristics, any of which may be specified on buyers' purchase orders and supplied by producers within acceptable tolerances, are sufficient evidence of the high degree of sophistication reached in materials technology. The advances of the next few years will produce new requirements and new characteristics. All this explains why universities and other institutes establish departments for Materials Engineering, why engineers are hired for positions as purchasing agents, and why some companies, knowledgeable in materials, succeed where less knowledgeable ones do not.

One of the most perplexing questions to ask is, "Which is the cheapest material to use?" In this age of rapid progress, there is no definitive answer. Consider the following case.

A steel part must be machined, then welded to the end of a steel shaft. The cheapest raw material is mild steel. But mild steel does not machine well. A leaded steel will be slightly more expensive than a mild steel but will machine at half the cost of a mild steel. It is therefore cheaper in terms of raw material plus machining costs. But a leaded steel is tricky to weld, since the lead boils out of the steel during welding. Which steel is now the cheaper, leaded or mild steel? One shop might select mild steel, and another shop leaded steel. Each shop would make its selection in the light of its own difficulties, resources, abilities, and experience, and each would presumably be correct in its selection. Materials selection always involves compromise, and compromises call for more skill and judgment than simple choices between black and white.

PROBLEMS

1 Explain the purpose of a getter.

2 Define a micron.

3 Why is purity critical to the proper functioning of a transistor?

4 Explain brittle and ductile fracture at the level of the space lattice of a single crystal.

5 In order to be sure of the strength of a butt weld, welders will build up the weld so that it is thicker than the adjacent plate. Discuss the implications of this practice for both brittle fracture and for fatigue failure.

6 By and large, which is the best choice in the design of metal fabrications, a butt weld or a fillet weld? Why?

7 What is an endurance limit?

8 What metals or other materials can you name that will creep at room temperature, given a sufficient period of time?

9 Differentiate between abrasion and impact.

10 Is the Rockwell hardness test a suitable one for a perfectly elastic material such as glass? Why not?

11 What is the relationship between coefficient of friction and angle of repose?

12 What reasons can you give why Rockwell hardness does not correlate well with machinability ratings?

13 How does sulfur contribute to machinability of metals?

14 What is the meaning of springback?

15 Tool steels have poor weldability. If their thermal conductivity were higher, would their weldability be improved?

Steel is the basic material on which the Western World has built its technical culture. Though steel has been known and used in limited quantities for a few thousand years, it did not come into extensive use until about a hundred years ago, at which time methods were finally established for producing steel in tons rather than in pounds. Since then steel has been the colossus among metals, and nothing yet indicates that it will lose its dominating position in the future. While other materials such as aluminum, concrete, and plastics, have made some inroads into the markets served by steel, nevertheless far more steel is consumed than the total tonnage of all other metals and plastics combined. Annual consumption of all steels in the United States exceeds 135,000,000 tons, in Canada 10,000,000 tons, and in the whole world half a billion tons.

The remarkable versatility of steel in part explains its wide use. There is a steel for almost every purpose: soft and hard steels, steels of low conductivity and high conductivity, ferromagnetic and paramagnetic steels, weldable and heat-treatable steels, wrought and cast steels, steels to resist heat, cold, corrosion, impact, and abrasion. Notable too is the readiness with which most other metals can be blended with steel to provide an almost infinite variety of useful alloys.

Though by no means the largest group of steel alloys by tonnage, the tool steels deserve special attention. Just as the toolmaker may be con-

STEEL

10

sidered the most critically important of all the skilled trades in a society that values its high standard of living, the tool steels, which are the toolmaker's raw materials, must be accounted the most critically important group of metals. These are the special steels from which are made the tools, forms, dies, gauges, and machinery that produce finished consumer goods. And just as toolmakers are high-paid craftsmen, so their tool steels are among the most expensive of the steels.

Only limited quantities of elemental iron are used in industry. Instead, iron is alloyed with a small amount of carbon, the resulting alloy being a *steel*. There are always present in steel small percentages of sulfur and phosphorus originating from the iron ore and the coke fuel used to reduce the ore. However, these are not counted as alloying elements, since they are usually not advantageous but detrimental. In addition, almost all steels include small amounts of silicon and manganese, which are added to the steel in the steel mill. Except in larger amounts, these too are not counted as alloying elements. The most commonly used alloying metals in steels are nickel and chromium. A *carbon steel* therefore will contain carbon and minor percentages of sulfur, phos, silicon, and manganese. A *low alloy steel* will contain carbon plus a few percent of another metal or metals such as nickel. A high alloy steel will contain over 10 percent of alloying metals.

Those steels which contain more than 2 percent carbon are usually called irons, and the group of such irons includes gray cast iron, white cast iron, malleable iron, and ductile iron. These are all cast products of the iron foundry and not rolled products from a steel mill.

The total number of steel alloys in use is probably not known, but is unquestionably in the thousands. New steel alloys are developed every year. In the last ten years particularly, steel technology has seen rapid development.

10.2 the extraction of iron
from its ores

Most ores of iron having industrial importance are iron oxides, and most of these are magnetic. Iron ore occurs quite commonly over the earth's surface, particularly in low-grade deposits, but the steel industry operates on such a large scale that only the largest ore bodies are developed. In 1965 the American steel industry consumed 140,000,000 tons of ore, supplemented by an unknown quantity of scrap steel. Some statistics of the large Hull-Rust open-pit mine in Minnesota dramatically suggest the magnitude of iron ore operations. One billion tons of ore and overburden have so far been excavated from this mine, leaving a hole in the ground measuring $3\frac{1}{2}$ square miles in area with a maximum depth of about 540 ft.

Typical iron ores include the following three:

1. *Magnetite*, Fe_3O_4, brown in color, strongly magnetic, containing about 65 percent iron. This is a rich ore, and therefore less commonly found than lower-grade ores.
2. *Hematite*, Fe_2O_3, red in color (hematite, hemorrhage, and hematology have the same derivation), paramagnetic, containing about 50 percent iron.
3. *Taconite*, usually green, strongly magnetic, containing about 30 percent iron and much silica. Such low-grade ores must be beneficiated or upgraded at the mine site by removal of silica.

One ton of ore is worth just over $10 delivered, or 0.5 cents a pound. After conversion into iron in a blast furnace, the resulting pig iron is worth about $70 a ton, or 3.5 cents a pound. When this iron is converted into a steel shape, such as a bar or plate of mild steel, the steel is worth over 5 cents a pound at mill prices. The low price of steel is another of its outstanding characteristics and makes it the cheapest of all metals by a considerable margin.

It is not yet commercially possible in the United States to convert iron ore directly into steel in a single-process operation. Such a method is called "direct reduction". Direct-reduction methods have been the subject of aggressive research since 1950. A few small direct-reduction plants are operating in other countries, and there is some likelihood that in the near future direct-reduction methods will be used for the making of steel in North America. At present, however, the process from iron ore to steel takes two stages:

1. The ore is converted into hot metal (raw iron, or pig iron) in a blast furnace.
2. The hot metal is refined into steel in a steel refining furnace such as an open-hearth furnace.

The blast furnace, Fig. 95, is the largest of all the big industrial furnaces, though the rotary kilns used for the manufacture of cement clinker are longer. A blast furnace, of which there are about 200 in the United States, is a vertical shaft furnace about 200 ft high, with a diameter inside the firebrick lining of about 30 ft, and shaped like an oversize Coke bottle. It requires for its refractory lining a supply of refractories by the trainload rather than the carload. High heat duty firebrick is employed, except that carbon brick is used to line the hearth walls below the molten metal line. The furnace itself weighs about 10,000 tons, and is supported on steel piling and a 12-ft-thick pad of reinforced concrete about 60 ft in diameter. Refractory concrete is poured on top of the foundation concrete, and about 15 ft of large firebrick is laid on the refractory concrete. The cost of this sort of construction explains why the steel industry is more interested in

Fig. 95 Blast furnaces on Route 30 through Pittsburgh.

methods of increasing production from existing blast furnaces than in
building new installations. A single blast furnace installation may cost
$30,000,000, but its product sells for only 3–4 cents a pound.

Raw material is charged into the top of the furnace by means of skip
cars. Production rate for a blast furnace may run to 3000 tons of metal
per 24-hr day, and each finished ton requires the charging into the furnace
of 3350 lb of iron ore, 570 lb of limestone, and 1350 lb of coke, for a total
of about 5300 lb of raw materials. In addition, about 40 tons of cooling
water must be passed through the furnace per ton of product, and $3\frac{1}{2}$ tons
of combustion air. Nothing can match the awesome continuous appetite
of this ugly monster.

The limestone serves as the slagging material to remove sulfur and
phosphorus. The coke burns principally to carbon monoxide, which
reduces the iron oxide by combining with its oxygen at a temperature of
about 3000°F to form carbon dioxide. This is the essence of the chemical
reactions of the blast furnace, though a complete understanding of the
chemistry is still somewhat beyond our grasp. The carbon found in steel is,
of course, derived from the coke originally charged into the blast furnace.

Once the blast furnace is fired, it is never cooled down until the refractory lining must be replaced. This means continuous operation for at least
five years. The molten iron, called hot metal or pig iron, is tapped from
the furnace periodically throughout the day.

The hot metal thus produced is actually an impure and low-quality cast iron containing about 4 percent carbon. This high carbon content makes the metal unusable as a steel. With so much carbon it has no ductility and cannot be rolled into finished shapes such as plate, sheet, or bar. This is the reason why the blast furnace iron must be further processed: among other considerations, the steel refining furnace must reduce this carbon content.

10.3   steel-refining practice

The principal function of a steel-refining furnace is to control the amount of carbon, impurities, and alloying elements in the steel. This is done under a basic slag using lime, since an acid slag using silica does not remove sulfur and phos. The hot metal delivered to the steel-refining furnace contains 4 percent carbon, and the steel furnace will reduce this to less than 1 percent by oxidizing the carbon. At the same time, any alloy metal additions will be made to the molten steel, such as small percentages of manganese or nickel. Certain ingredients such as aluminum are too readily oxidized and would disappear into the slag, but these can be added to the finished steel after it is poured from the furnace into the pouring ladle.

Only three types of steel-refining furnace are important enough to deserve mention here. These are:

1. the open-hearth furnace, invented about 1860
2. the electric arc furnace, invented about 1900
3. the oxygen converter, invented in Austria, first used in North America in 1954

Small quantities of steel are also made by other methods, including the nearly obsolete Bessemer converter. The time seems to be approaching when the open-hearth furnace will be obsolete too, since steel companies are retiring these furnaces in favor cf the much faster oxygen converter. At the time of writing, about 10 percent of all steel production comes from electric furnaces, another 25 percent from converters, and the remainder from open-hearths. Converter production seems certain to reach 50 percent in a very few years.

The specialty steels such as tool steels and stainless steels are reserved for the electric arc furnace, which also is used in geographical areas which are not served by blast furnaces.

All three refining furnaces may be charged with either hot metal or steel scrap, but each shows some preferences. It is not usual to charge blast furnace iron into an electric furnace. This furnace uses virtually 100 percent scrap. The converter is not charged with more than 25 percent scrap, since it does not have a burner or other external source of heat and cannot therefore melt steel. The open-hearth furnace uses either hot metal or scrap, employing more scrap when scrap steel prices are low and less when prices are high.

The basic oxygen process was first used in Austria in 1952. The furnace (Fig. 96) is a pear-shaped vessel open at the top. No source of heat is supplied. The converter is first charged with hot metal. Then a retractable water-cooled lance, actually a pipe, is lowered into the converter above the surface of the bath. Pure oxygen at about 150 psi is directed from the lance onto the bath. The stream of oxygen burns out the carbon in the hot metal as carbon monoxide in a very short time as compared with other steel-refining methods. This chemical reaction is the only source of heat during the operation. As the temperature of the process increases, it frequently must be held back by additions of scrap steel. The open-hearth and electric furnace require a few hours to melt and refine a heat of steel. The oxygen converter prepares a heat of steel at a furious rate of 45 minutes or less; an early problem with this method was getting an analysis of the steel back from the laboratory by the time the heat was ready to pour. Indeed, the converter works so vigorously that it burns out its firebrick lining in a week.

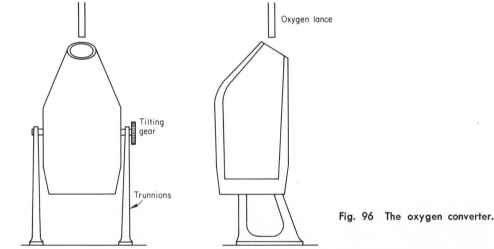

Fig. 96 The oxygen converter.

Typical capacity of a converter is 100 to 200 tons of steel per heat. The older open-hearth furnaces are much larger, more complicated in construction and operation, and more expensive than the converter. There are however still about 900 open-hearth furnaces in the United States. Neglecting any description of its complicated gas flues, the open-hearth furnace is a shallow melting bath with an arch roof, melting 200 to 400 tons or more steel per heat. This furnace is heated by a large gas flame for several hours; this may be supplemented by oxygen lancing.

Lime or limestone is first charged into the open-hearth furnace, then scrap metal. The scrap is melted, and the slag floats. Hot metal is then charged about two hours after the beginning of operations. Refining of the steel commences after melting is completed. During the refining stage, the carbon content is lowered and sulfur and phosphorus reduced to lowest possible levels. Common practice is to reduce the carbon below the required level, finally recarburizing by adding hot metal, coke, or coal just before tapping the furnace. If the carbon must be reduced to very low levels, say 0.03 percent for culvert steel or porcelain enamelling steel, then the use of oxygen lancing is necessary. Since alloy metals melt at lower temperatures than pure metals, as the carbon is burned out of the steel the melting temperature constantly rises. Low carbon steels therefore impose severe temperature conditions on the furnace. The refining operation requires considerable time, and the total heat time may be 10 hours by the open-hearth method. Burner heat requirement per ton of steel exceeds 3,000,000 Btu in the open-hearth furnace.

Electric arc-melting furnaces operate on scrap metal. Such furnaces are simply large-scale arc welders, using three-phase electric power brought to the furnace by means of three large graphite electrodes that enter vertically through the dome roof of the furnace (Fig. 97). Current travels down

Fig. 97 Electric arc melting furnace. The three electrodes are partially withdrawn from the furnace while the furnace crew makes up a slag. (Courtesy American Bridge Division, United States Steel Corp.)

one electrode, arcs through the scrap and up another electrode with much noise. While arc furnaces as small as half-ton capacity are available, for tonnage steel the capacity ranges from 30 to 150 tons or more.

Electric transformer capacity for an arc furnace may be of the order of 30,000 kva. As in arc welding, conditions approach short-circuiting. Melt-down begins at about 200 v, and even a modest size furnace may draw 25,000 amps per electrode. While carbon electrodes are much cheaper, graphite is used because of its lower electrical resistance and greater current capacity. Electrode diameters range from about 12 to 24 in. The electrodes are slowly consumed by the heat of the arc at their ends, usually at a rate of about 15 lb of electrodes per ton of steel. A new electrode can be screwed onto the top end of the one in use.

Operation of the furnace begins by raising the electrodes, then swinging the roof of the furnace to one side. A charging bucket then dumps scrap into the furnace, usually filling the furnace to the top. The roof is swung back and the electrodes lowered. Each electrode is automatically positioned at the proper level of about one inch above the charge. Arcing begins with much heavy noise until the charge is melted. Thereafter the furnace is quieter. Melting requires 400 or more kilowatts per ton of steel.

In the refining operation that follows melting, the carbon content of the steel is brought to the desired level. Iron ore or oxygen lancing are used to reduce the carbon; coke or scrap electrodes can be added to increase carbon.

Generally a double-slag method is used in electric refining of steel. This method is perhaps best explained in terms of a heat of stainless steel containing about 20 percent chromium. The chromium is added to the melt in the form of ferrochromium, an alloy of two-thirds chromium and one-third iron. The first slag is a basic (lime) oxidizing slag with the purpose of oxidizing phosphorus, silicon, manganese, and carbon. But chromium is a readily oxidizable metal also, and much chromium will also be removed by such a slag. To recover this chromium, a second slag is made up of lime, silica, fluorspar, and coke. The coke and lime react to form calcium carbide, which yields a reducing slag. This slag reduces and returns to the bath such reducible metals as manganese and chromium.

Besides alloy additions, certain other additives are used for quality control of the steel. All steels must contain a minimum of about 0.3 percent manganese. The manganese combines with any residual sulfur in the steel to form harmless manganese sulfide inclusions of microscopic size. Without manganese, sulfur in steel would cause the steel to crack during rolling-mill operations, sulfurized steels being "hot-short" at rolling temperatures. A second additive is silicon, which is used to deoxidize the steel. Molten steel dissolves oxygen, one of the interstitial elements that promote brittle fracture. Sometimes aluminum is added, either to deoxidize the steel or to produce a fine-grained steel. Some of these additives may be added after the steel is poured from the furnace into the holding ladle, especially if they are readily oxidizing, as aluminum is.

Whether the heat of steel is refined in an open-hearth furnace, a converter, or an electric furnace, the laboratory must provide a chemical analysis of the steel before it is poured. The methods of analysis are discussed in Chapter 17. The analysis reports carbon to the nearest hundredth of a percent, plus all other significant constituents of the steel, of which there may be as many as 20, including the interstitials hydrogen, nitrogen, and oxygen. If the heat meets the requirements of the analysis, the steel is tapped into the holding ladle in preparation for pouring into ingots.

Thus steel is born. The instruments of its birth are furnaces — massive, dirty, ugly, and noisy. Yet in these fiery hellholes, whose chemistry we only dimly understand, men can formulate steels with a precision that the druggist in his pharmacy cannot match. Science did not invent steel. Rather, steel is a heritage of Western culture, for it required the work of practical men for over 600 years to develop these steel-making processes.

10.4   rolling-mill practice

The molten steel at a temperature of about 2900°F has been poured into the ladle. The ladle contains a pouring nozzle at the bottom. A long steel stopper rod running from the top of the ladle holds a refractory stopper on its bottom end to close the nozzle. The stopper rod can be raised with a lever when the steel is to be poured. The steel stopper rod does not melt in the molten steel, first because it is protected by refractory sleeves, and second because it is made of pure iron, which melts at a higher temperature than steel. The pouring of the steel must be done with care, since splashing metal could seriously injure personnel.

The steel is poured into ingot molds and freezes. The molds are tapered to facilitate stripping of the mold from the solid ingot.

Plain carbon steels are made in three grades: rimmed, semikilled, and killed. A killed steel is deoxidized by ladle additions of silicon or aluminum. These two metals are strong oxide formers, and remove the dissolved oxygen in the steel as silicon or aluminum oxide inclusions. Since there is no evolution of dissolved gas when the molten steel cools in the mold, such steels lie quiet in the mold, and the steel man calls them "killed". A semikilled steel is partially deoxidized. A rimmed steel does not receive this deoxidation treatment and is named for the very characteristic rim of parallel crystals that grow inward from the mold surface as the steel freezes. Killed steels are more resistant to brittle fracture than rimmed steels and are commonly rolled into plate and structurals. Rimmed steels are chiefly used for drawing-quality sheet.

The killing process removes only oxygen from the steel. The oxygen remains as ceramic inclusions visible under the microscope. For some steels these inclusions are harmful, one of their effects being a reduction in the fatigue resistance of the steel. Such inclusions, for example, cannot be tolerated in ball and roller bearings. Where the inclusions cannot be tolerated, and when other dissolved gases such as hydrogen must be removed (hydrogen causes cracking in heavy forgings), the steel is degassed by pouring in a vacuum. The improvement in quality gained by vacuum degassing is considerable and degassed steels have been increasingly in demand.

A more recent development in pouring techniques is continuous casting, a technique that will be increasingly integrated with the oxygen converter process. The ingot mold for continuous casting is a water-cooled copper mold open at the bottom. Casting is carried on without interruption as the long frozen ingot is pulled out of the mold by pinch rolls and cut into lengths. Killed steels because of their high shrinkage are not produced by continuous casting.

The steel lies in the ingot mold until frozen. The molds are then stripped. The ingots are reheated in soaking pits until they are at a uniform temperature throughout for hot rolling into finished shapes. During hot rolling the coarse grain structure produced in the slowly cooling ingot is broken up to make a finer-grained steel.

While hot rolling between roll stands is the principal method of reducing ingots, other methods are used for special products. The ingot may be forged on a large hydraulic press. Seamless tube is extruded from ingots through an extrusion die with hydraulic pressure. In hot rolling, the ingot is passed through a succession of rolls until it is reduced to the desired shape and size. The final shape may be rods for reinforced concrete, bar, structural shapes, rail, strip, sheet, plate, or skelp (plate for welding into pipe). A larger proportion of steel is rolled into sheet than into any other form, and sheet may be obtained in either the hot-rolled or cold-rolled condition. Hot-rolled sheet is cheaper and therefore more commonly used, and can be recognized by its black coat of mill scale. Cold-rolled sheet is rolled at lower temperature in the final pass. It has a bright finish but is less ductile and thus not suitable for more severe forming operations. The thinner gauges of sheet are only produced in the cold-rolled condition.

10.5 carbon in steel

The most important alloying ingredient in steel is carbon. This element is very potent in its effect on steel characteristics, and few steels contain more than 1 percent carbon. Those steels in which carbon is the only significant alloying element are termed carbon steels. Low carbon steel, also called mild steel, is produced in greater tonnages than all other steels combined. It is cheap, soft, remarkably ductile, and readily welded. It cannot be usefully heat-treated however. This is the material from which ships, tanks, pipe, car bodies, household appliances, bridges, culverts, and building frames are made.

Steels are designated according to their carbon contents in the following classification:

1. low carbon steel   0.03 to 0.30% carbon
2. medium carbon steel   0.35 to 0.55% carbon
3. high carbon steel   0.60 to 1.5% carbon
4. cast iron   over 2% carbon

The medium carbon steels are used for reinforcing rods for concrete, harrow teeth, shafting, and other components of agricultural implements and automobiles. High carbon steels are employed in knives, files, springs, concrete reinforcing bars, piano wire, hammers, axes, and chisels. Very low carbon is necessary in some steels, which are therefore virtually irons. These include many stainless steels, porcelain enamelling sheet, and some types of welding rods.

A small increase in the carbon content of a steel, even as little as a tenth of a percent, has a strong effect on all the properties of the steel. If the carbon content is increased, these are some of the effects:

1. the melting point of the steel is lowered
2. the steel becomes harder
3. the steel has a higher tensile strength
4. the steel is less ductile
5. the steel becomes more wear-resistant
6. the steel becomes less easily machined
7. the steel is more difficult to weld without cracking
8. the steel becomes heat-treatable
9. the steel is more expensive, due to the smaller volume of production

There is virtually no change in the modulus of elasticity with carbon content. If a mild steel and a high carbon steel are both loaded to the same stress, both will show the same strain. The higher carbon steel, however, will have a higher yield stress, higher tensile strength, and less elongation at rupture.

Carbon has a powerful effect on the melting point of steels. A pure iron melts at 2800°F. Increasing carbon reduces the melting point until at 4.3 percent carbon the melting point falls to 2065°F. The high melting point of pure iron makes severe demands on the refractory linings of steel melting furnaces and is one reason why pure iron is not in common use. By leaving a little carbon in the steel the melting point is lowered substantially, and so is the cost of the steel.

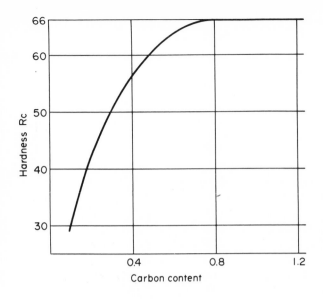

Fig. 98 Rockwell C hardness vs carbon content for carbon steels heat-treated to highest possible hardness.

The effect of carbon on the hardness of steel is shown in Fig. 98. The hardness of any steel may be varied by suitable heat treatments; this graph shows the hardest possible condition at any carbon content. The graph indicates that the maximum hardness is reached at 0.8 percent carbon. This raises the question of the purpose served in going to still higher carbon contents. Carbon above 0.8 percent gives increased wear-resistance of the steel, and is necessary in such tools as files, knives, wood-cutting tools, and hard-facing welding electrodes.

While carbon dissolves in molten steel, and in steel at red heats, only a few thousandths of a percent of carbon will dissolve in the space lattice of iron at room temperature. In steels cooled to room temperature the carbon is found to be combined with iron as iron carbide, Fe_3C, distributed through the steel. If a hard or wear-resistant steel is required, this is obtained by high carbon content to increase the amount of hard ceramic carbide.

An easily welded steel will have a low carbon content, and steels specially formulated for welding, such as tank and ship plate or welding

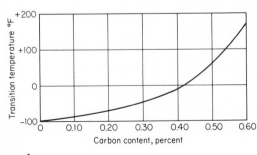

Fig. 99 Fifteen ft-lb Charpy transition temperature vs carbon content for plain carbon steel. Few standard steels will match the optimum performance shown in this graph.

steel
214

electrodes, will have only one or two tenths of a percent carbon. If, however, the steel must be heat-treatable, a minimum carbon of 0.3 percent is needed. This gives the minimum amount of carbides required for heat-treating purposes.

Figure 99 shows the performance of steels of different carbon contents under conditions of the Charpy impact test.

Figure 100 is the phase diagram for iron-carbon alloys. Notice that for a pure iron, the transformation temperature separating the fcc iron phase from the lower bcc iron phase is 1666°F. As the amount of carbon in the iron is increased, this transformation temperature falls, reaching 1333°F at 0.8 percent carbon. The fcc phase of steel is termed *austenite*, and the bcc phase termed *ferrite*. Since carbon enlarges the austenite range, it is an austenite promoter, at least up to 0.8 percent carbon. The composition 99.2 percent iron, 0.8 percent carbon, though in the solid state, corresponds to a liquid eutectic, in that it represents the lowest transformation temperature. It is referred to as the *eutectoid* composition. Steels containing less than 0.8 percent carbon are referred to as hypoeutectoid. Most carbon steels are hypoeutectoid. A carbon steel with 0.8 percent carbon is referred to as a eutectoid steel; greater carbon than this amount produces a hypereutectoid steel. When other alloying elements are added to steel, the eutectoid composition moves from the 0.8 percent position, usually to lesser carbon.

This transformation diagram of Fig. 100 is the basis for heat-treating of steels. Most heat treatments, either for hardening or softening the steel, require that the steel be first heated above the transformation temperature into the austenite phase, followed by cooling at some controlled rate — fast cooling for hardening, slow cooling for softening.

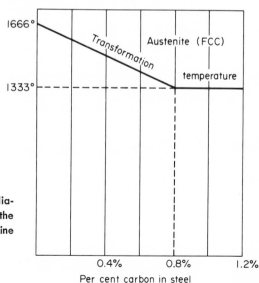

Fig. 100 Transformation diagram for carbon steels. Above the transformation temperature line steel is austenitic (bcc).

10.6 elements in steel other than carbon

The presence of minute amounts of hydrogen, oxygen, and nitrogen dissolved in the iron space lattice interstitially, even a few thousandths of a percent, is harmful, and promotes cracking, flaking, and brittleness. These elements are rarely used as alloying elements, though nitrogen is occasionally used as an austenite promoter in a few stainless steels.

Most of the alloying elements added to steels are metals. It is rather confusing to try to remember the specific effects of each element on the properties of steel. Instead, it is best to begin with the following simpler and more generalized approach to these matters.

By and large, all alloying elements fall into two groups. They either (1) dissolve in the iron space lattice by replacing iron atoms in substitutional solid solutions, or (2) form carbides with the carbon in the steel. A few elements such as manganese may show both tendencies, but even so one effect will predominate over the other, so that this simple approach is substantially true.

A second important effect of alloying elements must be borne in mind. One of the effects of carbon was austenite promotion, or the enlargement of the austenite range. Any alloying element must promote either austenite or ferrite. A ferrite promoter will reduce the austenite field and raise the transformation temperature; an austenite promoter such as carbon will do the reverse.

Silicon is used in small quantities to produce a killed steel. Larger silicon additions produce electric steels with higher electric resistance for such uses as transformer cores. Silicon dissolves in ferrite, replacing iron atoms in the space lattice. Since this means a change in interatomic distance where a silicon atom is located, the space lattice will be distorted and the metal will show higher tensile strength, higher hardness, and decreased ductility.

Aluminum is not added to steel except in small quantities for killing the steel and for producing a fine grain. The fine grain size produced by aluminum inoculation results in a tougher and somewhat stronger steel. Aluminum dissolves in ferrite and is a ferrite promoter, like silicon.

Nitrogen dissolves interstitially in the iron space lattice. It is an austenite promoter, and is added to certain stainless steels for this purpose.

Manganese is added to all steels to make them easier to roll, as previously discussed. Manganese dissolves in ferrite and is a powerful austenite promoter. The addition of 12 percent manganese results in a steel which is austenitic at room temperature.

The ferromagnetic metals *nickel* and *cobalt* both dissolve in the iron space lattice. Cobalt is used in high alloy steels such as the high speed steels and in heat-resisting alloy formulations. Nickel is one of the most important alloy additions to steels, and is used in a wide range of steels in amounts as little as 1 percent or as much as 50 percent. Like manganese, nickel is a powerful promoter of austenite; by adding sufficient amounts of either alloy, an austenitic steel at room temperature can be produced. Nickel improves most of the characteristics of steel, notably low-temperature toughness, heat resistance, and corrosion resistance. The most important high nickel austenitic steels are the 300 series stainless steels.

The above alloy additions all dissolve in ferrite. The following alloy metals do not dissolve in ferrite, at least to any notable degree, but tend rather to combine with carbon in the steel to form hard carbides. They are therefore usually associated with higher carbon contents. These metals are to be found chiefly in tool steels and hard-wearing steels. The carbide-formers also share the effect of decreasing the austenite field and raising the transformation temperature. This group includes the metals chromium, molybdenum, tungsten, vanadium, columbium, and titanium. Of these, titanium has the greatest affinity for carbon, though this metal is found in only a few steel alloys.

Columbium is added to a number of structural steels in very small amounts to increase the tensile strength. Typically, the addition of 0.02 percent Cb provides an increase of 10,000 to 15,000 psi in tensile strength.

Vanadium is not used in large amounts in any steel alloy. It promotes a fine-grained condition and increases strength. It is a frequent constituent of tool steels.

Both *tungsten* and *molybdenum* are used in large amounts, up to 18 percent, in high speed steels, and in lesser quantities in other types of hot-working steels, such as forging die steels. The presence of the carbides of these metals enables such steels to maintain hardness even at red heats.

Chromium is the most common of the carbide formers. Low alloy steels may contain as little as 1 percent chromium. In addition to providing hardness and strength, chromium in amounts of 12 percent or more produces the corrosion-resistant steels known as stainless steels. Corrosion resistance, however, is provided by chromium, not by chromium carbide. To avoid the formation of chromium carbides, those stainless steels which are not intended for heat-treatment have extremely low carbon content, and are really stainless irons.

Phosphorus, copper, lead, sulfur, and boron are used in certain special steels. Both phos and copper form substitutional solid solutions in the iron lattice and therefore have a strengthening effect. Phosphorus is added to produce a free-machining steel; copper gives corrosion resistance. Lead does not dissolve in steel, nor does it form carbides. It is distributed through free-machining steels in the form of microscopic globules. The only use for sulfur is likewise to produce a free-machining steel containing inclusions of manganese sulfide. Boron is added to steels in amounts of a few thousandths a percent to improve the hardenability of steels which are to be heat-treated. Too much boron, like too much phosphorus or sulfur, will make the steel impossible to roll.

10.7   industrial iron

Commercially pure iron has limited uses in industry. Armco iron is an iron of 0.01 percent carbon, which is used for its corrosion resistance in rolled products such as culverts. Iron, like any other metal, is more resistant to corrosion than its alloys. Iron powder is pressed and sintered in molds to produce finished small parts such as components of office machines.

A special type of iron that has been in use for centuries is *wrought iron*. This is an iron with slag stringers distributed through it, some of which are visible to the naked eye. These stringers are silicate slag, and form effective barriers to corrosion of the iron. Though not produced by the methods used in melting steels, wrought iron is rolled and shaped by the usual steel mill equipment, as its name suggests. Carbon content is minimal, rarely as high as 0.035 percent. The strength of wrought iron is lower than that of structural steels. When broken in flexure, it shows a fibrous break resembling a similar break in a piece of hardwood. Most wrought iron is formed into pipe.

Pure iron, like wrought iron, has an ultimate tensile strength less than that of steels, about 36,000 psi, which is the strength of the weldable grades of aluminum. Structural steels and mild steels have strengths from 60,000 psi up. Ductility of pure iron is unusually high, however, and its corrosion resistance superior to steel's.

10.8   cast steels and irons

While most steels are converted into wrought products, any steel may also be formed by casting; indeed all steels must first be cast into ingots before being rolled. About 2 percent of steel production goes into finished castings. While this is a small fraction of total steel consumption, steel castings are of critical importance in primary and heavy industry. The rolls used in rolling steel shapes are made of cast steel. Such complex shapes as pump casings and large valve bodies cannot be formed by any other economical method than casting.

While most steel castings are low carbon steels, nickel and other alloy steel castings are used for special purposes. Most heat-resistant and corrosion-resistant castings are made of stainless steel alloys. The high melting temperatures of steels require that steel castings be formed in sand molds, although it is a standard practice to use graphite molds for cast steel railroad wheels.

A steel containing in excess of 2 percent carbon is called an iron. Such steels have almost no ductility and must be shaped by casting.

Fig. 101 Micrograph of gray cast iron, showing graphite flakes in a pearlite structure.

The commonest type of cast iron is *gray cast iron*, containing about 3 to 3.5 percent carbon and over 1 percent silicon. These are relatively large amounts of both carbon and silicon. With so much carbon, all of the carbon cannot be taken up as iron carbide. A considerable fraction of the carbon separates out as long graphite flakes distributed through the cast iron, as illustrated in Fig. 101. These graphite flakes produce the characteristically dark appearance in a freshly broken surface of gray cast iron. The reason for the high silicon is that this element promotes such graphitization of the carbon.

Gray cast iron has almost no ductility, and if heated or cooled too rapidly it may crack. The graphite flakes make for some difficulty in welding, for it is not possible to make weld metal bond to graphite. Another of their effects is a lower modulus of elasticity, about 18×10^6 compared to about 30×10^6 for steel. A fourth deficiency of gray cast iron is its low tensile strength compared to steel. This is explained again by the graphite flakes, which have the effect of a network of cracks within the metal. The strength of graphite in cast iron is no better than its strength in a lead pencil.

However, gray cast iron is not without its virtues. It is a low-melting steel and easy to cast into complex shapes. It can withstand higher temperatures than steels without warping or oxidizing, even as high as 1000°F, hence its use for doors and other furnace parts. It is readily machinable due to the lubricating effect of graphite. The graphite network also provides a considerable degree of corrosion resistance. Still another advantage of cast iron is vibration-damping. The graphite network rapidly damps out vibra-

Fig. 102 A molybdenum ductile iron.

tions and "whip" in the metal, so that gray cast iron is frequently selected for crankshafts and machine bases.

Much gray cast iron is melted in foundry cupolas, which are miniature blast furnaces ranging from three to six feet in inside diameter. Cupolas are charged from the top with scrap iron, coke, and limestone. A better quality cast iron can usually be produced in an electric arc furnace such as is used for melting steel, or in an induction furnace.

Gray cast iron results from relatively slow cooling in the sand mold. Fast cooling by such methods as the use of steel or graphite "chills" (inserts) in the mold produces *white cast iron*. White cast iron is extremely hard and abrasion-resistant, unmachinable, and unweldable.

Nodular iron, also called ductile iron, is a special type of gray cast iron. This iron has a microstructure that overcomes many of the limitations of gray cast iron. When the iron is poured from the melting furnace or cupola into the ladle, it is inoculated with a small amount of magnesium. As a result of this treatment, the graphite takes a nodular (almost spherical) form. The result is a cast iron of considerable ductility and high tensile strength. The operation of inoculating the iron is one of the more dramatic routines of industry: a blinding white flare is produced.

Malleable iron is a cast iron which by special heat-treatment acquires a degree of ductility, 10 percent or more in a 2-in. gauge length. The graphite in malleable iron is somewhat nodular in shape.

Ni-Resist is a 15 percent nickel cast iron for corrosion resistance. For wear resistance, the alloy cast iron *Ni-Hard* is employed.

Low alloy steels are those steels containing not more than 5 percent of any alloying metal or metals. Such steels are used for applications requiring either extra toughness or higher strength. High alloy steels contain over 10 percent of alloying elements, and find their chief applications under conditions of wear, heat, and corrosion.

Until about twenty years ago, the method of building great strength into equipment was simply to make the equipment from heavier sections. This method is in general neither efficient nor economical, and indeed for an increasing number of products, not possible. The high strength required in the frame and skin of a supersonic aircraft cannot be obtained by indefinitely "beefing up" structural sections. If a truck body can be made lighter in weight by one ton through the use of high strength, low alloy steels, then an extra ton of revenue-producing payload can be carried on each truck haul for the life of the truck. Again, consider the case of a high-rise building of 50 stories. If the use of high strength, low alloy steel permits a reduction in the depth of floor beams of 2 in., then the total building height is reduced by over 8 ft. This represents 8 ft less of curtain wall covering the building

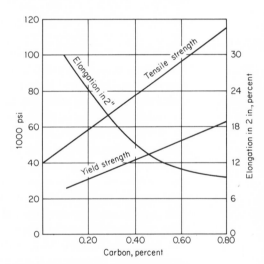

Fig. 103   Effect of carbon content on ultimate tensile strength, yield strength, and elongation on annealed hot-rolled steel.

of steel framing, of fireproofing, ducting, piping, insulation, and installation labor, not to mention lower foundation costs. In the final result, those 2 in. per story represent savings of many thousands of dollars after allowing for the slightly higher cost of the alloy steel.

These are the considerations that explain the growing popularity of low alloy steels. Every year sees a number of new steels introduced, and the number now available is perhaps confusingly large.

To sort out the whole field of low and high alloy steels in general, they can be grouped into six classes:

1. high strength, low alloy (HSLA) steels, chiefly used as construction steels in buildings, cranes, construction machinery, etc.
2. American Iron & Steel Institute (AISI) and Society of Automotive Engineers (SAE) steels, chiefly used as machine parts in automobiles, aircraft, and other machinery
3. alloy tool steels for tooling, either low alloy or high alloy
4. stainless steels
5. special heat-resisting steels
6. electric steels, chiefly alloyed with silicon or aluminum

10.10 high strength, low alloy steels

The standard structural steel in use for the last 60 years was simply called "structural steel". It was made to ASTM (American Society for Testing and Materials) standard A7. It was a low carbon steel, but the specification did not require the steel to have a definite chemical analysis. The specification laid down requirements for strength and ductility. Yield strength was 33,000 psi, ultimate tensile strength 60,000 psi, and elongation about 20 percent in a 2-in. gauge length, all these being minimum values. The design stress used with this steel was 20,000 psi.

The newer high strength, low alloy steels have made rapid inroads into the applications formerly filled by A7 steel. These are all "lean" steels, that is, very low in alloy content, with ultimate strengths as high as 120,000 psi. By keeping alloy additions lean, the cost increment over A7 steel is held to a minimum, and the steels do not raise any unusual difficulties for the welder, though the higher strength levels require the use of welding rods with commensurate strength. Such HSLA steels are rolled into plate, sheet, bar, and structural shapes.

To ensure toughness and weldability, the HSLA steels for construction purposes have carbon contents of 0.20 percent or less. The alloy formulation of these steels is arranged to give them maximum resistance to atmospheric corrosion, and occasionally such steels have been left unpainted. Of the wide range of these newer construction steels, over 300 brand names, perhaps the best known are "Cor-Ten" and "T-1". These two steels are typical of the HSLA steels as a group. They contain small amounts of the ferrite strengtheners, including manganese, silicon, nickel, and copper, and still lesser amounts of the carbide-formers, such as titanium, vanadium, and columbium.

These are machinery steels which have been catalogued by number by the American Iron and Steel Institute (AISI) and the Society of Automotive Engineers (SAE). An AISI 8620 is the same steel as SAE 8620. The steels have a number system which is in part descriptive of the alloy; although it seems simple in principle, the system is in practice a bit complicated, and only the bare bones of the scheme will be discussed here. For example, consider AISI 2345. The latter two digits, in this example xx45, always designate the carbon content, or 0.45 percent. The first two digits designate the alloy. In this example 2xxx indicates a nickel steel, and x3xx indicates approximately 3 percent nickel. A designation such as 10100, with five digits, would indicate 1.00 percent carbon or more. The basic digits in the system are the following:

10xx	plain carbon steels
11xx	sulfurized free-machining carbon steels
12Lxx	leaded free-machining steels
13xx	manganese 1.75%
23xx	nickel 3.50%
25xx	nickel 5.00%
3xxx	nickel-chromium steels (not stainless steels)
40xx	molybdenum 0.20–0.30%
41xx	low chromium-molybdenum
4xxx	nickel 1–4%, chromium to 0.55%, moly 0.20–0.30%
5xxx	up to 1% chromium
6xxx	low chrome-vanadium steels
7xxx	not used
8xxx	low nickel-chromium-molybdenum
9xxx	usually nickel-chromium with low molybdenum

The letter B in the middle of the number, such as 81B45, signifies a minimum of 0.0005 percent boron for hardenability.

The 2xxx and 3xxx series of AISI-SAE steels are no longer in common use. Most of the other steels of this series have a wide range of uses in automobiles, agricultural equipment, and aircraft. In general these steels are fabricated into small tools and hand tools, and machine components, including those of the family automobile. The following list is a selection of uses:

1010 and 1015	— steel tubing for general use
1022	— piston pins of automobiles
1040	— connecting rods of automobiles
1055	— gardening tools
1065	— spring wire
4140	— socket wrenches

4130	— small rocket motors
4340	— highly stressed aircraft parts, such as landing gear
52100	— ball and roller bearings
8620	— automobile gears and parts of universal joints

10.12 tooling and tool steels

The subject of tooling appears not to be well understood by personnel outside the field of production technology. Tooling is often confused with hand tools, which are not tooling, but are produced by tooling. The word "tooling" embraces the special equipment which is used to shape materials into finished components. Such equipment adapts the capacity of a production machine to the requirements of the part to be produced. A simple example of tooling is the combination of a punch and a die, which if mounted in a large press can produce holes in sheet metal or plastic.

Tooling materials are not consumed in massive tonnages, yet probably are the most critically important of the industrial materials, since without them almost nothing can be manufactured except by prohibitively expensive hand methods.

While it is possible for almost any industrial material to be used for tooling purposes, tooling materials are generally restricted to a relatively small group of materials. Dimensional stability is one of the dominant requirements for a tooling material, for without it, identical and interchangeable parts cannot be made. Most of the special tool materials are the select group of steels known as tool steels, but epoxies, polyurethane rubber, silicone rubber, magnesium plate, and cast irons serve useful functions in tooling, and these accessory additions to the toolmaker's repertory will be examined in their appropriate chapters.

The service requirements to be met by a tool steel may be most conveniently discussed in terms of punching 1,000,000 holes in 16-gauge mild steel sheet, not an especially demanding service for tool steels. The operation is performed on a punch press. In the punch press a standard tooling item called a standard die set is mounted. This is a pair of heavy steel plates carefully aligned, as shown in Fig. 86. The male punch is attached to the upper plate of the die set, the punch plate; the female die containing the hole is attached to the lower plate or die shoe. The rigidity of the die set ensures that the punch will always be aligned with the hole. Misalignment will break the punch.

Suppose the holes to be punched are 1 in. in diameter. To punch a hole, the steel sheet must be sheared all the way round the 1-in. periphery for a shearing length of 3.14 in. The sheet is 16-gauge, or approximately $\frac{1}{16}$ in. thick. The punch must therefore shear approximately $\frac{3}{16}$ sq in. of steel to produce the hole. The mild steel sheet has a shear strength of perhaps 45,000 psi. But there are friction and binding effects to account for, and to take care of these conditions the shear strength of the sheet is often taken to be the ultimate tensile strength, which perhaps is 60,000 psi. The total shearing force required to punch the hole is then

$$\frac{3}{16} \text{ sq in.} \times 60,000 \text{ psi} = 11,000 \text{ lb (approximately)}$$

The compressive strength of the punch material must support this force of 11,000 pounds, plus any bending force that the operation may produce in the punch. Similarly, the die must withstand the punching force of 11,000 pounds through thousands of cycles without any mushrooming of the material around the hole. The punch and the die must not fail in fatigue. Further, when the blank is punched out of the sheet, the sheet will grip the punch and must be stripped off it by a stripper plate. This stripper operation, together with the punching operation, will wear away the surface of the punch, so that the hole size will become smaller after some thousands of punching operations. Such wear must not be excessive, or the punched holes will in time become too small.

The material for both punch and die must be readily machinable during toolmaking operations, but must also be heat-treatable, for after the toolmaking both punch and die must be heat-treated to exactly the required hardness, toughness, and wear-resistance. Further, these tooling materials must not distort or alter their dimensions to an excessive degree during the phase changes involved in heat treatment.

Fig. 104 High-speed steel milling cutter notching a small workpiece. For this application the cutter material requires the property of hot hardness.

This example represents a very simple case of tooling, yet only a special steel can meet such service requirements. More severe standards of performance are demanded of hot forging dies, or dies used to form vinyl plastics (which are corrosive to steels), or wire-drawing or extruding dies subjected to extreme pressures. As tooling practices become ever more exacting, users of tool steels demand ever better performance from these materials. The chief complaints made against tool steels are probably these four:

1. they wear out in service too soon
2. they chip or break during use
3. they change size during heat-treating
4. they distort or crack during hardening

From the previous remarks it should be apparent that progress in materials technology is as dependent on tooling materials as on materials progress in general, for no material becomes significant until it can be reduced to useful shapes by economic methods. Currently machining progress is handicapped by our general inability to produce metal-cutting materials that meet the demands of machine shops.

The several classes of tool steels are classified by letter designation:

type W water hardening. High carbon steels
O oil hardening. Lean alloy steels
A air hardening. Medium alloy steels
S shock-resisting steels
H hot working steels
T high speed steels containing tungsten
M high speed steels containing molybdenum

The simplest of the tool steel alloys are the high carbon water-hardening steels. These, as their name suggests, are hardened by fast quenching with water. These have limited uses in cold-working operations, such as the shearing of leather and paper. Plain carbon steels are capable of great hardness, but begin to lose hardness at the very low temperature of 300°F, so that they are not suited even for drill bits for drilling metals. As a result, the general trend has been away from type W steels.

All the other groups of tool steels use for their alloying elements the carbide-forming elements tungsten, molybdenum, chromium, and vanadium. To supply sufficient carbides, the carbon content of such steels must necessarily be high. Carbon therefore may be as little as 0.4 percent or as high as 2.25 percent. The hot-working and high speed steels, which must operate at elevated temperatures, must be rich in carbides because these are refractory and relatively insensitive to temperature. Because they are very rich in carbides, these steels can be hardened by relatively slow cooling in

Fig. 105 Micrograph of a tungsten high speed steel, showing the distribution of tungsten carbides in the annealed state.

air. Figure 105 is a micrograph of a high speed steel, showing the dispersion of hard carbides throughout the steel. These are largely tungsten carbides, since the steel contains 18 percent tungsten.

Shock-resisting steels are used in applications where toughness and shock resistance are paramount requirements. They are made into punches, chisels, pneumatic tools, and shear blades. These steels contain carbide formers, silicon to strengthen the ferrite, and sometimes manganese or nickel for increased toughness.

The oil-hardening type O steels are considered the most important group of tool steels because of their wide range of applications. Carbon content is about 1 percent, with about 0.5 percent chromium and 0.5 percent or more tungsten.

Type H hot-working steels are employed in forging dies, aluminum extrusion dies, and die-casting dies for plastics. These are medium carbon alloy steels, with 5 percent chromium or several percent tungsten.

The high speed steels earned their odd name in earlier days when they were substituted for carbon steel cutter bits on machine tools. They permitted the cutting speed of the machine tool to be greatly increased without losing their cutting edge. These steels can maintain their hardness to temperatures as high as 1200°F, which is a dull red heat. Originally the high speed steels were type T (tungsten), but in late years molybdenum has tended to displace tungsten. Molybdenum is not so heavy as tungsten, yet forms an equal amount of carbide, and steels of course are sold by weight, thus making molybdenum cheaper. A very high alloy, high speed steel may contain 18.5 percent W, 4 percent Cr, 1 percent V, 4 percent Co, and 0.8 percent carbon. Nowadays these steels can no longer meet the most stringent demands of the machining industries, which are better served by sintered carbide cutters.

Some of the hot-working tool steels have found occasional use in gas turbine engines as turbine blading by reason of their hot-hardness and hot-strength. Another alloy used both as a hot-working tool material and as a heat-resisting material is *stellite*. It is not a steel, as its name suggests, but a cobalt alloy. It is very hard, and is formed only by casting and grinding.

10.13   stainless steels

Heat-resistant alloy steel castings, designated type H, and corrosion-resistant alloy steel castings, designated type C, may be thought of as types of cast stainless steel. For improvement of both heat and corrosion resistance, generally the nickel content of these casting alloys must be increased, up to a maximum of 66 percent nickel. Such cast alloys are used in gas turbine engines and afterburners, discharge ends of cement kilns, fixtures and baskets for furnaces and heat-treating operations, furnace dampers, burner nozzles, centrifugal pumps, and agitators for mixing of chemicals.

Perhaps the most useful remark that can be made about the large group of stainless steels is that a little knowledge of these materials is of little value and is a cause of some regrettable errors in materials selection. The stainless steels are often viewed as the panacea for all steel ills. When an ordinary steel fails in service, a stainless steel may be substituted. Sometimes the substitution is successful, but there are occasions when the stainless steel does not perform as well as the previous material. Pious faith is not a desirable mental habit in materials selection.

Certainly the stainless steel group has some interesting characteristics. They even affect the relationship between the sexes. Consider the stainless steel kitchen knife. The wife likes it because it doesn't rust when left in the dishpan. The husband dislikes it because it doesn't keep its edge. Stainless steels are poor tool steels, an argument to which the female sex is impervious.

The use of stainless steels has been growing at a more rapid rate than that of most other steels. Annual consumption of stainless steels in the

United States is now about a million tons. These are somewhat costly steels, but their advantages and market acceptance outweigh their additional cost in a wide range of applications, such as kitchen knives. The stainless steels are a group of low carbon high alloy steels which offer the advantages of attractive appearance, low maintenance, great corrosion resistance against oxidizing chemicals (but not reducing chemicals or chlorides), oxidation resistance, and high strength and toughness at extreme temperatures. However, these are heavy steels: there is a double price premium in the higher cost per pound and the higher specific weight.

Thermal conductivity of the stainless steels is one-third that of carbon steels. Thermal stresses are therefore a more serious consideration when designing with stainless steel. The low thermal conductivity also makes these steels more damaging to machining cutters through inability to remove the heat generated during machining. The nickel-chromium grades have an expansion coefficient about a third higher than that of carbon steels, and produce more warping during welding operations.

The stainless steels, like the tool steels and construction steels, are not included in the AISI-SAE steel coding system. Instead, the stainless steels have a numbering code of their own which uses three digits instead of four. Neglecting a few 200 and 500 series stainless steels, all stainless steel compositions are assigned numbers in either the 300 or 400 range. The first step in understanding the characteristics of these steels is to differentiate clearly between the 300 and 400 groups. The second step is to break the 400 series into two groups, heat-treatable and not heat-treatable. The third step is to become acquainted with some of the more common grades in these groups.

The stainless steels may be summed up as very low carbon irons with a minimum of 12 percent chromium, although stainless 501 and 502, used in the oil industry where a lesser degree of corrosion resistance suffices, contain 4 to 6 percent chromium. The corrosion and heat resistance of these steels may be considered proportional to the chromium content, which for extreme service conditions may be as high as 35 percent. Unlike the high speed steels, this heat resistance of the stainless steels does not depend on the presence of carbides, but upon chromium metal itself uncombined with carbon. Chromium quickly acquires a thin skin of tightly adherent chromium oxide which blocks corrosion or oxidation of the stainless steel.

All stainless steels have considerably higher strengths than low carbon steel. A mechanical shear rated for $\frac{1}{4}$-in. steel plate will not safely cut $\frac{1}{4}$ in. of stainless steel, as is repeatedly proved by numbers of broken shears across the country.

The 400 series are straight chromium steels. The 300 series are chromium-nickel low carbon steels. Many of the 300 series contain approximately 18 percent chromium and 8 percent nickel, and used to be referred to as "18-8" stainless. This practice is hardly to be recommended.

10.14   the 300 series
stainless steels

The peculiarities of the 300 series may be thus summed up:

1. they are low carbon, none containing more than 0.25% carbon
2. almost all contain 16–20% chromium, 8–13% nickel
3. they are austenitic, face-centered cubic, paramagnetic
4. they are not heat-treatable
5. they work-harden when formed, shaped, or cut
6. they have an expansion coefficient a third higher than carbon steels

Because of work-hardening effects, these steels are machined with slow speeds and deep cuts to get underneath the work-hardened layer.

The most interesting and most used 300 series steels can now be discussed.

302.   This was the first of the stainless steels to come into common use, about 50 years ago, and is familiar in such articles as stainless steel sinks, restaurant and hospital equipment. Because of the high (for stainless steels) carbon content, 0.15 percent, there is a tendency to replace 302 with 304 nowadays. The harmful effects of carbon in 300 stainless steels will be discussed presently. This steel also contains 17–19 percent Cr and 8–10 percent Ni.

304.   This steel is identical to 302 except that its carbon content is 0.08 percent maximum. This is a general-purpose 300 stainless steel.

301 and 305.   The 300 series austenitic stainless steels all have an elongation of about 55 percent in a 2-in. gauge length. In sheet form therefore these steels are suitable for drawing and forming operations. However they work-harden rapidly and often require annealing (softening) between and after forming operations. Type 301, used for wheel covers on automobiles, has an unusually high elongation of 60 percent in 2 in. Where work-hardening is a problem, type 305 is employed. This alloy has an increased nickel content, 10–13 percent, to produce a lower work-hardening rate.

303 and 303Se.   These are free-machining grades. Type 303 contains 0.15 percent sulfur or more; type 303Se contains about 0.25 percent selenium.

308.   Type 308 is used in stainless steel welding rods. In Sec. 10.3 it was noted that there is a loss of chromium due to oxidation when steel is melted. The same loss will occur during fusion welding. Type 308 therefore contains a little extra chromium to compensate for chromium loss in welding operations.

316. This alloy contains 2–3 percent molybdenum for greater resistance to the attack of acids. This steel is used in the meat packing, food, and pulp and paper industries for such equipment as pumps, piping, and valves. In addition, the internal fittings of automatic control valves and other control instruments are often made of type 316.

304L and 316L. These are low carbon grades, maximum carbon 0.03 percent.

321, 347, 348. Type 321 contains a small amount of titanium; type 347, columbium or tantalum. Type 348, a variant of 347, is suited to the nuclear power industry. Its content of tantalum and hafnium (hafnium always accompanies columbium as an impurity) is held to low levels because of the high neutron absorption cross-section of these two metals. The explanation for the use of these three steels is given below.

THE AUSTENITIC STAINLESS STEELS

Type	C	Cr	Ni	Mn	Other
301	0.15 max	16–18	6–8	2	—
302	0.15 max	17–19	8–10	2	—
303	0.15 max	17–19	8–10	2	sulfur
304	0.08 max	18–20	8–10	2	—
305	0.12 max	17–19	10–13	2	—
308	0.08 max	19–21	10–12	2	—
316	0.08 max	16–18	10–14	2	2–3% Mo
321	0.08 max	17–19	9–12	2	titanium
347	0.08 max	17–19	9–13	2	Cb + Ta

If the 300 series steels are heated to or used in the range 800–1600°F, there is a rapid combination of chromium and carbon to form chromium carbides. These carbides tend to precipitate in the region of the grain boundaries of the stainless steels, and the effect is called carbide precipitation. Such loss of chromium impairs the corrosion resistance of the steel. There may be only 0.1 percent carbon in the stainless steel, yet this small amount of carbon can combine with a relatively large amount of chromium. Carbide precipitation can occur, for example, even in welding these steels. Carbide precipitation is significant only if corrosion resistance is significant; it would not be a matter of concern in stainless steel architectural facings on a bank building, or a stainless steel kickplate on a door.

One obvious method of preventing carbide precipitation is to employ the minimum possible carbon content. That is the explanation for the low-carbon grades 304L, 316L, 308L, etc. A second method is to add to the steel an alloy ingredient with a greater affinity for carbon than chromium has. Of all the metals, titanium has the strongest affinity for carbon. Type 321 contains titanium, so that the carbides precipitated in this steel are titanium carbides, leaving the chromium for corrosion resistance. However, this solution raises another problem. If 321 steel were to be arc-welded with 321 welding rods, all the titanium in the welding rod would be oxidized in the arc and none would be deposited in the joint. For this reason 321 welding rods are not available. Type 321 steel is welded with type 347 welding rods in which columbium is substituted for titanium and serves the same purpose as titanium.

10.15   the 400 series

stainless steels

The 400 series stainless steels contain no nickel. The absence of nickel, the austenite promoter, and the presence of chromium, a ferrite promoter, indicate that these steels cannot be austenitic. They are ferromagnetic and do not work-harden to an unusual degree. These steels do not possess quite the high levels of corrosion and heat resistance that characterize the richer 300 series. The 400 series actually includes two groups of steels, *martensitic* and *ferritic*.

Martensite is the hard phase of steel resulting from the fast quenching of carbides, and the word martensitic implies that a steel may be heat-treated. Martensitic stainless steels contain more carbon and during heat-treatment form chromium carbides. They are used for machine parts that must combine some degree of corrosion resistance with high strength levels. The most commonly used martensitic stainless steels are 410 and 416, containing 0.15 percent maximum carbon; others may contain as much as 1 percent carbon. Type 420, with 0.20 percent carbon or higher, is used for stainless cutlery.

The ferritic stainless steels cannot be heat-treated. They are low carbon, high chromium irons containing 16 percent or more chromium, commonly used in sheet form. Type 430 is used as a stainless steel chimney liner.

The 300 series, being austenitic (face-centered cubic), remain notch-tough down to absolute zero. On the other hand, the 400 series have poor impact strength at low temperatures. In the annealed (soft) condition the 300 series are slightly stronger (about 90,000 psi) and have greater ductility than the 400 series.

The two 200 series stainless steels 201 and 202 are interesting in that 0.25 percent nitrogen is substituted for nickel as an austenite promoter. These two steels substitute for 301 and 302.

10.16 maraging and 12 percent manganese steels

The maraging steels (pronounced "mar-aging") are a recent discovery but are rapidly finding new applications, especially in the aerospace industry. These are extremely low carbon iron-nickel alloys with a minimum of 18 percent nickel (manganese may be substituted), about 9 percent cobalt, 3 percent molybdenum, and small amounts of titanium and aluminum. Until the introduction of the maraging steels, it was not possible to heat-treat steels to tensile strength levels beyond 225,000 psi, because higher strengths were accompanied by dangerously low ductility. The maraging steels can be heat-treated to 300,000 psi and still retain minimum ductility, which is generally considered to be about 10 percent in a 2-in. gauge length.

Another steel of remarkable characteristics is 12 percent manganese steel, also called Hadfield manganese steel. This contains about 1 percent carbon besides the high manganese. Manganese, like nickel, is an austenite promoter, and this steel contains sufficient manganese to be austenitic at room temperature, like the 300 group of stainless steels. The austenitic steels work-harden more rapidly than other metals, and Hadfield manganese steel has remarkable work-hardening ability. It is used for such applications as excavator teeth, rock crushers, railroad frogs, and hard-surfacing welding rods, where constant battering will continually harden the steel. The work-hardening tendency is so powerful that the steel is virtually unmachinable, and must be formed by casting and grinding.

PROBLEMS

1 It is not impossible to produce stainless steel alloys in a basic oxygen converter. What might be the chief difficulty in this process, however?

2 What is the source of heat in an oxygen converter?

3 Why is the steel industry losing interest in the open-hearth furnace?

4 Explain the need for double-slagging in the melting of some steels.

5 Why is sulfur generally harmful in steels?

6 How does manganese overcome the harmful effect of sulfur in steel?

7 What advantage does vacuum degassing of steel offer?

8 What general characteristics are required of tool steels?

9 What purpose does chromium serve in a tool steel? in a stainless steel?

10 What are the general differences between 300 and 400 stainless steels with respect to:
(a) alloy content
(b) crystal structure
(c) magnetic properties
(d) low-temperature behavior
(e) work-hardening characteristics?

11 Why is a 304 stainless superior to 302 in a weldment? Why is 304L still better in this respect?

12 Account for the use of 308 stainless alloy in manual welding rods.

13 Why is 321 stainless not available in manual welding rods?

14 What influence does the graphite network have on the properties of gray cast iron?

15 What is a high speed steel?

16 What is meant by "carbide precipitation" in austenitic stainless steels?

17 For what uses is a Hadfield manganese steel suited?

11.1 metallography

Heat-treatment refers to the heating and cooling operations performed on a metal, a plastic, or a ceramic, for the purpose of changing its properties. Such property changes arise as a result of microstructural changes in the material. In the case of metals, some of these changes are on a sufficiently large scale to be observed under a microscope, though a few are not. Those microstructural changes that are not visible through the microscope may be observed by some of the techniques outlined in Chapter 17, such as X-ray or similar types of analysis.

The microscopic study of metals is called *metallography*, and has been one of the most important contributors to advances in metallurgy. Metallographic examination of a metal discloses a wealth of information quickly and economically, including such details as carbon content, grain size, identification of the metal, defects, inclusions, and its previous fabrication and heat-treatment history. Metallography is the detective work of the broad field of metallurgy.

Little of significance is disclosed by looking at a piece of unprepared metal under a microscope, however. To disclose the microstructure, the metal sample must first be carefully polished by suitable techniques, then etched in a suitable corrodent. The corrodent attacks the different microconstituents in the metal at different rates and attacks also the grain boundaries. As a result the separate grains are disclosed in outline and the different constituents appear in different colors or different shades of black, white, or gray. Thus in Fig. 105 the carbides in the steel appear dark due to the etch.

MICROSTRUCTURE
AND
HEAT-TREATMENT OF METALS

11

11.2 recrystallization and annealing

Above the transformation temperature carbon steel is in the austenite phase. When steel in the ferrite phase is heated into the austenite region, the original ferrite grains must be replaced with austenite grains. The new grains nucleate at grain boundaries or other regions of high energy concentration, and as heating continues, the grains grow to a size visible under the microscope, gradually consuming the original grain structure. If the heating is stopped at an early period, a fine-grained structure results, and except for metals to operate at high temperatures, this type of structure is the most desirable one for both highest strength and highest notch toughness. Prolonging the heating period will promote larger grains.

Now any metal can be made to recrystallize in the above fashion, even without a phase change, if it has previously been plastically deformed. The recrystallization temperature is defined as the lowest temperature at which grains free of the previous distortion stresses appear in the microstructure of the previously plastically-deformed metal. The recrystallization temperature is subject to many influences, the principal ones being these:

1. the severity of the plastic deformation
2. the temperature at which plastic deformation occurs
3. the presence of alloying elements and inclusions

Figure 106 shows the effect of prior deformation on the recrystallization temperature of low carbon steel. For zero plastic deformation the recrystallization temperature corresponds to the transformation temperature; increasing deformation lowers the recrystallization temperature.

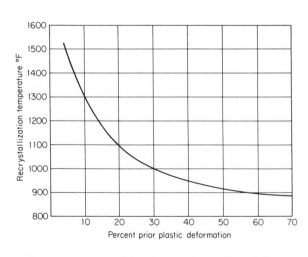

Fig. 106 Effect of plastic deformation on the recrystallization temperature of a low carbon steel.

lead	below 70°F	nickel	1110°
zinc	70°	molybdenum	1650°
aluminum	300°	tantalum	1830°
copper	390°	tungsten	2200°
iron	840°		

The above table suggests that minimum recrystallization temperatures are approximately proportional to melting points. It should be noted that the recrystallization temperature imposes some kind of a service temperature ceiling upon a metal. If the metal part is operated above its recrystallization temperature, it will tend to recrystallize into a single-grained metal part, a condition of great weakness and brittleness.

Plastic deformation followed by recrystallization provides a method of obtaining grain refinement in metals and alloys which do not undergo a phase change. The recrystallization serves also as an anneal, which is a relaxation or stress relief for deformation stresses.

11.3   annealed carbon steel

Below the transformation temperature, there are two constituents observable in hypoeutectoid (less than 0.8 percent carbon) carbon steel: iron which is called *ferrite* (bcc), and iron carbide, Fe_3C, which is called *cementite*. Figure 107a shows the appearance of ferrite under the microscope. Cementite contains 6.67 percent carbon. All the carbon in the steel can be considered to be taken up as cementite, since at room temperature only a few thousandths of a percent of carbon is dissolved interstitially in ferrite.

The cementite is found in grains of *pearlite* in a peculiar fashion. Pearlite grains are alternate laminations of ferrite and cementite. Figure 107b shows an AISI 1080 plain carbon steel. This steel contains only pearlite grains, the only ferrite present being in the laminations.

The amount of pearlite in a hypoeutectoid carbon steel is proportional to the carbon content. A pure iron can have no pearlite since it has no carbon or iron carbide. The composition of pearlite is 0.8 percent carbon, the eutectoid percentage. Therefore a steel with 0.8 percent carbon will show 100 percent pearlite under the microscope, like Fig. 107b. A steel with 0.4 percent carbon will be 50 percent pearlite and 50 percent ferrite. The metallurgist can thus estimate the carbon content of a carbon

microstructure and heat-treatment of metals

237

Fig. 107 (a)   Ferrite

Fig. 107 (b)   Pearlite

Fig. 107 (c)   Martensite

steel by a glance into the microscope and an estimate of the fraction of pearlite present. The method obviously is not applicable to hypereutectoid steels, but since these are less used, they will not be discussed.

We can now turn to the heat-treating processes of hardening and softening steels. Softening is called *annealing*, though annealing often has the additional purpose of stress-relieving. In annealing, a steel is first heated about 50°F above the transformation temperature (also called the critical temperature), held at that temperature a sufficient time to dissolve carbides in the austenite, then allowed to cool slowly in the furnace. The structure of an annealed steel is the mixture of pearlite and ferrite just discussed. This is the softest condition of steel and the condition in which steel usually is supplied to buyers by the steel mill or the warehouse. A brief scrutiny of Fig. 100 will reveal that the annealing temperature of a carbon steel can be closely estimated from the carbon content.

11.4   hardening of carbon steels

To harden a steel, the metal is heated to about 50° above the transformation temperature, held at that temperature for a sufficient time to dissolve carbides in the austenite, then quenched rapidly in water or oil. The difference between hardening and annealing therefore is entirely in the cooling rate after austenitizing. Because of the rapid cooling rate of hardening, there is not sufficient time for the austenite solution to dissociate into the usual ferrite and cementite. What comes down with sufficiently rapid cooling is a supersaturated solution of carbon atoms interstitially trapped in a body-centered tetragonal structure of iron. This suddenly frozen solution is called *martensite*. The microstructure of martensite is shown in Fig. 107c; it resembles a loose pile of straw in appearance.

The transformation from austenite to martensite does not occur at the transformation temperature between ferrite and austenite. Instead the martensite transformation occurs over a *range of temperature*. Austenite may begin to transform to martensite at 800°F for a low alloy steel. As the temperature continues to fall, more martensite is formed, until at room temperature the structure of the steel may be 99 percent martensite and 1 percent austenite. Complete transformation probably never occurs. With greater alloying additions to the steel, the temperature at which the martensite transformation begins is lowered, and the transformation may be less complete at room temperature. In a high speed steel, martensite may not begin to appear until a temperature of 600°F is reached, and at room temperature perhaps only 80 percent of the austenite will have transformed. Similarly, an austenitic stainless steel is austenitic by virtue of the fact that the temperature of initial transformation to martensite lies below room temperature.

The temperature at which the transformation to martensite begins is designated M_s. One of the many formulas for determining M_s is the following. Percentages of the various elements are substituted for the symbols in the formula.

$$M_s = 930-570C-60Mn-50Cr-30Ni-20Si-20Mo-20W$$

Note that all alloy elements in steel have the effect of lowering the M_s temperature.

The transformation to martensite ceases if cooling is interrupted, and will proceed further if cooling is resumed. Changing the cooling rate, say from oil-hardening to air-hardening, does not change the M_s temperature.

The hardness of martensite depends on the amount of carbon in the steel, that is, on the amount of carbides, as shown by Fig. 98. Thus the maximum hardness obtainable in a steel is built into the steel at the mill, and cannot be changed by the fabricator. The fabricator may, however, carburize or case-harden the exterior of the steel by allowing extra carbon to diffuse into the steel.

Certain tool steels will harden at relatively slow rates of cooling. These are called air-hardening steels. Air-hardening characteristics are obtained by the use of large amounts of carbide-formers such as chromium, tungsten, or molybdenum.

Martensite is hard and brittle, with no ductility, so that there is always danger of cracking due to thermal stresses. Worse still, there is a volume expansion when martensite forms. The part of the steel that is cooling but not transforming is contracting, while the fraction that is transforming is

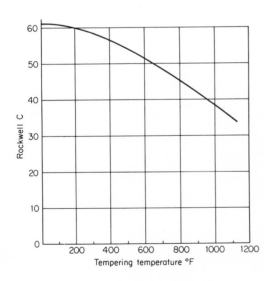

Fig. 108 Hardness vs tempering temperature for a water-quenched machinery steel with 0.4 percent carbon and 1.25 percent nickel. (Atlas Steels SPS)

microstructure and heat-treatment of metals

expanding. This makes for dangerous cracking possibilities, either during cooling or soon after the quenching operation. To prevent cracking, tempering is done immediately after hardening.

Tempering, or drawing, is a softening and toughening heat treatment performed immediately after hardening. Almost always the steel is drawn back to a hardness of R_C 60 or less from the original hardness of martensite, R_C 65. To temper a hardened steel, it is heated to some temperature below the transformation temperature, in the range of 300–1200°F. Since the transformation temperature is not passed, the rate of cooling back to room temperature is not significant. The higher the tempering temperature, the softer and tougher the steel will be. The effect of tempering temperature on the hardness of a carbon steel is shown in Fig. 108.

The purpose of tempering may be understood by contrasting it with hardening. In hardening, we obtain the maximum possible hardness in a steel, but no toughness or ductility. In tempering, we "sell" some of this hardness in order to buy toughness. If a great deal of toughness is required, then much of the hardness must be given up. If toughness is not especially critical, as in a scriber for marking metal, then most of the hardness can be retained, and we may temper simply for the purpose of relieving the hardening stresses, which may cause later cracking of the steel.

Tempering is a well-known operation because of the beautiful colors that appear on carbon steels at various tempering temperatures. These colors do not always appear on alloy steels. The list below shows how colors serve as a built-in thermometer:

straw yellow	400°F
brown	460
bright purple	500
dark blue	550
loss of temper color	700

There are no further temper colors until the temperature of the steel reaches about 1200°F, when a dull red heat begins to show. This is the start of the red-hot range. The colors result from the formation of transitory oxide films on the steel surface.

Tempering is actually a stress-relieving operation, but is not called stress-relieving unless the tempering temperature is taken above 1100°F, specifically for the stress-relieving of weldments or machined parts.

Tempering and annealing are both softening operations. However, tempering does not involve a phase change. Further, tempering is performed only after a hardening operation, and its purpose is not to soften but to toughen.

The heat-treating of carbon steels containing 0.9 percent or more carbon follows somewhat different procedures from these, and will not be discussed here.

11.5   normalizing

Normalizing is a heat treatment somewhat similar to annealing. In annealing, the steel is taken slightly above the critical temperature and then furnace-cooled or otherwise cooled very slowly. In normalizing, the steel is heated about 100°F above the critical temperature and then cooled in air. Hence the cooling rate for normalizing is between the cooling rates for hardening and for annealing. The purpose of normalizing is to produce a harder and stronger steel than annealing can produce and to refine the grain. Certainly the grain size of the steel ought to be finer with the faster cooling rate provided by a normalizing treatment. The microstructure of a normalized steel resembles that produced by annealing, except that the laminar structure of the pearlite grains is no longer visible under the microscope.

11.6   summary of the microconstituents of steel

The principal microconstituents of steel have been discussed at some length. The following list briefly summarizes them.

1. Ferrite. Essentially pure iron, body-centered cubic, soft, ductile
2. Cementite. Iron carbide, Fe_3C, 6.67% carbon, hard and brittle
3. Pearlite. Laminar ferrite and cementite, 0.8% carbon
4. Martensite. Interstitial carbon atoms in body-centered tetragonal iron. Hard and brittle quenched steel
5. Austenite. Ductile face-centered cubic iron existing above the transformation temperature

A heat-treatable steel must have two characteristics:

1. It must undergo a phase change across a transformation temperature.
2. It must contain carbides, either iron carbide or alloy carbides. Plain carbon steels with less than about 0.3 percent carbon have insufficient carbides to make possible any significant heat-treating effects.

All steels contain fractional percentages of silicon and manganese, but in small amounts these two elements are not important influences on the heat-treating characteristics of steels. Most of the other alloying additions made to heat-treatable steels are carbide-formers, and influence the heat treatment procedures.

The basic heat-treating theory of the plain carbon steels is somewhat complex. When this theory is extended to the alloy steels, the basic operations of hardening, annealing, and so on remain, and there are no new phases to consider beyond those already set out. For the alloy steels however, the heat-treating processes are somewhat modified.

Nickel and manganese lower the transformation temperature of a steel, both elements being austenite promoters. If these elements are present in sufficient amounts, the transformation temperature becomes so low that the steel becomes austenitic at room temperature, as in the case of Hadfield manganese steel and the 300 series stainless steels. The carbide-formers, titanium, chromium, etc. move the transformation temperature to ranges higher than those indicated in Fig. 100. Large amounts of tungsten, for example, move the transformation temperature to about 2000°F, as in the case of the high speed steels, some of which must be heated to 2400°F for heat-treating. Another effect of carbide-forming elements is more advantageous, in that the transformation to martensite can be made more slowly: by the addition of over 5 percent of carbide-formers the steel becomes an air-hardening steel. This much less severe type of quench reduces the risk of cracking. A third effect is the lower M_s temperature.

The carbide-forming elements such as tungsten and chromium have strong effects also on the tempering behavior of alloy steels. Figure 108 indicates that a carbon steel progressively softens as its tempering temperature increases — as is proven whenever a carbon steel drill bit becomes overheated. The presence of considerable amounts of carbide-formers, however, produces a tempering curve such as the one in Fig. 109. The

Fig. 109 Secondary hardness developed in tempering to 1000°F. The steel is a high-speed steel consisting of 1.30 percent C, 9.5 percent W, 5.2 percent Mo, 3.5 percent V, 4.3 percent Cr, 10 percent Co.

alloy steel may not soften at all until a temperature of 1000°F is reached, or it may actually increase in hardness in the region of 900°F. This highly advantageous effect is called "secondary hardening", and is explained as follows. The addition of large amounts of carbide-forming alloys reduces the start of martensite transformation and is a cause of incomplete transformation of austenite to martensite by the time room temperature is reached. On tempering to a high temperature such as 900°F, a temperature is reached at which the mobility of the constituents of the steel is improved, and the untransformed austenite completes its transformation to martensite, with increased hardness.

While nickel and manganese enlarge the austenite region, the carbide-formers restrict the austenite field. Chromium is one of the more common alloying additions to steel, and its effect on the austenite region may be considered typical. The effect is shown in Fig. 110. The lines marked 0 percent Cr are the boundaries of the austenite field for a plain carbon steel.

Fig. 110 Effect of chromium on the austenite range.

A steel may be hardened or annealed from any temperature within this austenite area, but only the lowest possible temperatures within the field are used, those just above the critical temperature, in order to prevent grain growth, scale formation, and loss of carbon by oxidation (decarburization). With the addition of 5 percent chromium, several effects are produced. The eutectoid carbon composition is moved from 0.8 percent to 0.5 percent carbon. The transformation temperature is increased to about 1500°F. Finally, the whole austenite region is narrowed. For example, there is no austenite region for 5 percent chromium and 1.4 percent carbon, which means that such a steel could not be heat-treated.

The next boundary shown is for 12 percent chromium. Again, the austenite region is reduced in area, the transformation temperature is raised to the neighborhood of 1600°F, and the austenite region pinches out at about 0.9 percent carbon. Type 410 stainless steel contains 12 percent chromium and 0.15 percent carbon. The diagram shows that this steel can be hardened, since it has an austenite region.

Going next to the boundary for a 15 percent chromium steel, it will be noted that a steel containing 15 percent chromium, 0.15 percent carbon, and no other alloying elements would not be martensitic (heat-treatable). The austenite region is being pinched out on both the left-hand and the right-hand side. Finally, the boundaries for a 19 percent chromium steel show that the austenite region has nearly disappeared; if such a steel is to be hardened, the carbon content must be very closely controlled, and so must the heat-treating temperature. Type 430 stainless steel, containing 14–18 percent chromium and a maximum of 0.12 percent carbon, is without an austenite region and the accompanying transformation temperature. This is a ferritic stainless steel and cannot be hardened, at least not by heat treatment.

Because chromium raises the transformation temperature, all the martensitic stainless steels have hardening temperatures in the range of 1700–1850°F. The ferritic stainless steels (type 430, etc.) cannot be hardened because they lack an austenite phase. Only the martensitic stainless steels have two phases separated by a transformation temperature, and only these stainless steels are hardenable. The 300 series austenitic stainless steels, however, may be work-hardened by deformation. The explanation for this effect is the transformation due to strain effects of a small amount of austenite to martensite.

11.8 heat-treatment of nonferrous metals

To reiterate, those steels are heat-treatable which provide the two requirements of carbides and a transformation temperature. While no nonferrous metal offers the wide heat-treating possibilities of steel (of which only the basic methods are discussed in these pages), some of the nonferrous alloys are heat-treatable. While the heat-treating approach is different from that of steels, there are similarities. A phase change is required for heat-treating, as well as an alloy ingredient which will deposit in different forms or phases, such as carbon does in steel.

No pure metal can be heat-treated, just as pure iron is not heat-treatable, although pure metals if work-hardened can be reannealed. Most nonferrous alloys do not undergo a suitable phase transformation on heating, while for others the phase transformation is too close to the melting point of the metal to be of practical use for heat-treating purposes. For such metals and alloys, heat-treating in order to change the hardness, strength, or ductility is not possible. The only hardening methods available in such cases are cold-working and alloying, though alloying is not a method available to the fabricator.

There is only one industrial alloy of importance that can be heat-treated in a manner similar to steel. This is aluminum bronze with a composition of approximately 10 percent aluminum and 90 percent copper. With furnace cooling this alloy gives an annealed structure like pearlite, and may be quenched to a martensitic structure for strength and hardness.

The more important of the heat-treatable nonferrous alloys, besides aluminum bronze, include the following:

copper with 2% beryllium
aluminum with 4% copper
zinc alloys of aluminum
aluminum alloys of magnesium
certain alloys of nickel

The method of hardening these alloys is termed *precipitation hardening* or *age-hardening*. Like other metals, heat-treatable or not, these alloys may also be softened by annealing. Two stages are involved in producing the hardening effect: *solution heat-treatment* and *aging*. The method of precipitation hardening will be explained here in terms of the aluminum alloy 2024, also named 24S, a high strength aluminum containing 4.5 percent copper plus lesser constituents.

It is a familiar fact that water dissolves more sugar as the temperature is raised. This is also true of many solid solutions of one metal in another, though certainly not true of all such solutions. More carbon can be dissolved interstitially in body-centered cubic iron at high temperatures (a maximum of 0.025 percent) than at room temperature (0.008 percent). This is also the case with the 4.5 percent copper in 2024 aluminum. Figure 111 is a part of the equilibrium diagram for copper alloys of aluminum. At 1018°F aluminum can dissolve a maximum of 5.65 percent copper. On cooling, aluminum can dissolve progressively less copper, as shown by the phase boundary displacing to the left at lower temperatures. The κ or kappa phase is a solution of copper in aluminum. The θ (theta) phase is the intermetallic compound $CuAl_2$. Now suppose the 2024 alloy is heated to 1000°F into the κ region. The copper is held in solution in the solid aluminum. To harden this alloy, it is rapidly cooled. This cooling does not produce a martensitic structure, but freezes the solution, holding the copper

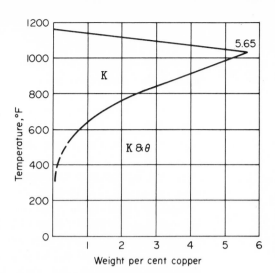

Fig. 111   Equilibrium diagram of aluminum alloyed with copper.

as a supersaturated solution by not providing time for the copper to precipitate out of solution. This action is called *solution heat-treatment*. The metal is not in its hardest condition yet, however. A second process called *aging* must follow. Aging occurs over a period of hours or days, during which the supersaturated copper gradually comes out of solution as copper aluminide, $CuAl_2$. By means of precipitation hardening, the ultimate tensile strength of 2024 aluminum may be doubled, from approximately 30,000 psi to approximately 60,000 psi.

These then are the requirements for precipitation-hardening. There must be a decreasing solubility of the alloy element in the base metal as the temperature is lowered, so that a supersaturated condition can be produced by rapid cooling. With time, the solute atoms precipitate out to form a separate phase which is an intermetallic compound, such as $CuAl_2$. The precipitation process may occur naturally over a period of time at room temperature, but sometimes it requires the extra energy provided by a temperature higher than room temperature.

Precipitation-hardening effects are quite pronounced with beryllium copper, which can be heat-treated to the remarkable strength level of 220,000 psi.

11.9   martensitic precipitation-hardenable steels

The martensitic precipitation-hardenable steels are a more recent development, and include certain precipitation-hardening (PH) stainless steels and the maraging steels.

The martensitic PH steels have a composition such that martensite forms in the usual manner at a temperature in the range of 100–250°F. This is obtained by using slightly lower nickel and manganese than the austenitic stainless steels. These steels have a lower carbon content than the usual martensitic steels, 0.12 percent maximum. The hardness of martensite depends solely on the carbon content (Fig. 98 on page 214). As a result of the low carbon in these PH steels, a martensite is produced which is soft enough to be machined, in the range of R_C 25 to 30 by using a hardening temperature of about 1900°F. The precipitation-hardening process precipitates a complex intermetallic compound usually involving titanium and aluminum, giving final strengths of about 200,000 psi with about 10 percent elongation in 2 in. and R_C 40 to 45.

The maraging steels, mentioned in the previous chapter, are heat-treated similarly to the PH steels, that is, they are first quenched like any hardenable ferrous alloy to produce martensite, then precipitation heat-treated (maraged) like any hardenable nonferrous alloy to produce the intermetallic compound dispersion. Strength levels of about 300,000 psi are possible with maraging steels, at the relatively low hardness level of R_C 50. The martensitic quench is produced simply by air cooling from 1500°F, with no risk of cracking and virtually no distortion. Machining is done in the martensitic condition, after which the steel is maraged at the low temperature of 900°F with minimal warping and oxidation.

The following table gives analyses of Stainless W, a PH stainless steel, of 18 percent nickel maraging steel, and of Inconel 718, a precipitation-hardening nickel alloy chiefly used in gas turbines. Certain similarities in these analyses should be noted. All contain nickel, aluminum, and titanium, the metals involved in the intermetallic compound that appears after precipitation-hardening of these alloys.

Element	Stainless W	18% maraging steel	Inconel 718
C	0.12 max	0.03 max	0.04
Mn	1.00 max	0.10	0.20
Ni	6–8	18.5	52.5
Cr	16–18	–	19
Fe	balance	balance	18
Al	1.0 max	0.10	0.6
Ti	1.0 max	0.40	0.8
Co	–	9.0	–

The chemical analysis of a steel reveals a great deal of information about the steel, including the following:

(a) M_s temperature
(b) the relative weldability, machinability, and hardenability of the steel
(c) the probable hardening temperature
(d) the quenching medium to be used in hardening
(e) the uses of the steel

This kind of metallurgical detective work requires a degree of practice, however. To see how to read a steel analysis, consider a few examples.

1. 0.80% C, 0.30% Si, 0.60% Mn

All steels contain fractional percentages of silicon and up to about 1.65 percent manganese. These two elements therefore disclose little about this steel, but if they dissolve substitutionally in the ferrite lattice, they strengthen the steel (they may instead combine with oxygen and sulfur). The significant element in this analysis is carbon.

(a) This is a high carbon steel, and therefore is presumably a tool steel.
(b) Being a plain carbon steel, it is water-hardening.
(c) Its critical temperature is 1333°F, therefore it should be hardened from about 1400°F.
(d) If annealed, its microstructure will be 100 percent pearlite.
(e) It has sufficient carbon to be hardened to R_C 65.
(f) Since the carbon is high, this steel will tend to crack if welded.

This steel might be used for cold chisel stock, or other cold-work hand tools such as scribers. It is a W-1 tool steel.

2. 0.90% C, 0.50% Cr, 0.50% W, 0.2% V, with small amounts of silicon and manganese

(a) The high carbon content, with small amounts of chromium, tungsten, and vanadium, all carbide-formers, indicates hard carbides when the steel is hardened. This must be a tool steel.
(b) Since it is almost a plain carbon steel, it is restricted to cold-working tools, such as punches and dies.
(c) The addition of small amounts of alloying elements signifies an oil-hardening tool steel.

(d) It will harden to the maximum steel hardness of R_C 65.

(e) Being little different from a plain carbon steel, presumably it would be quenched from about 1400°F.

This is an 0–1 cold-work steel.

3. 0.73% C, 18.0% W, 4.0% Cr, 1.1% V, with silicon and manganese

(a) Obviously a very high alloy steel. The alloy ingredients are all carbide-formers. This is a hot-working tool steel for such purposes as cutter bits for machining, or for forging dies.

(b) Because of the high alloy content, this steel will exhibit secondary hardening when tempered, and should not lose hardness below about 1000°F.

(c) With such a high tungsten content, it probably must be hardened from about 2200°F or higher.

(d) Carbide-forming alloy ingredients in excess of 5 percent usually indicate an air-hardening steel.

This is a T-1 high speed steel.

4. 2.25% C, 12.0% Cr, 1.0% V, 1.0% W, minor amounts of other elements

(a) This steel obviously is compounded to give large amounts (14%) of hard chromium carbides. It will therefore be a wear-resistant steel.

(b) It must be air-hardening because of the high chromium content.

(c) If tempered, it should remain hard at fairly high temperatures.

(d) Although it has almost as much carbon as a cast iron, the carbon must be in the form of chromium carbide rather than graphite.

(e) It must be hardened from a high temperature.

5. 0.08% C, 12.0% Cr

(a) This has the same chromium content as the previous steel. However there is little carbon. Chromium carbides cannot be formed in any significant amount. This cannot be a tool steel.

(b) The very low carbon suggests a stainless steel.

(c) This is a ferritic stainless steel.

6. 0.15% C max, 12.0% Cr

This is a martensitic stainless steel.

7. 0.15% C max, 13.0% Cr, 0.15% S.

(a) A martensitic stainless steel.

(b) The high sulfur content indicates a free-machining grade.

8. 0.10% C, 0.35% Mn, 0.15% Si, 0.25% Cu, 0.35% Ni, 0.10% Cr

(a) A very low carbon steel, with an almost complete absence of carbide-formers. This cannot be a tool steel. Neither can it be a stainless steel.
(b) Such elements as copper, nickel, and silicon form substitutional solid solutions in the iron lattice, their effect being to strengthen the steel.
(c) This is a high strength, low alloy, construction steel.

9. 0.13% C max, 9% Ni

(a) Low carbon with high nickel. Nickel does not form carbides, but lends toughness to a steel, especially at low temperatures.
(b) This steel is a construction steel used for cryogenic purposes.

10. 0.30% C, 1.0% Cr, 0.20% Mo

(a) There is sufficient carbon for heat-treating purposes, though the carbon is not high.
(b) There is not enough carbon for tool steel use. Also, the alloy content is small.
(c) This is a high strength machinery steel for automotive parts, agricultural equipment, etc. (Actually SAE-AISI 4130)

Now try interpreting the following steels. When in doubt, guess, and learn from your mistakes. Extract as much information as you can in the matters of end use, heat-treating temperatures, quenching media, hardness, M_s temperature, formability, etc.

1. 0.2% C, 0.55% Ni, 0.50% Cr, 0.20% Mo
2. 0.3% C, 3.0% Cr, 9.0% W, 0.3% V
3. 1.25% C
4. 0.75% C, 17.0% Cr
5. 0.18% C, 0.30% Si, 0.90% Ni, 0.60% Cu
6. 0.30% C, 3.5% Ni
7. 1.20% C, 1.75% W, 0.75% Cr
8. 0.50% C, 1.40% Mo, 5.0% Cr, 1.0% V, 1.5% Ni
9. 0.80% C, 18.0% W, 4.0% Cr, 2.0% V, 8.0% Co
10. 0.15% C max, 0.15% S min, 18% Cr, 8–10% Ni
11. 0.70% C, 0.25% Mo, 0.75% Cr, 1.50% Ni
12. 0.10–0.15% C, 0.50% Mn, 0.03% Si
13. 0.025% C (max), 1.8% Mn, 20.6% Cr, 9.7% Ni
14. 0.6% C, 13.0% Mn, 4.0% Ni
15. 3.0% C, 15.5% Cr, 0.7% Mo
16. 0.025% C max, 0.4% Si, 19.5% Cr, 9.0% Ni, 2.3% Mo, 0.7% Cb
17. 0.06% C, 17.2% Cr, 0.90% Mo
18. 0.11% C, 11.75% Cr
19. 0.19% C, 1.1% Mn, 0.30% Si, 0.4% Cu, 0.5% Cr
20. 0.10% C, 15.0% Ni, 34% Cr

PROBLEMS

1 What is the difference between tempering and annealing?

2 Microscopic examination of a plain carbon steel indicates that approximately 30 percent of the microstructure is pearlite. What is the approximate carbon content of the steel? (The carbon content of the steel is less than 0.8 percent.)

3 What purpose is served by tempering a steel?

4 A weld is laid down in two passes. Welding conditions are the same for both passes. Microscopic examination discloses that the first pass has a finer grain than the second pass. Can you explain why?

5 Explain the difference in appearance under the microscope between martensite and pearlite.

6 What are the two constituents of pearlite?

7 How is it possible that the martensite formed in a maraging steel can be easily machined?

8 Using Fig. 99, estimate the temperature at which you would set a hardening furnace for the purpose of hardening the following plain carbon steels:
(a) AISI 1020   (b) AISI 1040   (c) AISI 10100.

9 Calculate the M_s temperature of the following steels:
(a) stainless 304: 0.08% C, 18% Cr, 8% Ni, 2.0% Mn, 1.0% Si
(b) type O-1 tool steel: 0.90% C, 0.50% W, 0.50% Cr, 1.0% Mn
(c) type T-1 high speed steel: 0.70% C, 18.0% W, 4.0% Cr, 1.0%V

10 Give a metallurgical explanation of the secondary hardening effect found in some high alloy tool steels.

11 What is the usefulness of secondary hardening?

12 What similarities are there between the hardening of a steel and of a hardenable aluminum?

13 Explain how a maraging steel is fully heat-treated.

The light metals are considered to be those in the Periodic Table up to and including titanium: beryllium, magnesium, aluminum, titanium, and calcium, potassium, sodium, and lithium. Only the first four are employed as structural metals. The others are too soft and reactive, but because of their chemical reactivity may be used to extract metals from their ores in the manner that carbon is used with iron ores. Sodium and potassium are also used as molten metal liquid coolants in the sodium-cooled type of nuclear reactor

12.1   the extraction of aluminum
and beryllium

Though both are light metals, aluminum and beryllium seem to be totally unlike. A comparison of the two is instructive and illustrative of the infinite range of problems with which materials science must contend, particularly in extractive processes.

The most abundant metal in the earth's crust by a wide margin is aluminum. About 8 percent of any clay is aluminum, so that every excavation is a virtual aluminum mine. For a nonferrous metal, though not for iron, an ore with a concentration of 8 percent metal is a rich ore indeed. Unfortunately, while techniques for extracting aluminum from clay are available, clay is not the cheapest source of aluminum. Extraction costs are cheapest for bauxite ore, $Al_2O_3.3H_2O$, a hydrated alumina which is

THE
LIGHT
METALS

12

rather fortuitously distributed over the earth's surface. There is, for example, no bauxite in mineral-rich Canada, although this country is a major world supplier of aluminum by virtue of its water-power resources.

While there is no prospect of a shortage of aluminum, short of removing the first few miles of the earth's crust, the prospect is less favorable for beryllium. This is a comparatively rare metal, like tin, and, also like tin, its reserves will some day be exhausted. About 5 parts per million of the earth's crust is beryllium. The principal beryllium ore, and the only commercial source at present, is beryl; other ores are not important and are found in quantities too small to be mined. Beryl is a beryllium-aluminum silicate, $3BeO.Al_2O_3.6SiO_2$, containing about 5 percent beryllium, and is almost always found in association with lithium ores in pegmatite formations. Because processes for concentrating beryl have not been introduced, the only mining process is that of hand-picking large pieces of beryl with cheap labor, unless the beryl is separated as a by-product from lithium minerals.

Both beryl and bauxite are much more stable compounds than iron oxide, and coke will not reduce these minerals to metal in a blast furnace process of the type used for iron. Both metals are more expensive than iron, in part because of smelting costs.

Fig. 112 Electrolytic cell for extraction of aluminum from bauxite.

Alumina must be reduced in an electrolytic cell. Such a cell is sketched in Fig. 112. Since bauxite is a nonconductor of electricity, electrolytic reduction requires the addition to the cell of an ionizable material. Cryolite, a rare fluoride of aluminum, is placed in the cell and is melted by passing current through it. The bauxite is then added. The anodes of the cell, and the lining of the cell, which is also the cathode, are made of carbon manufactured from petroleum coke, an oil refinery product. The oxygen of the ore reacts with the anodes and is released as carbon dioxide. The operation makes heavy demands on the anodes and electric power: a pound of aluminum product requires about 10 kwhr of electric power and over half a pound of anodes. Aluminum smelters therefore are not located at sources of bauxite, but on tidewater near sources of hydroelectric power.

Aluminum then is more difficult to smelt from its oxide ore than iron is. Beryllium is even more difficult to extract. The beryl is converted to beryllium oxide, an oxide even more stable than alumina. The relative stability of these oxides is indicated by their melting points:

iron oxide	2800°F
alumina	3720°F
beryllia	4570°F

The converted beryllia is converted again to beryllium fluoride, and finally reduced to beryllium particles by magnesium in the following reaction. The reaction temperature is above the melting point of beryllium (2370°F).

$$BeF_2 + Mg \rightarrow MgF_2 + Be$$

This reaction is possible because beryllium fluoride is less stable chemically than beryllium oxide. The beryllium product is in particle size, and contaminated with over 1 percent magnesium. The alloying of magnesium with beryllium has adverse effects on the properties of beryllium, especially its ductility. Vacuum melting reduces the magnesium content to less than 0.1 percent and produces ingots of beryllium.

This method of reducing beryllium from its fluoride by means of magnesium is used in similar processes to reduce titanium and zirconium from their ores. These metals are reduced from their chlorides, however, in what is known as the Kroll process.

The beryllium, after vacuum melting, has a low level of magnesium, and being in ingot form, would appear ready for rolling or forming to final shape, as other metals such as iron and aluminum would be at this stage. This is not the case. Every operation with beryllium appears to be afflicted with "bugs", and the melting process, in solving or partly solving the magnesium contamination problem, has raised other problems.

First, beryllium, like titanium, is a reactive metal. Both must be melted under vacuum or inert gases, since oxygen, nitrogen, or hydrogen, even in minute quantities, embrittle these metals to the point of uselessness. Their reactiveness is not confined to gases, however. Both metals when molten are a kind of universal solvent and will react with any crucible material. If melted in a graphite crucible, considerable beryllium carbide is formed. If melted in an oxide crucible, even beryllium oxide, the metal will be contaminated with beryllium oxide. It is true that almost all metals will react in some degree with their melting refractories. If aluminum is exposed to refractory walls for a long period, it will reduce silica to metallic silicon, which will alloy with the aluminum. But these metal-crucible reactions are only serious with the reactive metals, chiefly beryllium and titanium. The other reactive metals such as tantalum have melting points so high that they are not extracted by melting.

Although no refractory is entirely satisfactory for melting beryllium, beryllia gives the best performance.

In keeping with the innate genius of beryllium for doing things wrong, still another melting problem arises. This metal freezes in large crystals of a size that must be seen to be believed. In a mold of square cross-section, the ingot may grow only four crystals, one from each side of the mold. Magnesium, cadmium, and zinc, also in Group II of the Periodic Table, tend also to form unduly large crystals, but not to the extent that beryllium does. Large crystals are inadmissible in metals, as they produce a condition of brittleness, especially in beryllium. This large crystal growth could be controlled in part by a rapid quench, but such quenches invariably split the ingot. There is no phase change or recrystallization that will permit heat-treating to produce small crystals.

There is only one possible solution to the problem of crystal size. The ingot is reduced to small particles, ground to about 200 mesh, then sintered with heat and pressure in dies to produce the required shape.

12.2   properties of aluminum
and beryllium

With problems such as these to contend with, and a production cost of $60 or more per lb, one might well ask what properties beryllium offers that warrant the effort of producing it. For comparison, consider first aluminum.

Pure aluminum is a soft metal without pronounced work-hardening properties and with remarkable ductility. It is not strong unless alloyed. Ultimate tensile strength is only about 10,000 psi for the pure metal, but alloying strengths of 75,000 psi are possible. The modulus of elasticity of aluminum is 10×10^6, one-third that of steel, and its weight also is one-third that of steel. Because of its uses in aircraft, space vehicles, trains, trucks, ships, conveyors, and shipping containers, aluminum has been termed "the transportation metal". Easy to machine, form, and weld, it is also easy to melt, though it tends to dissolve hydrogen with consequent porosity in castings and fusion welds. The melting point is only 1220°F for pure aluminum, less for alloys. It is a face-centered cubic metal, and therefore is not subject to brittle fracture.

By comparison, beryllium is brittle. There appears to be no inherent reason why it should be. It is a hexagonal close-packed metal. So are magnesium, titanium, and zirconium. These metals are ductile and can be rolled into sheet. The same operation should be possible with beryllium. After the expenditure of millions of dollars and 15 years on research, beryllium is still brittle, and rolling is impossible. Best ductility is given by extruded beryllium, but at best elongation is usually only a few percent.

However, beryllium is reasonably strong. Maximum strength is of the order of 100,000 psi, higher than aluminum alloys. The rigidity of beryllium surpasses that of steel, its modulus of elasticity being about 40×10^6. The very high modulus, high strength, and unusually light weight, two-thirds the specific weight of aluminum, make this an attractive metal for aerospace applications if the problem of brittleness can be solved.

While few if any aluminum compounds are toxic, all compounds of beryllium are dangerously toxic. While methods of industrial hygiene are now well understood and applied to the processing of beryllium, there were in earlier times a number of cases of berylliosis in industry. There is at least one authenticated case of a beryllium worker's wife afflicted with berylliosis, though the husband was not. She washed his plant clothing regularly, thus contracting the disease that passed the man by. This incident seems strangely in keeping with the peculiar "personality" of beryllium.

Aluminum can be alloyed with a great many metals. Beryllium is not especially receptive to alloying. Alloying cannot solve the brittleness problem, for an alloy is ordinarily less ductile than the corresponding pure metal.

12.3   properties of the light metals

The light metals, like all the light elements, share two other common characteristics in addition to low specific weight:

1. High specific heat, 0.22 Btu per lb for aluminum, 0.25 for magnesium, and a very high 0.52 for beryllium.
2. Low absorption for gamma radiation, high scattering cross-section for neutrons and low absorption for neutrons (with the exception of boron and titanium).

The light metals therefore are used as moderators and as fuel rods in nuclear reactors. Figure 113 is a photograph of typical fuel rods containing nuclear fuel. The uranium fuel particles cannot be exposed because they corrode and are pyrophoric; they must be canned. Zirconium, zirconium alloys, magnesium, beryllium, aluminum, and austenitic stainless steels are the preferred canning materials. Zirconium and stainless steels have suitable nuclear properties but are not light metals.

Beryllium, when used as a moderator, offers the possibility of some neutron multiplication, since it releases one neutron from its nucleus at a much lower energy requirement than any other metal. This characteristic is used in beryllium neutron-generating devices, which release small amounts of neutrons for analytical work.

Fig. 113 Bundles of fuel rod sections for a research nuclear reactor. The darker rods are zirconium, the lighter rods are sintered aluminum powder (SAP). (Courtesy Whiteshell Nuclear Research Establishment)

The low gamma ray absorption of the light metals indicates that they are easy to radiograph using either X-ray or gamma ray techniques. X-ray photography of these metals requires only very low voltages, which for aircraft X-ray inspection may be as low as 50 kv. Figure 17 on page 42 contrasts the high absorption of a steel insert for X rays with the much lesser absorption of the magnesium casting. Figure 114 compares the relative X-radiation absorption of beryllium with that of aluminum. Below 100 kv beryllium is much more transparent. Hence the use of beryllium as an X-ray "window" in an X-ray tube.

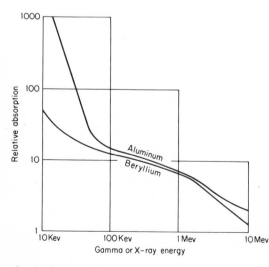

Fig. 114 Relative absorption of aluminum and beryllium for high-energy radiation. Both being light metals they are transparent to high-energy radiation above 1,000,000 electron-volts. Note that the differences in absorptivity between different materials become small above 1 Mev; for good contrast in X-ray radiography the lowest practical voltage is used.

the light metals
258

Since pure metals have better corrosion resistance and better electrical conductivity than alloys, commercially pure aluminum has for its principal uses those applications where corrosion resistance and electrical and thermal conductivity are primary requirements. Because it has a lighter weight than copper, aluminum has tended to make inroads into the wire markets served almost exclusively by copper heretofore, although aluminum has an electrical resistance about 50 percent higher than copper. The thermal conductivity of aluminum is about half that of copper, 1540 Btu/sq ft-in.-°F. It has, however, the significant disadvantages of low strength, and twice the thermal expansion of steel. The high thermal expansion makes for difficulties in the welding and casting of this metal.

Commercially pure grades of annealed aluminum have yield strengths in the range of about 4500 psi, ultimate strength 11,500 psi, elongation 40 percent or more, and low fatigue resistance. It may be cold-worked to strength levels as high as 23,000 psi but with considerable loss of ductility.

In commercial alloys, aluminum is alloyed with silicon, magnesium, manganese, copper, zinc, and chromium. Copper and zinc alloys are heat-treatable and can develop strengths in the range of 65,000 to 75,000 psi. The other types of alloys are hardened by cold-working. The magnesium

Fig. 115 A casting alloy of aluminum containing 13 percent silicon. Individual grains of silicon may be seen.

alloys, which are usually selected for welding, develop ultimate tensile strengths of about 40,000 psi. While only small percentages of alloying elements are used in wrought aluminum alloys, the casting alloys may contain as much as 17 percent silicon, 11 percent copper, or 10 percent magnesium. The hard alloys containing copper are the best machining aluminums, but have limited ductility for forming and bending.

The aluminum alloys are classified into two groups: the casting alloys and the wrought alloys. The wrought formulations are those used for rolling, extruding, drawing, and forging.

For the wrought alloys, two numbering systems are in use in Canada and the United States. In the latter country, the four-digit system is more common. In Canada, a two-digit system is used, the number being followed by the letter S to designate a wrought alloy. The following table compares the two systems.

99.6% purity aluminum	1S	1060
99.0% purity aluminum	2S	1100
manganese alloys	3S to 9S	3xxx
copper alloys	10S to 29S	2xxx
silicon alloys	30S to 39S	4xxx
magnesium alloys	50S to 69S	5xxx
magnesium-silicon alloys	50S to 69S	6xxx
zinc alloys	70S to 79S	7xxx

Some of the more important alloys of aluminum, with their principal alloy additions, are these:

1. 3S, 3003, with 1.0–1.5% Mn. The manganese addition provides 50% more tensile strength.
2. 24S, 2024, with 3.8–4.9% Cu, 1.5% Mg. A high strength, heat-treatable aluminum commonly used in aircraft work and parts requiring high strength or hardness. Corrosion resistance is poor. This alloy is not usually welded, since welding heat anneals it, causing loss of strength.
3. 28S, 2011, with 5–6% Cu. A free-machining alloy supplied in cold-drawn bar form.
4. 33S, 4043, with 4.5–6.0% silicon. Welding grade aluminum, available as welding wire.
5. 50S, 6063, with approximately 0.5% each of magnesium and silicon. This is an extrusion alloy, familiar as aluminum windows, doors, grilles, and trim.
6. C54S, 5154, with 3.1–3.9% Mg. Welding grade aluminum, chiefly supplied in sheet, plate, and shapes.
7. 65S, 6061, with about 1% Mg, 0.5% Si. Structural aluminum. The geodesic dome of Fig. 116 is made of 6061 aluminum.

Fig. 116 The geodesic dome over the headquarters of the American Society for Metals in East Cleveland, Ohio. The dome is made of aluminum 6061 tubing.

The temper designation follows the alloy designation, 65S–T6, for example. A "temper" refers to a condition produced in the metal by mechanical working or heat-treatment; the aluminum tempers are produced either by cold-working or age-hardening or both. Only the zinc, copper, and magnesium-silicon alloys however can be age-hardened.

The wrought alloys that are not heat-treatable may be supplied in the "O" or annealed temper, or the "F" as-fabricated temper. Mechanical properties are not guaranteed in the "F" temper. Other tempers include:

> H1 — work-hardened only
> H2 — work-hardened and partially annealed
> H3 — work-hardened and stabilized

There may also be a second digit in the temper number, such as H12. This second digit indicates the degree of work-hardening:

> 1 — eighth hard
> 2 — quarter hard
> 4 — half hard
> 6 — three-quarter hard
> 8 — full hard
> 9 — extra hard

Thus 6061–H12 indicates a magnesium-silicon alloy work-hardened to quarter hard condition.

The heat-treatable alloys such as 2024 (24S) may also be supplied heat-treated for hardness and strength, and this temper is indicated by T:

> T4 — solution heat-treated
> T6 — solution heat-treated and artificially aged

the light metals
261

12.5 aluminum casting alloys

Aluminum casting alloys are formulated for sand casting, permanent mold casting, and die casting. These alloys are designated by a three-digit number, such as 108, 356, etc. As was the case with stainless steel alloy numbers, there is little system in these numbers, and the problem is complicated further by the fact that casting alloys have more than one numbering system. Perhaps the most used system is that of the Aluminum Association. In this system, silicon casting alloys have numbers up to 99, silicon-copper casting alloys 100 to 199, magnesium casting alloys 200 to 299, and silicon-manganese 300 to 399. Copper alloys are preferred for their hardness when machinability is a factor; silicon alloys are useful when fluidity to follow intricate shapes is desired. The high magnesium alloys require care in melting to prevent excessive oxidation loss of the magnesium content.

Aluminum is prone to cracking and tearing when hot, that is, it is "hot short". Most aluminum casting alloys are not notably strong in tension, only a few exceeding 40,000 psi at room temperature. This low strength, which drops rapidly at higher temperatures, coupled with a high coefficient of expansion, indicates a tendency toward hot shortness. Aluminum also has a strong tendency to pick up hydrogen in the molten condition, and this is a cause of porosity in castings and welds. Moreover, aluminum castings are not pressure-tight, and to obtain pressure-tightness they must be impregnated with sodium silicate, epoxy, or other material.

12.6 use of aluminum

By and large, magnesium alloys of aluminum are selected for weldability, copper alloys for machinability, and silicon alloys for castability. For corrosion resistance or electrical conductivity, the commercially pure material is best.

Aluminum has some special welding problems. The high coefficient of expansion promotes distortion during welding operations. Because of the metal's very high thermal conductivity and low electrical resistance, it is difficult to resistance-weld (spot-weld) aluminum, and currents as high as 100,000 amps may be necessary for such operations. Another preoccupation in welding aluminum is the removal of the refractory oxide skin on the metal.

Under conditions of repeated stress, aluminum parts must be carefully designed against fatigue failure, especially in welded aluminum structures. This metal does not show a true endurance limit. Figure 117 shows typical fatigue curves for aluminum alloys.

Fig. 117 Typical fatigue curves of aluminum alloys. The absence of an endurance limit is a characteristic of these curves.

Aluminum has a high reflectivity for infrared and visible radiation. The metal is frequently deposited on reflectors by a process of evaporation and deposition under vacuum, as in the manufacture of sealed-beam headlights. The high reflectivity also accounts for the use of aluminum foil in insulation materials, the foil serving to reflect radiant heat.

In the form of finely divided flakes, aluminum serves as an excellent paint pigment, providing an impervious coating with excellent hiding power on either wood or metal.

The increased use of aluminum in automobiles deserves mention. As this book is written, aggressive efforts are being made to use aluminum 3003 and 6063 for automobile radiators, and one would assume that the efforts will bear fruit. The cast aluminum engine block has been successfully used; such blocks are usually high silicon alloys such as 356 (9 percent silicon, 3.5 percent copper). Considerable weight saving is possible by substituting aluminum for cast iron in diesel engines. Aluminum pistons are of course standard in automobiles.

As a final salute to aluminum and its alloys, we may note that this metal and United States Steel's T-1 low alloy steel made possible the design of a bulldozer for the U.S. Army that is light enough to be carried by helicopter or dropped by parachute. This flying bulldozer disassembles into three large pieces, which are individually dropped from the air, then quickly assembled on the ground. This remarkable creature weighs only 20,000 lb.

12.7   magnesium

Pure magnesium weighs two-thirds as much as aluminum, or 1 oz per cu in. The E-value is also two-thirds that of aluminum, 6.5×10^6. The melting point of magnesium is 1202°F, about the same as that of aluminum. The

Fig. 118 Micrograph of magnesium.

thermal conductivity is high, but not so high as in aluminum. Coefficient of expansion is 0.000016 in./in., a very high value. Like most of the light structural metals, magnesium is hcp. While aluminum alloys become too weak for use above 300°F, magnesium alloys can be used at twice this temperature. Figure 118 is a micrograph of pure magnesium.

Magnesium is an active metal. Its first extensive use was as incendiary bombs for strategic air warfare. Magnesium chips are readily ignited, though there is little hazard in gas welding of magnesium components. Such a metal of course has poor corrosion resistance. Its chemical activity, however, is turned to advantage in the use of magnesium anodes for the galvanic protection of hot water tanks, buried pipelines and other structures subject to galvanic attack. It is used also to reduce zirconium, titanium, uranium, and beryllium from their fluorides and chlorides in primary

Fig. 119 A magnesium dockboard providing access to a boxcar from a loading dock for lift trucks.

extraction processes. The use of magnesium in the production of ductile cast iron was noted in Chapter 10.

Most magnesium, however, is used for equipment where light weight is a principal requirement, as in aircraft (the pipe fitting of Fig. 17 is an aircraft magnesium component), space vehicles, ladders, portable power tools, luggage, or the dockboards used on warehouse shipping and receiving docks (Fig. 119). The large stiffening rings of moon rockets may be as large as 33 ft in diameter; these have been produced in magnesium alloys. Currently the lightest commercial alloy is a magnesium alloy containing 14 percent lithium and 1.25 percent aluminum.

Magnesium has recently taken a place among the tooling materials. The major cost of such tooling devices as fixtures and drill jigs lies not in the material but the manufacturing cost. Magnesium's light weight, weldability, and ease of machining may greatly reduce the cost of manufacture. In use, the light weight of such tooling reduces operator fatigue in handling the fixtures, and is especially convenient for women operators. Magnesium tooling plate is usually alloy AZ31B.

Alloy designations for magnesium follow a simple system. Two letters represent the chief ingredients, followed by two numbers giving respective percentages to the nearest whole number. A serial letter follows the digits. Thus AZ92A is an Aluminum-Zinc alloy with 9 percent Al and 2 percent Zn. These designations apply both to wrought and cast alloys. The alloy letter code is the following:

A	aluminum	M	manganese
E	rare earths	Z	zinc
H	thorium	T	tin
K	zirconium		

Most of the magnesium alloys are of the AZ type. Rare earth and thorium additions give improved strength at temperatures above 500°F. The amount of thorium used is usually about 3 percent and does not produce a radiation hazard. Zirconium additions of about 0.5–0.7 percent provide grain refinement. Alloy AZ92A is used for normal temperature applications, including sand casting and welding wire. The alloys of highest strength may have ultimate tensile strengths as high as 55,000 psi in extruded articles. Elongation, however, is limited in all magnesium alloys.

12.8   titanium

This is the heaviest of the hcp light metals. Only two minerals are of commercial importance: ilmenite, an iron-titanium oxide, and rutile, TiO_2. The industrial uses of rutile were outlined in an earlier chapter.

Fig. 120 Micrograph of pure titanium sheet.

Titanium is a highly reactive metal above 1000°F. Like beryllium, molten titanium will attack any refractory oxide: the practice of welding metals as they lie on a firebrick is not possible with titanium.

Titanium can be identified by its light weight, 60 percent of steel, its bluish or silvery tinge, and its blue grinding sparks.

Titanium first began to compete in the metals market when higher strengths at higher temperatures were demanded in high speed aircraft early in the 1950's. A switch in emphasis from aircraft to missiles almost ruined the market for titanium. However, production now is at a rate of about 15,000,000 lb annually, and the metal is steadily making inroads into the civilian market, where its light weight, strength, and remarkable corrosion resistance at room temperature offer possibilities that compensate for its high price of over $5 per lb. This reactive metal is corrosion-resistant by virtue of an adherent oxide skin such as protects aluminum and the stainless steels.

Titanium has an E-value of 15.5×10^6, half that of steel, and higher than the E-values of aluminum and magnesium. It can be alloyed and heat-treated for strengths exceeding 200,000 psi. Pure titanium melts at 3035°F, above the melting point of iron. Thermal expansion and thermal conductivity are quite low, and fatigue strength excellent.

Figure 121 shows a stress-strain curve for commercially pure titanium sheet. Both the strength and the elongation, 27.5 percent in 2 in., are excellent.

Titanium undergoes a phase change to bcc when heated above 1620°F. The low temperature hcp phase is termed alpha, the bcc phase beta. It is strengthened and embrittled by minute amounts of carbon, oxygen, and nitrogen. Certain alloying additions such as chromium, molybdenum,

the light metals

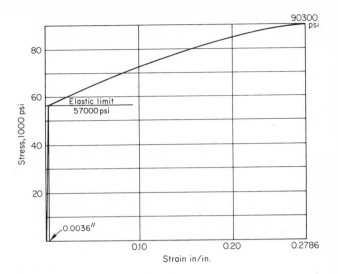

Fig. 121   Stress-strain curve for a commercially pure titanium sheet, aircraft quality.

vanadium, and iron are beta stabilizers, causing a lowering of the transition temperature. Alloying additions which raise the transition temperature are called alpha stabilizers. These are aluminum, carbon, oxygen, and nitrogen. These elements form solid solutions and are employed in nonheat-treatable alloys. Aluminum is a common alpha stabilizer in amounts up to 8 percent, and is also found in the solution heat-treatable beta alloys.

12.9   beryllium

The use of beryllium is still severely limited by its poor ductility. About 80 percent of beryllium production goes into copper alloys, which are discussed in the following chapter. The beryllium coppers are precipitation-hardening alloys, indicative of beryllium's noteworthy capacity as a precipitation-hardening alloy element. Though beryllium nickel has only limited commercial use, it can be heat-treated to a tensile strength of 270,000 psi, with an elongation of 9 percent in 2 in., a combination that almost no steel can match except for the newer maraging steels. This ability to produce hardenable ferrous and nonferrous alloys is interesting when compared with two metallurgical characteristics of beryllium: the beryllium atom is too small to form substitutional solid solutions with other commercial metals, and too large for interstitial solid solutions. The hardenable alloys of copper and nickel are possible because of substitutional solid solution at higher temperatures.

A final oddity of beryllium is its low Poisson's Ratio. For most metals Poisson's Ratio is about 0.3. For beryllium it is about 0.1.

the light metals
267

PROBLEMS

1 Explain why powder metallurgy methods must be employed with beryllium.

2 If beryllium were both nontoxic and ductile, what advantages would it offer in the market for metals?

3 List the general characteristics of the light metals other than low specific weight.

4 Suggest two reasons why aluminum is not easy to spot-weld.

5 What alloying ingredient is added to aluminum for (a) high strength, (b) weldability, (c) machinability?

The large group of nonferrous metals and alloys has a very wide range of applications.

The radioactive metals *uranium*, *thorium*, and *plutonium* are chiefly used as nuclear fuels, and are therefore discussed in Chapter 16. Thorium however has limited applications an as alloy element in high-temperature magnesium alloys and in tungsten alloys for welding and electronic applications. Uranium was used as an alloy element in steels for improved fatigue strength, but is no longer employed for this purpose. *Zirconium* also finds its major applications in the nuclear power field, but is also a useful alloying element for a range of other metals.

Nickel and *lead* are as versatile in their applications as steel, though not consumed in the same large tonnages. The uses of *copper* stem chiefly from its high conductivity for heat and electric current, and its remarkable capacity for alloy formation. *Cadmium* and *tin* on the other hand are more limited in their uses, which are largely in bearing metals, plating, soldering alloys, and copper alloys. *Zinc* has much the same applications as these two metals, and in addition is well adapted to the die-casting process. *Cobalt* is an alloying element in ferrous and nonferrous alloys and a binder or matrix material in carbide tools. *Manganese* is not used in pure form, but as an alloying element.

The most important industrial application of *silver* is its use in the silver-copper brazing alloys, which can braze most metals together. *Gold* is an occasional alloying element in such brazing formulations. Silver, gold, and the *platinum* group of metals are also used as contacts in instru-

METALS
WITH SPECIAL PROPERTIES
AND APPLICATIONS

13

ments and electrical switching devices. *Mercury* is a fluid electrical conductor.

The *refractory metals*, with melting points above 3600°F, are most notable for their high strength, hardness, and stiffness, especially at high temperatures. Finally the *rare earths* include 14 metals very similar in properties, which have not yet fully revealed their industrial possibilities.

13.1   nickel

A review of the properties and applications of nickel quickly discloses that this is a most remarkable metal, and perhaps the closest approach to an ideal metal. A catalogue of its physical properties makes it appear as a twin brother to steel, however — both mild steel and nickel have approximately the same modulus of elasticity, tensile strength, ductility, endurance limit, coefficient of thermal expansion, thermal conductivity, and electrical conductivity. Both metals also are ferromagnetic. The melting point of nickel is 2651°F, in the same range as the low carbon steels. If this were the complete personality of nickel, it would be a little-used metal, for it would offer the same properties as steel, but at a higher price, for nickel is not an easy metal to extract from its ores.

Most of the world's nickel is supplied by Canada and Russia from sulfide ores, chiefly pentlandite, an iron-nickel sulfide. The ore is always a copper-nickel ore. Since copper and nickel are similar both chemically and physically, it is difficult to separate the two metals during smelting. This difficulty accounts for the higher price of nickel, about ten times that of steel. In addition to copper and iron, the platinum groups of metals, silver, gold, cobalt, selenium, and tellurium are associated with nickel in the ore and are recovered. Even the sulfur may be recovered as sulfuric acid. The percent of nickel in pentlandite, amid this surfeit of low-grade materials, is only about 1 percent.

The end uses of nickel have the following approximate distribution: about 80 percent of nickel is used in steel alloys such as low alloy and stainless steels, about 10 percent is used in nickel plating, and 10 percent for nickel and nickel alloy uses. Most of the AISI-SAE low alloy steels contain small amounts of nickel. Nickel therefore is an integral element in our complex steel technology, and indeed, steel without nickel is difficult to envisage.

Nickel and steel are alike in the effect of sulfur on these metals. As with steel, sulfur in nickel forms nickel sulfide, which like iron sulfide, melts at a low temperature. Nickel sulfide in a nickel ingot is the last component to melt, and therefore deposits in the grain boundaries. When the ingot is rolled, this low strength intergranular material causes cracking and crumbling. The problem is cured as it was in the case of steels: man-

Fig. 122 A high nickel alloy combustion chamber of a 60-hp gas turbine engine.

ganese is added to combine with the sulfur as manganese sulfide, which deposits as inclusions instead of a grain boundary network. Magnesium may also be used to remove sulfur in nickel. Nickel is severely corroded by sulfur compounds, such as those in crude petroleum or sulfur gases.

While steels and iron are bcc, nickel is fcc. Nickel therefore has no tendency toward brittle fracture at low temperatures (see Fig. 79 on page 180). Indeed most alloys for cryogenic applications contain considerable amounts of nickel for toughness. At the other end of the temperature spectrum, nickel has high creep strength and a notable resistance to oxidation and general corrosion. Nickel therefore is the usual constituent in cryogenic alloys and in the superalloys needed in gas turbine and rocket engines. No other metal is equally suited to both high- and low-temperature applications.

Nickel is perhaps the most important metal for electronic and low-current electrical applications. Some of its many electrical uses have been mentioned before — magnetostriction, for example, or permanent magnets. A wide variety of nickel alloys are employed in vacuum electronic tubes, notably for cathodes. Nickel in sheet or other form is used as anodes in low-power tubes and in photocells. A great many thermocouple materials are also high nickel alloys.

Of the nonelectronic commercial grades of nickel, A nickel (Nickel 205) is the purest, with 99 percent nickel. It is used in the chemical industries for evaporators, kettles, and other processing equipment. Tensile strength is 55,000 psi, yield strength 15,000 psi, hardness R_B 64. The great interval between yield and ultimate strength is of course indicative of good ductility.

metals with special properties and applications
271

Nickel with about 4 percent cobalt is used for magnetostrictive transducers for such purposes as ultrasonic cleaning. Nickel with 4 percent manganese has improved corrosion resistance at higher temperatures, particularly against sulfur compounds. This material is used for spark plug electrodes.

13.2   nickel alloys

Nickel, like copper and iron, is capable of producing a wide range of alloys peculiarly adapted to the demands of special applications, and as with these other two metals, these alloys are available in heat-treatable and non-heat-treatable types. Most of the nickel alloys to be discussed have been developed either for high-temperature use or for resistance to specific chemicals.

Nickel and copper are solid-solution soluble in each other in all proportions. The equilibrium diagram for these solutions is given in Fig. 22 on page 49. Thus an infinite number of nickel-copper and copper-nickel alloys is possible. The names of these alloys, like many of the other copper alloys, is somewhat confusing. If the percent nickel exceeds the percent copper, the alloy will likely be termed a *monel*. If the nickel content is in the range of 12 to 30 percent, the alloy will be termed a *cupronickel*. Nickel coinage contains 75 percent nickel and 25 percent copper, but coinage nickel is not called monel.

The *monels* may be considered to be two-thirds nickel and one-third copper. Monels are more resistant to reducing chemicals than nickel and more resistant to oxidizing chemicals such as chlorides and nitrates, than copper, hence they have better corrosion resistance than either constituent. Resistance to attack by both freshwater and saltwater is outstanding, and the monels are therefore used as piping and pumps for brines and seawater, steam condensers, ships' propellers, and shafting.

R Monel (Monel R-405) contains 66 percent Ni, 31.5 percent Cu, and 0.05 percent S. The sulfur addition is made, as in the case of sulfurized steels, for machinability. This monel then is selected for parts that must be machined. Other monels may contain from 44.5 to 84 percent nickel. The standard monel is Monel 400 containing 66 percent Ni, 31.5 percent Cu, and about 1 percent each of iron and manganese.

The presence of half a percent or more of aluminum or titanium or both in a high nickel alloy indicates a precipitation-hardening alloy. The nature of the compound precipitated is a little uncertain; it may be an intermetallic nickel-aluminum and nickel titanium, $Ni_3(Al, Ti)$.

Permanickel, 98.6 percent Ni, 0.50 percent Ti, and Duranickel with 4.5 percent Al, 0.50 percent Ti, are thus heat-treatable nickels. The 500

Monels, K-500 and 501 both contain 2.80 percent Al and 0.50 percent Ti. Inconel superalloys are all heat-treatable and contain even more aluminum and titanium.

The demand for metals with high strength and high creep and oxidation resistance at high temperatures has so far been met not so much by the refractory metals, which oxidize too readily, but by the nickel superalloys. These are complex alloys usually based on nickel, and used at temperatures remarkably close to their melting points. They are expensive metals to develop; the overall research costs of extending their temperature range probably approximate a million dollars per degree F. Strength at high temperatures is contributed by the precipitated $Ni_3(Al, Ti)$ phase, which cannot be found under the microscope. Prominent among the superalloys are the Inconels, which are complex nickel-chromium-iron alloys. Inconel X-750 is employed for gas turbine blading and afterburner combustion chambers, and has been used in high-stress applications at temperatures of 1700°F or higher. The fuselage of the famous Bell X-15 rocket aircraft was also fabricated of Inconel X-750. Figure 123 compares the microstructure of Inconel X-750 with that of pure nickel. Ultimate strengths of the superalloys at room temperature may exceed 200,000 psi after hardening. Their machinability ratings are low, in the range of about 20 compared to B1112 as 100.

Analyses of a selection of the superalloys are given in the table on page 275. Some of these alloys contain molybdenum and cobalt, two elements

Fig. 123 (a) Pure nickel, showing twinned structure.

metals with special properties and applications

Fig. 123 (b)   A hardenable high nickel Inconel superalloy.

that contribute strength at high temperature. Cobalt forms solid solutions with nickel, while molybdenum forms carbides.

The Hastelloys are nickel-chromium-irons or nickel-molybdenum-irons, developed for great corrosion resistance to chemicals, especially acids, but also used as superalloys. Hastelloy A (see table) is austenitic and thus not heat-treatable.

The alloys constantan, alumel, and chromel P in the table are the commonly used thermocouple materials for temperature control of industrial furnaces. Other chromel alloys are used as electric heating resistances for such applications as household appliances. A very wide range of other high nickel alloys are available with high specific resistance for electric heating, with values for ohms/mil-foot ranging from 10 to 800. For small wire-wound resistors as used in electronic circuitry, the standard alloy is Nichrome, 73 percent Ni, 20 percent Cr, but for precision miniature resistors Karma is preferred, 80 percent Ni, 20 percent Cr, with a specific resistance of 800 ohms per circular mil-foot. Both materials have extremely low temperature coefficients of resistance.

Nilvar and Invar, 36 percent nickel with iron, have the lowest coefficients of thermal expansion of all known materials, 0.000001 in./in. By variation of the nickel percentage in iron-nickel alloys it is possible to tailor an expansion coefficient to any practical requirement. The wire leads of vacuum tubes, for example, can be made to match the thermal expansion of the glass tube.

metals with special properties and applications

Elinvar is a high nickel alloy with a constant E-value over a considerable temperature range. Such an alloy is invaluable for hair springs and balance wheels in watches and for other instrument components. Finally the Alnico permanent-magnet nickel alloys should be mentioned again. These are nickel-chromium-aluminum-cobalt alloys.

Beryllium nickel was mentioned in connection with beryllium in the previous chapter. This alloy contains 1.95 percent Be, 0.50 percent Ti, and is marketed by the Beryllium Corporation as Berylco Nickel 440. It is hardenable to remarkable strength, fatigue resistance, and wear resistance, with a maximum R_C of about 50. Its uses are in the field of instrumentation.

NICKEL ALLOYS

	Ni	Cr	Fe	Al	Ti	Mn	C	S	Cu	Other
A Nickel	99.5		0.15			0.25	0.06	0.005	0.05	
Permanickel	98.6		0.10		0.50	0.10	0.25	0.005	0.02	0.35 Mo
Duranickel	94.0		0.15	4.50	0.50	0.25	0.15	0.005	0.05	
Monel 400	66.0		1.35			0.90	0.12	0.005	31.5	
Monel R-405	66.0		1.35			0.90	0.18	0.050	31.5	
Inconel 600	76.0	15.8	7.20			0.20	0.04	0.007	0.10	
Inconel 700	46.0	15.0	0.70	3.00	2.20	0.10	0.12	0.007	0.05	28.5 Co, 3.75 Mo
Inconel X-750	73.0	15.0	6.75	0.80	2.50	0.70	0.04	0.007	0.05	0.85 Cb
Incoloy 800	32.0	20.5	46.0	0.30	0.30	0.04	0.04	0.007	0.30	
Rene 41	balance	19	2.5	1.65	3	0.30	0.10			11 Co, 9.75 Mo
Hastelloy A	53		22			2				22 Mo
Hastelloy C	balance	16	5							16 Mo, 4W
Constantan	45								55	
Alumel	95.3		0.1	1.6		1.75				1.2 Si
Chromel P	90	9.5	0.2							0.4 Si
Inco-Weld A	71	16.4	6.6		3.2	2.3	0.03	0.007	0.04	

Special nickel alloys of importance in the fabrication of metals are those formulated for welding and brazing. Such nickel alloys are especially useful for joining metals other than nickel. Cast irons are commonly welded and repaired with high nickel alloys, usually Ni-Rod, 95 percent nickel, or Ni-Rod 55, 53 percent nickel. Inco-Weld A (see table) resembles an Inconel in composition, but was developed for the welding of dissimilar metals, such as ferritic stainless steel to high nickel alloys. It is used also in the welding of cryogenic steels such as 9 percent nickel steel and has even welded zirconium alloys. Brazed joints that must resist high temperatures require nickel-base brazing alloys, usually nickel-chromium. These brazing alloys have solidus temperatures close to 2000°F.

In sum, the nickel alloys embrace a remarkably wide range of specialty uses. Nickel is critically important, therefore, in meeting the specialty requirements of our steel technology.

metals with special properties and applications

13.3 copper

Copper is similar to nickel in its ability to alloy with a wide range of metals, and like nickel is face-centered cubic. The ores of copper, too, are usually sulfides.

Copper is noted for its high conductivity for both heat and electric current. Much copper production therefore goes into busbars and other types of electrical conductors. The thermal conductivity of copper, about 2700 Btu/°F/in., is almost ten times that of steel. Copper is the preferred material for chills, continuous-casting molds, and other equipment that must remove heat. The high thermal conductivity, however, is a disadvantage in the fabrication of copper. The pure metal is almost unweldable because of the difficulty of retaining sufficient welding heat in the area of the weld. It is rarely resistance-welded.

Pure copper has an E-value of 16×10^6 psi, a yield strength of 9000 psi and ultimate strength of 32,000 psi. Elongation is about 50 percent in 2 in. The wide difference between yield and ultimate strength indicates that copper has considerable work-hardening capacity. The metal is too soft to be readily machinable.

The melting point of pure copper is 1981°F. However, copper cannot be used at temperatures very much above room temperature due to loss of strength and oxidation. The oxide formed at high temperatures is black, but after long exposure to atmospheric conditions copper turns green (so does nickel). The copper industry has devoted much effort to surface treatments that will preserve the original surface appearance of copper, and has recently developed treatments that may prove suitable for that purpose.

The current-carrying grades of copper must be relatively pure, since alloying additions, even in minute amounts, greatly increase the resistivity. Silver, gold, and cadmium, however, have lesser effects on resistance. Electrolytic tough pitch copper (ETP grade) containing 0.04 percent oxygen is used for conductors. Oxygen-free high conductivity copper (OFHC grade) is the best grade available. A micrograph of oxygen in furnace copper is shown in Fig. 30 on page 56. The inclusions are Cu_2O. Such copper is not welded, since release of the oxygen produces cracks in the copper. To remove oxygen, phosphorus is added to molten copper as small phosphorus-copper shot.

Though much copper is used for tubing, pipe, and heat transfer equipment, it is not used in the food-processing industries in contact with foods because many copper compounds are toxic.

The copper alloys are numerous indeed, but their nomenclature is often inconvenient and confusing. Zinc, tin, aluminum, and silicon all serve as solid-solution hardeners in these alloys. By suitable alloying, a wide range of metallic colors, from copper to white, is available. In general, *brasses* are alloys of copper and zinc, *bronzes* are alloys of copper and elements other than zinc.

The brasses are, of all metals, the most ingratiating ones to machine, so that the word "brass" is almost synonymous with machinability in the minds of production personnel.

The portion of the copper-zinc equilibrium diagram that embraces the brasses is given in Fig. 124. Note that the diagram indicates the brasses to be nonheat-treatable: no phase boundary line indicates decreasing solubility of one material in another. The alpha brasses contain up to 36 percent zinc, ranging in color from red to yellow as the zinc content is increased. The alpha plus beta brasses contain 38 to 46 percent zinc. Since copper is fcc, alpha brasses are fcc. The beta phase is bcc. Zinc is hcp.

Fig. 124 Copper-zinc equilibrium diagram.

The alpha brasses are good cold-working materials, while the alpha plus beta brasses are not especially ductile at room temperature but are excellent hot-working alloys.

A familiar alpha brass is the yellow *cartridge brass*, 70 percent copper, which is used in a wide range of products from electric light sockets to flashlight casings to rifle shells. Figure 125 is a micrograph of this brass.

The red brasses have less alloy content and better corrosion resistance than the yellow brasses. Red brasses are used for plumbing pipe. Alloys such as muntz metal and admiralty metal are formulated for corrosion resistance to freshwater and seawater, and find their uses in marine hardware and condenser tubing for thermal power plants.

metals with special properties and applications

Fig. 125 Micrograph of a leaded cartridge brass. The twinning commonly found in wrought fcc metals can be found here.

TABLE OF BRASS ALLOYS

	Cu	Zn	Sn	Pb
1. electrolytic tough pitch copper	99.92			
2. gilding brass	95	5		
3. commercial bronze	90	10		
4. red brass	85	15		
5. low brass	80	20		
6. admiralty metal	71	28	1	
7. cartridge brass	70	30		
8. yellow brass	65	35		
9. free machining brass	61.5	35.5		3
10. muntz metal	60	40		
11. naval brass	60	39.25	0.75	

The usual effect of alloying is increased strength and reduced ductility as compared with the pure metal. Copper-zinc alloys are an exception. The remarkable combination of increased ductility with increased strength in copper-zinc alloys is shown in the following table. Note that the ductility decreases when the beta phase appears. The table gives comparative values only for one grain size and degree of working, and does not indicate the maximum strengths of these alloys. A standard $\frac{3}{4}$-in. diameter bar of yellow brass breaks at about 75,000 psi.

metals with special properties and applications
278

PROPERTIES OF COPPER-ZINC ALLOYS

Zn, %	UTS, psi	Elongation % in 2 in.
0	32,000	46
5	36,000	49
10	41,000	52
15	42,000	56
20	43,000	59
25	45,000	62
30	46,000	65
35	46,000	60
40	54,000	45

The brasses present difficulties in welding due to loss of zinc, which boils at the low temperature of 1665°F. The brasses therefore are gas-welded or brazed rather than arc-welded.

13.5   bronzes

The *phosphor bronzes* are actually tin bronzes containing 1 to 11 percent tin. Phosphorus is used in small amounts as a deoxidizer. These bronzes are used in sheet and bar form for their high tensile strength, toughness, formability, fatigue strength, and corrosion resistance. Tensile strength may be as high as 100,000 psi. Phosphor bronzes are frequently specified for instrument parts such as diaphragms, bellows, springs, and electrical contacts.

Cast bronze plumbing fittings are a common article in domestic and commercial plumbing lines strung in copper pipe. A commonly used alloy for casting these fittings is a tin bronze analyzing 81 percent copper, 3 percent tin, 7 percent lead, 9 percent zinc. The tin and zinc provide castability while the lead gives machinability.

Silicon bronzes are more familiarly known by their trade names, such as Everdur and Herculoy. These also are high strength alloys, with strengths as high as 110,000 psi.

The *cupronickels* contain up to 30 percent nickel. Since copper and nickel are completely soluble in each other, these are single phase alloys like the monels, incapable of heat treatment. They are chiefly employed for tubing which must have resistance to fresh- and sea-water attack.

Aluminum bronzes contain from 4 to 11 percent aluminum. The alloys containing over 8 percent aluminum are heat-treatable to give microstructures similar to steel. Slow cooling gives a lamellar soft structure like pearlite; fast cooling produces a martensitic structure. The aluminum bronzes are used for a wide range of articles, including electrical hardware, marine hardware, propellers, tubing, and pumps. Tensile strength may exceed 100,000 psi after heat treatment, but ductility is then minimal.

Beryllium copper is another heat-treatable bronze, giving the highest strengths of all the copper alloys, together with remarkable fatigue resistance, formability, corrosion and wear resistance. Its uses cover a wide range, including instrument parts, springs, diaphragms, dies, firing pins, electrical hardware, and because of its hardness, nonsparking hand tools such as wrenches. A maximum hardness of about R_C 42 is possible. A range of beryllium bronzes is available, from 0.4 percent to 1.9 percent beryllium. Cobalt plus nickel is included in the alloy for grain refinement.

Zirconium copper and *chromium copper* are heat-treatable, used chiefly for instrument work and electrical hardware such as resistance welding tips and switch parts.

Copper and many of these copper alloys are supplied as cold-drawn leaded bars for ease of machining, and in this form can often be machined at the maximum speed of a lathe. Besides lead, tellurium and sulfur may be added for machinability.

The copper brazing alloys include, besides pure copper, high zinc alloys and high phosphorus (5–6 percent P) alloys containing some silver. These will braze most of the copper alloys.

BRONZE ALLOYS

	Cu	Sn	Si	Zn	Ni + Co	Other
phosphor bronze	90+	1.25–10				
silicon bronze	98		1.5–3			
architectural bronze	57	3		40		
cupronickel	70				30	
aluminum bronze	90+					4–11 Al
nickel silver	65			17	18	
beryllium bronze	97.9				0.2	1.9 Be
chromium copper	99.1					0.9 Cr
zirconium copper	99.85					0.15 Zr

13.6 zinc

Zinc is used for an anodic coating on steels, applied usually by hot-dip galvanizing or electrogalvanizing. In sheet form zinc is most familiar

metals with special properties and applications

as dry cell casings. Other important uses include die castings and the alloying of nonferrous metals.

Zinc melts at 787°F and boils at 1665°F at atmospheric pressure. Its low boiling point indicates its unsuitability for use under vacuum conditions in industry or outer space. When melted or welded, special techniques are required to reduce zinc losses by evaporation, even in brasses.

Die castings require the use of high purity zinc. The presence of more than trace amounts of cadmium, lead, or tin promotes corrosion in zinc die castings, though die casting alloys may contain a few percent of aluminum or copper. Perhaps the most familiar die castings are the carburetors and fuel pumps of automobiles.

13.7 cadmium

Cadmium is used for the plating of steel hardware and fasteners and as an alloy in bearing metals. The uses of *tin* are similar to those of cadmium. Since cadmium compounds are toxic, this metal is not permitted in food-processing equipment. Because of its high neutron capture cross-section, cadmium is used in the control of nuclear reactions.

13.8 cobalt

Cobalt is a hard, ferromagnetic metal melting at 2719°F. The uses of cobalt largely arise from its strength at high temperature; it is used therefore in superalloys, heat-resistant castings, hot-working steels, and as a binder in sintered carbide cutting tools. It is also found in Alnico and other permanent magnet alloys. The best known of the cobalt alloys are the *stellites*, which contain also chromium, tungsten, and carbon.

Advances in isotope techniques have made Cobalt-60 one of the more important industrial (and medical) metals. This radioactive cobalt contains an extra neutron, which makes the atomic nucleus unstable. Probably more Co-60 is used in industry and medicine than the total of all other radioisotopes. It is produced in the nuclear reactors at Chalk River and Oak Ridge. Aside from medical therapy, Co-60 is used as a source of deep-penetration (over 1 Mev) gamma radiation for the examination of welds, forgings, and castings. It is not suitable for the lighter metals with lower absorptions, such as aluminum. Like all radioisotopes, it is sold by the curie (Sec. 2.11) and not by weight.

13.9 lead

Pure lead melts at 621°F. This versatile metal has applications that derive from its special properties of high atomic weight and density, softness, ductility, low strength, low melting point, corrosion resistance, and ability to lubricate. Its fatigue strength is poor, so that it cannot be used under conditions of vibration. It will creep even at room temperatures. Still another disadvantage is the toxicity of its compounds. The chief uses of lead include the following:

1. tank linings for corrosion protection
2. storage batteries of the lead-acid type
3. pipe and drainage fittings such as closet bends for toilet bowls
4. machinability additive to free-cutting steels and brasses
5. biological shielding against gamma radiation (but not against neutrons)
6. lead sheathing of electric cable
7. low-melting solders
8. bearing metals
9. fusible alloys and low-melting alloys for various purposes (see Fig. 126)
10. type metal for the printing trade
11. terne plate (lead-tin coated steel)
12. tetraethyl lead anti-knock ingredient in gasolines
13. lead compounds in paints

In general lead does not form useful alloys except with other metals with low melting points. In the free-machining leaded alloys the lead is not an alloy ingredient but an inclusion. For corrosion resistance and for gamma ray shielding, pure lead gives best performance.

To increase the low strength of lead, two types of alloys are in use: tellurium lead and antimonial lead. The addition of less than 0.1 percent tellurium improves the work-hardening capacity of lead. Pure lead has a tensile strength of only 2500 psi, but antimony improves this strength. A maximum of 11 percent antimony may be used, resulting in an increase in strength of about three times. Alloying, however, reduces the already low melting temperature of lead.

The solders are alloys of lead and tin, the amount of tin used ranging from 5 to 50 percent. The equilibrium diagram for these solders is given in Fig. 24 on page 51. Tin additions are necessary to enable the lead to wet the metal to be joined. The lead-base babbitt bearing alloys are somewhat similar to solders, containing about 10 percent each of tin and antimony. Terne plate, used for gasoline tanks on automobiles and other mobile equipment, is steel sheet coated with a lead solder alloy of about 20 percent tin.

The thickness of lead is usually referred to by weight in pounds per square foot. One square foot of lead $\frac{1}{64}$ in. thick weighs 1 lb. Thus an 8-lb sheet lead is $\frac{8}{64}$ in. thick.

Fig. 126 Experimental aircraft panel under buckling test. The top and bottom of the panel are supported by cast cerrobend, a low-melting-point alloy.

13.10   silver and gold

These precious metals have a limited range of uses in industry. Silver is the more useful. Both metals have a tensile strength of about 18,000 psi, though neither is used for structural purposes. Silver has slightly better electrical conductivity than copper, while gold has lower conductivity. Both metals are fcc and ductile.

Gold has occasional uses as a reflecting surface, as attachments to transistors, and a few brazing alloys contain gold in amounts up to 40 percent.

Silver is plated onto low-voltage electrical contacts, but not for its conductivity. When arcing occurs, the contact surface oxidizes. Silver is used because the oxidized silver readily reduces back to silver. Silver is also occasionally used as a corrosion-resistant lining in chemical process vessels. However, it is readily corroded by sulfur.

Silver may be hardened by a few percent of copper, the copper acting as a solid-solution strengthener which permits precipitation heat-treatment. The most important of the silver-copper alloys are the silver solders, brazing alloys which contain considerable silver with copper and zinc. These have solidus temperatures between 1000 and 1500°F.

The photosensitivity of silver salts is the reason for their use in photographic emulsions. When development of photographic film is done on a large scale, silver can be recovered from the emulsion.

Both silver and gold and their brazing alloys are sold by the troy ounce, twelve ounces to the pound. An ounce of silver is heavier than an ounce of lead (avoir.), while a pound of lead is heavier than a pound of silver.

metals with special properties and applications

13.11   the platinum group

This group of six metals is extracted from nickel ores. Platinum is probably the most useful member of the group. Platinum, palladium, iridium, and rhodium, are face-centered cubic, while osmium and ruthenium are body-centered cubic. Osmium and iridium, having twice the specific weight of lead, are the heaviest of all metals, while platinum is almost as heavy. The other platinum metals are slightly heavier than lead. All six of the platinum group have high melting points, above 3000°F.

In addition to being the heaviest metal, osmium has the highest modulus of elasticity, 80×10^6. This, however, is no virtue because of the remarkable brittleness of osmium. The others of the platinum group also have high E-values.

The platinum group collectively shows a high degree of corrosion and oxidation resistance compared to other metals. Iridium is considered the most corrosion-resistant of all the metals.

Platinum is the most ductile of the group. Its uses include laboratory apparatus such as small crucibles and dishes, thermocouples and other instrument components, spinning and wire-drawing dies, components of high-power vacuum tubes, glass-working equipment, and electrical contacts. Platinum alloys readily with many metals, and is usually solid-solution hardened by ruthenium, iridium or rhodium.

Palladium is used principally in telephone relay contacts. A billion interruptions of current are expected before the relay wears out. Palladium offers for such service freedom from oxidation, sulfidation, and spark erosion.

Iridium is chiefly used as the radioisotope Iridium-192. Together with Cobalt-60, it satisfies most of the requirements of industrial radiography, Cobalt-60 being used for penetrating heavy sections of heavy metals, while Iridium-192 is used for lighter sections in both heavy and light metals.

13.12   the rare earths

The rare earths are a large group of 14 metals, actually about a quarter of all the metals. Most of this group are hexagonal close-packed. They are blessed with such exotic names as praseodymium, dysprosium, neodymium, etc., which may or may not explain why they presently lead a disoriented life on the fringes of the society of respectable metals.

Mixtures of the rare earths have been called "mischmetal" since earlier times, and are added to stainless steels to provide ease of rolling. Their use as an alloying element in magnesium has been noted. An yttrium alloy of aluminum has been developed.

General Motors Corporation has used a radioisotope of samarium for gammagraphing engine castings. The oxides of cerium, praseodymium, and lanthanum have been considered for the thermoelectric generation of power, and in electronics gadolinium ferrites have been studied. Most, but not all, the rare earths have remarkably high neutron absorption cross-sections, and therefore have possibilities for control of nuclear reactors. A few of the rare earths have been employed as doping materials in lasers. By and large, however, interest in the rare earths has developed only in recent years, and it is difficult to predict what uses will be found for these materials. The developmental uses outlined above suggest that they may well settle into the more glamorous areas of engineering.

13.13   zirconium

Zirconium is another reactive metal: extraction of the metal from the ore therefore proceeds in the usual method of converting the ore to zirconium chloride and then reducing the chloride with magnesium. Like titanium, molten zirconium reacts with crucible materials, reducing their oxides to metal.

Zirconium melts at 3366°F. It is not characterized by good hot strength, however, and oxidizes readily above 1000°F. Fine zirconium powder or machining chips may even ignite spontaneously, though the metal is not hazardous in massive form.

Crystal structure of zirconium is hcp at room temperature, with a bcc phase above 1590°. In sheet form, zirconium somewhat resembles stainless steel, though it has a somewhat lower specific weight. It has a low thermal conductivity, like stainless steel, but a much lower coefficient of expansion — 0.000 004 in./in. Like stainless steel its corrosion resistance is remarkable, though not as good at high temperatures. Small amounts of carbon, oxygen, nitrogen, and hydrogen greatly reduce the corrosion resistance, and strengthen and embrittle the metal.

Most zirconium is consumed in the manufacture of fuel rods for nuclear reactors. For such an application the amount of impurities of high neutron absorption must be held to very low levels. Zirconium ores invariably contain over 2 percent hafnium, which is a neutron absorber; this hafnium must be removed during processing of the metal. The content of boron and cadmium is held to a maximum of 0.5 parts per million for the same reason.

The only alloys of zirconium are zirconium-2.5 percent niobium (i.e., columbium) and the Zircaloys. Zircaloy-2 contains 1.2–1.7 percent tin with small amounts of iron and nickel. Both tin and niobium have low neutron absorption and offset the detrimental influence of impurities such

Fig. 127   Micrograph of Zircaloy-2, a tin alloy of zirconium.

as nitrogen. Zircaloy-2 has a tensile strength of 66,000 psi and elongation of 20 percent in 2 in. A micrograph of a zirconium alloy is shown in Fig. 127.

13.14   the refractory metals

The refractory metals are by definition those metals with melting points above 3600°F. Such a definition should include osmium, iridium, and ruthenium, and should exclude chromium. The first three, however, fall into the group of platinum metals. The refractory metals include only chromium, columbium, hafnium, molybdenum, rhenium, tantalum, tungsten, and vanadium.

The refractory metals have melting points as high as 6150°F, somewhat beyond the useful temperature range of refractories and melting furnaces, and therefore they cannot be melted and cast like most metals. These metals must be prepared by sintering them in powder metallurgy processes similar to those in use with beryllium and zirconiun.

It would appear that such metals could be used at temperatures beyond the reach of lower-melting metals. The refractory metals have remarkable strength at unusually high temperatures, but oxidize catastrophically at rather low temperatures. With respect to oxidation properties, these metals are far inferior to the platinum metals or even nickel.

It is ironical and frustrating that low-melting metals such as magnesium, aluminum, and calcium, should have highly refractory oxides, while the refractory metals usually have oxides that melt below the melting point of the metal. The following table presents the melting points of the refractory metals and their oxides.

MELTING POINTS OF REFRACTORY METALS AND OXIDES

chromium	2822°F	chromia	4230°F	(Cr_2O_3)
hafnium	3866	hafnia	5140	(HfO_2)
molybdenum	4730	molybdenum oxide	1465	(MoO_3)
niobium	4380	niobia	2500	(Nb_2O_5)
rhenium	5730	rhenia	565	(Re_2O_7)
tantalum	5425	tantalum oxide	2500	(Ta_2O_5)
tungsten	6152	tungsten oxide	1830	(WO_3)
vanadium	3450	vanadia	1270	(V_2O_5)

The lowest-melting oxide is reported in the table. Note that the melting point of the metals tends to increase in alphabetical order. The actual relationship of the melting points is disclosed by arranging these metals as they appear in the Periodic Table:

Ti	V	Cr
Zr	Nb	Mo
Hf	Ta	W

The melting point increases toward the bottom of each of the three columns.

Relative oxidation rates at higher temperatures are shown in Fig. 128.

Many of the refractory metals are familiar carbide-formers in steel technology. Comparative properties of the pure metals are listed in the table on page 288.

Fig. 128 Relative oxidation rates of refractory metals at temperatures in the range of 2000°F. Oxidation loss of tungsten is approximately 0.10 in. per 15 hrs.

metals with special properties and applications

PROPERTIES OF THE REFRACTORY METALS

Metal	Structure	E(70°)	E(2000°)	Ductility	UTS(70°)	UTS(2000°)
Hf	hcp	20×10^6		Fair	60,000	
V	bcc	20×10^6		Good	70,000	5,000
Nb	bcc	16×10^6	12×10^6	Good	40,000	10,000
Ta	bcc	27×10^6	24×10^6	Excellent	100,000	20,000
Cr	bcc	42×10^6	30×10^6	None	70,000	10,000
Mo	bcc	46×10^6	40×10^6	Poor	80,000	25,000
W	bcc	60×10^6	50×10^6	None	100,000	35,000
Re	hcp	66×10^6	50×10^6	Good	160,000	75,000

A review of the properties tabulated above shows why niobium (columbium) and tantalum are the preferred refractory metals at the present time. This preference is based on their combination of good ductility and high melting point of the oxide, combined with minimum cost. Hafnium has a favorable spectrum of properties, but its cost greatly exceeds that of columbium and tantalum.

Because the properties of these metals are strongly affected by such factors as trace elements, grain size, processing procedures, and even the method of measuring the properties, the values listed above must be viewed as only approximate. This is even true for E-values. The table above applies to the "pure" metals, but this means rather the purest available. The presence of 0.01 percent oxygen in a refractory metal might, for example, double the ultimate tensile strength.

All of the refractory group except two are body-centered cubic, and therefore show a ductile-to-brittle transition temperature. This transition temperature is well above room temperature for tungsten, molybdenum, and chromium.

Hafnium is present in all zirconium ores, and this is the only source from which it is extracted. But while zirconium is commercially available, hafnium is not. It has had limited review for aerospace programs, but its use is limited to rectifiers and a few electronic applications.

Rhenium is probably the metal with the most pronounced work-hardening characteristics. This is a high strength material with good ductility, high melting point, and high E-value, a splendid combination spoiled by its strong oxidizing tendency. This metal has been reviewed for aerospace applications with little success, and future applications for it, as for all the refractory metals, seem likely to lie in electronics, for filaments in high-power vacuum tubes and for structural components under vacuum where its oxidation deficiencies will not be a handicap. It is also used in rhenium-tungsten high-temperature thermocouples. When alloyed with molybdenum and tungsten, it greatly improves the room-temperature ductility of these metals.

The chief uses of *chromium* lie in chrome-plating and in steel alloys, to which it contributes hardness, strength at high temperature, and corrosion resistance. Though a relatively abundant metal, its brittleness may relegate it to the role of an alloying element in the foreseeable future. The research effort devoted to solving the problems of chromium is much less aggressive than that expended on the more promising metals columbium and tantalum.

Vanadium has many ores, and is present in crude oils up to a maximum of 0.06 percent by weight. It is added to steels in small amounts up to 1 percent for the purpose of grain refinement. Some promising high strength alloys of vanadium have reached the development stage, but are not yet in use.

13.15   columbium and tantalum

These two metals are distinguished by excellent ductility, even at low temperature, tantalum probably having the best ductility of the body-centered cubic metals. It is not certain that tantalum has a ductile-to-brittle transition temperature. Both metals occur together in ores, and as was the case for zirconium and hafnium, they must be separated for nuclear use, since tantalum has a high neutron absorption and that of columbium is low.

Until interest developed in the refractory metals after World War II, columbium was used only as an alloy addition in stabilized stainless steels such as 347 and 316Cb. Tantalum, which has a very low work-hardening capacity, was used for piping, heat transfer coils, and similar applications in chemical process industries, its corrosion resistance being almost identical to that of glass. It has also been used as a melting crucible material for melting reactive metals under vacuum. While columbium is not yet employed in electrical or electronic devices, tantalum is used for anode and grid elements in medium- to high-power tubes, in capacitors, and in tantalum-foil rectifiers. Tantalum oxide has a rectifying effect on alternating current.

Columbium shows promise for high temperature applications. Alloy development work has produced alloys capable of short-time exposure to temperatures of 2500°F in air, though the objective of these programs is a temperature of 3000°F. Compared to columbium, tantalum has the disadvantages of high specific weight and less abundance in ores. Typical commercial alloys of these metals, all formulated for hot strength, creep resistance, oxidation resistance, and ease of fabrication, are these:

Columbium alloys:

FS82	33% Ta, 1% Zr
FS85	28% Ta, 1% Zr, 11% W
Cb-6	10% W, 8% Ti

metals with special properties and applications
289

Tantalum alloys:

Ta-10W	10% W
Ta-8W-2Hf	8% W, 2% Hf
Ta-12.5W	12.5% W

Several other columbium alloys are commercially available, but only these three tantalum alloys. The Ta-10W alloy has a tensile strength of 50,000 psi at 2500°F, almost the melting temperature of stainless steels. The columbium alloys are used in the nose components and leading edges of hypersonic aerospace vehicles.

13.16 molybdenum and

tungsten

These two metals and tantalum have had industrial uses over many decades. Thomas Edison experimented with tungsten wire in his 98-percent-perspiration, 2-percent-inspiration invention of the incandescent lamp. Molybdenum and tungsten are among the chief carbide-formers in high speed steels, molybdenum tending to replace tungsten in this application because of its lower weight. Though both metals have unusual strength, hardness, and stiffness, even in pure form, and especially at high temperatures, they both have the serious defects of great brittleness at room temperature and pronounced oxidation at relatively low temperatures. Alloying to reduce oxidation of these metals has not been as successful as in the case of columbium.

Room temperature applications for these metals are numerous. Tungsten has the following applications:

1. electrodes for inert-gas welding (TIG welding)
2. lamp and electron tube filaments
3. anodes for X-ray tubes and electron tubes
4. electric resistance elements
5. wire-drawing dies
6. rocket nozzles

Tungsten is too hard to machine, except by grinding. Molybdenum is machinable. It is also cheaper than tungsten. Its applications include:

1. electron tube anodes
2. grids for high-power electron tubes
3. dies for die-casting, extrusion, and upsetting of metals
4. components in processing molten glass

metals with special properties and applications
290

5. corrosion-resistant valves and piping
6. supports for tungsten filaments in light bulbs
7. resistance-heating elements

The addition of alloying elements to tungsten has little advantage, and tungsten therefore is usually employed in relatively pure form. Molybdenum has a few commercial alloys, chiefly two:

TZM	0.5% Ti, 0.08% Zr
Mo-0.5 Ti	0.5% Ti

Mo-50W, with 50 percent tungsten, is used only as wire in electron tubes. TZM has outstanding strength up to 3000°F and has a range of uses for aerospace vehicles and metal-forming dies.

The refractory metals will come into wider use when their price is reduced somewhat and when methods of purifying metals are improved. Their shortcomings can be overcome, but probably only to a limited degree. Although they are popularly viewed as exotic metals, their future areas of application will probably be those in which they are presently established:

(a) electricity and electronics
(b) chemical processing
(c) metal fabrication
(d) aerospace

PROBLEMS

1 Compare iron and nickel as to (a) *E*-value, (b) sulfur control during melting operations, (c) melting point, (d) crystal structure.

2 Given the analysis of Monel R-405 (see Table of Nickel Alloys), how do you know that this alloy is not heat-treatable?

3 Distinguish between brasses and bronzes.

4 Give the crystal structure of copper, alpha brass, beta brass, and zinc.

5 Why is zinc gas-welded, but rarely arc-welded?

6 What is the thickness of a sheet of 6-lb lead?

7 Summarize the uses of the platinum metals.

8 Why must hafnium be removed from nuclear-grade zirconium?

9 What advantages do the refractory metals offer?

ORGANIC
MATERIALS

Part **IV**

14.1 a little history

The technical culture of the Arctic Eskimos, now rapidly being forgotten, was at least as gifted as ours in its use of materials. Except for one inland tribe, the Eskimo lived in a country without resources other than rock and snow. The land provided him with insufficient food and materials for survival, so he turned to the resources of the sea for materials. Except for snow as a winter shelter material and stone for tools and a small cooking hearth, the Eskimo used the organic materials of sea animals to survive. Even his fuel had to be animal oils.

Most early civilizations, however, used wood as an industrial material. It was employed principally as a construction material, and still is. Wood and other organic materials such as canvas, hemp, manila fiber and oakum, made possible the sailing ship, the invention that more than any other raised man's standard of living, for it made worldwide trading possible. Until 125 years ago, the sailing ship was man's most powerful machine. The great sailing "clippers" of the golden age of sail might carry as much as 10,000 square yards of canvas, which propelled them at top speeds of about 25 miles per hour. Such windpower is equivalent to 1000–1500 horsepower.

The peculiar influence of organic materials on historical development does not end with the sailing ship, the archery that turned the tide in medieval battle, or the wooden palisades of early North American forts. Radar made it possible for the Royal Air Force Fighter Command to win the most

THE
ORGANIC
MATERIALS

14

crucial battle of World War II, the famous Battle of Britain, but what is less well known is that polyethylene insulation made radar possible. Two years after the Battle of Britain, Japanese forces overran the sources of natural rubber that were to supply the vehicles of American armies, but again new synthetic rubbers saved the day. In the same war years the plastic Teflon, used as a corrosion-resistant lining, made possible the processing of materials for the atom bomb.

Wood is a natural organic material, while polyethylene and most rubbers are synthetic. The scope of application of natural organic materials has tended to decline, beginning about the year 1900 (with the notable exception of paper, the raw material of bureaucracy), while on the other hand the chemist's ability to produce new synthetic organics has exceeded the capacity of markets to absorb them.

14.2 general characteristics

The organic materials are the innumerable substances based on carbon chemistry. Parallel to them is the variety of ceramic materials based on silicon, which is in the same column of the Periodic Table. The large organic group includes the natural materials wood, coal, petroleum, natural gas, natural rubber, animal fibers, and food. Synthetics include the larger group of solvents, adhesives, metal and wood finishes, synthetic fibers, rubbers, plastics, explosives, lubricants, dyes, soaps, cutting oils, zeolites, and countless others.

If we compare the structural organic materials, which are wood, rubber, and plastics, with the structural metals and ceramics, we find a number of differences.

1. The organics are soft, and have lower strengths.
2. Moduli of elasticity are lower, from a maximum of about 2×10^6 for hardwoods to as low as 200 for the common soft rubber band.
3. The ductility of most organic materials is remarkable, often exceeding 100 percent. The plastics tend to deform plastically, the rubbers and wood deform elastically, although both will creep at room temperature.
4. Temperature limits for the organic materials are low, generally below 500°F. Many are combustible.
5. Because of the presence of hydrogen in the molecule, specific heats are high for organic materials, in the range of 0.3–0.4 Btu/lb/°F.
6. Thermal and electrical conductivity are both very low. Many of the organics are excellent insulators.
7. Specific weight of any organic material is low.
8. Many organic materials, notably wood and nylon, undergo dimensional changes with changes of relative humidity.

By and large, then, the chief deficiency in the properties of the solid organic materials as a group is a *lack of dimensional stability* under the influence of stress and environment.

Many of the organics of interest in this book are polymers, including the woods, rubbers, plastics, finishes, adhesives, fibers, and foods.

Most of the industrial organic materials are *petrochemicals*. A petrochemical is, roughly speaking, an organic chemical derived from petroleum or natural gas. The petrochemicals, like other organic compounds, are chemicals containing carbon and hydrogen (hydrocarbons), but frequently also contain oxygen and nitrogen. An exact explanation of what constitutes a petrochemical, however, is apt to produce either confusion or hilarity. Some petrochemicals aren't petrochemicals, and some are petrochemicals sometimes. Consider sulfur, which is produced from oil and gas. Sulfur is not a petrochemical, because it is not a chemical at all, but an elemental substance. But carbon black, also an elemental substance, is a petrochemical, because a processing operation is required to make it from oil or gas. Benzene, xylene, and toluene can be made from crude oil: these are petrochemicals. But benzene, xylene, and toluene can be distilled from coal: these are not petrochemicals. Ammonia, NH_3, which contains no carbon, is a petrochemical. Most rubbers are petrochemicals, but natural rubber is not.

14.3 wood

"Wood is universally beautiful to man. It is the most humanly intimate of all materials. Man loves his association with it, likes to feel it under his hand". Thus the American architect, Frank Lloyd Wright, expresses the appeal of wood to man. For the reasons noted by Wright, wood persisted as a raw material in the industrial arts shops of public schools long after the general usefulness of such training had disappeared.

Fig. 129 The wooden pallet, which created a revolution in material-handling practices, material-handling equipment, and warehouse layout. The style of pallet shown is known as a four-way pallet, since it allows the forks of a lift truck to enter the pallet from any of the four sides. The 40 × 48-deck is the commonest size.

Although wood has lost many applications to metals and plastics, its uses are still highly diversified. Its chief products are paper and lumber. Second to these is the use of wood as a packaging material for crating, wirebound boxes, wood boxes, skids, and pallets like the one shown in Fig. 129. Other uses for wood are perhaps of lesser importance: cellulose filaments, chemicals, laminated timbers, fine-art objects such as furniture, and a variety of special products such as timber piles, power poles, railroad ties, foundry patterns, cribbing, wood pipe and tanks, fisherman's floats, matches, charcoal and other luxury fuels.

It is not possible to conceive of wood as becoming obsolete because of its unique advantages over other materials:

1. it is a self-perpetuating natural resource
2. its relative abundance in most geographical areas
3. the ease with which it can be processed
4. its light weight
5. its inherent beauty
6. it is the strongest of the cellular materials, and the cheapest

A remarkable property of wood is its capacity to survive fires. The fire resistance of wood is promoted simply by using large timber sections. A 12 × 12 timber might require days to burn through: no accidental fire lasts more than hours. Wood also has a low thermal conductivity and a high specific heat. Wood therefore must be considered much more fire-resistant than steel, the latter material having a high thermal conductivity and considerable loss of strength at elevated temperatures. Wood will not ignite until its temperature reaches about 550°F.

Wood has a high degree of corrosion resistance, but will slowly "weather" if exposed continuously to the atmosphere. In weathering, its surface turns gray and roughens. Weathering apparently is a very slow corrosion process, the rate of weathering being cited as a quarter-inch per century.

The woods are broadly divided into two groups, hardwoods and softwoods. In this classification, the relative hardness of the woods is unimportant, though all the very hardest woods are indeed hardwoods. Some softwoods, however, are harder than some hardwoods. *Softwoods*, which tend to flourish in colder climates or higher altitudes, are those trees which grow needles instead of leaves and bear cones instead of fruit. The softwoods tend to grow in huge stands of relatively few species, a characteristic that the hardwoods do not share. The softwoods are *conifers*, cone-bearers. Hardwoods are most commonly found in hotter climates, though a few species grow in subarctic areas. The hardwoods bear fruit and leaves which fall off in the autumn season. Spruce, fir, pine, hemlock, and tamarack are typical softwoods; aspen, willow, oak, maple, and walnut are hardwoods. About 30 softwoods and 50 hardwoods are of commercial importance in this country.

Typical uses of some softwoods

1. pines — foundry patterns. Easily shaped, non-splitting, dimensional stability
2. Western White Pine — matches, boxes, crates
3. Southern Pine — railroad ties, boxes, tanks, millwork
4. Sitka Spruce — aircraft. Strong, few defects, light weight
5. Douglas Fir — plywood, wood tanks. Strong, tending to become brittle with age
6. Cypress — tanks, vats, and silos. Decay resistant
7. Cedar — pencils. Easily whittled, rot-resistant, but splits readily and has little strength or hardness

Typical uses of the hardwoods

1. hickory — handles for impact tools. Hard, strong, and tough
2. ash — long tool handles (e.g., shovels), baseball bats
3. birch — butcher blocks, desks. Rots readily
4. oak — railroad ties, posts, industrial floors, pallets. A poor wood for dimensional stability
5. maple — flooring, bowling pins, boxes and crates
6. basswood — drafting boards, boxes and crates
7. aspen — pallets. A tough wood

The first trees to appear in the long history of the earth were the softwoods, which date from about 200,000,000 years ago. The hardwoods are about half as old as the softwoods in geological history.

14.4   the structure of wood

In the temperate zones, tree growth is rapid early in the season. As the season advances, the growth is slower. The spring growth (springwood) can be distinguished from the summer growth (summerwood) by its lower density and lighter color. The growth rings in a cross-section of the tree trunk can be distinguished as a result of these color variations.

The structure of wood is cellular. A piece of wood is thus a bundle of thin-walled tubes. This structure explains the anisotropy in the properties of wood.

The chemistry of the walls of these wood cells is of great industrial importance, especially for the pulp and paper industry. From 55 to 70 percent of the cell wall is *cellulose*, a long-chain fibrous polymer resistant to acids. It is estimated that the cellulose polymer is composed of 5000 to 10,000 monomer units. Such a long molecule would be visible under the microscope if only the molecule were somewhat wider that it is.

From 15 to 35 percent of the cell wall is *lignin*. This is the chemical that produces the brown color of corrugated cardboard cartons and causes the yellowing of newsprint with age. Secondary constituents of wood include volatile (distillable) materials, gums, and ash.

The property of anisotropy is a design consideration in the use of wood. The tensile strength of wood on a plane perpendicular to the grain is about ten times better than the strength parallel to the grain. Shear strength parallel to the grain is poor, while shear strength perpendicular to the grain is very high. The dimensional changes in wood due to variations of moisture content are likewise influenced by the cellular or tubular structure of wood. Changes in length parallel to the grain as a result of moisture variation are negligible. The anisotropy of wood may be reduced by laminating it as plywood, with the grain running in different directions in the several laminations. Lamination, however, reduces the apparent modulus of elasticity.

14.5 physical properties of
wood

The physical and mechanical properties of wood are considerably affected by the moisture content of the wood, including hardness, strength, and electrical resistance. The moisture content in the air-dried condition at equilibrium with the atmosphere is 12–15 percent.

Moisture content in percent is measured as

$$\frac{\text{weight of moist wood} - \text{oven-dried weight}}{\text{oven-dried weight}} \times 100\%$$

Generally the lighter woods can hold more moisture than heavy woods. South American balsa wood, specific gravity 0.2, may hold 400 percent moisture in the saturated condition. Very heavy hardwoods may have saturated moisture contents of only 30 percent.

Shrinkage due to moisture changes is about 0.1–0.2 percent in the longitudinal direction. Shrinkage tangential to the growth rings is almost twice the shrinkage radial to the rings for equal changes in moisture content. Woods of high lignin content, such as mahogany, show less shrinkage than woods low in lignin, such as basswood.

The specific gravity of a wood is defined as

$$\frac{\text{oven-dry weight of 1 cu ft of wood}}{62.4}$$

The specific gravity of the oven-dry cell wall material of any wood is about 1.5. The specific gravity of any species of wood must then depend on the size of the wood cells and the thickness of the cell walls. The specific gravities of most North American woods are in the range of 0.35 to 0.65.

The anisotropy of wood shows in its thermal conductivity: conductivity for heat is twice as great parallel to the grain as in the other two directions. Thermal conductivity is increased with higher moisture content. Actual K-values per inch of thickness are about 1 Btu per hour more or less, depending on moisture content, direction of heat flow, and type of wood. The heaviest hardwoods have about twice the conductivity of the lightest softwoods.

Since the electrical resistivity of wood depends on moisture content, moisture meters usually measure the electrical resistance of the wood between probes and correlate these electrical values to moisture content.

Tensile and compressive strength of wood increases with specific gravity. The strength will be lowered by increased moisture content, however. Under long-term stress, wood will creep at room temperature. On the other hand, wood withstands impact stresses well, this feature accounting for its use in tool and implement handles.

Wood must be selected for freedom from its many possible defects. The more common defects are these:

1. *Checks.* Cracks running parallel to the grain and across the growth rings. Checks usually result from the seasoning of wood from the green condition and are especially troublesome in certain hardwoods such as oak.
2. *Cross-grain.* The grain does not run parallel to the length of the board in cross-grained lumber. Such lumber will be weak.
3. *Knots.* These occur where a branch intersects the tree trunk.
4. *Pitch pockets.* These occur between annual growth rings, and are filled with wood pitch.
5. *Warp.* Any variation from two-dimensional flatness.
6. *Insect damage.*
7. *Bark pockets.* Small patches of bark embedded in the wood.
8. *Rot.* There are many forms of wood rot. Repeated drying and wetting of wood promotes one kind of rot. Another kind is promoted by the use of steel fasteners in wet wood.

TYPICAL PHYSICAL PROPERTIES OF WOOD

	Sp Gr	Modulus of Elasticity	Compression Parallel to Grain, psi	Tension Parallel to Grain, psi
Ponderosa Pine	0.37	1.34×10^6	5200	9700
Eastern Spruce	0.39	1.2×10^6	5200	
Douglas Fir	0.46	1.6×10^6	7200	13,200
Balsam Fir	0.38	1.3×10^6	5200	
Redwood	0.38	1.25×10^6	7200	8800
Maple	0.60	1.9×10^6	7600	

14.6   paper products

It is customary to think of paper as newsprint or office material. Such a concept does no justice to the wide panorama of paper usage in industry, where it is even used as a structural material. The author would hazard the educated guess that the "Big Three" automotive manufacturers consume well over 100 tons of paper per day in industrial operations, not including office paper.

The paper industry defines paper as "all kinds of matted or felted sheets of fiber . . . formed on a wire screen from water suspension." Paper products are divided into two broad groups: paper and paperboard, the latter being a heavier and more rigid type of product. These two categories are produced in roughly equal amounts in the United States, about 20,000,000 tons of each. The actual consumption of paper in the United States exceeds the consumption of any metal other than steel. About 50,000,000 tons of paper is the annual consumption. In Canada the annual production of paper in tons is approximately equal to the annual production of steel. This huge paper industry consumes annually over a million tons of salt cake, half a million tons of sulfur, and a million tons of china clay.

The U.S. Bureau of the Census, Industry Division, divides statistics of paper production into 8 groups of products distributed approximately as follows:

newsprint	12%
book & magazine papers	28
fine & writing papers	10
wrapping papers & bags	24
tissue papers	2
sanitary papers	11
building papers	9
other papers	4
	100%

About one-third of this production goes into industrial and packaging uses.

14.7   paper-making materials

In addition to wood pulp, paper is made from waste paper and rags, and occasionally other raw stock such as bagasse (sugar cane waste). Waste paper is a difficult raw stock to use because of the presence of such foreign materials as trash, adhesive cements, and plastic film, and the problems of de-inking and bleaching the waste paper. Rag paper was exclusively used as raw material until a hundred years ago. The poorest grades of rag stock are used for roofing felt papers, though most rags are converted into specialty papers for the following purposes:

1. legal documents, insurance policies, share certificates, bonds, and bank notes
2. drafting and blueprint papers
3. high-grade letterhead bond papers and special stationery
4. cigarette and carbon papers (light-weight papers)

The two chief chemicals in wood are cellulose and lignin. Paper-making from wood pulp is based on the fact that cellulose fibers adhere to each other to form continuous sheets. Indeed cellulose is the basic raw material for seven types of adhesives, including cellulose nitrate, cellulose acetate, and ethyl cellulose. Cellulose is a carbohydrate, a substance composed of carbon, hydrogen, and oxygen. The cellulose monomer is a type of sugar, $C_6H_{10}O_5$, having the structure illustrated in Fig. 130. Lignin is present in newsprint pulp, which is basically groundwood prepared by grinding the wood fibers out of the wood with large grinding wheels. Permanent papers must be prepared by removing the lignin with chemicals.

Cellulose monomer

Fig. 130   Structure of cellulose.

Wood pulp fiber is remarkably strong: about 80,000 psi tensile strength.

Neglecting special methods that produce only limited tonnages of paper, paper pulp is produced by three principal processes:

1. the kraft process, which produces the greatest tonnage
2. the sulfite process
3. the groundwood process, its most important application being the production of newsprint in Canadian paper mills.

An average kraft pulp mill produces 500 tons of paper pulp per day. For this output the daily consumption of wood will be almost 1000 cords, or a pile of wood four feet high, four feet wide, and a mile and a half long.

PAPER PULP CHARACTERISTICS OF SOME WOODS

	Bark, %	Cellulose, %	Lignin, %	Fiber Length, mm
White Spruce	12	60.5	29.0	3.5
Eastern Pine	12.5	60.0	27.5	3.5
Hemlock	10	59.5	30.0	4.0
Paper Birch	13	60.5	25.7	1.2
Sugar Maple	14	60.8	23.2	1.0
Aspen	18.5	65.5	23.4	1.2

14.8 wood pulp processes

Chemical pulp is produced by dissolving the lignin with chemicals, thus freeing the cellulose fiber. The *sulfite process* uses sulfurous acid and bisulfites to defiber the wood after it is cut into chips, by forming complex lignin sulfonic acids. This process was the most important pulping method

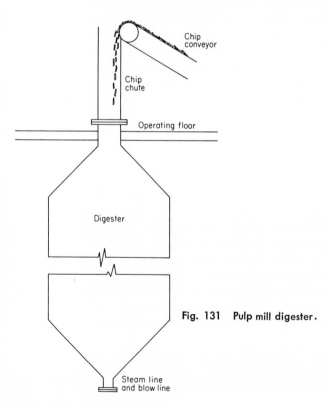

Fig. 131   Pulp mill digester.

until about 30 years ago, when the kraft process overtook it. The kraft method could pulp woods that were not suited to the sulfite process, such as many hardwoods and resinous woods like pine. The sulfite reaction on the wood chips is carried out in cylindrical vessels, usually of stainless steel, called *digesters* (Fig. 131). These are about 16 ft in diameter and about 50 ft high, with a conical bottom. Several digesters, with chip and pulp handling equipment, will be housed together in a digester building at the mill.

The *kraft*, or sulfate, process uses alkaline caustic soda and sodium sulfide to remove the lignin. The pulp produced by this method is a stronger pulp, hence the name "kraft", the German word for "strong". Most of the kraft pulp mills of the United States are in the South, since this process can pulp both the pines and hardwoods of that area. The cooking is done in digesters of much the same construction as those used for the sulfite process.

The sulfite and sulfate processes produce chemical pulp. The ground-wood process produces mechanical pulp by grinding the wood in the presence of water. Groundwood pulp is produced for newsprint, for tissue, towelling, and board paper, and for molded packaging materials such as egg containers and paper plates.

The raw pulp produced by these methods may require bleaching. In addition the pulp must be put through a beating process, as it is called: actually it is a brushing process. This improves the strength and other properties of the finished paper. The pulp also requires various additives, such as sizing agents, dyes, and clays to improve brightness and printing characteristics. The use of fluorescent dyes is becoming common. Commonly called optical whiteners, they function by absorbing radiation in the ultraviolet and reradiating in the visible blue range, with the effect of making the paper appear whiter.

14.9   paper making

Paper is made on a woven wire belt in a long paper machine. The pulp stock is pumped onto the woven wire of the paper machine in the form of a thin flat ribbon from a suitable nozzle. Moisture in the stock is drained through the supporting wire mesh, after which a series of pressure rolls and a dryer remove further moisture. The paper sheet is then calendered, that is, passed through a series of rolls stacked vertically. The calendering operation controls the sheet thickness and smoothness. Finally the sheet of paper is reeled.

Figure 132 is a sketch of the Fourdrinier type of paper machine. The Fourdrinier wire belt is usually of bronze wire or synthetic fiber woven into a 55 to 85 mesh. Coarser mesh is used to make paperboard, and finer

Fig. 132 Fourdrinier paper machine.

mesh for special papers such as cigarette paper. The wire must be kept clean, otherwise the paper will be blemished. Due to abrasion and corrosion effects, the wire has a rather limited life.

Paper may have to be coated with a sizing material such as starch. The sizing operation has the purpose of restricting penetration of printing inks into the paper and producing a hard and attractive surface. Sizing and other liquid coatings are applied by means of a flat metering blade and a puddle of the liquid coating extending across the width of the paper.

14.10 *converting of paper*

Various converting operations may be performed on the paper in order to produce the desired finished product. The word "converting", as used in manufacturing industries, refers to operations that convert semifinished products, such as paper, into manufactured articles. Converting operations on paper include laminating, coating, or forming into bags.

Coating is required for the many types of printing papers to enable the paper to receive the printing ink and to reproduce the printed design with sharpness, fidelity, and attractive appearance. Quality white clay (kaolin) in a starch binder is the usual coating for this purpose. Titanium dioxide, which is added to paints and porcelain enamel for whiteness, is also used in paper coatings. A waxed paper is first coated, printed, and then waxed. Building papers and roofing felts are made of paperboard coated with asphalt, this construction providing a barrier against moisture and water vapor.

Lamination provides a paper with a combination of properties or surfaces, or is used to produce a heavier or stronger paper or paperboard. The lamination of paper and aluminum foil is familiar in the packaging of chocolate bars and other products. Any difference in tension between the laminates during lamination will produce a curled product; this is prevented by independent tensioning controls for each sheet material.

Many papers are *creped*, especially decorative papers, sanitary papers such as towelling, and packaging papers. Creping begins by wetting the paper in a thin sizing solution and passing it through a heated roll. The paper is peeled from the roll with a blade called a creping knife. The setting of the knife, its contour, the speed of production, and the amount of size, all control the amount of creping or stretch produced in the paper. The creped paper must not be tensioned before drying, otherwise the creping will be lost.

Corrugated paperboard is made of three webs of kraft paperboard, the middle one being corrugated on rolls and the outer laminations being coated to it with a suitable adhesive such as starch. The corrugated structure is highly resistant to bending or crushing. Corrugated paperboard was probably the first of the "sandwich" structures which now find applications in aerospace vehicles and highway trailers, using expanded metal or foamed plastic for the sandwich core. Larger structural paper sandwiches can be made using paper honeycomb cores bonded to a suitable outside facing material.

The chief types of paper bags are the *multiwall shipping bag* of the type used to bag portland cement, and the brown *kraft paper grocery bag*. These are made on high-speed bag machines, where they are first formed into tubes, after which a bottoming machine closes the bottom.

Cylindrical concrete forms are made of heavy paperboard. They are produced in various large diameters and lengths of 12 ft, with a wax coating, and are chiefly employed in the casting of concrete building columns. After the concrete has set, the paper is peeled away from the concrete.

The use of shipping and protective papers has increased markedly in recent years. Car liner papers are used to protect goods loaded into boxcars. Large unit loads of lumber are often shipped on flat cars wrapped in weather-proof covering paper.

Fig. 133 Strippable tape showing reinforcing fibers.

the organic materials
307

Strippable tapes, shown in Fig. 133, are an ingenious laminated tape for closing cartons. These tapes are laminated with two sheets of kraft paper bonded with asphalt or starch. The outer paper lamination has a reinforcing fiberglass weave embedded in it to give strength to the paper against damage during shipping. To open the carton, this outer lamination is stripped off, the fiberglass reinforcement being stripped with it. The single layer of paper remaining is then easily cut and the carton opened.

14.11 the dimensional stability
of paper

The dimensional changes of paper due to absorption or loss of water are a familiar problem to draftsmen. Such lack of dimensional stability is a matter of concern in many industrial operations. It may affect register in multicolor printing operations, or registering of the punched holes in punched cards. In one commonly used method of automatic oxyacetylene cutting of steels, a photocell follows a line drawn on a sheet of drafting paper while automatic controls cause the cutting torch to reproduce the shape drawn on the paper. For this type of operation, a drafting paper of suitable dimensional stability must be used.

Because of tension applied to the longitudinal dimension of paper during its manufacture, paper is anisotropic like the wood from which it is made. Longitudinal dimensional changes due to humidity variations are minor, but in the cross-direction such changes are more troublesome, though they vary between grades of paper.

Most papers will not elongate more than 5 percent when tensioned to rupture. Special grades will elongate more than this amount, especially creped papers.

14.12 petroleum and
natural gas

The organic natural resources deposited in the earth's crust may be solid, liquid, or gas — coal, petroleum, or natural gas. Each of these three materials is a mixture of large numbers of hydrocarbons. Many specific hydrocarbons, such as the gas methane, may be found in all three types of deposits. In particular, some petroleum hydrocarbons are always found in natural gas deposits, and natural gas is always found in petroleum. The basic difference between natural gas and petroleum is simply that petroleum has a greater content of liquid hydrocarbons than natural gas, while natural gas has a greater content of gaseous hydrocarbons.

The word "petroleum" means rock oil, signifying oil found in sedimentary rock deposits. Rock oil became an industrial material in the 1860's, the decade that gave us cheap steel, paper from wood, and the decimation of the whale population of the oceans. Whale oil was the principal illuminant at that time, and as it became less available due to scarcity of whales, the less popular coal oil had to be substituted. Coal oil was kerosene made from coal. Kerosene is a constituent of petroleum, and speculation about the potential use of rock oil for illumination produced the first oil industry north of Pittsburgh and in southern Ontario about 1860. The kerosene fraction was distilled from the petroleum and sold, while the gasoline, asphalt, and natural gas fractions, having no market, were discarded. But the turn of the century brought two inventions that needed the oil industry for engine fuel and for paving: the automobile and the aircraft. A truly gigantic market for gasoline and asphalt was born. This was an ideal market configuration for petroleum, for the "light ends" or light constituents of the crude petroleum could be used in gasoline, and the heavy ends in asphalt.

Later another very important group of products was developed from petroleum and gas. These were the petrochemicals. Though only a few percent of all petroleum production goes into petrochemicals, this group of products serves a spectrum of applications that is simply too vast for brief summarization and extends far beyond the more familiar plastics and rubbers. The history of petrochemicals may be said to date from 1916, when a method of making propyl alcohol from petroleum was discovered. The synthetic plastics and rubbers joined the list of petrochemicals in limited production in the 1930's, barely in time to serve the critical needs of the first war that was fought with materials technology, World War II.

14.13 petroleum deposits

Petroleum and natural gas are products of the organic remains of plant and animal life, generally deposited in marine sediments. It is believed that the geological formation of petroleum is not dependent on high pressure or temperature. Vanadium and nickel occur in limited amounts in crude oil in compounds called porphyrins, which are the geological remains of plant chlorophyll. Sulfur is always present in sedimentary oils and natural gas. It reacts slowly with the oil constituents to form hydrogen sulfide. If sulfur compounds are present in considerable amounts, the deposits are referred to as "sour crudes" or "sour gas". Much sulfur production is derived from these deposits. Finally, most petroleum deposits also contain both salt and water.

The analysis of all crude oils appears to correspond approximately with the following:

carbon	83.9–86.8%
hydrogen	11.4–14.0%
sulfur	0.06–2.0%
nitrogen	0.11–1.70%

However the mixture of chemical compounds may vary greatly from one well to another. Some deposits contain much gas and light oil compounds, others are heavy and asphaltic. The lighter crudes are preferred because of the higher content of light gasoline fractions. Most of the nitrogen and sulfur is found in the heavier constituents of the crude, which are therefore more likely to be sour.

TYPICAL CRUDES FROM VARIOUS OIL FIELDS

Area	Specific Gravity	Gasoline	Kerosene	Sulfur	Asphalt
Pennsylvania	0.80–0.90	30–40%	15%	0.1%	4%
Gulf Coast	0.86	5	8	0.15	4
California	0.96	11	10	3.8	50
Leduc, Alberta	0.82	35	10	0.4	7
Venezuela	0.95	7	19	2.2	55
Russia (Urals)	0.95	25	0	5.0	45
Kuwait	0.87	27	17	2.5	25

The weight of crude oils in this table is expressed as specific gravity referred to water as 1.0. The oil industry uses also the API (American Petroleum Institute) gravity scale. This API gravity (the units are called degrees) is related to specific gravity by the following formula:

$$\text{API gravity, degrees} = \frac{141.5}{\text{sp gr}} - 131.5$$

Thus water has an API gravity of 10. Gasoline has an API gravity of 52 to 70, SAE #10 lube oil 22 to 33. Crude oil API gravities may range from 4 (unpumpable at 70°F) to 85.

Whether the well is an oil well or a gas well, the mixture that reaches the wellhead consists of gas, oil, and water. These components must be separated. The line from the Christmas tree (i.e., the group of wellhead valves, which doesn't resemble a Christmas tree) runs to a gas and oil separator. The separator is a vertical cylinder which allows the gas to rise out of the oil for collection. The top line out of the separator removes the gas, the bottom line removes the oil. If water is also present, it is allowed to separate out in a field storage tank by gravity.

Raw natural gas is collected in a gas conservation plant for processing. Hydrogen sulfide is removed by contact with ethanolamine and the useful gas constituents separated by distillation processes in three parts. One part is dry gas, methane with some ethane, nitrogen, and carbon dioxide, which is sold as natural gas for heating. Liquified petroleum gas or LPG is the second part, consisting of propane or butane and is sold as bottled fuel. Natural gasoline or casinghead gasoline is removed as the third part and converted to motor gasoline at an oil refinery.

Almost all oil and gas is transported either by tanker or "big-inch" pipelines from the producing field to the market areas.

14.14 hydrocarbon components of petroleum and gas

The number of hydrocarbon chemicals in petroleum may well be almost infinite. The lighter gaseous and liquid hydrocarbons can be identified and separated from petroleum without difficulty, but the great multitude of compounds are in the heavier fractions. The individual heavy hydrocarbons cannot be identified, nor can they be separated. Instead, they are divided into groups or "cuts" at the oil refinery. The problem may be understood by an illustration. The common gasoline hydrocarbon, octane, which gave its name to the octane number of gasoline, contains 8 carbon atoms and 18 hydrogen atoms. These 26 atoms can be rearranged to form 17 other hydrocarbons. By reducing the number of hydrogen atoms attached to the 8 carbon atoms, still more hydrocarbons are possible. Twenty-five carbon atoms offer the possibility of about 40 million different hydrocarbons, and 25 is by no means the maximum number of carbon atoms in any petroleum molecule.

Most of the hydrocarbons in petroleum can be classified into four groups: paraffin, olefin, naphthene, and aromatic.

The *paraffins* have the general formula C_nH_{2n+2}. Methane, the chief constituent of natural gas and the lightest of the paraffins, has the formula CH_4. The names of specific paraffins end in -ane: ethane, hexane, heptane, etc. The paraffins are saturated hydrocarbons, the term "saturated" meaning that they contain the maximum possible number of hydrogen atoms in each case. For this reason they are rather inactive chemically. The carbon atoms in paraffins tend to form long chains in polymer fashion. Those which form a straight chain without branches are termed normal or *n-*paraffins; those with branches are isoparaffins. See Fig. 134 on page 312.

```
                                              H
                                            H C H
   H          H H       H H H      H H H H    H │ H
 H C H     H C C H    H C C C H  H C C C C H  H C C C H
   H          H H       H H H      H H H H    H H H
Methane    Ethane     Propane   Normal butane  Isobutane


   H H H H H        H H H H H H
 H C C C C C H    H C C C C C C H        Fig. 134  Paraffins.
   H H H H H        H H H H H H
 Normal pentane    Normal hexane
```

Fig. 134 Paraffins.

Paraffins with four or less carbon atoms are gases at ordinary temperatures, those with 5 to 15 carbon atoms are liquid, those with over 15 are waxes. Figure 134 identifies some of the paraffin series. The normal paraffins have low octane numbers and are undesirable in gasolines. Their good burning characteristics, however, make them preferred constituents of diesel and gas turbine fuels and fuel oils. Gas turbine fuels are largely kerosenes, the original commodity extracted from petroleum a hundred years ago. Isoparaffins are the preferred constituents of gasolines, including aviation gasoline.

The uses of the lighter paraffins may be briefly summarized as follows:

1. methane — chief constituent of natural gas
2. ethane   — converted to other organic materials such as polyethylene
3. butane   — fuel for refinery boilers, or added to winter gasoline, cigarette lighter fluid, or converted into petrochemicals
4. pentane, hexane, heptane, octane, etc. — raw materials for gasoline

The *olefins*, Fig. 135, are unsaturated. If two hydrogen atoms can be added to an olefin to saturate it, it is a mono-olefin, C_nH_{2n}. The mono-olefins have names that correspond to those of the paraffins to which they are related, with the ending -ene or -ylene. If four hydrogen atoms can be added for saturation, the olefin is a diolefin, C_nH_{2n-2}, with a name ending in -diene (pronounced dye-een). Olefins are chemically reactive and serve as the principal raw materials for the petrochemical industry in the manufacture of plastics, rubbers, and other materials. Actually olefins are not

```
   H H H H
 H C-C-C-C H
   H H H H
   Butane

   H H H H
 H C-C=C-C H
   H       H
   Butylene

   H H H H          Fig. 135   Olefins.
   C=C-C=C
   H       H
   Butadiene
```

Fig. 135   Olefins.

the organic materials

common in crude petroleum, but are formed in the course of oil refinery operations. Gasolines contain considerable amounts of high-octane mono-olefins. The diolefins are undesirable in gasolines because they form gums. The olefins have the straight-chain structure of the paraffins.

Naphthenes are saturated ring-shaped hydrocarbons with the general formula C_nH_{2n}. The names of the naphthenes begin with cyclo-. The molecule of cyclohexane is shown in Fig. 136.

Fig. 136 Benzene, an aromatic, and cyclohexane, a naphthene.

Aromatics are found in coal and to a lesser extent in crude oil, especially in California crudes. These are ring-shaped compounds like the naphthenes, but are unsaturated. Figure 136 includes a sketch of the structure of benzene. Benzene, toluene, and xylene, often referred to in the industry as BTX, are the most important of the aromatics. Aromatics are chemically active, and like the olefins are the starting-points for the synthesis of a wide range of organic chemicals, including explosives, drugs, solvents, dyes, and polystyrene. They are desirable components of gasolines, but not of diesel and gas turbine fuels because they tend to smoke. The aromatics are excellent solvents, though they present a fire hazard.

14.15   the refining of petroleum

Crude petroleum may sometimes be burned as bunker fuel in ships' boilers, but in general it cannot be used as a commercial product. It is therefore pumped by pipeline to oil refineries for conversion into fuels, lube oils, asphalts, petroleum coke, and chemical intermediates, the latter being further converted in chemical plants.

Crude petroleum represents a mixture of a wide range of oil and gas components which differ from well to well. These must be converted into products of fixed characteristics and standard quality, regardless of variation in characteristics of the crude oil delivered from the pipeline. The petroleum product in greatest demand and of greatest profit is gasoline, though the gasoline fractions in the crude may be small and the heavy asphaltic fractions large.

The first refinery operation is the separation of the crude into various "cuts", using distillation methods. For flexibility of operation, two other basic refinery processes are needed. First, there must be a process for "cracking" or breaking up the larger molecules into shorter gasoline molecules. Second, there must be a method of polymerizing small gas molecules into longer molecules. The first process is called cracking, and the second polymerization. These processes will provide the basic operational flexibility to meet changes in market demand for petroleum products and variations in the type of crude oil received from the pipeline. Other refinery processes will be incorporated with these either to improve product quality or to produce special products such as greases, coke, or chemical intermediates.

Distillation. Distillation is the first step in reducing the multitude of hydrocarbons in petroleum to usable products. After the crude oil is separated into distilled fractions, these fractions can be refined or converted. The separation of liquid mixtures by fractional distillation is possible because of differences in boiling points, a difference put to use by Allied soldiers in Italy in 1943, who did not like Chianti wine and therefore fractionally distilled it into alcohol and water. The several fractions into which petroleum is usually converted and their boiling ranges are given below.

Fraction	Boiling Range, °F	Ultimate Use
methane	−259.5	natural gas
ethane	−128	ethylene
propane	−44	liquified petroleum gas
butane	+11 to 31	motor gasoline, rubber, etc.
light naphtha	30–300	motor gasoline
heavy naphtha	300–400	motor and gas turbine fuels
kerosene, C_{11}–C_{15}	400–500	gas turbine fuel
stove oil	400–550	gas turbine and oil fuel
light gas oil, C_{15}–	400–600	furnace and diesel fuels
heavy gas oil, C_{20}–	600–800	gasoline and fuel oil
vacuum gas oil, C_{30}–	800–1100	gasoline, fuel oil, lube oil
pitch	1100+	asphalt

The fractions to and including heavy gas oil are separated by distillation at atmospheric pressure. The heavier fractions must be distilled under vacuum conditions, using a pressure of about 50–100 torr (1 torr = 1 mm mercury pressure). At atmospheric pressure distillation temperatures would be so high that there would be damage to the product, including depolymerization and excessive formation of coke. The individual hydrocarbon chemicals may be separated from one another by distillation only if they are very light ends from C_1 to C_4. In the heavier fractions there are too many compounds with identical boiling points.

Petrochemicals are manufactured from light ends such as ethane and butane, while gasoline is made from both the lighter fractions and the heavier gas oils.

Catalytic cracking. Cracking is the process by which fractions boiling in the gasoline or light naphtha range are produced from heavier fractions. The larger molecules are divided into fragments of lower molecular weight basically by means of heat, but with the assistance of pressure and catalysts. A catalyst is a material which promotes a chemical reaction without being consumed in the reaction: its effect has been compared by chemists to that of moonlight on young love. Without the catalyst, excessive amounts of methane and ethane are produced by cracking, that is, the cracking occurs too close to the ends of the chain of carbon atoms.

Petroleum hydrocarbons are cracked at temperatures above 650°F. Higher temperatures are required to crack larger molecules. The resulting cracked product is a mixture with much the same boiling range as the crude from which it is made, containing fractions from gases to tar and coke. But the cracked material will contain perhaps twice as much material boiling in the gasoline range, that is, pentane, C_5, and heavier. The cracked material has no fractions suitable for kerosene, lubricating oils, waxes, or asphalts. These products therefore are not cracked; gasoline, diesel fuel, and furnace oil are cracked. The cracked hydrocarbons are more olefinic than the original crude hydrocarbons. If a C_{12} (dodecane) paraffin is cracked into two parts, one part will probably be a hexane paraffin and the other a hexane olefin. Besides olefins, the cracked material will contain aromatics. All these nonparaffinic components improve the octane rating of the cracked product. Straight-run distillate gasolines made of the pentane, hexane, heptane, octane, etc. of crude oil cannot be burned in the modern automobile, though they were used in the past.

A special type of cracking process used to upgrade the quality of gasolines is called *reforming*. Reforming produces greater amounts of naphthenics and aromatics, converting hexane, for example, into benzene. The products of the reforming process may also be converted into petrochemicals.

Polymerization. Cracking and reforming processes produce large amounts of gaseous hydrocarbons. These light ends may be put through a *poly unit* to produce polymer gasoline. This operation is of course the reverse of cracking.

Lubricating Oils. Lubricating oils must meet a wide range of service conditions, and consequently a wide variety of these oils must be produced. Vegetable oils and synthetic oils fill certain special needs, but by and large petroleum oils are the only materials with the necessary properties and low cost for lubrication applications.

The primary requirements for a lube oil are lubricity and resistance to oxidation. Special requirements also apply however. In particular, the viscosity must match the application. A low viscosity is needed for a sewing-machine oil, while high viscosity is necessary for the more severe demands of a worm gear speed reducer. In the case of a fluid power hydraulic system, a low-pressure system will be filled with a low-viscosity oil, perhaps SAE #10, to reduce the horsepower requirements of the pump. But a high-pressure hydraulic system will require a higher viscosity to reduce leakage through the valves of the system. Refrigeration equipment requires an oil suited to low-temperature operation and wax-free, while a steam turbine requires a high-temperature oil which contains antioxidants.

Cutting and drawing lubricants are formulated for thread cutting, drilling, and other machining operations on metals, and for such forming operations as the shaping of sheet metal in dies. Two severe requirements are imposed on such lubricants:

1. The maintenance of a lubricating film between the tool or die and the work, under pressures that may often exceed 100,000 psi.
2. Dissipation of the heat of machining or forming.

Many of these forming lubricants are water-soluble oils or water emulsions.

Greases. These are lubricating oils thickened by fatty acid soaps. The soap holds the oil to the surface requiring lubrication, and is dispersed in the oil in the form of fibers too small to be distinguished under an optical microscope. Soaps are produced by chemical combination of a metal hydroxide with a fat or a fatty acid. The chief hydroxides used in grease manufacture are those of calcium, sodium, lithium, and barium. The type of fat will influence the properties of the grease, but not to the degree that the metal hydroxide will. Calcium greases are limited to temperatures below 200°F while sodium greases may be used above this temperature. Barium and lithium greases are suitable for both high and low temperatures, and are usually designated as multi-purpose greases.

Petroleum waxes are used in the packaging industry for waxed paper and waxed containers. A heavily waxed paper may contain as much as 35 percent wax by weight.

Petroleum asphalts are used in asphalt concretes for paving, and for roofing, paints, varnishes, and insulating compositions.

Insulating oils serve for insulation purposes in transformers, X-ray tubes, and oil-filled cables. Such oils must have a high flash point and low vapor pressure, with high dielectric strength.

Petroleum coke is the residue from the destructive distillation of petroleum, and may be found in car engines that "carbon up". Petroleum coke is not pure carbon, but contains up to 16 percent of volatile petroleum compounds, and is oily in appearance. It is sometimes used as a fuel in the Eastern States and Minnesota, though it requires special furnace designs and has a very high ignition temperature of over 1000°F. Its chief use, however, is in the manufacture of carbon electrodes for aluminum refining and other such metallurgical processes.

For blast furnace operation, coke is made by distilling coal in coke ovens. Coke is made more cheaply than petroleum coke. But coal contains much sulfur, which is present in coke-oven coke, since no process is in use to remove sulfur from coal or coke. On the other hand it is standard practice to desulfurize petroleum, and petroleum coke thus has almost no sulfur content. The harmful effects of sulfur in metals have been discussed in earlier chapters. Arc-melting electrodes must therefore be made of petroleum coke.

14.17 solvents

The industrial solvents used for the cleaning of metals and paint stripping are petrochemicals with a small molecule that enables them to penetrate into surface coatings. Three types of solvent are in use: paraffins, aromatics, and chlorinated solvents, listed in the order of increasing solvent power. The paraffin solvents are simply members of the paraffin family, such as diesel fuel or gasoline. These have rather limited solvency. The aromatic solvents include such chemicals as benzene and xylene. The chlorinated solvents such as trichlorethylene (C_2HCl_3), methyl chloride (Ch_3Cl), or carbon tetrachloride (CCl_4) are paraffins with the hydrogen atoms partially or wholly substituted by chlorine atoms. The following table compares the characteristics of these three groups of solvents.

SOLVENT COMPARISON TABLE

	Paraffins	Aromatics	Chlorinated
cost	low	medium	highest
solvency	limited	good	best
flammability	high	very high	none
toxicity	low	high	high
paint removal	poor	better	excellent

14.18 petrochemical intermediates

These are the chemicals such as ethylene, manufactured from petroleum and natural gas, which are further processed into finished products. They are the raw material for most rubbers and plastics, and numberless other chemicals for industry. Despite their importance, they consume only a few percent of oil and gas production.

Petrochemical intermediates may also be manufactured from coal, which is rich in aromatic hydrocarbons. This is done in Europe, where local resources of petroleum are relatively limited. Coal chemistry in this country will remain of secondary interest until oil and gas become considerably more expensive.

The most important of the intermediates is ethylene. Besides such products as engine antifreeze (ethylene glycol), many plastics and rubbers are produced from ethylene. The chief feed stocks used for cracking into ethylene are ethane and propane, but butane, naphthas, and gas oils may also be used. In principle, any organic chemical can be made from any fraction of petroleum or natural gas.

Other olefin intermediates are acetylene (which is also a finished product), propylene, butylene, isobutylene, and butadiene. Most of these are used in the production of rubber, among other things. Nylon may be produced from butadiene. Acetylene can be converted into such plastics as polyvinyl chloride and Orlon.

Next to the olefins, the most important group of intermediates is the aromatics, chiefly the BTX trio benzene, toluene, xylene. Of the cyclic naphthenes, the most significant intermediate is cyclohexane, used in the production of nylon.

Insecticides, detergents, solid rocket fuels, photographic films, pharmaceuticals, solvents, explosives, and alcohols are a partial listing of some of the end uses of the olefin, aromatic, and naphthene intermediates mentioned.

14.19 organic polymers

Most of the industrial polymers are *plastics* and *elastomers*. Plastics are those synthetic resins characterized as a group by plastic deformation under stress; elastomers or rubbers are those which are capable of extensive elastic deformation. This will do as a general statement provided we note that there are many exceptions to it. Some plastics are highly elastic, and any rubber can be deformed plastically under certain conditions. Moreover, it is not unusual to copolymerize a plastic monomer with a rubber monomer, a common technique to overcome the brittleness of some plastics.

The plastics themselves are classified into two groups: *thermoplastics* and *thermosets*. The thermoplastics, of which polyethylene, polystyrene, and asphalts are examples, can be softened repeatedly with heat and will reharden when cooled. Thermosetting plastics harden or "cure" with heat and then cannot be resoftened by heating. Typical thermosets are Bakelite, epoxy, silicones, and rubbers.

There are three general methods of polymerization:

1. addition polymerization
2. condensation polymerization
3. copolymerization

In *addition polymerization*, the polymer is produced by adding a second monomer to the first, then a third monomer to this dimer, a fourth to the trimer, and so on until the long polymer chain is terminated. Polyethylene is produced by the addition polymerization of ethylene monomers, as indicated in Fig. 137. Addition polymerization always results in a thermoplastic.

Fig. 137 Vinyl and related thermoplastics.

Condensation polymerization occurs in the combination of a compound with itself or other compounds, accompanied by the elimination of some simple compound such as water as a result of the polymerization. The molecular formula lacks certain atoms present in the monomer from which it is made. Thus when phenol and formaldehyde monomers are polymerized, water is released, and the resulting product is a polymerized phenol-formaldehyde (Bakelite). Condensation products may be either thermosets or thermoplasts.

Copolymerization is the addition polymerization of two or more different monomers. Many monomers will not polymerize with themselves, but will copolymerize with other compounds. One of the more important copolymers is butadiene-styrene, a rubber used in tires.

A polymer is a long-chain compound, and when represented in diagrams polymers are drawn as straight chains. Actually these compounds are not linear since the monomers link at slight angles to each other, and the actual polymer may have the form of a coil. Under the application of a stress, the polymer molecule straightens. This flexibility in the molecule accounts for the remarkable elongations possible with some plastics and rubbers. The diagrams in this book show all polymers as straight chains without side chains, but any polymer will grow some side chains.

Many thermosetting plastics, such as Bakelite or hard rubber, have only limited elongation. Their freedom of movement under stress is limited by *cross-linking*. This is the linking of one long molecule to another.

Fig. 138 Condensation polymerization of phenol-formaldehyde.

Thus Fig. 138 shows two molecules of phenol-formaldehyde cross-linked with carbon atoms. In rubbers, this cross-linking is called vulcanization, the cross-linking agent usually being sulfur. Many paints and finishes harden as oxygen in the air cross-links the molecules. The effect of cross-linking is to make a network polymer, reducing the plasticity of the material while retaining its elasticity. The number of cross-linking bonds is always relatively small compared to the total number of possible cross-linking sites, and the rigidity or hardness of the material is proportional to the amount of cross-linking.

A polymer with the shape of a coil spring and with side chains, attached methyl (CH₃) groups or aromatic rings, has a shape that is incompatible with the ordered arrangements of crystal structures. It is not surprising that many of these materials are amorphous. Sometimes a degree of crystal ordering is possible on a submicroscopic scale. Such regions are termed *crystallites*. The whole molecule, because of its length, may well extend through several crystalline and non-crystalline regions. Polymers with simple structures, such as those of Fig. 137, will show a considerable degree of crystallinity. The greater the crystallinity or number of crystallites, the greater the specific weight of the polymer, because of the closer packing of molecules in the crystalline phase. Thus low-density polyethylene has a crystallinity in the range of 55–70 percent, while values for high-density polyethylene are 75–95 percent. The chief advantage of crystallinity is that the polymer product may be used at higher temperatures. Generally a more crystalline polymer will have better resistance to water absorption and to solvent attack. The crystalline regions are closely ordered segments while the amorphous regions present an open and random arrangement which can be penetrated by water, solvents, or permeating liquids.

The molecule of polypropylene is shown in Fig. 139. If the methyl unit (CH₃) is attached at random locations above and below the carbon chain, the polymer cannot crystallize. Such an irregular orientation is termed the atactic structure. A regular arrangement of the methyl group makes crystallinity possible. The tactic and atactic structures are produced by different catalysts and processing conditions during polymerization.

Fig. 139   Polypropylene, atactic, and isotactic structure.

In the isotactic structure all the methyl units are located on one side of the carbon chain; they alternate on both sides in the syndiotactic configuration. Such regular arrangements of polymer structure are produced by what is called stereospecific polymerization.

Although only the more important industrial polymers will be discussed in the following pages, those we shall mention comprise a sizable list. In the case of the rubbers, about a dozen need concern us, if attention is restricted to the important rubbers. Comparing the thermosetting and thermoplastic materials, the differences may be briefly summarized. The thermosets will not soften, but will char. They will withstand higher temperatures than the thermoplasts, if we ignore such exceptions as polytetrafluoroethylene (Teflon) and inorganic polymers. Their strength, creep properties, and modulus of elasticity are higher than the same properties of thermoplastics. Such converting operations as vacuum-forming and extrusion are not possible on thermosets, which have no softening temperature.

Additives. Additives are the ingredients added to polymers to alter their properties, to plasticize them, protect them from deterioration, or for any other reason. Cross-linking agents are one type of additive.

Plasticizers are non-volatile solvents which make the more brittle plastics such as polyvinyl chloride softer and more plastic. Unplasticized polyvinyl chloride is used as rigid pipe, but when plasticized it makes an excellent flexible garden hose. The polyolefins such as polyethylene, polystyrene, plexiglass, and the thermosets are rarely plasticized.

Reinforcing fillers such as carbon black and clay are added to rubbers. Carbon black is also added to polyethylene in amounts of about 2 percent for protection against the depolymerization effects of ultraviolet radiation. Polyethylene pipe is almost invariably blended with carbon black.

14.20 natural polymers and
their derivatives

Asphalt, cellulose, lignin, shellac, natural rubber, casein, and starch are natural polymers of great importance to industry. Starch is used chiefly as a paper-product adhesive. Natural rubber will be discussed with the synthetic rubbers. Shellac is used as a protective and decorative coating. It is an excretion of the lac bug of Asia. It can be compression-molded, and is one of the materials used for phonograph records. Casein is the chief protein in milk. Its industrial importance is declining, but it is still used as an adhesive and for small molded articles.

A considerable number of thermoplastic materials can be made from cellulose, which is itself a thermosetting plastic. *Cellulose nitrate* (or celluloid), discovered about 100 years ago, was the first of the synthetic polymers to be introduced. It is used in paints and finishes, combs, toothbrush handles, and billiard balls. Its chief disadvantage is its high flammability. In the past, when it was used as motion-picture film, it had a remarkable capacity for setting movie houses on fire.

Cellulose acetate, used as an adhesive, packaging film, and photographic film, has a crystal-clear transparency, and permeability to water vapor and gases. Such permeability makes it an excellent choice for the packaging of fruits and vegetables that must "breathe".

Cellulose acetate butyrate is molded into pipe, telephone housings, small tool handles, and automobile steering wheels. These uses arise from its resistance to oils, greases, and perspiration.

Several other synthetic polymers are made from cellulose.

Research work on inorganic polymers is spurred by the pressing need for polymers that can withstand higher temperatures. The carbon polymers soften above 200–300°F and oxidize readily, though the fluorocarbon and silicone polymers have met some of the higher-temperature requirements. A number of inorganic polymers have adequate resistance to elevated temperatures, but fall short in other properties such as brittleness or deterioration.

Fig. 140   Phenyl-butyl borimide, an inorganic polymer.

$$-N-B-N-B-N-B-$$

with substituents C_6H_5 above each B and C_4H_9 below each N

Every student of chemistry knows that sulfur will polymerize to rubbery plastic sulfur if heated to about 500°F and cooled. Selenium also will polymerize; so will sulfur trioxide. No commercial possibilities are apparent from such sulfur polymers. Boron, aluminum, tin, titanium, and phosphorus-nitrogen polymers have been developed, but few have any applications as yet. Figure 140 shows the structure of the boron polymer phenyl-butyl borimide.

14.21   *formaldehyde thermosetting polymers*

A wide range of thermosetting plastics of considerable industrial importance is produced by reacting urea, melamine, phenol, and other compounds with formaldehyde.

The first of the plastics was the thermoplastic cellulose nitrate, previously discussed. About 50 years ago phenol-formaldehyde, the first of the thermosetting plastics, was developed. It was named Bakelite, and this trade name is still applied to phenol-formaldehydes as a group. The phenol plastics are strong, elastic, and quite brittle. A sampling of their many uses would include the following articles, most of them familiar to everyone:

1. wall plates for electric toggle switches and the toggle itself
2. mechanical parts of electric motor starters
3. miscellaneous electric hardware such as lamp bases and receptacles
4. radio and appliance knobs
5. toilet seats

The urea and melamine formaldehydes may also be used in the manufacture of these articles. Phenols are usually brown in color, and color limitations have restricted their range of uses. Phenolic, urea, and melamine resins are also used as impregnating, bonding, and laminating agents, especially in plywood and chipboard manufacture and in bonded grinding wheels. The brown color of the phenolic adhesive is not objected to by consumers of such commodities. The heat resistance of these materials makes them suitable also for the bonding of brake linings and clutch facings.

Melamine-formaldehyde provides improved impact strength and durability over phenol-formaldehyde, but is somewhat more expensive. The general characteristics of melamine resins are familiar from their use in plastic tableware. Cellulose, wood flour, asbestos, rag, and glass fiber filler are often added to melamine and other molded formaldehydes to provide increased strength. Resorcinol-formaldehyde resin adhesive is preferred when a low-temperature cure is desired, and is selected for diffi-cult bonding operations on wood, such as the fabrication of glued laminated timbers and arches.

Figure 141 shows the stress-strain curve for a typical Bakelite phenol-formaldehyde. The absence of plastic deformation in this "plastic" material should be noted, and is, of course, explained by the rigidity arising from cross-linking. The small elongation at failure is indicative of great brittle-ness.

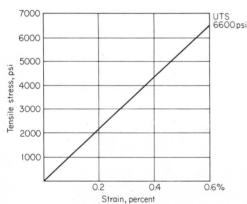

Fig. 141 Stress-strain curve for one grade of Bakelite. This is a brittle and elastic "plastic ma-terial".

14.22 polyesters

A polyester is any organic material produced by a condensation reaction between an alcohol and an acid. The alcohols will usually be ethylene glycol, propylene glycol, diethylene glycol, glycerol, or allyl alcohol; the acids are usually either maleic, phthalic, adipic, or terephthalic. These raw materials will produce two types of polyesters: saturated or unsaturated. Some of the saturated polyesters are cross-linked and therefore thermo-setting. Such a polyester is polyurethane, which will be discussed in the section on rubbers. Many unsaturated polyesters are termed *alkyds*, the abbreviation of the words alcohol and acid. The alkyd resins are chiefly used for wood and metal paints and enamels.

Dacron and Terylene are polyester fibers familiar in the garment industry. Most gloss or enamel paints, such as those used on automobiles, are alkyd-base formulations. A third and equally familiar application of polyesters is their use in reinforced plastics.

Reinforced polyesters (and other reinforced plastics such as phenolics and epoxies) find use in many applications where a high strength-to-weight ratio and strong corrosion resistance are required, such as tooling, molds, fixtures for production, pressure tanks, septic tanks, piping, rocket fins and ablative nose cones, auto bodies, hard hats, boats, photographic develop-ment tanks, trays, and roof sheeting. Glass fiber mat is the usual reinforcing, though asbestos or metal wire may be used. Glass fiber has a tensile strength of 150,000 psi, and filament-wound reinforced plastics with high glass content have unusual tensile strength. For highest strength the fibers must be oriented in the direction of the maximum tensile stress. The strength is directly proportional to the amount of glass reinforcement used. Strengths as high as 50,000 psi are possible in reinforced plastic, with E-values of 1.6 to 3.3 $\times$ 10^6.

14.23   epoxies

The word "epoxy" is made up of scraps from an ancient and a modern language, the Greek word for "between" and "oxy" from oxygen. Epoxy means "oxygen between the compounds". More explicitly, an epoxy is a polymer with oxygen atoms in the polymer chain, though other polymers, such as silicones, may have oxygen in the main chain also.

The epoxies are strong and brittle thermosetting plastics produced by a condensation reaction between (typically) bisphenol A and epichlorhydrin, as shown in Fig. 142. The polymer chain terminates in a C-O-C group. A thermoplastic variant of the epoxies are the phenoxy plastics, which are ductile.

The epoxies are principally used as potting, encapsulating, and casting resins which are cast and cured, rather than molded with heat and pressure. They are equally important in the form of surface coatings for metals, producing hard, adherent, abrasion-resistant and corrosion-resistant surfaces. Three of the notable advantages of the casting epoxies are low shrinkage, excellent adhesion to metals, and great versatility in curing

Epichlorhydrin   Bisphenol A   **Fig. 142 Epoxy monomers and polymer.**

Monomer

procedures. Curing may be done at room temperature or by heat, and both one-component and two-component epoxies are available.

The use of epoxies as adhesives will be discussed in the next chapter.

The epoxies seem to have found a place in industry that resembles the position of nickel among the metals. Most of the uses of the epoxies are specialized, like those of nickel, but the epoxies can meet requirements served by no other plastic. Most industries now take the epoxies for granted in the following and other applications:

1. *Civil engineering and construction.* Bonding of concrete, repairs to concrete, durable epoxy surfaces for industrial floors, bonding of insulation board to concrete.
2. *Electrical engineering.* Potting and encapsulating of electrical hardware, epoxy moldings, epoxy insulation.
3. *Aerospace engineering.* Reinforced fiberglass plastics, adhesive for aircraft bulkheads, floors, wing flaps, and sandwich panels.
4. *Mechanical engineering.* Epoxy tooling, jigs, dies, and foundry patterns, epoxy paints.

14.24 tooling epoxies

The epoxy casting resins supplement the tool steels in tooling applications. Whether a tool steel or an epoxy will be selected for a tooling application depends on certain factors which are best illustrated by an example.

Suppose a plant is to "tool up" for the production of two formed sheet metal products. One is a cheap shallow-drawn ashtray to be sold for 5 cents each (at the manufacturing level); the other is a large curved panel for an aircraft fuselage.

Cheap ashtrays are produced by the millions, and must be pressed out at high production rates. Each ashtray produced will add its small increment of wear and abrasion to the sheet-forming dies, male and female.

No plastic die material could be expected to endure for a million press cycles. The male and female dies for the ashtray would therefore be made of a cold-work tool steel.

The case of the fuselage panel is different. Aircraft production involves only short runs, so that an epoxy tooling resin may be expected to survive the run. Further, the fuselage panel, unlike the small ashtray, must be formed on a die of very large area. If it measures something like 6 by 6 ft, the cost of the material and tool-making labor for die-making in tool steel will be prohibitive, especially if this cost must be paid out over a short production run. The fuselage panel will require nothing more than a shallow draw, for which an epoxy tool will be entirely suitable. The panels will presumably be produced on stretch-form dies, in which the metal will be grasped by its edges and pulled over the die profile at a stress exceeding its elastic limit. Epoxy tooling resins are economically suited to such manufacturing operations.

Plastic dies, being softer, are more easily and quickly machined than steel dies. Major or minor changes in die shape are usually readily accomplished in plastic dies, which can sometimes be rebuilt by adding more resin and reinforcement (epoxy will bond to itself). Equally important, steel tooling requires a long lead time for its design and manufacturing stages, so that for prototype work, plastic tooling may be demanded in order to save time. Plastic dies, however, cannot withstand the more severe stress

Fig. 143 An epoxy metal forming die. (Courtesy Rezolin, Inc., Santa Monica, Cal.)

the organic materials
327

and wear of high production rates, high press speeds, and deep-drawing operations, and require more care in their handling.

Typical uses for epoxy tooling are soft jaws for lathe chucks, core boxes for foundry work, shallow-drawing dies, stretch-form dies, and assembly jigs (Fig. 143). Tooling epoxies are usually formulated with filler materials such as aluminum or iron powder. Such fillers control the hardness and machinability, reduce shrinkage, lower the coefficient of thermal expansion, and reduce exothermic heat of curing. Excessive exotherm may cause warping in the tooling, and tooling always requires the best dimensional stability obtainable.

14.25   nylon, polyacetal, and
polycarbonate resins

The formaldehyde, polyester, and epoxy resins are all thermosetting. The three types of resin discussed in this section and following sections are all thermoplastic.

Approximate structure of
Polyacetal

Monomer

Polycarbonate

Hexamethylene–diamine

Adipic acid

Fig. 144 Polyacetal, polycarbonate, and nylon.

Nylon

Polycarbonate, polyacetal, and nylon thermoplastic resins are not chemically related. They are grouped together here because all three have sufficient hardness, toughness, strength, creep resistance and a combination of other characteristics to make them suitable as replacements for metals in mechanical items from gears to fasteners, especially in automobiles. These are "high-performance" plastics.

The *nylons* are polyamides. Most nylon is produced by a condensation reaction of hexamethylene diamine and adipic acid as shown in Fig. 144. There is strong attraction between the polymer molecules, resulting in a high degree of crystallinity and high heat resistance. Crystallinity of course results in a sharp melting point in a polymer.

Nylon came to fame by driving natural silk and the Japanese silkworm out of the hosiery market soon after World War II. Stockings have been referred to as "nylons" since that time. Nylon has an impressive list of industrial virtues: light weight, moldability, abrasion resistance, hardness, heat resistance, strength, low friction, solvent and chemical resistance, and excellent machinability. However, nylon will absorb moisture, producing a slight expansion and some deterioration of electrical and physical properties. The effect of moisture on strength is indicated in Fig. 145. Nylon is also sensitive to ultraviolet radiation.

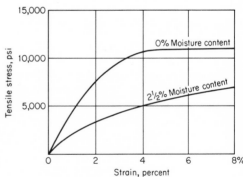

Fig. 145   Stress-strain curves for dry and moist nylon, tested at 70°F.

Nylon polymer has a creamy color, but is occasionally pigmented. It has a very broad spectrum of uses:

1. film and coatings
2. fibers — rope, parachutes, safety belts for aircraft and cars, brushes, fishing lines, sieves, tire cords, surgical sutures
3. adhesive
4. printing inks for high adhesion and abrasion resistance
5. gears for abrasion resistance and silent running
6. bearings, small shafts, wheels, runners, wire feeders for automatic welding machines, cams, conveyor chains
7. high-pressure hose and tubing
8. strapping

the organic materials
329

Nylon strapping is competitive with the steel strapping used in shipping and packaging of materials. If several sacks of cement are strapped together with tensioned steel strapping, the jolting movements of the shipping vehicle will compact the cement to a smaller volume. The steel strapping will then no longer fit the bundle and fall off. This deficiency in steel strapping is due to its limited elongation, which is only 1 percent. Nylon strapping has an elongation of several percent, and as the load compresses, the tensioned nylon strapping relaxes and continues to bind the load.

The *polyacetals*, of which the most familiar brand name is Delrin, are polyformaldehydes. The acetals are used in automobile moldings and instrument housings, pump impellers and fan blades, cams, hinges, business machine housings, and aerosol cans.

Polycarbonates (Fig. 144) are transparent. They have exceptional notched-bar impact strength, toughness, and elongation. They are virtually impossible to break in service, though polycarbonate can be pulled apart in a tensile testing machine after a remarkable display of ductility. Creep resistance is better than that of any other thermoplastic. Polycarbonate has been made into nails, screws, and fasteners. Other uses include unbreakable kitchen utensils, tail lights for automobiles, hard hats, housings for portable power tools, light globes, and pump impellers.

14.26 the polyolefins

The polyolefins are produced by the polymerization of unsaturated hydrocarbons, and include the plastics polyethylene and polypropylene, and the rubbers polyisoprene and polyisobutylene. The polyolefins belong to the large group of vinyl and other polymers produced by the addition polymerization of relatively simple monomers in a straight carbon chain. These are shown in Fig. 137. The regular and simple monomer of polyethylene, ethylene, a gas boiling at $-104°C$, permits a considerable degree of crystallization, about 60 percent in low-density polyethylenes. The crystal structure is orthorhombic. The angle between the carbon bonds in the polymer chain is 109°. The degree of crystallinity decreases with temperature, until at about 250°F no crystallinity can be detected in low-density polyethylene. The presence of branching, of course, inhibits crystallinity.

Polyethylene contains more hydrogen atoms per unit volume than water. This makes it an excellent material for shielding against neutrons. Neutron shielding capacity is improved by blending about 1 percent boron compounds into the polyethylene.

Polyethylene has poor strength, high creep even at room temperature, low elastic modulus, and high expansion and mold shrinkage. It is therefore not used in applications demanding a high degree of dimensional stability. Despite these very serious limitations, this plastic material has developed remarkably large markets within the fields of application of plastics.

Polyethylene is produced in three grades: low density, intermediate density, and high density. Low density grades are polymerized at exceedingly high pressures, over 15,000 psi, while high density grades are produced at low pressures. The specific gravities of the three grades are

0.912–0.925
0.925–0.940
0.940–0.965.

The degree of crystallinity is approximately proportional to the specific gravity, and the heat resistance improves with the crystallinity. The higher densities are less waxy in appearance and to the touch.

Where resistance to weathering and ultraviolet radiation is a requirement, polyethylene is blended with about 2 percent carbon black.

The largest outlet for polyethylene is film. Most film is consumed by the packaging industry, but the construction and agricultural industries use the film as a building vapor barrier, for temporary heated enclosures to protect construction workers in cold weather, as protection for wet concrete, for protection of plants from frost, and a multitude of other uses. Most film is made of low-density material, though the high-density plastic is a much better vapor barrier.

Other uses include coatings on paper or other materials, injection-molded articles such as kitchenware, laboratory apparatus, and toys, and blow-molded bottles, containers, and squeeze bottles. Such corrosive chemicals as hydrofluoric acid, ammonia, and rust-removing compounds are now supplied in polyethylene containers. Low-density polyethylene pipe is now familiar in cold-water service. High-density pipe is preferred for use in chemical plants because of its greater rigidity and superior chemical resistance. The superior dielectric properties of polyethylene explain its use for electrical insulation on wire and cable.

Polyethylene, like other thermoplastics, may be made to cross-link by means of gamma radiation in very heavy doses. In the course of radiation, hydrogen is liberated and carbon atoms cross-link between molecules. The polyethylene becomes infusible and withstands prolonged aging at temperatures of almost 300°F.

Propylene is a gas boiling at −48°C at atmospheric pressure. Its polymer *polypropylene* is the lightest plastic so far produced, with a specific gravity of 0.90. General physical and electrical properties of polypropylene are similar to those of high-density polyethylene. Polypropylene, however, is harder and has a higher softening point and lower shrinkage.

Polypropylene film is not as limp as polyethylene film. In addition to film, polypropylene is molded into domestic hollow ware, toys, bottles, and automobile distributor caps.

Fig. 146 Polyethylene protection on unit loads of plywood.

14.27 *vinyl and related polymers*

The chemical structure of these plastics is given in Fig. 137. "Vinyl" or polyvinyl chloride (PVC), derived from ethylene, is a hard and rather brittle thermoplastic if unplasticized. Type TW Flameseal electric wire is vinyl-insulated. Many phonograph records are made of PVC also.

Overheating of PVC releases hydrochloric acid, which is toxic and corrosive. Processing machinery for PVC, such as extrusion screws, must be made of materials that will resist such corrosive attack.

Other vinyl resins include:

1. a range of vinyl copolymers
2. polyvinyl alcohol, chiefly formed into tubing
3. polyvinyl butyral, the adhesive that bonds automobile safety glass
4. polyvinylidene chloride, better known as Saran, used in foil, textiles, and corrosion-resistant tubing and valves
5. polyvinyl acetate, a thermoplastic adhesive

Polystyrene is the addition polymer of styrene, which is another ethylene derivative. Polystyrene is a clear, hard, and rigid plastic, but in its more familiar domestic uses polystyrene articles are made of high-impact formulations which have greater elasticity.

The styrene copolymer *acrylonitrile-butadiene-styrene*, or ABS, is a tough material, corrosion-resistant and dimensionally stable. It is used for chemical piping, and for component parts of items which are subject to impact, such as vacuum cleaners, telephones, refrigerator liners, and football helmets.

the organic materials
332

The most important of the acrylic plastics is *polymethyl methacrylate*, more familiarly known by the trade names Plexiglas and Lucite. This thermoplastic has excellent weathering characteristics, high transmittance for light, hardness, and strength. The cast product has better properties than extruded products, with higher strength and better optical characteristics. The acrylics are brittle, however. Though used as aircraft glazing, they are not suitable for windows of buildings because they are easily scratched. But the acrylics are used for outdoor signs because they lend themselves to intriguing lighting effects. The Rohm & Haas Company, the producer of Plexiglas, claims to have supplied the material for 150,000,-000 Plexiglas automobile tail lights.

14.28   polysulfones and polyimides

These are relatively new families of high-performance plastics.

The *polysulfones* can be used at temperatures as high as 320°F or as low as −150°F, with the additional properties of great strength and dimensional stability. The rate of creep is unusually low for a thermoplastic material. Because of the unusual temperature stability of polysulfone, it must be formed at temperatures above 600°F.

The capabilities of the polyimides such as Kapton exceed those of the other thermoplastics discussed. Temperature limits for these materials are absolute zero to 500°F, or as high as 1100°F for short-time exposures. At 750°F the strength of polyimide is twice the strength of any polyethylene at

Fig. 147 One-inch thick polymethyl methacrylate plate. The transducer shoe on top of the plate is made from the same material and is used for ultrasonic flaw detection in welds.

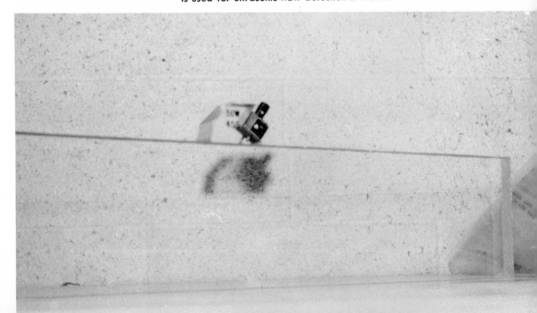

room temperature. Such polymers cannot be processed by the methods used with other thermoplastics, but require proprietary methods. Polyimide is chiefly used as film. Its resistance to ionizing radiation is remarkable for an organic polymer, and this property has found several aerospace applications.

14.29   fluorocarbons

In the remarkable fluorocarbon polymers some or all of the hydrogen attached to the paraffinic carbon chain is replaced by fluorine (Fig. 137). In order of decreasing fluorine content, the fluoroplastics include:

1. polytetrafluoroethylene (PTFE or Teflon), which is a polyethylene formula with fluorine substituted for every hydrogen atom
2. fluorinated ethylene-propylene (FEP), a copolymer. This has properties similar to PTFE, but is not so difficult to process
3. polychlorotrifluoroethylene (CTFE), with one chlorine and three fluorine atoms in the monomer
4. polyvinyl fluoride and polyvinylidene fluoride, which are fluorovinyls

Increasing fluorine content in these polymers is accompanied by improved electrical characteristics, higher service temperatures, lower coefficient of friction, and better corrosion resistance. The best combination of properties is therefore provided by PTFE.

PTFE is a crystalline (over 90 percent crystallinity) thermoplastic, opaque, soft, waxy, and white in color. Though its monomer boils at $-106°F$, the polymer has a service temperature for continuous exposure from absolute zero to 500°F. It has little strength, and creeps readily at room temperature. Specific electrical resistance is over 10^{18} ohm-cm, and dielectric strength is also high. PTFE is almost immune to chemical attack, except for molten alkali metals such as sodium, and a few fluorine compounds. It provides the lowest unlubricated coefficient of friction of any material: about 0.04.

Though a thermoplastic by reason of absence of cross-linking, PTFE is almost a thermosetting resin in its behavior and processing. It can be extruded or injection-molded only by sintering methods employing powders.

The electric industry uses PTFE for a wide range of specialty applications, including insulation, coaxial cable components, tube bases, plugs and sockets. The chemical and instrumentation industries value its chemical resistance for gaskets, tubing, valve packings, O-rings, valve linings, flexible couplings, and diaphragms. Its low friction and nonstick characteristics explain its numerous applications for rollers, bearings, conveyor coatings, etc.

CTFE is somewhat less corrosion-resistant and stronger than PTFE, and may be processed on standard equipment for thermoplastics. It has a continuous service temperature of 400°F, less than that of PTFE, and the same nonsticking characteristics. FEP has the same general characteristics of CTFE, being tough and strong in the temperature range of −450 to +450°F.

14.30 general properties of plastics

Creep and weathering characteristics are frequent considerations in the specifying of plastics. Some of the thermoplastics are depolymerized by ultraviolet radiation and must either be used indoors or protected by suitable additives such as carbon black. The creep performance of the plastics resembles that of metals: an initial high rate of creep, succeeded by a slower linear rate of secondary creep with time, and finally a rapid tertiary creep to failure. Because of excellent corrosion resistance, the plastics find many applications in process equipment, while their excellent electrical properties lead to a wide range of uses in electrical and electronic hardware. Best corrosion and electrical properties are provided by plastics without additives or plasticizers.

The following tables of properties are illustrative only. The materials are formulated in various grades for various service conditions, and in various molecular weights, so that properties may vary widely, depending on the grade, the method of manufacture, the presence of fillers and additives, and other variables.

THERMOSETTING PLASTICS

Mechanical Properties	Phenol-Formaldehyde	Cast Epoxy	Polyester
1. Tensile strength (1000 psi)	7–10	12	4–10
2. Elongation, %	0.5–1.5	–	–
3. Modulus of elasticity, psi	1×10^6	0.45×10^6	1.5×10^6
Electrical properties			
4. Dielectric strength, v/mil	350	400	400
5. Dielectric constant	5–6.5	3.6	6.0
6. Resistance, ohm-cm	10^{11}–10^{12}	10^{16}–10^{17}	10^{14}
Other properties			
7. Specific gravity	1.3	1.2	2.0
8. Temp. limit, °F	250	300	300

THERMOPLASTICS

Mechanical Properties	Cellulose Acetate	Poly-styrene	Meth-acrylate	Teflon	Low-Density Polyethylene
1. UTS	6000	7000	14,000	4000	1300
2. Elongation, %	15–50	1–2	5	–	200–750
3. E-value	$0.8–3.5 \times 10^6$	0.45×10^6	0.4×10^6	–	20,000
Electrical Properties					
4. Dielectric strength, v/mil	300	500	350	1500	500
5. Dielectric constant	5.5	2.5	3.0	2.0	2.3
6. Resistance, ohm-cm	$10^{11}–10^{13}$	$10^{17}–10^{19}$	10^{15}	10^{15}	10^{15}
Other Properties					
7. Specific gravity	1.3	1.05	1.2	2.2	0.92
8. Temperature limit, °F	200	200	200	500	200

NYLON, POLYCARBONATE, POLYACETAL

Mechanical Properties	Nylon	Polycarbonate	Polyacetal
1. Tensile strength	9000	10,000	10,000
2. Elongation, %	90	60	15
3. E-value	0.4×10^6	0.35×10^6	0.4×10^6
Electrical properties			
4. Dielectric strength, v/mil	400	400	2000
5. Dielectric constant	3.5	3.0	3.7
6. Resistance, ohm-cm	$10^{13}–10^{14}$	10^{16}	10^{14}
Other properties			
7. Specific gravity	1.1	1.2	1.4
8. Temperature limit, °F	300	250	150

14.31 cellular foamed plastics

Several of the plastics are made into plastic foams, including polystyrene (as Styrofoam), polyethylene (Ethafoam), PVC, polypropylene, and poly-urethane. These materials can be foamed to give various densities from 1 to 60 lb per cu ft. The strength of such plastic foams decreases with decrease in density, but the lighter foams have the best thermal insulating properties. A market consumption of 600,000,000 lb of foamed plastics is predicted for 1968. Almost half of present consumption is used in the bedding and furniture industries for cushions, pads, cores, carpet paddings and underlays, and related applications.

Fig. 148 Foamed polystyrene protective packaging for a slide projector.

Refrigerators and freezers use poured-in-place polyurethane as an insulating material. Other applications include trucks, trailers, and railroad cars. Polystyrene foam may be used for the same purpose and also as a building insulation. Other uses for foamed polystyrene include insulated containers, disposable cups for hot coffee, and packaging such as that shown in Fig. 148.

14.32   elastomers

Rubber and aluminum are transportation materials. Aluminum is employed as a structural material for transportation vehicles, while rubber is molded into articles that provide the frictional traction without which transportation is impossible: soles and heels of footwear, vehicle tires, cleats, conveyor belting, rubber hose for the movement of pumpable fluids, and insulation for the electric cables that transport power. While most rubber is consumed in such transportation applications, it has a variety of other uses, including such strange applications as tooling, pumps, and bearings for shafts. The uses of foamed rubber were briefly discussed in the preceding section.

Because they are not cross-linked, the thermoplastics are characterized generally by plastic behavior under stress, while the cross-linked thermosets are generally elastic and brittle. The rubbers are usually addition-polymerized from unsaturated monomers such as butadiene, and cross-linked (vulcanized) with sulfur at approximately every 500th carbon atom. In-

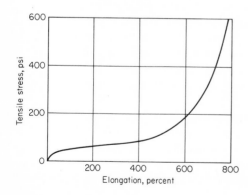

Fig. 149 Vulcanization of rubber.

creased cross-linking gives increased stiffness and reduced elongation. The structure of the cross-linking is shown in Fig. 149. However, in the case of the rubbers, elastic strain is not proportional to stress, and in addition there is a definite time lag between the stress and the corresponding strain. A characteristic stress-strain curve for rubber is shown in Fig. 150: the S-curve is a typical feature. The linear middle portion of the stress-strain curve is due to the development of crystallinity in the rubber due to stretching. The maximum possible strain of several hundred percent shown in the figure is characteristic of all rubbers except hard rubber.

At least three-quarters of all rubber consumed in this country is synthetic rubber. Given the present state of rubber technology, natural rubber has certain advantages which require its use in a limited range of articles, chiefly special vehicle tires. Natural rubber is stronger than the synthetic rubbers so far developed. Even more important, the heat generated in natural rubber when flexed is not so great as that generated in synthetic rubber (this type of heat generation is referred to as hysteresis). While automobile tires can be made of synthetic rubbers, the larger tires for off-the-road heavy construction vehicles and aircraft tires must be made of natural rubber. Most rubber goods, however, are made of SBR, styrene-butadiene rubber.

Fig. 150 Typical stress-strain curve for a polyisobutylene rubber.

While the major component of a car tire is SBR, several other kinds of rubber may be used in such a tire. An inner tube is made of butyl rubber, or if the tire is tubeless, the tire may be lined with butyl rubber. A large proportion of the weight of the tire is carbon black. This material, also derived from petroleum, provides strength, abrasion resistance, hardness, and ultraviolet protection to the rubber.

14.33 types of rubber

The more important rubber monomers, isoprene, styrene, isobutylene, acrylonitrile, butadiene, and chloroprene, are shown in Fig. 151. The polymers are usually addition polymers. Natural rubber corresponds to *polyisoprene*. Synthetic polyisoprene is also produced, but is not identical to natural rubber.

1. **Natural rubber.** Low hysteresis and high strength were noted as the virtues of natural rubber. However, it is readily attacked by solvents, gasolines, and minute quantities of ozone in the air. When vulcanized and reinforced with carbon black, tensile strength lies in the range of 3500–4500 psi and elongation 550–650 percent.

2. **SBR (Styrene-Butadiene Rubber).** This is the standard synthetic rubber, used for car tires, rubber hose and tubing, and conveyor belts. Tensile strength after vulcanizing and compounding with black is 2500–3500 psi, elongation 500–600 percent.

Fig. 151 Rubber monomers.

Isoprene

Acrylonitrile

Chloroprene

Butadiene

Styrene

Isobutylene

3. Butyl rubber. This is a copolymer of isobutylene and a small amount of isoprene or butadiene. Permeation of gases through butyl rubber is only 10 percent of the permeation through natural rubber, hence the use of this rubber for inner tubes and liners. It is also used as a mastic sealant, especially for curtain-wall construction of buildings, and has occasional uses as a solid fuel for rockets. This is a low-density rubber of low strength and high elongation.

4. Nitrile rubber. A copolymer of butadiene and acrylonitrile. Such rubbers have excellent adhesion to metals and resistance to oils and solvents. Uses include gasoline hose and hose linings, aircraft fuel tanks, printing rollers, and O-rings. An interesting use is that of nozzles for aerosol cans to resist the fluorinated hydrocarbon gas which pressurizes the can.

5. EPR (Ethylene-Propylene Rubber). These rubbers are made from low-priced monomers which yield a very light-weight rubber. EPR has excellent resistance to aging, ozone, and chemicals, and good electrical properties. It is incompatible with other rubbers.

6. Polysulfide rubber (Thiokol). A rubber of low mechanical strength but with outstanding resistance to solvents and low permeability to gases. Polysulfide rubber adhesives have excellent adhesion to metals. The uses of thiokols are all specialty uses, including rocket fuel, aircraft fuel tanks, gaskets, and caulking material for curtain wall construction.

7. Polychloroprene (Neoprene) rubber. Neoprene, as it is usually termed, is resistant to oils and paraffins, ozone, and abrasion. It is not highly flammable. Its best known use is in electrical cable covering, but it has a variety of other uses as gaskets, hose, engine mounts, bearing pads in bridge construction, protective clothing such as gloves and aprons, conveyor belts, and adhesives.

8. Fluoroelastomers. The many fluorine-containing rubbers are low strength rubbers with high dielectric strength and dielectric constant. Most of these rubbers are saturated and therefore are not vulcanized. Like the fluoroplastics they may be used at both high and low temperatures. Kel-F, Viton, Fluorel, and other fluoroelastomers therefore have specialty uses, including aerospace applications.

9. Silicone rubbers. Silicone rubbers may have fluorine, nitrile, or phenyl groups in the monomer. Unlike most rubbers, these are unaffected by ultraviolet radiation or ozone. Like other silicone products, the silicone rubbers are resistant to heat, cold, and solvents. Their tensile strength is quite low at room temperature, but at higher temperatures they are the strongest of the elastomers.

Fig. 152 An ingenious use of a material. Caterpillar Tractor Co. inspects the contour of internal gear teeth with the use of Dow Corning Silastic RTV silicone rubber. The silicone rubber when cast in place, accurately reproduces the tooth contour. The rubber molding is removed and inspected (instead of the gear tooth) by optical methods. (Courtesy Dow Corning Corp.)

Silicone rubbers can be vulcanized at room temperature. This feature, together with a temperature limit of 500°F or higher, has made possible the use of silicone rubber as a tooling and mold material (Fig. 152).

10. Reclaim rubber. Reclaim rubber is scrap rubber. It is a convenient raw material since it is already blended with required antioxidants and other additives. It is used in large amounts in rubber goods because of its low cost. It should not be inferred that the use of reclaim rubber is confined to second-quality products — neither does the steel industry produce low-quality steel from scrap.

11. Polyurethanes. The polyurethanes have some special characteristics and uses, and are discussed in a later section.

14.34 rubber as an engineering material

Rubber must no longer be considered as a special material with uses confined to specific products such as vehicle tires which alone can exploit its unique properties. The uses of rubber have expanded into many new applications, especially in civil and mechanical engineering, and the future will see more new applications. The polyurethanes discussed in the following section emphasize the broad utility of rubber in our present technology, for these rubbers serve as competitive materials for metals in some applications.

Rubber is, of course, virtually irreplaceable for some products. The soft rubber eraser, worth a nickel or a dime, saves dollars in the correcting of embarrassing mistakes. The rubber O-ring, simple as it may be, is a critical component in liquid and gas systems: its composition must be properly formulated to enable the ring to form a proper seal, while its chemical properties must provide resistance to the chemical attack of the liquids or gases conveyed.

In the field of civil engineering, probably the most important uses of rubber are the following:

expansion joints	rubber floor tile
water stops	hose
sealers and seals	gaskets
adhesives and tapes	O-rings
belt conveyors	vehicle tires
	work boots and apparel

The chemical engineer uses rubber as corrosion-resistant coatings, linings, pipe, and containers. The electrical industry uses rubber chiefly to cover wire and cable. It is in the mechanical engineering field that rubber has the greatest diversity of application. Many of these applications were listed under individual rubbers in the previous section. Using the automobile as a specific example, rubber is employed in its tires, vibration mounts, power belts, hose, sealers, adhesives, electric wire, upholstery, and weather-stripping.

Rubber is an excellent material for engine mountings and vibration-damping devices. Its damping factor is unusually high, and it can store more energy than a comparable steel spring. Furthermore, it attenuates sound, which a steel spring would transmit readily between its two seats.

No rubber presently developed has a sufficiently broad range of properties to serve as an all-purpose elastomer. The less saturated elastomers such as natural rubber and SBR are susceptible to weathering effects, such as ozone and oxygen attack, and are less resistant to solvents. Butyl rubber, with only a few percent of the unsaturation of natural rubber, is a better rubber with respect to these properties, but does not have the strength or abrasion resistance of natural rubber. The creep or "cold flow" of synthetic rubbers is usually higher than that shown by natural rubber, though the synthetic grades may be used at somewhat higher temperatures than natural rubber. For very low- and very high-temperature applications the silicone rubbers and fluoroelastomers must be used.

The following summary may serve to clarify some of the confusion arising from the multiplicity of rubbers:

1. natural rubber	strength, low heat of deformation
2. SBR	general-purpose rubber
3. butyl	low gas permeability, solvent resistance
4. silicone rubber	high- and low-temperature uses, low strength
5. chloroprene	electrical uses
6. polysulfide	solvent resistance
7. polyurethane	abrasion resistance

The classification of metal alloys such as low alloy steels, stainless steels, tool steels, aluminums, and welding rods, by numbering systems serves many useful purposes. A similar classification of rubbers has been set up by the SAE and ASTM societies, and has been adopted by many industries. The full system is explained in ASTM Standard D735.

In this classification the following prefixes are used:

1.	R	synthetic or natural compounds not oil-resistant
2.	SA	synthetic compounds with very low oil swell (polysulfides or acrylonitriles)
3.	SB	synthetics with low oil swell
4.	SC	synthetics with medium oil swell
5.	TA	synthetics with maximum resistance to high and low temperature (silicone rubbers)
6.	TB	synthetics with outstanding resistance to both dry heat and oils at high temperatures

A three-digit number follows the prefix. The first digit indicates hardness (e.g., 6 indicates 60 durometer), the last two digits indicating tensile strength (e.g., 20 for 2000 psi). Finally, a letter suffix indicates special tests; for example, B indicates compression set and C weather resistance. A typical full designation might be Grade R 635G. This would indicate a rubber not oil-resistant, 60 durometer hardness, 3500 psi, the letter G indicating tear resistance.

14.35 polyurethanes

The uses of polyurethane as a foamed polymer were discussed in an earlier section; here attention will be given to the rigid or molded polyurethanes. Polyurethane rubber, however, is also used as a high gloss and hard paint with excellent weathering characteristics and as an adhesive.

Polyurethanes are produced by reacting a diisocyanate, which is a complex aromatic compound containing nitrogen, with an alcohol. Molded polyurethane articles are usually two-component systems that are mixed and poured to cure in a mold. Polyurethanes can be formulated to give various grades of durometer hardness without the use of extenders or additives such as carbon black. A typical polyurethane rubber has a tensile strength of 5000 psi — higher than natural rubber — high elongation, Shore A hardness of 65, great tear strength, and remarkable abrasion resistance. Tensile strengths of 8000 psi and very high hardness are possible. Other remarkable properties of the polyurethanes will be noted presently.

The high strength and abrasion resistance of polyurethane rubber suggest that this rubber would make an excellent tire material. This is true, except for the high heat build-up in polyurethane during flexing of the tire as it rotates. Polyurethane also is more expensive than other standard rubbers. Nevertheless polyurethane tires have proved their worth on the wheels of lift trucks and other warehouse trucks, and are often specified for such equipment.

Other uses of polyurethane include long-wearing shoe heels, printing rollers, mallet heads, oil seals, diaphragms, vibration mounts, gears, pump impellers, bowling pins, duct liners, gaskets, and even football helmets. In some of these applications polyurethane competes with metals.

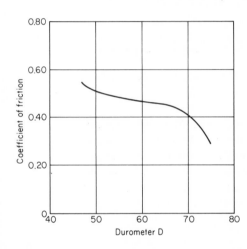

Fig. 153 Typical coefficient of friction property of polyurethane rubber. (After Du Pont, *Engineering Properties of Adiprene*)

Polyurethane has the unusual property, for a rubber, of a low coefficient of friction in the unlubricated condition. The friction coefficient decreases with hardness, as shown in Fig. 153. While these friction values are higher than those obtainable with bearing metals, they are low enough for the use of hard polyurethane in special bearings and bushings. Other characteristics are resistance to aging and a temperature range from about −125° to 200°F.

Polyurethane, like the epoxies, belongs to the select group of materials which are used for tooling applications. A typical tooling application is

Fig. 154 A block of polyurethane used as a female bending die. The rubber block conforms to the shape of the male die.

shown in Fig. 154, where a block of polyurethane is used as a female braking die. This application makes use of the principle that rubbers are virtually incompressible — actually they have about the same compressibility as water. When the steel male bending die forces the workpiece into the polyurethane, the rubber yields under the die but bulges around it, forcing the workpiece up against the die to form a 90° bend in the workpiece. Obviously the block of polyurethane can serve as the female die for a wide range of male forming dies, since it will conform to the shape of the male die in bending and drawing operations. There is little difficulty with spring-back in this method of forming; often the male die can be machined to a 90° angle if a 90° bend is required. Hard polyurethanes are used for such metal-forming, Shore A hardness of 80 or higher.

14.36 foods and refrigerants

Probably foods must be regarded as the most important group of materials. They are not usually industrial materials in the sense that they are used as raw materials, but the food-processing industries are an important, large, and interesting group of industries. A few foods serve as industrial raw materials, including starch, milk, peanuts, soybeans, and sunflower seeds.

Most foods approximate the specific heat and latent heat of water and ice, since 80–90 percent of any food is water. All foods freeze between 28 and 35°F. Because of the high heat storage of water, the refrigeration and freezing of foods involves the removal of large quantities of heat and the use of refrigeration equipment of large capacity. Storage of foods also requires close control of relative humidity; this aspect also is an expensive part of food technology. All fresh fruits respire, using stored chemical constituents in the food, chiefly sugars, and oxygen from the air, to produce carbon dioxide and heat.

The specific heat of foods above their freezing points is approximated by the following formula:

$$\text{Sp ht} = 0.008W + 0.20$$

where $W = \%$ water content.

The following table gives the thermodynamic properties of several foods. The large amount of water even in such foods as celery and carrots should be noted.

PROPERTIES OF PERISHABLE PRODUCTS

Commodity	% Water	Freezing Point	Sp Ht Above Freezing	Sp Ht Below Freezing	Latent Heat, Btu/lb
apples	84	29	0.87	0.45	121
bread	35	–	0.70	0.34	46–53
carrots	88	–	–	0.46	126
celery	94	31	0.95	0.48	135
corn	74	31	0.79	0.42	106
butter	16	–	0.33	0.25	23
ice cream	62	–	0.70	0.39	89
milk	87	31	0.90	–	125
eggs	66	28	0.74	0.40	96
lettuce	95	32	0.96	0.48	136
potatoes	78	31	0.82	0.43	111
tomatoes	94	31	0.95	0.48	134
fish	62	28	0.80	0.40	89–122
beef	62+	28	0.70–0.84	0.38–0.43	89–110
pork	32+	28	0.48–0.54	0.30–0.32	50–60
poultry	74	27	0.79	–	106

The refrigerants are used as heat transfer materials to move heat from a low-temperature region, the refrigerator, to a high-temperature region, the refrigeration unit. Refrigerants, especially the Freons, are also used to pressurize aerosol cans. It was noted earlier that the refrigerants are imperfect gases; therefore refrigerant tables are available for the determination of temperature, pressure, volume, and weight. These tables are similar to the Steam Tables of Chapter 4 and need not be explained again. A selection from the tables for Freon-12 is given below. But whereas the enthalpy of water is taken as zero at $+32°F$ in the Steam Tables, for refrigerants the enthalpy of the liquid, h_f, is taken to be zero at $-40°F$.

FREON-12, LIQUID, AND SATURATED VAPOR

Temperature	psia	v_g	h_f	h_g
−40	9.31	3.875	0.0	72.913
−20	15.27	2.443	4.235	75.110
−10	19.19	1.972	6.372	76.196
0	23.85	1.609	8.521	77.271
+10	29.34	1.324	10.68	78.335
+20	35.74	1.099	12.86	79.385

A few refrigerants such as ammonia are inorganic. The important group of refrigerants known as the Freons are chlorinated or fluorinated hydrocarbons, the basic hydrocarbons being methane and ethane. The American Society of Heating, Refrigeration, and Air Conditioning Engineers (ASHRAE) designates the refrigerants based on methane with numbers below 100; those based on ethane have numbers from 100 to 200. Thus Freon-12 is a methane refrigerant.

The actual system designation for refrigerants may be illustrated using F-114. The chemical formula for F-114 is $C_2Cl_2F_4$, dichlorotetrafluoroethane. The last digit gives the number of fluorine atoms in the molecule (4 fluorine atoms). The last digit but one is one more than the number of hydrogen atoms. Since there are no hydrogen atoms in F-114, this number is a 1. The last digit but two is one less than the number of carbon atoms, but if the carbon atoms number only 1, this number is omitted, as in Freon-12.

ASHRAE STANDARD DESIGNATION OF REFRIGERANTS

Number	Name	Formula
12	dichlorodifluoromethane	CCl_2F_2
22	monochlorodifluoromethane	$CHClF_2$
40	methyl chloride	CH_3Cl
50	methane	CH_4
114	dichlorotetrafluoroethane	$C_2Cl_2F_4$
160	ethyl chloride	C_2H_5Cl

Refrigerants can deteriorate by three mechanisms:

1. pyrolysis — destruction by heat
2. hydrolysis — destruction by reaction with water
3. oxidation — destruction by reaction with water

Both pyrolysis and hydrolysis will reduce Freons to hydrogen chloride or hydrogen fluoride. Both compounds are highly corrosive to refrigeration systems.

A large number of characteristics are desired in a refrigerant:

1. no odor, since odor may contaminate food
2. no toxicity, so that food will not be harmed
3. no explosion hazard in any concentration in air
4. no corrosive attack on the metals of the refrigeration system
5. chemical stability at both the low and high temperatures in the refrigeration system
6. insolubility in water
7. ease of leak detection
8. high electrical resistance. Many motors of refrigeration condensing units are exposed to refrigerant vapor
9. good thermal conductivity
10. low viscosity
11. ability to dissolve lubricating oil, to prevent solidification of heavy oil waxes on heat transfer surfaces
12. low cost
13. low specific volume to allow the use of equipment of small size

This is rather a demanding list to impose on any material.

Ammonia is only used in large industrial refrigeration systems. Its name is derived from Ammon, the Egyptian sun-god. If moisture is present, ammonia forms ammonium hydroxide which is corrosive to copper and copper alloys. Freon-12 is a common refrigerant in small installations. It is corrosive to natural rubber, but neoprene gaskets are resistant to it. Carbon dioxide is often selected for hospitals and ships because of safety considerations. In the form of dry ice it makes an excellent and cheap expendable refrigerant.

PROBLEMS

1 How is the anisotropy of wood overcome?

2 Why is paper anisotropic?

3 How does moisture content affect the several properties of wood?

4 Explain why a sandwich structure can be so strong when none of its components separately may be able to carry much load.

5 What is the weight in pounds per cubic foot of a crude petroleum with an API gravity of 6? of a jet engine fuel with API gravity of 38?

6 Explain the purpose of the basic oil refinery operations of fractional distillation, cracking, and polymerization.

7 What is a grease?

8 What are the principal uses of petroleum coke?

9 Explain the difference in stress-strain behavior between an elastomer and a thermoplastic.

10 What is the difference in chemical structure between a thermoplastic and a thermoset?

11 Explain the meaning of cross-linking.

12 Explain why it is difficult for a synthetic polymer to crystallize.

13 What advantages do the epoxies offer?

14 List the favorable properties of nylon as an industrial material.

15 Why is a higher degree of crystallinity associated with greater density in a thermoplastic?

16 List the favorable and the poor properties of PTFE plastic, including its frictional and electrical characteristics.

17 In what applications is natural rubber preferred over synthetic rubber?

18 Explain the method of metal-forming in rubber tooling.

19 Why is polyurethane rubber preferred for such tooling applications?

20 For what reason is reclaim rubber an excellent raw material?

21 Which of the rubbers is (a) an automotive rubber, (b) a cryogenic rubber, (c) a rocket fuel, (d) a high-temperature rubber, (e) an electrical rubber, (f) a rubber for tires of large earth-moving vehicles?

22 What are the characteristics of an SB 620C rubber?

23 What is the specific weight in pounds per cubic foot of F-12 gas at $0°F$ and 23.85 psia?

Adhesives and surface coatings may be related materials. Many of the organic materials are formulated for either use, such as the epoxies. In both cases a thin film must be attached to a substrate material. The adhesive must bond only. The coating must bond, but has the additional functions of protecting the substrate and providing an attractive appearance.

The range of surface finishes is very wide, and includes organic materials as well as inorganic coatings such as porcelain enamels and anodized finishes. Few manufactured parts can dispense with a finish of some kind in their manufacturing process; the durability of the part or its market acceptance may be dependent on the coating process.

15.1   substrates and surface films

No coating or adhesive adheres to a surface unless it can "wet" the surface. A classic example of a non-wetting material is a drop of mercury on a steel plate. The mercury has no attraction to the steel plate and draws into a tight sphere which can easily be rolled along the steel plate. Mercury, then, cannot be used to bond the steel plate to another material. A drop of a wetting material will spread over the plate until the edge of the drop forms an equilibrium angle θ with the plate, as in Fig. 155. Good wet-

ADHESIVES
AND
SURFACE FINISHES

15

Fig. 155   Wetting angle.

ting is indicated by a small angle; if the drop spreads over the whole plate to give a contact angle of zero, then the wetting is ideal.

Whether a coating material can wet a surface depends also on the condition of the surface. No paint or adhesive bond would be expected with an oil-covered or rust-covered steel plate. But there are other, more subtle surface difficulties.

Suppose the steel axle of a vehicle breaks. If the two broken parts are put together in proper alignment, the axle is not thereby mended. We take it for granted that nothing can be mended in this way. Yet it is rather remarkable that this simple repair method does not work. If the atoms of the axle attracted each other so powerfully that a large force was required to rupture the axle, then an equal force should bring the two broken parts into close enough proximity for the interatomic forces to mend the break. Yet this method of repair fails completely.

First of all, the deformation accompanying the fracture will make it impossible to bring the atoms of the two broken pieces together to the required interatomic distance of 4 Angstroms approximately. The two pieces may appear to the eye to mate well; on an atomic scale they will be a hopeless mismatch. They may be joined together only by a very large force which more or less mashes them together with considerable change of section, in the welding method called "cold welding". Such joining sometimes happens fortuitously, as when an engine shaft seizes, or when pressure and heat weld a machining chip to a cutting tool.

There is a second difficulty. All metal surfaces act as getters, or absorbers of gas molecules, particularly for water vapor. The two fractured surfaces become freshly exposed to the air and instantly absorb a layer of water vapor. This layer makes metal-to-metal contact impossible, for a film of gas intervenes which unfortunately does not possess adhesive properties.

These surface considerations help to explain the action of coatings and adhesives. Such materials must cover the surface to establish continuous contact, and must in addition remove or dissolve surface impurities or gases to establish contact with the original material of the substrate. Usually a bond to the surface of metals is impossible without first cleaning the surface. Bonding to porous materials such as paper or brick may not require a cleaning operation if the adhering material can enter the pores of the substrate and thus obtain anchorage.

In outer space, repair of broken surfaces would be easier, since there are no gases to adsorb on the broken surfaces. But in space there is the possibility of a wrench seizing to a nut, a hammer to a nail, and certainly the hazard of shafts seizing to bearings.

adhesives and surface finishes

351

15.2 metal cleaning

Metal surfaces are always contaminated with unwanted matter of various types, usually referred to as *soil:*

> mill scale and rust
> adsorbed water vapor
> oils and lubricants such as cutting oils and drawing compounds
> perspiration deposits such as fingerprints
> paints and other finishes

Before the application of paints or adhesives, such materials must be removed to produce what is called a "clean" surface. What is actually produced is a "sufficiently clean" surface, since what may be clean for one application may not be so for another.

The various metal cleaning methods may be classified as either *mechanical* or *chemical:*

> mechanical: grit-blasting, barrel-finishing, scratch-brushing, ultrasonic cleaning,
> grinding, steam-cleaning, etc.
> chemical: solvents, electrocleaning, acids, alkalis

For many applications the water-break test can be used as a test of surface cleanliness. In this simple test, if the surface will hold an unbroken film of water, it is considered clean.

15.3 mechanical cleaning

Small parts may be tumbled in a barrel for purposes of cleaning, degreasing, descaling, deburring, finishing, burnishing, or coloring. The method is also used to give a luster to metals and plastics. This *barrel-finishing* operation may be done wet or dry and with or without a tumbling medium.

Deburring of parts is done by adding an abrasive compound to the contents of the barrel. Without an abrasive, burrs tend to be peened over rather than removed from the part. The pH of the tumbling liquid must be controlled; for most operations on steel a pH of about 9 is used. Typical products which use barrel-finishing methods are roller bearings, cutlery, jet engine blades, gears, and many plastic products.

Ultrasonic cleaning is a remarkably effective method of cleaning, even for paint stripping. The equipment requires a bath of solvent, equipped with ultrasonic transducers. The cleaning is performed by ultrasonic energy produced in a separate generator. The frequencies in use range from 20 to 40 kc, and ultrasonic power may range from 100 w in a small unit to

5 kw in a large unit. The acoustic energy produces voids in the liquid which collapse to produce cavitation pressures which are estimated at over 1000 psi. The cleaning tank must be made of hard and rigid material so that acoustic power is reflected and not absorbed by it. Typical products that are cleaned ultrasonically include printed circuit boards, transistors (for removal of soldering flux), spray nozzles, and typewriter parts.

Abrasion methods of cleaning may employ a wire brush, a powered scratch brush, sand, or grit-blasting. Ordinary carbon steel brushes are usually not suitable for this purpose, especially for stainless steel parts, because steel particles may embed in the work and later rust. Abrasion methods using grit or shot are the usual methods of cleaning weldments, castings, and large fabrications. Grit may be fired from a nozzle or thrown centrifugally off a rapidly rotating wheel, the latter method using considerably less power.

Steam cleaning uses a steam nozzle and a portable steam generator. Low-pressure steam is not effective. High-pressure steam at about 100 psig is used, often with a cleaning compound added. Steam cleaning is often used for paint stripping and for cleaning supermarket shopping carts.

Flame-cleaning uses a gas flame to remove mill scale from steel or paints from metals.

15.4   chemical cleaning

The choice of chemical cleaner depends on the specific resistance of the metal to corrosion. Aluminum products, zinc die-castings, brass, and copper are all attacked by alkaline cleaners. Magnesium, on the other hand, will be attacked by cleaners which are not strongly alkaline, and requires a *p*H of about 10.5.

Acid cleaners are corrosive and difficult to handle. Alkaline cleaners do not share this disadvantage, and are preferred for additional reasons:

1. There is usually no chemical attack on the metal.
2. A less corrosion-resistant material may be used for tanks.
3. There is no hydrogen embrittlement of the metal to be cleaned.

Since metals, including steels, are embrittled by hydrogen, many specifications forbid the use of acid cleaning because of the presence of hydrogen. However, acid cleaners, when conditions permit their use, are cheaper and faster, and are better scale removers. In addition, the etching effect of an acid cleaner will improve the adhesion of paints and adhesives.

Acid cleaning is often termed pickling, presumably because in earlier times vinegar (acetic acid) was used for the purpose. Acid cleaning is standard practice for the removal of mill scale from steel. The cheapest of the acids is sulfuric acid. Hydrochloric acid (muriatic acid), diluted by water three to one, is used at room temperature. If used hot, its fumes corrode nearby equipment. It is a faster cleaner than sulfuric acid, but requires a nonmetallic tank such as rubber, fiberglass, or polyethylene. Nitric acid being more expensive is used only when other acids are not effective. Phosphoric acid is used either hot or at room temperature, in concentrations of 15 to 30 percent weight.

Alkaline cleaning is used with aluminum. Sodium hydroxide, sodium carbonate, trisodium phosphate, or other alkaline cleaners are used. A black smut may be produced on the surface of aluminum by alkaline cleaners, especially in the case of certain alloy aluminums. This smut is removed by an acid dip.

The oxide surface of aluminum must sometimes be removed, for anodizing, spot welding, or other purposes. This may be done in a sulfuric acid-sodium fluoride solution, or a phosphoric acid-chromic acid solution.

Chemical cleaning is carried out by several methods: hand wiping, dip tanks, spraying, vapor degreasing, and electrocleaning. Hand wiping is not efficient and produces imperfect results. Problems of toxicity prevent the use of hand wiping with chlorinated solvents. The latter are used in the *vapor degreasing* method. In this procedure the metal to be cleaned is suspended above the cleaning tank. The solvent in the tank is heated and its vapors condense in droplets on the cooler metal workpieces. The droplets drip back to the tank, carrying soil with them. Drips from a workpiece hung higher up must not be allowed to fall on any workpiece suspended below.

In *electrocleaning* the part to be cleaned is an electrode in a solution which carries electric current. The effect of the electric current is to electrolyze the water of the solution, hydrogen being released at the cathode and oxygen at the anode. This generation of gases provides agitation. Alkaline solutions are usual. The work may be either anode or cathode, or may be switched from one to the other. Metals that form protective oxide skins, such as stainless steel or nickel, are cleaned cathodically. Brass also is cleaned cathodically to avoid loss of zinc at the anode.

After cleaning, the parts must be rinsed in hot water, since residual amounts of acids or alkalis may attack metal surfaces. The rinse water is dried from the surface as quickly as possible, often with the use of infrared lamps.

Adhesives and surface coatings are applied as soon as possible after final rinsing.

15.5 conversion coatings

Conversion coatings are inorganic films produced by some kind of chemical reaction with the metal surface of the workpiece. They are produced either

Fig. 156 Micrograph of a zinc phosphate coating on steel sheet. There is porosity between the phosphate crystals, and the coating by itself does not protect the steel.

for corrosion protection or as a base for surface finishes. Though they are extremely thin, usually much less than 0.001 in. thick, they are tightly bonded to the part since they are chemically formed from the original metallic surface. The most commonly employed conversion coatings are *phosphate*, *chromate*, and *anodic* (anodized) coatings.

Phosphate coatings are applied to steel or galvanized steel. The corresponding method for aluminum is usually a chromate treatment. These coatings offer the following possibilities:

1. Paint makes a strong bond to phosphate coatings.
2. While the phosphate coating by itself offers minimal corrosion protection, the addition of a finishing paint coat provides excellent protection.
3. A phosphate coat makes an excellent lubricant for the drawing of steel in presswork operations.
4. Some of the phosphating chemicals serve also as cleaners. Phosphating is applied to domestic appliances, automobile bodies, military items, and metal furniture, to name only a few applications. Such coatings are applied by brush, spray, dip, or tumbling.

For paint bonding purposes, crystalline zinc phosphate coatings ($Zn_3PO_4 \cdot 4H_2O$) are produced on metals. There is no reaction with the steel in this method, and therefore a true conversion coating is not produced. The coating is soft, and being a hydrated compound, paint baking temperatures must not be too high or the phosphated coating will be damaged. The porosity of the phosphate coat allows paint to penetrate and adhere strongly to the surface. However, too coarse a phosphate crystal structure may produce a deposit that does not adhere well to the metal surface.

adhesives and surface finishes
355

An iron phosphate coating is a true conversion coating, since the phosphate is provided by a phosphoric acid solution and the iron of the part being treated. Unlike zinc phosphate, iron phosphate coatings are amorphous. The iron phosphate dip may be used both for cleaning and phosphating. Compared to zinc phosphate, such a coating has somewhat better corrosion resistance even though it is thinner, since it is less porous. After phosphating the part is usually rinsed.

Several types of conversion coatings are applied to aluminum:

1. chromate-phosphate coatings from acid solutions
2. chromate coatings
3. oxide coatings produced by electrical methods (anodizing)
4. crystalline zinc phosphate coatings, similar to those used on steels

Chromate coatings are more widely used as prepaint treatments than the other types. Like phosphate coatings on steel, these conversion coatings will not flake or chip, not even during forming of the metal sheet.

15.6 anodizing of aluminum

In the anodizing method, a light or heavy oxide coating is produced on aluminum by making the aluminum part the anode in an acid electrolytic bath. The anodic coating is porous and must be sealed by immersion in boiling water or linseed oil. Such coatings are applied to aluminum windows and doors, aluminum trim on highway buses, and the aluminum scales and other parts of drafting machines. Anodizing may be done for any of the following reasons:

1. improved corrosion resistance
2. paint adhesion
3. decorative and color effects — the porous oxide coat can be impregnated with dyes
4. electrical insulation
5. improved emissivity of the surface
6. abrasion resistance (hard anodizing)

The oxide coat on aluminum can be thickened by cheaper methods of chemical oxidation, but anodizing provides a more predictable and controllable quality of oxide coat and better corrosion resistance.

Many variables control the properties of the anodic film:

1. the alloy of aluminum — silicon alloys anodize to a gray color, chromium alloys tend to a yellowish color, etc.
2. prior heat treatment or welding

3. type of electrolyte
4. concentration of the electrolyte
5. voltage of the bath
6. current density in amps per square foot
7. a.c. or d.c.
8. temperature of the bath
9. anodizing time

The thickness of the oxide film is controlled by most of these variables, but chiefly by the anodizing time (Fig. 157). There is a practical maximum thickness, because while the film grows from the inside out, as a conversion coating must, the electrolyte dissolves the film already formed. As a result of this chemical dissolution, the rate of film growth steadily decreases, until finally the rate of film formation and dissolution become equal, and no further increase in thickness can occur. For most applications a film of 0.5 to 2 mils is developed. By comparison, the usual thickness of the natural oxide surface of aluminum sheet is of the order of 0.000002 in.

Fig. 157   Growth of an anodic coating.

Because the outer surface of the oxide film is attacked by the electrolyte for the longest time, it is more porous than the innermost section of the film.

The electrolyte for anodizing may be sulfuric acid, chromic acid, oxalic acid, or boric acid. The latter two acids are used only for special effects. Oxalic acid produces a yellowish tint in the oxidized surface. Boric acid is largely restricted to the production of thin and impermeable dielectric films on electrical condenser foil (the dielectric strength of an anodized film is very high). Aircraft parts may use a chromic acid electrolyte.

The sulfuric acid process is the usual one employed, in an acid concentration of 15 to 25 percent. The process is performed at room temperature, usually in a lead-lined steel tank, the lead lining acting as cathode for the circuit. Voltages of 12 to 24 v are employed, with current densities of 12 to 18 amps per sq ft and anodizing times of about 30 min. The use of higher temperatures has the effect of reducing the film thickness and increasing the porosity of the film.

adhesives and surface finishes

"Hard anodizing" or "hard coating" is the production of an anodized coat specifically for wear resistance. The hard coat is the same oxide produced by any other anodizing process and has the same hardness, but the coating is thicker and less porous. The process is operated at a lower temperature to reduce the extent of chemical dissolution of the oxide film. Coatings as thick as 0.004 in. are produced in hard coating: such a coating will significantly increase the overall dimensions of a part produced to tolerances. Such articles as automobile pistons are hard-coated.

15.7 other inorganic finishes for
metal surfaces

A range of colors is presented by *copper* and its alloys. Eleven standard colors are available, from the red of pure copper, through the golds of the brasses, to the silver of nickel silver. Until recently, these color effects in copper have been difficult to exploit because no surface treatments were available as permanent protection against tarnishing of copper. Newest developments have resulted in copper treatments with a degree of permanency against exterior exposure. These should result in more extensive decorative use of copper without the penalty of repeated cleaning treatments.

Patterned and textured sheets in copper, aluminum, and stainless steel are available in wide variety. Such finishes are produced by chemical etching, grinding, brushing, polishing, or by impressing a textured pattern from embossing rolls. An embossed pattern can control the reflectivity of the sheet, strengthen it by cold-working, and provides visual appeal beyond that provided by the unrelieved flat sheet. Embossed patterns are not usual with stainless steel sheet however. The most commonly used finishes for stainless sheet are #2B and #4:

#2B — cold-rolled, annealed, pickled, then given a cold-finishing pass to produce
a smooth and mildly reflective surface
#4 — this is the polished finish, produced by belt-grinding with 150–180 grit

Porcelain enamelling was discussed in Chapter 7. Such enamels are capable of remarkable decorative effects, including murals, by the use of techniques such as stencilling, printing rolls, silk-screening, etc.

Today there is a strong trend toward the use of *clad steels*. These are composed of a mild steel core to provide strength and ductility, with a surface cladding to supply other service characteristics such as corrosion resistance. The cladding may be a factory-produced paint or plastic coating, a metal dip-coat such as a galvanized coat, or a metal surface bonded to

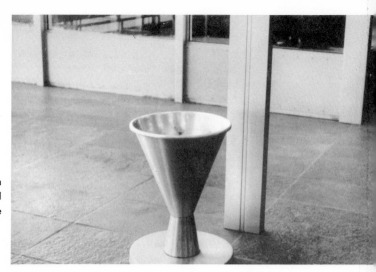

Fig. 158 Anodized aluminum architectural work and anodized aluminum ashtray at the entrance to a building.

the base steel. The familiar stainless steel cookware is a clad steel, actually a mild steel clad with stainless. Such a clad steel is superior to solid stainless steel for cookware, since stainless steel has low thermal conductivity.

Zinc coating, or *galvanizing*, is a cheap and effective method of protecting steel from atmospheric corrosion. The zinc coat is usually applied by hot-dipping the steel in a bath of molten zinc. Various coating weights can be applied, the usual minimum weight being 1.25 oz per sq ft, which is the sum of the coatings on the two sides of a steel sheet.

Tin-plating is a more expensive coating, usually reserved for food containers. *Terne sheet* is cheaper than tin plate, being an alloy of 80 percent lead and 20 percent tin. The tin is required because lead will not wet the surface of steel and hence will not bond. Most terne sheet is used for such items as fuel tanks for large and small engines and construction equipment.

Aluminized steel is sheet steel with an aluminum coating on both sides, produced by a hot-dip process. In appearance, this product somewhat resembles aluminum. Two grades are produced. Heat-resistant aluminized steel has an aluminum coat 0.001 in. thick on each side, while corrosion-resistant aluminized steel has a coating of 0.002 in. per side. Aluminized steel may be found in automobile mufflers and exhaust piping, ducting, and heating appliances.

Electroplating is the deposit of metal coatings from electrolytic baths. Plating may be done for any of several purposes:

1. appearance
2. corrosion protection
3. wear resistance
4. increasing the size of worn parts

adhesives and surface finishes
359

and may be performed on any of the common metals. The part to be plated is made the cathode in the bath, and the anode is a bar of the metal to be plated. Electroplating is subject to many of the problems of anodizing, such as coating porosity and uniformity of the deposit. A heavy deposit may be plated on projections while recesses may receive only a thin deposit. Thus an electrodeposit on a screen of round wire will produce wires of elliptical section. Many electroplating processes also release hydrogen at the cathodic workpiece, a cause of embrittlement which may or may not be of concern in the service of the part.

Instead of galvanizing, zinc may be electroplated from cyanide baths. Cadmium plating is common on small hardware items; it provides corrosion protection inferior to that of zinc and may result in hydrogen embrittlement. Cadmium-plating is not permitted on food-processing equipment because its compounds are toxic.

Nickel tarnishes on exposure to atmosphere. Chromium does not tarnish, but electroplated chromium is porous. Best protection and appearance therefore is provided by first plating a thin film of nickel a few ten-thousandths of an inch thick, followed by a heavier electroplated film of chromium.

Vacuum plating, also called vacuum metallizing, is a method of depositing thin metal films by deposition from the vapor phase under high vacuum. Under high vacuum conditions the metal to be deposited has a high vapor pressure and a low boiling point. The vacuum deposition of cadmium avoids the hydrogen embrittlement problem of electroplated cadmium. Vacuum deposition is performed on plastics as well as metals; capacitors are made by the vacuum deposition of zinc or aluminum on paper. This is the best method for the production of reflective surfaces such as are found in sealed-beam headlights.

15.8 organic finishes

Despite the variety of metallic and ceramic finishes discussed in the previous sections, most surface areas are finished with various types of paints, lacquers, varnishes, and enamels. These organic finishes (which may contain inorganic pigments such as titanium oxide) contain a binder or "vehicle" which is either an oil or a synthetic resin and which usually hardens by cross-linking to produce a thermosetting finish.

There is a surprisingly large number of reasons for the painting of surfaces:

1. surface protection
2. decorative effects
3. cleanliness or "good housekeeping"

4. marketability of the product
5. advertising
6. identification (as in color coding)
7. safety and traffic control (as with traffic paints)
8. improved working conditions or morale
9. camouflage

In general, different types of finishes are required for these different objectives.

A simple type of coating, suitable for surface protection only, is the strippable coating shown on the lathe center of Fig. 159. Such coatings are tough, plasticized polyvinyl or cellulose acetate butyrate resins, and serve primarily for the protection of the product during shipping and storage. The parts to be protected are sprayed or dipped into a hot tank of the coating, which deposits a heavy thickness on the parts. When the part is to be put into use, the coating is easily stripped. Such a coating material contains a vehicle only, without other additives such as pigments.

Fig. 159 A strippable coating on a lathe center.

The vehicle in a more complex paint has the function of binding together the pigment particles in the paint. The binder can produce an adherent, glossy, and impermeable surface film; the pigments cannot. The pigments provide both color and hiding power. Hiding power may be defined as the ability to hide or obliterate the background material, and is tested by applying a known thickness of paint over a test card with a black-and-white design. Such hiding power charts are shown in Fig. 160. The proportion of pigment to vehicle determines the gloss of the paint; low pigment ratios result in a gloss paint, and high pigment ratios in a non-reflective paint.

Besides binder and pigment, the paint will require solvents to adjust the volatility of the paint mixture. Volatility roughly corresponds to the evaporation rate or the drying time of the paint, and must be adjusted to the requirements of the painting method. Thus spray painting will require higher volatility than brush application.

The differences between paints, varnishes, enamels, and lacquers are somewhat indeterminate, but are approximately as follows. A *paint* is a mixture of a vehicle and a pigment. A *lacquer* is a finishing material that

Fig. 160 Three types of hiding power charts. A paint coat has been applied to the chart on the right.

dries quickly by evaporation of solvents and forms a film from its non-volatile constituents. *Varnish* contains no pigment. A strippable coating could therefore be termed a varnish. An *enamel* is a blend of a paint and a varnish.

The formation of the paint film occurs by either of two methods: solvent loss as in lacquers, and cross-linking as in linseed oil or epoxy finishes. In the terminology of the paint industry, the method of solvent loss characterizes a non-convertible finish; cross-linking is the characteristic of a *convertible* finish.

The most familiar example of a non-convertible finish is a mixture of shellac and alcohol. This is a rapid-drying lacquer. Such a finish has a number of disadvantages:

1. The loss of solvent introduces shrinkage stresses in the film, which may affect film adhesion.
2. The absence of cross-linking indicates that the solvent resistance of the film is poor.
3. A second coat will tend to redissolve the first coat.
4. Only a thin coat can be deposited from a nonconvertible finish because of solvent loss.
5. The rapid drying rate is suited to spray-painting but not to brushing.

This system may now be compared with convertible systems, which include linseed oil paints, baking enamels, and two-component paints, the latter having a synthetic resin in one can and a curing agent (also called a hardener or a catalyst) in a second can. The oil paints contain an unsaturated oil such as linseed oil which cross-links by using atmospheric oxygen as a cross-linking agent. In the case of an epoxy paint, one can contains a low-molecular-weight liquid epoxy resin, the other can a curing amine perhaps, such as diethylene triamine. These two components are mixed in the proportions required for the chemical reaction. The paint must be applied before the curing reaction has advanced too far. This may be only half an hour. Material not used within this curing time must be scrapped. The *pot life* is the length of time between initial mixing and the final stiffening of the mix. Such a system will have good adhesion and chemical resistance, but will tend to run or sag, since the viscosity increase must follow the curing reaction. Actually the viscosity of such a system must be adjusted with volatile solvents.

15.9 application methods

Although most paints are applied by brush or spray gun, a wide variety of other application methods is available.

Brushing is the most expensive application method. For brush application the paint must remain fluid long enough for brush marks to disappear, yet not so long that the paint will sag. Special thixotropic paints are available for brushing, which have lower viscosity under the shear stresses of brushing but stiffen when not sheared. If the paint is not thixotropic, it will still remain on a vertical wall if the paint film is not too thick. This simply indicates that its own weight does not exceed its yield strength.

In *flow coating*, paint is pumped in streams to flow over the article to be painted. This is a production line method, since if a different article is to be painted, the configuration of paint flow must be altered. In this method and in dip-painting, the highest quality of finish is not possible.

Compressed-air spraying is the method that best suits a wide range of articles. The paint is introduced into a stream of high-velocity air to atomize it. The resultant paint stream is fanned out to cover a suitable area of the article. Paint is fed to the spray nozzle either by suction feed (subatmospheric pressures) or by pressure feed. Suction feed is not especially effective on heavy-paint materials, but is employed in the automotive, furniture, and appliance industries.

To prevent sagging, paints for gun use require larger amounts of solvents, which are volatilized during spraying to give a rapid increase in viscosity. Spraying is done by holding the gun perpendicular to the surface of the work and 6 to 10 inches from it, and applying the paint in straight lines.

Spray booths are expensive installations, and require costly ventilation arrangements. In addition, much of the paint in the spray fails to deposit on the workpiece. To reduce spray losses, *electrostatic spraying* may be used. In this method the paint is spun off the edge of a rapidly rotating disc. A high-voltage electric field charges the paint particles, which are

adhesives and surface finishes

attracted to grounded workpieces on a conveyor. The workpieces need not be uniform in size or shape, and the paint spreads uniformly over the workpiece because of mutual repulsion of the charged paint particles.

Dip tanks may be used for large or small articles, and are particularly effective where the back, front, and inside of the article must be painted.

Roller coating applies a surface finish by means of a roll, and is closely related to printing processes. This method is, of course, restricted to flat sheets, including sheets for food cans and bottle caps.

Aerosol spray cans are used to apply small amounts of surface coatings. The can of spray material is pressurized with a Freon or other refrigerant to a maximum of about 40 psi. The Freon is the propellant for the spraying operation.

15.10 emulsion paints

An *aerosol* is a dispersion of a liquid in a gas. An *emulsion* is a suspension of fine particles of a liquid within another liquid. Latex paints are emulsions of organic resins in water. The spherical particles of paint, which are not soluble in the water, are simply distributed throughout the water medium. On application to the surface being painted, the water evaporates and the resin particles coalesce to form the final paint film. Such paints are popular in the consumer market for use on wood, plaster, and concrete walls, but also have limited use in industry. Styrene-butadiene latex paints are sold in largest volume. Ceiling acoustic tile is one of the industrial applications of these emulsion paints. The industrial advantages of an emulsion paint are the reduction in fire hazard, low odor, and reduction in thinner costs.

Average particle size in an emulsion paint is about 0.1 micron (50 microns is the smallest size that can be distinguished by the naked eye). The emulsion formed must, of course, remain stable with the passage of time. Generally the particle size of an emulsion will increase with age as small particles combine into larger ones. This coalescence causes an increase in viscosity.

Unlike emulsion paints, most paints are solvent-type coatings, and a wide range of solvents is available for the adjustment of paint properties such as wetting, viscosity, and drying time. Because the continuous phase of an emulsion paint is water, it is more difficult to adjust the properties of such paints. Compared with other paint solvents, water would be classed as a low boiling-point solvent like toluene, ethyl alcohol, or methyl ethyl ketone. Water, however, evaporates much more slowly than these organic solvents, and its latent heat is very much higher than that of any other paint solvent.

It was observed in the previous section that butadiene-styrene is the most popular resin in emulsion paints. In this resin butadiene is the plasticizer for the styrene. Butadiene-styrene is not confined to emulsion coatings, nor is any other organic resin. The following list includes the more common synthetic paint resins. The natural resins such as linseed oil are not included.

PAINT RESINS

Acrylic	Phenolic
acrylonitrile-butadiene	Polyimide
Alkyd	Polyester
amino	Rubber
phenolic	chlorinated
styrenated	neoprene
Amino	Silicone
Bituminous	Styrene
Cellulose	butadiene
nitrate	Urethane
ethyl	Vinyl
butyrate	acetate
Chlorinated polyether	butyral
Epoxy	chloride
amine	
phenolic	
polyimide	

Alkyd resins are widely used in synthetic finishes. A number of materials can be incorporated into the alkyd molecule, including alcohols, oils, and fatty acids. Further, the alkyd resins have the capacity to improve the properties of other surface coatings, and for such purposes they are blended with styrene-butadiene, polyvinyl acetate, phenolics, and acrylics to improve water resistance, adhesion, and flexibility. Two large markets for the alkyd paints are automotive and appliance finishes.

Most of the alkyd finishes are made by reacting phthalic anhydride with a polyalcohol such as glycerol (Fig. 161). Short-oil alkyd resins contain about 40 percent oil such as linseed oil or tung oil; long-oil resins contain about 60 percent oil. The long-oil resins are slower drying and give a softer film with better durability and flexibility. Generally speaking, long-oil alkyds are used in the maintenance, marine, and architectural markets, while short-oil alkyds are used on household appliances and furniture.

As with many of the synthetic plastics and coatings, the alkyd resins ultimately deteriorate under ultraviolet radiation. The degree of gloss failure is roughly proportional to the amount of such radiation received.

Glycerol   Phthalic anhydride

Fig. 161 Typical alkyd resin.

Acrylic resins are also used as automobile finishes, since they retain their gloss unusually well.

Epoxy resins offer the following outstanding properties:

1. no primer coat is required
2. they adhere well to metals, wood, concrete, and brick
3. they are resistant to solvents and cleaning fluids
4. they are flexible and resistant to abrasion
5. they may be used at temperatures as high as 300°F

For best resistance to chemical attack, as much as a 5-mil thickness of epoxy may be applied, in two or more coats. Good epoxy finishes are required to withstand 5 percent sulfuric acid or 20 percent sodium hydroxide for 72 hours without evidence of deterioration, and impacts of 30 in.-lb or more without cracking.

Cellulose nitrate is chiefly used in quick-drying lacquers. *Ethyl cellulose* provides highly flexible films with good acid and alkali resistance. *Cellulose acetate butyrate* has the best resistance to hydrocarbons.

While most of the synthetic resins (most notably the epoxies) have good adhesion and suitable properties for metal surfaces, metal surfaces in general pose unique problems and have special requirements such as corrosion resistance. Unlike concrete, wood, and wallboard, metals have surfaces that are nonporous. Nevertheless, paint vehicles bond well to steel. However, paint vehicles adhere somewhat less effectively to less reactive metal surfaces. Adhesion to aluminum is still more difficult, and few paints will adhere to copper. In the protection of metal surfaces, paint films cannot exclude moisture, but provide corrosion resistance by imposing an electrical resistance to the currents of galvanic corrosion. In severe environments the standard paints cannot give adequate protection to metals, and special formulations such as bituminous coatings must be used. Heavy coal-tar epoxy or other coal-tar base coatings are used to protect buried steel tanks and pipes. However, coal-tar coatings are far from beautiful and cannot therefore be used to protect the inside of a household refrigerator from condensation. Instead, porcelain enamels and vinyl plastics are used for refrigerator interiors.

Aluminum paints give excellent protection and adhesion to metals, and are used both for priming and finishing coats. Such a paint carries a dispersion of fine thin flakes of aluminum, smaller than 100 mesh size, which forms an impervious film in layers of perhaps a dozen flakes deep, bonded together with the vehicle. The arrangement is known as "leafing" (Fig. 162) because of the analogy with falling leaves. Such aluminum paints have remarkable hiding power and a reflectivity of about 75 percent.

Fig. 162 Leafing of aluminum paint.

Metal substrate

A film of aluminum paint 0.0005 in. thick will completely hide any colored surface. Asphalt-base varnishes are often used as the vehicle, and this makes the paint appear black in the can until the aluminum is stirred and dispersed.

Silicone resins are used in paints which must have great resistance to heat, moisture, oxidation, and ultraviolet radiation. They are used on ovens, boilers, and smokestacks for heat resistance, and on masonry and concrete as water repellants.

Fire-retardant paints reduce the spread of fire by foaming. Heat breaks down the paint film to produce gas which is trapped in the film, causing it to foam and insulate the surface against heat. Such paints are not decorative paints, but may be given a topcoat.

Red Lead (Pb₃O₄) or lead oxide primers are used on steel surfaces. These may be red lead in linseed oil, or red lead in a vehicle of linseed oil and a long-oil alkyd resin. Because of the large linseed oil content, small amounts of tight rust or mill scale on the steel surface do not usually harm the integrity of these primer coats. Any of the primer coats used for steels may be used for aluminum except those containing red or white lead.

Zinc chromate is used as a corrosion-inhibiting primer on light metals such as magnesium and aluminum. Heavy coats are not employed, a coating of a third of a mil thickness giving better service than one of several mils. The chromate has a light yellow-green color, with poor hiding power, though hiding power is not the purpose of zinc chromate. Xylene or toluene thinners are used. These evaporate quickly, giving a drying time of about 5 minutes for the chromate primer.

15.13   paint testing

In paint testing, what is actually tested is the paint-substrate combination. Some of the more important paint tests are outlined in the following remarks.

1. **Flash point.**   This test is discussed in the next chapter.

2. **Hiding power.**   The hiding power chart has been mentioned earlier in this chapter.

3. **Corrosion resistance.**   A 1-mil thickness of the paint is applied to a steel panel and allowed to dry for 24 hours. Pools of acids or alkalis of the desired concentration are applied, covered with watch glasses and allowed to remain in contact for at least 6 hours. The corrodants are then removed, the surface is washed under a stream of water, and the surface examined for any change of appearance. The paint is then removed by solvent and the steel panel examined for corrosion. The line of contact of the watch glass is disregarded in the examination.

4. **Flexibility and adhesion.**   There are many tests for these properties. The paint may be applied to a metal panel, the panel being bent 180° around a mandrel of specified diameter. Or a conical mandrel may be used, and the diameter at which cracking of the paint film first occurs is noted.

The impact test uses a steel ball with a 1-in. radius. This is dropped from varying heights and the inch-pounds of energy recorded. The direct impact test is made on the painted face of the panel; the reverse impact test drops the ball on the unpainted side of the panel. The latter test is a more severe one. Alternately, the Erichsen or Olsen cup test described in Sec. 9.17 may be used to test for flexibility and adhesion.

Still another method is used to test for adhesion. A steel rod $\frac{5}{16}$ in. in diameter with a rounded end is used to mar the panel in two directions at right angles to each other. The rod is held perpendicular to the face of the panel and the rounded end of the rod is drawn across the finished surface using sufficient pressure to indent the film. The paint film is examined along both indentations. A less severe test requires cutting into the paint film in a cross-hatch pattern and then applying a piece of pressure-sensitive tape to the paint film. The tape is stripped, and any removal of the paint from the cross-hatched surfaces is noted.

Special apparatus is required for the testing of the abrasion, scratch, and weathering resistance of finishes.

15.14 adhesive bonding

Adhesive bonding, like metal finishing, requires careful surface preparation, and in general the same metal cleaning methods apply. Many of the synthetic rubbers and plastics used in metal finishes are also employed as adhesives.

Adhesive bonding has certain disadvantages when compared to other joining methods such as welding or the use of fasteners. Surface preparation is one disadvantage. Another is the relatively long time required for the adhesive to cure. The curing operation also may require heat or pressure or both. Finally, most adhesives, with the exception of sodium silicate and ceramic adhesives, have service temperature limitations of about 300°F.

Against these disadvantages must be set these significant advantages:

1. Absence of stress concentrations such as occur at rivet and bolt holes.
2. Uniform stress distribution over the large bonded area (this may not be entirely true of a lap joint).
3. Dissimilar materials may be joined, such as rubber to glass, or glass to metal.
4. Adhesive joints have excellent resistance to fatigue stresses.
5. An adhesive joint can provide electrical insulation or a moisture barrier.
6. Small particles can be bonded, such as abrasive grains to paper backing.
7. Adhesives are especially advantageous in the bonding of thin foils of paper and metal.

Structural adhesives are available for the dependable bonding of virtually any material. Their reliability is attested by their considerable use in aircraft and rocket construction, for wing flaps, bulkheads, floor panels, helicopter rotor blades, and in joining aircraft skins to fuselages. As much as 800 to 1000 lb of adhesives may be used in a single aircraft. Aerospace uses for adhesives include the bonding of sandwich structures made by joining thin metal faces to lightweight cores. Such construction offers unusual strength-to-weight ratios.

A general classification of adhesives would divide the very great number of adhesives into the following five groups:

1. animal, fish, and vegetable glues
2. thermoplastic adhesives
3. thermosetting adhesives
4. elastomeric adhesives
5. ceramic adhesives (chiefly mortars and sodium silicate)

The animal and vegetable glues include hide glue, bone glue, blood glues, starch, and casein glue. Most of these adhesives are used in the paper and packaging industries. Since paper has little tear strength or moisture and heat resistance, no especially stringent requirements are imposed on paper adhesives. Most of the sodium silicate adhesives likewise find their chief applications in paper products, but are also used in the briquetting of iron ore, the flux coatings of manual welding rods, and the bonding of abrasive grinding wheels. The following list is suggestive of the multitude of uses for adhesives in paper and packaging:

1. corrugated cardboard (corn or potato starch)
2. gummed kraft paper tapes (bone glue or starch)
3. hand luggage
4. bottle labelling
5. paper laminating
6. bookbinding
7. paper milk cartons
8. sandpaper (animal glue)
9. paper tubes (starch adhesives)
10. envelopes and stamps
11. paper bags

There are two other applications of interest to cigarette smokers—the bonding of the abrasive to match-book covers, and the bonding of the seam of a cigarette paper. Both joints require water resistance and a rapid-curing joint to meet the speed of manufacturing operations peculiar to these two products. Casein glues are suitable for both applications.

Automatic packaging lines require close control of adhesive viscosity and setting time, and these more stringent demands promote the use of the synthetic adhesives over the natural adhesives, even at higher prices for the former. The plastic and rubber cements also tend to be reserved for more special applications, again because of their higher price. The synthetic adhesives, however, are used in large volume, supplying approximately 50 percent of the adhesive market.

While this author prefers to term our civilization the Steel Age, others have called it the Light Metals Age or the Plastics Era. But if we are to give names to our present technology, perhaps it might also be termed the Paper and Adhesives Age. Statistically, every person in the USA consumes annually three times his weight in paper, a surprisingly large proportion of which is bonded with adhesives.

15.15 characteristics of adhesives

Adhesives have become a science of considerable topical interest and have developed an appropriate terminology. Adhesive requirements and specifications cannot be understood without a knowledge of the following terms.

1. **Substrate.** The material on which a coating is spread. If the coating is an adhesive, the substrate may be called the *adherend*.

2. **Adhesive.** A substance which joins materials by attachment of their surfaces. A *cement* is the same thing as an adhesive.

3. **Pressure-sensitive adhesive.** An adhesive that will adhere to a surface by a briefly applied pressure alone.

4. **Set.** To convert a liquid adhesive to a hardened condition. If setting occurs by polymerization or cross-linking, the operation is often referred to as a *cure*. A catalyst may be used to accelerate the cure.

5. **Tack.** Tack is the property of an adhesive which causes a surface coated with the adhesive to form a bond on immediate contact with another surface. Tack is thus the "stickiness" of an adhesive.

Fig. 163 Stressing of an adhesive joint by shear, peel, and cleavage forces. Adhesive joints are strong only in shear.

6. Peel strength. This measures the resistance of the adhesive to stripping (Fig. 163), and is expressed in pounds per inch width. While many adhesives have shear strengths exceeding 5000 psi, the peel strength of any adhesive is limited, and adhesive joints must generally be protected against peeling.

For adhesives used in lap joints there is a best film thickness, and adhesive films thinner or thicker than this optimum will be less strong. Soldered and brazed lap joints have this characteristic also. For maximum bond strength, joint thickness ranges from 2 to 5 thousandths of an inch, varying with the adhesive. Usually the thinnest possible joint is used, provided that the joint is not starved of adhesive.

Bond strengths of lap joints are proportional to the width of the joint but are not directly proportional to the joint length or overlap. As the length of overlap increases, the unit strength decreases. The first inch of overlap will carry most of the stress.

Tack is the most important characteristic of a pressure-sensitive tape, such as "Scotchtape", electrician's friction tape, drafting tape, and masking tape. These tapes have adhesives which are permanently soft, viscous, and tacky, and can be peeled from a surface without leaving any residue.

Fig. 164   Typical joint strength of a synthetic adhesive.

Pressure-sensitive tapes do not "wet" a surface and cannot therefore be employed in heavy-duty applications or structural service. Most of the pressure-sensitive adhesives are rubber cements blended with a tackifying agent in equal amounts, such as coumarone-indene. Unmodified rubber cements have poor tack. A keying coat is used to bond the pressure-sensitive adhesive to the tape, since the two must adhere well and not strip when the tape is removed from a surface. On the side of the tape opposite to the adhesive coat a release coat is applied to allow unwinding of the tape from its roll. These details of its formulation suggest that pressure-sensitive tape is one of the more ingenious inventions of our time.

The *mastics* used in the laying of floor and wall tile, linoleum, and countertops, also require a high degree of tack. These mastics may be rubber-base, synthetic resin, epoxy, or linoleum paste with solvents. Asphalt tile and vinyl-asbestos tile may use rubber or asphalt-base mastics. The mastic is applied either by the buttering method, in which the adhesive is applied to the tile, or the floating method, in which the adhesive is applied to the surface with a trowel. The trowel is notched along one side in order to make ridges in the adhesive coating. The covering or tile is laid when the solvent has evaporated from the mastic. A typical floor tile adhesive may contain, besides reclaim or other rubber adhesive, coumarone-indene for tackifier, an antioxidant, clay, and calcium carbonate.

Of the various types of sealants and caulking compounds, the polysulfides or thiokols are probably the all-round best. Sealants are used as void fillers, usually for weather-proofing in building construction, and must be permanently flexible, chemically inert, and of course must adhere to a wide range of materials. Modern curtain-wall construction of buildings, with great expanses of panel construction, requires a versatile sealant to keep out rain and wind and to take up expansion movements at the joints in the curtain wall construction. These expansion movements call for elongation in the sealant which can be met only by elastomeric materials such as the polysulfides.

15.16 miscellaneous applications of adhesives

The various cellulose compounds make good general-purpose adhesives which set by solvent evaporation. Cellulose nitrate and cellulose acetate use organic solvents, while methyl cellulose is water-soluble. Cellulose acetate will not bond metals, rubbers, or glass satisfactorily. Cellulose nitrate is more versatile, but does not bond rubber and is not among the best metal adhesives. The boot and shoe industry relies heavily on nitrocellulose adhesives.

Other thermoplastic adhesives include polyvinyl alcohol (water-soluble), asphalts, acrylics, polyvinyl acetate, and polystyrene. None of the thermoplastic adhesives are considered satisfactory for use as structural adhesives. All have poor creep strength and low temperature limits.

Adhesive uses consume much polyvinyl acetate. This adhesive is used in milk cartons, paper bags, gummed tapes, and shipping bags, in competition with animal and vegetable adhesives. The building trades employ polyvinyl acetate for tile mastics and cements, white caulking compounds, and drywall joint cements.

Polyvinyl alcohol is one of the few water-soluble synthetic adhesives, and therefore can be used as a remoistenable adhesive like the animal and vegetable adhesives.

The most familiar use for the phenolic adhesives is the bonding of plywood veneer and particle board. Phenolics will also bond metal and glass. Chemically related adhesives include urea-formaldehyde, phenol-resorcinol, and melamine-formaldehyde. Melamine adhesives offer the best durability against general weathering, with high bond strength. Phenol-formaldehyde is used to bond abrasive grit into grinding wheels, giving sufficient wheel strength to allow peripheral speeds as high as 15,000 ft per min in cutoff wheels used for sawing metals. However, where the wheel must have more shock resistance, an elastomeric adhesive is selected.

The thermosetting adhesives, alkyds excepted, have high bond strengths and are suitable for structural adhesives. It is generally true that the thermosets are superior in bond strength and creep to thermoplastics, elastomeric, animal, or vegetable adhesives. The epoxies provide high bond strength to almost all materials, though their peel strength is limited.

Probably the elastomeric adhesives are the most interesting and versatile group of adhesives. It is estimated that 5 percent of all rubber production is consumed in adhesives. If this be true, it represents a substantial tonnage of rubber.

The elastomeric adhesives are frequently applied as solvent cements. They are especially useful for joining two materials of widely different thermal expansions. They do not bond well to metals but are suitable for joining tile, glass, wood, rubber, flooring, leather, and for bristle setting in brushes. Rubber cements are used in automobile assembly to bond weatherstrip, plastic trim, brake bands, clutch facings, and motor mounts.

All the following rubbers have adhesive applications: reclaim, natural, SBR, butyl, polyisobutylene, neoprene, acrylonitrile-butadiene, thiokol, and silicone. Natural rubber has the best resilience and tack. Thiokol (polysulfide) has the best solvent resistance. Acrylonitrile adhesives bond to metal better than the other rubbers. The silicone adhesives have high-temperature applications, and will bond to polyethylene and Teflon. Styrene-butadiene rubber has only limited usefulness as an adhesive.

PROBLEMS

1   Explain the necessity for an adhesive in bonding together two surfaces.

2   What cleaning method would be used to remove (a) rust on steel, (b) paint on steel, (c) the oxide surface of aluminum, (d) fingerprints on titanium?

3   What is meant by the term "conversion coating"?

4   What is the drying method in a nonconvertible and a convertible finish?

5   What purposes are served by anodizing aluminum?

6   What limits the maximum thickness of an anodized coating on aluminum?

7   What is meant by the term "hard anodizing"?

8   What is the purpose of the binder and of the pigment in a finish?

9   What is a hiding power chart?

10 What is a thixotropic liquid? What is the advantage of thixotropy in a paint finish?

11 Why should an aerosol spray can never be incinerated?

12 Define an aerosol, an emulsion, and a latex paint.

13 What are the outstanding properties of epoxy finishes?

14 How does a fire-retardant paint function?

15 Give some of the advantages and disadvantages of adhesive bonding as compared to the use of fasteners and welding.

16 What is the meaning of "tack"?

17 Describe the composition of a pressure-sensitive tape.

18 What properties are required in a caulking compound?

16.1   the scope of fuels

A fuel is any material which can be made to oxidize at a sufficiently rapid rate, with release of adequate heat of oxidation. The possible number of fuels then is virtually unlimited. Though most fuels have been, and continue to be, hydrocarbons, many inorganic fuels have been tried. Though no longer used, boron hydride, a ceramic material, was a solid rocket propellant, and quite literally thousands of fuels have been tested as potential rocket fuels. One of the finest of solid fuels is the set of tires on an automobile. Scrap tires are actually used as a fuel in municipal incinerators to assist in the burning of wet garbage and refuse (which are used as fuels in some cities). Other types of rubber are used as solid rocket propellants. In World War II the strategic air forces of Germany, Britain, and the United States used magnesium as a fuel in small incendiary bombs designed to ignite the cities of their adversaries. Sewer gas is burned to heat sewage treatment plants. Phosphorus serves as a fuel in matches and mortar bombs. Explosives are fuels designed to create destructive pressures as a result of their combustion. Uranium on the other hand is employed as a nonoxidizing radioactive fuel and plutonium as a radioactive explosive. These random examples should serve to indicate the scope of fuels and fuel technology.

Mankind first used fuels to keep warm and for heat in the processing of meat for food. Later explosive fuels transformed methods of warfare. Today improvements in fuels and fuel technology of rockets are the means of projecting exploratory vehicles into the empty reaches of space.

FUELS
AND
RADIOACTIVE MATERIALS

16

Neglecting the more peripheral fuels, such as explosives, radioactive and metallic fuels and rocket fuels, the two most important uses of standard fuels are space heating and steam production for power or process use. Fuels for these two purposes may be solid, liquid, or gas.

The commoner solid fuels include:

1. peat, a primitive fuel
2. cordwood
3. bagasse, waste sugar cane
4. hog fuel, which is wood chopped or "hogged" in a wood chipper or hog. Hog fuel is burned at pulp mills for process steam generation
5. sawdust, a poor fuel because of its high moisture content
6. municipal garbage and refuse
7. lignite, or brown coal
8. bituminous or soft coal
9. anthracite, or hard coal
10. petroleum coke

Most fuel coal is consumed in large steam generating plants for the production of electric power in huge amounts. Such a plant may burn a few hundred tons of coal every hour.

The usual liquid fuels are fewer in number than the solid fuels. The liquid fuels are commonly produced by oil refineries.

1. light fuel oils of low viscosity, #1 and #2 fuel oils chiefly for domestic use
2. heavy fuel oils of high viscosity, #4, #5, and #6 (#6 is also called bunker oil or bunker C), which are sold at low prices in large quantities for consumption in heating boilers and ships. These heavy fuels require special burners to atomize them
3. internal combustion engine fuels:
   (a) gasolines for spark-ignition engines equipped with spark plugs
   (b) diesel fuels for compression-ignition (diesel) engines
   (c) kerosene blends for gas turbine engines
   The rocket engine is also an internal combustion engine, but is not restricted to liquid fuels.
4. black liquor, a heavy black gunk which is a residue from wood pulp operations, requiring a special type of furnace called a recovery furnace

Finally, the commoner gaseous fuels are the following:

1. acetylene, for oxyacetylene welding and thermal cutting of metals
2. liquid hydrogen, a rocket fuel
3. blast furnace waste gas
4. coal gas from coking operations at steel mills
5. refinery waste gas from oil refining operations
6. liquid petroleum gas, LPG, chiefly propane, sometimes butane
7. natural gas, which is chiefly methane

16.2 the proximate analysis of fuels

The utilization of fuels cannot be understood except in terms of their proximate analysis. Fuels may be analyzed for their chemical elements or compounds, but such an analysis has limited usefulness to fuel technology. Instead, the proximate analysis, though relatively unscientific, provides immediate insights into the method of employing a fuel and its combustion problems. The proximate analysis simply gives the percentage breakdown of a fuel in terms of four broad components:

1. moisture
2. volatile matter
3. fixed carbon
4. ash

1. Moisture.   Moisture may be formed from hydrogen and oxygen in the fuel, but this is not counted in the moisture analysis. The moisture is the free water or absorbed water in the fuel as delivered. To determine this moisture content, a sample of the fuel is dried at a temperature slightly above 212°F. The difference in weight between the original fuel sample and the dried weight is expressed as a percent.

The moisture in the fuel is a handicap. It is a component in the freight and handling charges. Further, when the fuel is charged into the furnace, about 1000 Btu will be lost from the useful heat of combustion for every pound of moisture to be evaporated. Indeed, it is possible for a fuel to be too wet to be self-burning. Fuels with excessive moisture content, such as hog fuel, lignite, or bagasse, require special types of furnaces which contain drying grates for evaporation of moisture.

2. Volatile matter.   If the dried sample of fuel is next heated to 1700°F *in the absence of air*, the volatile hydrocarbons in the fuel will be boiled out. The difference in sample weight as a result of this operation is expressed as percent of volatile matter. In the case of liquid fuels from wells, such volatile matter is chiefly straight-chain hydrocarbons, saturated or unsaturated. In the case of coal, which also contains large amounts of volatile matter, these hydrocarbons tend more to cyclic or aromatic hydrocarbons such as benzene.

The smoke that results from fuel burning is either black or silvery gray. The clouds of condensed steam that issue from chimneys should not be confused with smoke — all fuels contain hydrogen, therefore all chimneys transport steam. Black smoke results from inefficient firing, such as a cold furnace or insufficient air, and can be produced from volatile matter or fixed carbon. Black smoke can be prevented by proper combustion practice. Most true chimney smoke, however, is silvery gray, like the exhaust from a smoky automobile that needs new piston rings. This smoke results from the burning of volatile matter, and arises from the serious practical difficulties of getting a thorough mix of air and volatiles within the furnace or engine and the complex combustion chemistry associated with these volatiles. Burning of volatile compounds at temperatures below 1400°F not only produces simple carbon dioxide and steam but also yields complex oxygenated aldehyde compounds. A typical smokeless fuel is charcoal, which is made smokeless by distillation of volatile matter from wood.

3. Fixed carbon. This is the solid carbon residue remaining after the volatile matter is boiled out of the fuel. If the moisture and volatiles are driven from the fuel sample, the remainder of the sample can be burned, leaving only ash, and the percent of fixed carbon can be determined by weight loss.

Fuels with high percentages of fixed carbon, such as anthracite coal or petroleum coke, require special furnace shapes to ignite the fixed carbon. Volatiles have ignition temperatures below 1000°F and are in consequence relatively easy to burn, but fixed carbon ignites only at temperatures exceeding 1200°F. In order to burn fixed carbon, a furnace has surfaces suitably disposed to radiate heat onto the fuel bed. At the opposite extreme, a furnace that burns volatile matter simply requires adequate volume for combustion, and may be merely a rectangular or cylindrical box. Volatile matter must be burned with *overfire air*, that is, air admitted to the furnace above the grate or hearth level. Fixed carbon is more efficiently burned using *underfire air*, or air admitted through the hearth or grates. Hence, an experienced person can examine a furnace design and make a shrewd guess about what fuel will be burned in it.

Improper combustion can produce fixed carbon in a furnace. Furnaces operated at too low a temperature will produce fixed carbon from volatile matter. This is familiar in automobile engine cylinders which are driven at low speeds in city driving. They are said to "carbon up". The author once had the pleasant task of removing about 150 lb of carbon (petroleum coke?) from an improperly fired boiler burning #6 oil fuel.

4. Ash. Ash consists chiefly of metallic oxides. The ash content of a fuel may be an advantage or a disadvantage. Ash may be used to protect the furnace grates from heat damage. But ash must be collected and removed. Some ash is collected in hoppers below the grates, but in large furnaces most ash travels toward the chimney as flyash and must be collected in flyash hoppers at the top of the furnace.

Sometimes ash imposes restraints on the operation of a furnace. In a municipal incinerator, if the furnace becomes too hot, the ash will fuse into large clinkers which are difficult to remove and which block the flow of combustion air through the grates. Other types of furnaces operate at temperatures high enough to fuse the ash so that it can flow from the furnace as a liquid.

CHARACTERISTIC PROXIMATE ANALYSES OF
SOME FUELS

Fuel	% Moisture	% Volatile Matter	% Fixed Carbon	% Ash
petroleum coke	2	16	82	0.05
charcoal	1	22	73	4
lignite	10	45	35	10
natural gas	0	100	0	0
garbage	30	40	10	20
newspaper	4.8	78.0	16.3	0.75
bond paper	6.85	76.0	13.13	4.15
corrugated cardboard	5.05	78.5	16.0	0.53

16.3 other fuel properties

Chemical analyses of fuels provide specific items of information, such as the sulfur content of the fuel. The amount of sulfur is a measure of the tendency of the combustion gases to corrode the engine or furnace passages. Gas turbine engines in particular cannot tolerate more than 0.5 percent sulfur in their fuels, since such engines use high nickel alloys which are susceptible to sulfur attack. High sulfur fuels would be equally harmful in furnaces used to heat steel products.

The fire hazard of a fuel, solvent, or other liquid is often measured by its *flash point*. The flash point is defined as the lowest temperature at which the product gives off sufficient vapor to form a flammable mixture with air. Thus if the flash point were room temperature the fuel would present a significant fire hazard.

The *specific gravity* of a liquid fuel is referred to water as 1.0; the specific gravity of a gaseous fuel is referred to air as 1.0. The specific gravity of liquid fuels is used to convert volumes to weights and in general to evaluate petroleum products, since other properties are related to specific gravity. It is more usual to use the API gravity than specific gravity for petroleum products. The API gravity is related to specific gravity by the formula

$$°\text{API} = \frac{141.5}{\text{sp gr at } 60°\text{F}} - 131.5$$

As the API gravity increases

(a) the viscosity increases
(b) the heat content per pound increases
(c) the heat content per gallon decreases
(d) the carbon content decreases
(e) the hydrogen content increases

The *heating value* of a fuel is expressed as the heat released by combustion per pound or per gallon. One of the chief products of combustion of hydrocarbon fuels is water vapor. If the combustion products are cooled back to room temperature, this water vapor condenses, releasing its latent heat. The addition of this latent heat of water vapor to the heating value gives the gross or higher heating value. If such latent heat is not included, the net heating value results. Most heating values are expressed as the gross heating value.

FUEL OIL GRADES AND APPROXIMATE PROPERTIES

Fuel Oil	Flash Point	API Gravity	Sp Gr	Btu/lb (gross)
1	100°F	35	0.85	19,590
2	100	26	0.89	19,270
4	130	25	0.90	19,230
5	150	12	0.99	18,640
6	180	10	1.0	18,540

The values in this table are only typical, and vary between geographical areas of the United States and Canada.

16.4   engine fuels

The three types of internal combustion engine, spark-ignition, diesel, and gas turbine, do not in general burn the same type of fuel. The spark-ignition or gasoline engine is used only to supply small amounts of power in mobile equipment. The fuel for this engine is a cracked gasoline containing olefins and aromatics. For ease of starting, a more volatile (i.e., lower boiling) gasoline fuel is supplied for winter operation in colder climates; this is customarily supplied by blending lighter ends such as butane into the winter gasoline. Aviation gasoline, however, has only a small olefin content, and is never blended with butane. At high altitudes any low-boiling components might boil in the fuel tanks.

Gasoline requires a sufficiently high octane number to resist detonation during combustion. Octane number is expressed as follows. Isooctane is a hydrocarbon with an octane rating of 100; it is arbitrarily assigned this octane number because it has excellent combustion characteristics. Normal heptane on the other hand is a poor fuel which will knock severely if used in an engine. Normal heptane may be considered to have an octane number of zero. A blend of 80 percent isooctane and 20 percent normal heptane is assigned an octane rating of 80, that is, an octane rating is the percent isooctane in a mixture of isooctane and normal heptane. An unknown fuel is assigned the octane rating that gives the same engine performance that the unknown fuel itself does. Octane ratings must be determined in special test engines that burn mixtures of octane and heptane and also the fuels requiring octane ratings. Branched-chain hydrocarbons and aromatics have the highest octane numbers, while straight-chain paraffins have the lowest. Typical octane numbers (note normal octane and isooctane):

butane	95	normal octane	0
pentane	62	isooctane	100
hexane	25	cyclopentane	100
heptane	0	benzene	100
		toluene	107

The octane ratings of the natural gasolines pentane, hexane, heptane, are so low that these compounds are unusable in modern gasoline engines.

Aircraft gas turbine engines may operate at altitudes where the temperature may be $-60°F$ or more. They therefore require fuels which do not solidify at these temperatures. Also, since an aircraft gas turbine is expected to operate above 20,000 ft, light fractions that may boil under vacuum conditions in the fuel tanks cannot be employed. High sulfur fuels cannot be used because of their corrosiveness. The gas turbine engine, however, is basically not a fuel-sensitive engine like the spark-ignition engine, and can be made to burn a wide range of fuels, liquid or gas. Two types of aviation turbine fuels are in general use: JP-1, an aviation kerosene, and JP-4, a wide-cut aviation gasoline. Cheaper fuels are used in stationary gas turbines.

Diesel engines rotate at low speeds and can tolerate a rather wide range of fuels, but the viscosity of the fuel must be suited to the fuel injection system. High compression diesel engines often burn fuel gases.

Knocking is possible in diesel engines as well as in gasoline engines. The cetane number of the diesel engine corresponds to the octane number of the spark-ignition engine. The two hydrocarbons which are blended to give the cetane number are cetane, rated 100, and alpha-methyl-naphthalene, rated zero. A fuel with a cetane number of 40 would have the same ignition quality as a mixture of 40 percent cetane and 60 percent AMN. Cetane numbers for good diesel fuels are not as high as the octane numbers of quality gasolines.

These special fuels have a variety of applications, from harpoon guns, infantry bazooka weapons, and jet-assisted take-off of aircraft, to large manned space vehicles. Smaller rocket engines use solid fuels, while at the present stage of rocket technology the largest rocket vehicles are confined to liquid fuels.

The most important property of a rocket fuel is its *specific impulse*. This is defined as the propulsive thrust in pounds obtainable from the burning of one pound of propellant per second. Solid fuels do not provide as high a specific impulse as liquid fuels.

A liquid propellant is pumped into a combustion chamber where it is burned; the products of combustion then leave the rear of the rocket engine by expanding to a high velocity through a nozzle. The momentum of the exhaust gases provides the reactive force that drives the rocket.

A solid propellant is cast in place in the propellant chamber. A hollow space along the axis of the chamber has the proper cross-section for the required burning rate, usually a star-shaped section so that a uniform amount of propellant is burned every second. If the propellant simply burned radially outward to the motor casing, the rate of consumption would increase with time. See Fig. 165. The exhaust gases expand through a nozzle as in the case of a liquid propellant. The disadvantage of the solid propellants is their low specific impulse compared to liquid fuels. Higher specific impulse is possible only by using unstable fuels, that is, explosives which might detonate at the wrong time.

The exhaust velocity is given by the following equation:

$$c = I_{sp}g$$

where c = exhaust velocity, fps
I_{sp} = specific impulse
g = gravitational acceleration, ft/sec^2

The increase in velocity due to consumption of the propellant is found from

$$\Delta v = c \log_e \frac{m_0}{m_f}$$

where Δv = increase in velocity, fps
m_0 = launch weight of the vehicle
m_f = final weight of the vehicle after propellant consumption.

The thrust in pounds = wI_{sp}, where w = propellant consumption in pounds per second. The thrust is increased simply by increased propellant consumption.

Fig. 165 Two cast rocket fuel sections and their thrust characteristics.

LIQUID PROPELLANTS

Oxidizer	Fuel	Combustion Temperature	Specific Impulse
lox	ethyl alcohol	5700°F	276
lox	hydrazine	5660	300
lox	hydrogen	4800	388
lox	JP-4	6100	285
fluorine	ethyl alcohol	7250	318
fluorine	hydrazine	8050	334
fluorine	hydrogen	6700	388
fluorine	JP-4	7340	306

SOLID PROPELLANTS

Fuel	Specific Impulse
$KClO_4$ + thiokol rubber	170–210
NH_4ClO_4 + thiokol rubber	170–210
NH_4ClO_4 + polyurethane	210–250

Consider the problem of obtaining 6,000,000 lb of thrust for a manned space vehicle, assuming a specific impulse of 300. This will require an enormous consumption rate:

$$\text{thrust} = wI_{sp}$$
$$6,000,000 = 300w$$
$$w = 20,000 \text{ lb/sec}$$

fuels and radioactive materials
384

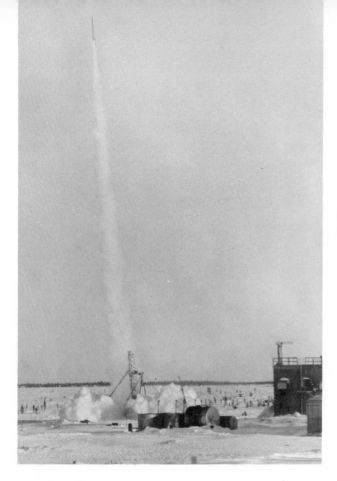

Fig. 166 Firing of a Black Brant rocket at the Fort Churchill rocket range.

16.6 explosives

Explosives are materials which decompose rapidly and violently, producing large volumes of gases. Like most materials, explosives are available in a variety of properties to meet their wide range of uses, which even includes the explosive forming and explosive welding of metals.

A widely used explosive for such purposes as removing tree stumps is the homemade recipe of a mixture of Elephant brand fertilizer and diesel fuel oil. This is detonated with a blasting cap. The fertilizer mentioned is an ammonium nitrate, which is a constituent of explosives. Cellulose nitrate, the first of the plastics, is also a constituent of explosives (and the most flammable of the plastics).

Military explosives are organic nitrates such as TNT (trinitrotoluene) formulated for the purpose of violent shock. Commercial explosives include:

1. detonating explosives, which explode almost instantaneously
2. high explosives such as nitroglycerin (dynamite), which burn over a brief period
3. low explosives such as black blasting powder, which have an action between detonation and combustion

fuels and radioactive materials
385

Fig. 167 Some of the products offered by Du Pont's explosives department to fill needs of the mining, construction, and quarrying industries. From the left, front row: NBL-413, a water-gel blasting agent for open pit work; Special Gelatin dynamite, used mainly in construction; "Trimtex," for use in controlled blasting procedures; various types of "Hi-Det" primers used in priming "Tovex" water gels; "Gelex" semigelatin dynamite, used chiefly in underground mining but also on construction projects; "Nilite" blasting agent (dyed ammonium nitrate prills and oil) widely used in underground mining, open pit mining, quarrying, and construction (when used underground it normally is loaded by pneumatic loaders); back row: a larger size of Special Gelatin; "Tovex" water gel products, largely used in open pit work; "Cor-Det" primers, a larger type of "Hi-Det" primers; and "Energex" dynamite, chiefly used on construction projects.

These several types present a graduated series in terms of the rapidity with which the gas pressure of the explosion products is developed. An explosion even slower than that of a low explosive would probably be termed combustion, such as occurs in a gasoline engine cylinder.

Five properties of explosives that are of chief interest here are: strength, velocity of detonation, fume production, density, and water resistance.

fuels and radioactive materials
386

The *strength* of an explosive is its energy content. The energy of an explosive, as with any energy, is its ability to perform work. For an explosive, this strength is measured as the percentage by weight of nitroglycerin in dynamite. A 40 percent dynamite contains 40 percent liquid nitroglycerin (or the equivalent in some other explosive) with 60 percent of other gas-producing material such as wood pulp, ground meal, sodium nitrate, etc. Commercial explosive strengths range from 15 to 90 percent.

The *velocity of detonation*, expressed in feet per second, is the speed at which the detonation travels through a column of the explosive. Greater velocity produces greater shattering effect, and when increased fragmentation is desired, higher velocity explosives are selected. Velocities may range from 1500 to 25,000 fps.

Density is expressed as "cartridge count", or the number of $1\frac{1}{8} \times$ 8 in. cartridges contained in a 50-lb case.

Fume production is important only in underground work. The bulk of the explosive gases are the usual products of combustion: carbon dioxide, water vapor, and nitrogen. But a proportion of these gases, such as carbon monoxide, are toxic. Dangerous concentrations of toxic gases must not be used underground.

The high explosives include nitroglycerin dynamites, ammonia dynamites, and gelatin dynamites. The most used are the ammonias. Blasting powder, a low explosive, is a black powder containing sodium nitrate with some sulfur. It is the slowest of the explosives, giving a heaving action that does not shatter, and is valued because it does not produce excessive fines when breaking stone or coal.

The use of explosives requires such accessories as safety fuses and blasting caps. Safety fuses are used to ignite the blasting caps, which in turn detonate the explosives. A commercial safety fuse burns at a rate of about 1 yard every 2 minutes. The explosive may also be detonated electrically by means of a blasting machine wired to electric blasting caps.

16.7   nuclear fuels

Combustion reactions utilize the energy released from rearrangement of the electron clouds of the atoms. Such energy is of the order of a few electron-volts per atom. Nuclear fuels use dissociation of the atomic nucleus for energy. The energies associated with nuclear reactions are measured in millions of electron-volts per atom. Fission of an atom of U-235 releases about 200 Mev; oxidation of a carbon atom produces only 4 ev.

Nuclear fuels are spontaneously fissionable materials. The only nuclear fuels presently in use are three: Uranium-235, Uranium-233, and plutonium.

Natural uranium is distributed in the earth's crust in amounts of about 3 grams per ton, but is mined from more concentrated ores such as pitchblende or carnotite. It is usually extracted from the ore by conversion to uranium tetrafluoride, with magnesium reduction of the fluoride, a method similar to that used with titanium, zirconium, and beryllium. Natural uranium is composed of two isotopes, 99.3 percent U-238 and 0.7 percent U-235 (neglecting 0.005 percent U-234). Plutonium does not occur in nature, but is produced by neutron irradiation of U-238. U-233 is produced by similar irradiation of thorium.

For nuclear reactor use, uranium may be enriched in U-235, or used as oxide or carbide. In the United States and Russia, uranium enriched with U-235 is frequently selected. A reactor using such enriched fuel is of very compact design; an enriched fuel therefore must be used in atomic submarines or ships. Enriched fuels, however, are expensive. In Canada, natural uranium is employed. Since only the small U-235 content of the natural uranium can undergo fission, Canadian reactors have the problem of careful design for effective use of the small amount of U-235. On the other hand natural uranium is a very cheap fuel.

The reactor fuel is formed into pellets or some other shape and loaded into fuel rods of zirconium or aluminum, such as those shown in Fig. 113 on page 258. These canning materials protect the nuclear fuel from corrosive attack, for the nuclear metals are highly reactive.

Uranium has a half life of 4.5 billion years. It has three solid phases:

α phase, orthorhombic, up to 660°C (1220°F)
β phase, tetragonal, 660–770°C (1220–1420°F)
γ phase, bcc, 770–1132°C (1420–2065°F)

Its melting point is 1132°C. The alpha phase is soft and plastic, so that many forming operations such as rolling are performed in this phase. The tetragonal beta phase is brittle, while the gamma phase is soft. Extrusion is performed in the gamma range.

Uranium is quite reactive and attacks crucibles and forming dies. It work-hardens readily, especially at temperatures below 750°F. It develops large dimensional changes from thermal cycling, and being strongly anisotropic, expansion effects are not completely reversible.

Uranium forms three principal oxides: UO_2, UO_3, U_3O_8. There are also other oxides. Because of the reactivity of the metal, the oxide is often employed as a nuclear fuel. The most stable oxide, UO_2, is preferred.

Hardness and strength of uranium are increased by radiation. Radiation also produces a decrease in thermal conductivity and dimensional increase along certain crystal axes, though such growth can be controlled by suitable heat treatment. The dioxide, however, is dimensionally stable under irradiation.

Since there are no ores of plutonium, this metal must be manufactured by irradiation in a nuclear reactor. Plutonium exists in six solid phases, the transformation temperatures between phases depending somewhat on heating and cooling rates:

α phase, monoclinic, up to 122°C (252°F)
β phase, monoclinic, 122–205°C (252–400°F)
γ phase, orthorhombic, 205–318°C (400–606°F)
δ phase, fcc, 318–450°C (606–840°F)
δ' phase, tetragonal, 450–480°C (840–896°F)
ϵ phase, bcc, to melting point

The coefficients of thermal expansion of some of these phases are remarkable. The alpha phase has the highest expansion coefficient of any metal, while the delta and delta prime phases have a negative expansion coefficient (as has the metal polonium). The electrical resistance of the phases is also remarkably high for a metal, and this resistance decreases with temperature as occurs with semiconductors, but not with other metals.

Thorium is a rather soft metal, fcc up to 1400°C (2550°F) and bcc above this temperature.

The dimensional changes and loss of thermal conductivity due to irradiation of solid nuclear fuels present serious problems in their utilization. Other difficulties arise from the nuclear reaction itself. In the fission of an atom, two fission-product atoms are produced, both daughter atoms being foreign atoms. Thus neutron irradiation of U-235 may result in the transformations shown in Fig. 168. The generation of new atoms in these nuclear reactions results in a volume increase. About 10 percent of the product atoms are xenon and krypton, which can collect to form small gas pockets.

Fig. 168 Typical transformation due to neutron irradiation of U-235.

$$_0n^1 + {}_{92}U^{235} \longrightarrow {}_{92}U^{236} \Big\langle \begin{array}{l} {}_{40}Zr^{98} \longrightarrow {}_{41}Cb^{98} \longrightarrow {}_{42}Mo^{98} \\ {}_{52}Te^{136} \longrightarrow {}_{53}I^{136} \longrightarrow {}_{54}Xe^{136} + 2\,_0n^1 \end{array}$$

Plutonium has a high neutron absorption cross-section for slow neutrons, so that unless the plutonium fuel elements have a very thin section, the outermost plutonium will absorb the neutrons and the core material would not participate in the nuclear reaction.

Neutron irradiation of nonfissile materials knocks atoms out of the space lattice, resulting in vacancies. Most metals are hardened, strengthened, and embrittled by irradiation with neutrons. Body-centered cubic metals develop an increase in transition temperature in Charpy tests after heavy irradiation. Polyethylene develops a degree of cross-linking and hardening under heavy doses of irradiation.

fuels and radioactive materials

16.8 radioactive isotopes

The availability and use of radioisotopes since 1950 has brought remark-able benefits to science, industry, medicine, and agriculture. The utility of radioisotopes is constantly being expanded, and these materials must be considered standard factors in industrial and scientific activity.

SOME INDUSTRIAL RADIOISOTOPES

Isotope	Radiation, Mev	Half Life
Radium (no longer used)	12 rays, 0.24–2.20	1620 years
Cobalt-60	1.33 and 1.17	5.3 years
Iridium-192	0.61, 0.58, 0.468, 0.316, 0.308	74 days
Thulium-170	0.084	124 days
Xenon-113	0.081	5.3 days
Ytterbium-169	0.052	32 days

The use of radioisotopes began with the natural one, radium. This had limited use for the gamma ray inspection of welds and castings, and as a somewhat dubious treatment for terminal cancer in the medical field. It was also used, with great carelessness, for luminous watch dials. The invention of the nuclear reactor, with its unlimited supply of neutrons, opened up the possibility of producing artificial isotopes uniquely suited to specific requirements.

There is no interest in a general-purpose radioisotope. For any partic-ular purpose, two properties are of especial importance to the user of iso-topes: (1) the energy or wavelength of the radiation, and (2) the half-life. For flaw detection in a thick steel casting, high-energy radiation such as that provided by Co-60 is desirable; for similar work on the light metals, such radiation is too powerful to be sufficiently absorbed by the metal, and an isotope with less potent radiation is used, such as Ir-192. In the matter of half-life, there is again some divergence in requirements. An isotope used for gauging the thickness of paper or metal sheet as it comes off the rolls must have a long half life, so that its emission strength will be sub-stantially constant with time, but for the leak testing of a pipeline a short half-life is better because safety precautions need not be enforced for an inconveniently long period.

Thulium-170 and Ytterbium-169, whose constants are given in the table above, are used for radiographing thin sections of light materials such as are processed in the aerospace industries. Note that Ytterbium-169 has characteristic radiation approximately the same in wavelength as a 50 kv X-ray tube, which is the smallest standard voltage available in industrial X-ray tubes. Xenon-113 is used for leak testing. The method of leak testing is to inject a few millicuries of Xe-113 into the pressure vessel to be tested, and to search the exterior of the vessel with a radiation-monitoring instrument such as a Geiger-Müller counter.

Hydrogen has three isotopes: H-1, H-2 or deuterium, and H-3 or tritium. Deuterium is used as a neutron moderator, but is not radioactive. Tritium is radioactive. Its most familiar use is in luminous watch dials, where it is used to activate a phosphor. It is not an especially dangerous isotope, since most of the emission is beta radiation which is rapidly absorbed by air or by the back metal panel of the watch casing. Radium too is occasionally used for such watches, however, and is more dangerous than tritium because it emits penetrating gamma radiation of sufficiently high energy to penetrate the metal of the watch. Although luminous watches must not be considered especially dangerous, if several brands of such watches are monitored with a radiation detector, a surprising variation in radiation will be noted between brands. The European Nuclear Energy Agency has proposed the following maximum quantities of radioisotopes for watches. They are an indication of the relative hazards of these materials.

radium	0.15 microcuries
tritium	7.5 millicuries
prometheum	150 microcuries

The Radiation Protection Division of the Canadian Federal Department of National Health and Welfare found in a recent survey that perhaps 5 percent of watches have amounts of radium exceeding these values. Watches of Swiss manufacture will in the future conform to the limits given here.

A great many isotope installations are used for measurement and control in industrial processes, such as the gauging and automatic control of sheet thicknesses. For this purpose a small isotope source is positioned on one side of the sheet, with a radiation detector such as a cadmium sulfide cell on the opposite side. The thickness of the sheet can be monitored by measuring the relative absorption of gamma rays by the sheet. Alternately the detector may be mounted on the same side of the sheet as the source, in which position it will measure the backscattered secondary radiation, which is almost linear with sheet thickness.

16.9 radiation hazard

Much ignorance and misunderstanding surround the matter of radiation hazard. Most of the more melodramatic aspects of radiation hazard, such as malformed births and sterility, are sheer fiction. Indeed, an intelligent person, after a comprehensive survey of the facts of radiation hazard, might well conclude that there is little danger from radiation short of a lethal dose. This would not be quite true, however. Facing a future of increased radiation for the human race, the medical profession realizes the consequences of wrong decisions, and is wisely reluctant to make definitive statements in the matter of radiation hazard. Radiation hazard may well be much less than we once suspected, but we are not yet certain of this, and a quarter of a century is an insufficient experimental period. Certainly radiation can be dangerous if the exposure dose is high enough, and there is always the possibility of accident due to inadvertence, unawareness, and carelessness, and a history of radiation disease due to such errors in the past.

The curie, the unit of radioactivity, was defined early in this book. The number of curies is of course halved in every half life. The curie, however, does not measure the amount of radiation received. This is measured by the *roentgen*, abbreviated r. To understand the roentgen, consider Fig. 169.

Figure 169 is a sketch of a simple apparatus which may be used to demonstrate the effects of radiation. A dry cell is connected through a current meter to a sheet metal cylinder. A concentric wire within the cylinder is connected to the positive terminal of the dry cell. Since the circuit is definitely an open circuit, no current will flow.

Suppose however that the air between cylinder and wire is exposed to gamma radiation. A weak current will be indicated on the meter.

This apparatus illustrates perhaps the most basic characteristic of radiation: *radiation ionizes atoms*, whether the atoms are in air or the human body or elsewhere. Radiation passing through the insulating air of this little apparatus frees electrons from their energy levels within the atom. These ionized electrons and the positive air ions are attracted to the wire and the cylinder respectively, and thus a current is produced. This apparatus can be considered a crude radiation meter, for increased radiation dosage of the air produces a larger current through the meter. Ionization of the air can be produced by any type of radiation of sufficient energy to remove electrons: alpha, beta, gamma, neutrons, protons, or cosmic ray products.

Current meter

Fig. 169 A simple radiation meter.

Dry cell

fuels and radioactive materials
392

The amount of radiation received is measured in roentgens. If 2080 million ion pairs, that is, electron plus positive ion, are produced in a cubic centimeter of air measured at 0°C and 14.696 psi as a result of radiation, then the radiation dose is 1 roentgen. Ionization requires the expenditure of energy, and 1 roentgen represents 87 ergs in air. This is a minute amount of energy: 1 joule $= 10^7$ ergs, and 1 joule per second $= 1$ watt.

From the point of view of health hazard we are more concerned with damage caused by a radiation dose of 1 roentgen to the human body than to air. The human body is composed of somewhat denser material than air and hence has a higher absorption for radiation than does air. Exposure of the body to 1 roentgen results in an absorbed dose of 95 ergs per gram of soft tissue. More damage therefore is done to the human body than to air.

Individuals vary in their resistance to specific diseases and environmental conditions, and this is true for radiation. A lethal dose of radiation would be several hundred roentgens if the whole body were exposed to this dose for a short period such as 1 hour. An exposure to 1 roentgen for 1 hour presumably would produce no medically discernible effect. Some typical exposures are these:

X-ray chest plate	0.02–0.5 r
luminous watch dial	perhaps 40 mr/year
atmospheric fallout	perhaps 3 mr/year
uranium in the ground	perhaps 40 mr/year
cosmic rays	perhaps 20 mr/year

where 1 mr = 1 milliroentgen. Regulations allow radiation workers an exposure of approximately 1 roentgen total per quarter year from X-ray and gamma ray apparatus in addition to the background radiation received by the whole population.

PROBLEMS

1 What is the difference between a fuel and an explosive?

2 What are the differences between the liquid fuels employed in gasoline, diesel, and gas turbine engines?

3 Discuss the uses of the proximate analysis of a solid fuel.

4 Estimate the proximate analysis of cigarette tobacco.

5 Gas turbine engines are constructed of high-nickel superalloys. Fuel specifications for such engines generally limit sulfur content in the fuel to 0.5 percent. Why?

6   Why is butane blended into winter gasoline in more northern climates?

7   Why can an aviation gasoline not be blended with butane?

8   Why are straight-chain natural gasolines not burned in automobiles?

9   How is the strength of an explosive measured?

10   What problems are circumvented by using uranium in the form of its oxide?

11   What are the two most significant properties of an industrial isotope?

12   Define the roentgen.

THE PROCESSING
OF
MATERIALS

Part **V**

Some of the simpler tests used to assess materials properties have been discussed in previous chapters of this book, although the treatment has in all cases been cursory. A sufficiently comprehensive treatment of test methods is provided in the series of standards of the American Society for Testing and Materials. The latest edition of the complete set of these testing standards occupies the shelf space of a good multivolume encyclopedia, and it is not for book writers to attempt to gild a lily of this caliber. It remains for this chapter to discuss certain testing, analytical, and control methods that are not strictly relevant to other chapters but which are developed from fundamental materials properties. Consideration of these methods serves also to show the power and usefulness of fundamental materials concepts in the field of automatic control. The chapter concludes with a brief discussion of nondestructive testing methods. Nondestructive testing is yet another area of materials technology making rapid progress and often exerting a powerful influence on methods of manufacturing.

17.1 the thermal conductivity gas analyzer

This instrument serves as an example of the application of a fundamental materials property, thermal conductivity, to perform a difficult process control function.

ANALYSIS AND TESTING

17

Suppose it is necessary to sense continuously, either for purposes of record or process control, the amount of nitrogen or hydrogen or both in a mixture of the two gases. Such information might be needed in the manufacture of ammonia. However, the method may be applied to any gas mixture.

The thermal conductivity analyzer actually senses the thermal conductivity of the two gases. The thermal conductivity of nitrogen is 0.167 Btu/sq ft-°F-in.-hr, that of hydrogen 1.06 Btu. Hydrogen will conduct six times as much heat as nitrogen under standard conditions of temperature and pressure, 20°C and 14.7 psia.

Suppose a mixture of nitrogen and hydrogen at a constant temperature and pressure to be passed through a conduit, the proportions of the two gases varying with time. To determine the relative amounts of the two gases, a bridge circuit (Fig. 170) is set up and current passed through the resistance bridge to heat the four resistances. One of the resistance filaments is installed in the gas conduit. At a certain known proportion of the two gases, the bridge circuit is balanced. Now suppose the proportion of hydrogen is increased. Hydrogen has a higher thermal conductivity and therefore more heat will be conducted away from the filament R_p in the conduit. The filament temperature will decrease and so will its resistance.

Fig. 170 Thermal conductivity gas analyzer bridge circuit.

The bridge must then be rebalanced. If a relationship is determined between the resistance of R_p and the proportion of hydrogen in the mixture, the proportions of the mixture can be continuously monitored. In an actual installation, balancing of the bridge and recording of the mixture proportion will be done automatically using a balancing motor. By the addition of amplifiers and feedback control to the instrumentation, the sensing bridge may be used to hold the gas mixture automatically to a fixed proportion.

The thermal conductivity gas analyzer is typical of virtually all control instruments, in that it has a simple operating principle (a resistance bridge) and is based on a simple scientific concept (thermal conductivity). The important place held by materials science in automation engineering is even better understood by a discussion of flame-sensing devices, the safety devices which protect every home and building in the country.

17.2 flame-sensing devices

Boilers rarely explode, but furnaces occasionally do. The cause of a furnace explosion is usually a human or instrument error that allows unburned oil, gas, or coal, to accumulate in the furnace. A furnace full of raw fuel is a bomb ready to explode. If the operator, or the automatic control system, then attempts to relight the furnace, it explodes. Such dangerous conditions are prevented by maintaining a constant flame at the burner to consume the fuel as fast as it is delivered to the furnace, or if the flame fails, by detecting the absence of a flame promptly and using the flame-sensing device to shut down the fuel supply.

Flame failure in small furnaces and boilers may be detected by a stack switch installed in the chimney ducting. The stack switch has a helical expansion element. After ignition occurs and the flame is established, the temperature of the flue gases rises. The expansion element expands, tilting a mercury switch. Failure of the flame will cause the helix to contract, opening the mercury switch and its associated circuitry and shutting off the fuel.

Such an instrument has a slow response. On a house furnace burning only 1000 Btu per min, this slow response can be tolerated since the energy quantities being controlled are small. On a larger heating boiler, burning 100,000 Btu per min (not a large boiler, by the way), tremendous quantities of energy are being handled and the "bomb" effect has more sobering possibilities. If the flame fails, the fuel must be shut off in about a second.

Now an obvious method of sensing a flame is to use a photocell, connecting the photocell to an amplifier which can close a solenoid valve in the fuel pipe. But what if the photocell cannot tell the difference between a flame and hot refractory? If the flame fails, the photocell will faithfully "read" the radiation from the brickwork, reporting it as flame.

Four types of flame-proving devices are in use:

1. the flame rod
2. the lead sulfide cell
3. the photocell
4. ultraviolet detectors

analysis and testing
399

All four sensors make ingenious use of the peculiar materials properties of flames, and the life of every person in this country depends on the effectiveness of flame-sensing devices.

1. The flame rod. A flame can conduct electric current because at flame temperatures there is a small degree of ionization of the flame gases. The limited ionization results in a high electrical resistance in the flame, about 2 to 80 megohms for the total conducting flame path. A flame rod can be inserted into the flame to conduct current to it. Because of the high flame resistance, the current will be in the microamp range, and an amplifier will be needed to operate the valve in the fuel line. If the flame is extinguished, an open circuit is established and the fuel line will be closed by a spring in the fuel line valve.

A flame has a rectifying effect on current. Because of this rectification, the flame rod must be at the positive end of the flame circuit.

2. The lead sulfide cell. The lead sulfide cell is a photosensitive semiconductor cell. Radiation incident on this cell will reduce its resistance, producing increased current through its associated circuitry. Its maximum sensitivity is in the infrared and visible red regions, indicating that it will respond to hot refractory as well as the flame. Refractory radiation has a constant intensity. On the other hand, the radiation intensity of a flame fluctuates at frequencies in the range of 12 cycles per second. To restrict the control circuit to flame sensing, an electric filter circuit is used to filter out frequencies below 10 cps. Thus sensitivity to hot refractory is removed from the control circuitry.

3. The photocell. The flame photocell is most sensitive to the blue portion of the flame radiation. Blue predominates in the radiation spectrum of an oil flame, so that photocells are chiefly used with oil fuel. The photocell, then, does not "read" the infrared radiation from hot brickwork.

4. The ultraviolet detector. The ultraviolet detector is more familiarly described as "purple people-eaters" in the industry. Since this cell reads only ultraviolet radiation in the flame, there is no problem from infrared interference. The ultraviolet radiation passes into the cell through a quartz window.

17.3 X-ray analysis

The mixture of elements that constitutes a stainless steel, a cold-working or hot-working tool steel, or a high nickel superalloy, is a complex one involving perhaps a dozen metals. A method must be available for analyzing the constituents of such complex alloys and their percentages, from the 0.002 percent of nitrogen to the 90 percent of the dominant metal. Any such method must also be convenient, fast, and economical, for *every* heat of such alloys must be analyzed.

Similar analytical requirements arise in almost every industry. An oil refinery may need to know the amounts of sulfur, sodium, nitrogen, and vanadium in crude oils. The refractory industry must be able to determine the amounts of trace oxides in refractories, including those of iron, titanium, sodium, and potassium. Criminal investigation laboratories must be able to analyze minute items of evidence such as hair, clay, paint, or dirt, such items perhaps being recovered from the clothing of a victim or suspect.

There is a multitude of analytical methods for such needs. Few of them employ the often inconvenient wet methods of test-tube analysis. Perhaps none can match X-ray analysis in its convenience, versatility, and speed. There are almost a dozen X-ray analytical methods, using X-ray instruments costing over $10,000. These X-ray analytical methods irradiate a small specimen of the unknown material with long-wave X-radiation. The wavelength and intensity of secondary X-radiation excited in the sample are automatically measured, and the percentages of chemical elements in the sample are plotted mechanically by a pen on a chart. Sample analysis by X-ray methods may take less than 5 minutes.

The sample to be analyzed can be made the anode for a beam of electrons. This anode is given a high voltage with respect to the electron gun (i.e., cathode) that produces the electrons. Suppose that the accelerating voltage applied to the electrons is 100 kv. Then electrons strike the sample anode with an energy of 100,000 ev. This is a rather sizeable energy to apply to an electron, though not so high as that used in industrial X-ray tubes. The electron under the influence of such an accelerating voltage will strike the target sample with a velocity of the order of half the speed of light. Suppose that such an electron strikes an atom in the target and that the atom absorbs the whole 100 Kev. This energy will move an electron in the target atom from an inner energy level to a remote level. Then if the same electron falls back to the inner energy level from which it was removed, it will release a 100 Kev fluorescent (photoelectric) photon with a wavelength of 0.12 A. This will be the minimum possible wavelength emitted from the sample under such an accelerating voltage.

Actually only a few X-ray photons of this maximum energy will be emitted. The energy of the bombarding electron is usually absorbed by several atoms in several impacts as the electron gradually decelerates. The electron jumps will be smaller, and the radiation wavelengths will be longer than 0.12 A. Also, if an electron in the target is removed from the K level to the O level, for example, it will not usually return again to the K level, especially if it is ionized. An electron from the L level may move into the empty K position, and an M or N electron may then fill the vacancy in the L level, and so on. As a result, there will be a continuous spectrum of X-rays, ultraviolet, visible, and infrared, lower in energy than the 100 Kev and 0.12 A maximum. Typical wavelength distribution is shown in Fig. 171.

In addition to this continuous spectrum of radiation, the target sample will produce characteristic radiation, so-called because such radiation is specific to the target material. If the sample is pure tungsten, the two narrow emission lines of characteristic radiation shown in Fig. 171 are produced. For tungsten these characteristic wavelengths are 0.187 and 0.216 A and are always present at any accelerating voltage above 70 kv. These characteristic wavelengths are the identifying and unique "finger prints" for this element. The minimum voltage at which these lines will appear is termed the excitation potential. Similar lines are found in the radiation spectrum for any target material. For molybdenum they are 0.71 and 0.63 A. The wavelength in Angstroms of the characteristic radiation for any element is given roughly by

$$\frac{1200}{(Z - 1)^2} \quad \text{where } Z = \text{atomic number of the element}$$

The characteristic radiation is simply the radiation corresponding to an electron jump from the L, M, or N levels to the K level. The energies corresponding to these levels in the tungsten atom are

K level	69.3 Kev
L level	12.1 Kev
M level	2.8 Kev
N level	0.6 Kev

The electron jumps and their corresponding photon energies are:

L to K	$69.3 - 12.1 = 57.2$ Kev
M to K	$69.3 - 2.8 = 66.5$ Kev
N to K	$69.3 - 0.6 = 68.7$ Kev

The corresponding wavelengths are (Angstrom wavelength $= 12,340/\text{ev}$):

L to K $\quad \dfrac{12,340}{57,200} = 0.216$ A $\quad$ called the Kα line

M to K $\quad \dfrac{12,340}{66,500} = 0.187$ A $\quad$ called the Kβ line

N to K $\quad \dfrac{12,340}{68,700} = 0.18$ A $\quad$ called the Kγ line

These wavelengths agree with the wavelengths of the characteristic radiation shown in Fig. 171.

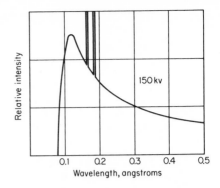

Fig. 171   Radiation spectrum from a tungsten target, showing the two characteristic lines for tungsten.

The excitation voltage necessary to produce this characteristic radiation is simply the electron-volt energy necessary to displace an electron from the K shell, creating a vacancy for an electron jump to that shell.

Now if the X-ray wavelengths of the characteristic radiation can be determined by some means, the elements in the sample are immediately identified. The relative amounts of elements in the sample can be determined by the intensities of the characteristic lines. Such intensities can be determined by a radiation meter such as a Geiger-Muller counter. Determination of wavelengths is no great problem, at least in principle. The means for doing so is suggested in Sec. 2.17, using the Bragg equation

$$L = 2d \sin \theta$$

The distance d must be a known interatomic distance in some perfect crystal. The X-ray instrument has the arrangement shown in Fig. 172. A

Fig. 172   X-ray fluorescence apparatus.

Fig. 173 X-ray diffraction and spectrograph apparatus. X-ray diffractometer on the left, vacuum spectrograph on the right, and strip chart recorder in the middle. (Apparatus supplied by Philips Electronics, Inc.)

beam of X rays causes elements in the specimen to fluoresce with characteristic radiation. X-radiation from the specimen is collimated by the fine tubes of the collimator, then diffracted off the crystal analyzer. The analyzer and the radiation detector are rotated to read all the characteristic radiation diffracted at various angles from the crystal analyzer. The entire apparatus is shown in Fig. 173; a chart record of a metallurgical analysis appears in Fig. 174.

If the purpose of the X-ray instrument is the identification of a material from its crystal structure, or the determination of crystal structure or interatomic distance, then the Bragg equation is again used but the interatomic distance d is the unknown quantity. A monochromatic beam of X rays of known wavelength must be used. An instrument for this purpose is called an X-ray diffraction unit or *diffractometer*. Since this instrument can measure interatomic distances, it may be used to determine elastic strains in metals, including residual stresses from welding and machining, by measuring these strains on an interatomic scale. It is not possible to measure plastic strains by this method.

The X-ray spectrograph and the X-ray diffractometer do not exhaust the possibilities of X-ray analysis. An X-ray *absorption* unit can be used to identify materials by means of the different absorption characteristics of materials. In such an instrument the X rays from an X-ray tube are split, part being passed through the specimen. The part passed through the specimen is compared in intensity with the part of the beam that is not absorbed. Still another X-ray analysis method is the *electron probe microanalyzer.* Here a very fine beam of electrons is focussed on a square micron of the target specimen, causing it to fluoresce. The X rays thus produced can be analyzed by the usual method of analyzing the crystal and detector of Fig. 172. This instrument is invaluable in the study of inclusions in metals, thin films, corrosion products, diffusion in metals, etc.

Fig. 174 Part of a chart recording of a spectrographic analysis using an X-ray tube with a molybdenum target. (Philips Electronics, Inc.)

While these methods do not exhaust the list of X-ray analytical methods, they perhaps suggest the power and importance of X-ray methods to industry in routine analysis and control and in materials research. The use of X-ray radiography for the detection of material defects requires a different type of X-ray tube, and will be discussed later in this chapter.

The electron microscope also uses a beam of electrons, but does not use the resulting X-radiation for analysis. The optical microscope reaches its limit of performance at about 2000 powers, because then the wavelength of light is of the same order of magnitude as the detail size that can be resolved. The use of ultraviolet light with its somewhat shorter wavelength extends the magnification only to a limited degree. By using electrons in place of visible photons, with an associated wavelength about 50,000 times smaller than that of visible light, the useful magnification range is extended beyond $100,000\times$. Like the beam of light, the beam of electrons must be focussed, but by the use of magnetic coils.

17.4   the electric resistance
strain gauge

The electric resistance strain gauge is a simple electrical strain-measuring device which can be adapted to measure strain, stress, load, torque, pressure, vibration, acceleration, modulus of elasticity, yield stress, and other physical variables. It is even used as a sensor in automatic control systems. Its use has become so widespread that it has developed a technology all its own.

This little gauge, Fig. 175, is a grid of fine wire, about 0.001 in. in diameter, on a suitable paper backing, that is cemented to the specimen to be tested. The specimen may be anything from an aircraft wing to an accelerometer. If the specimen strains, then the strain gauge must strain equally. Suppose the strain is a tensile strain. Then the resistance grid must elongate and the wire must reduce in diameter. The resistance of the strain gauge then increases. The increase in resistance, or the change in voltage across the strain gauge, varies linearly with strain. The relationship between resistance change and length change (strain) of the resistance grid is expressed as the *gauge factor* of the gauge; this gauge factor is supplied by the manufacturer.

$$\text{Gauge factor} = \frac{\Delta R/R}{\Delta L/L}$$

where L = gauge length, inches
R = gauge resistance, ohms.

Fig. 175 An electric resistance strain gauge, exaggerated in size.

Paper backing

Grid

Leads

The strain gauge can be used to measure strains to the millionth of an inch, to an accuracy of 1 percent or better. However such sensitivity of resistance measurement will read out small changes in ambient temperature as strains. Temperature change therefore must be automatically compensated for. This is done by including a compensating gauge in the electric circuitry. The compensating gauge is not strained, but is included in a resistance bridge circuit to buck the active gauge and hence cancel out temperature effects.

A typical resistance gauge has a nominal resistance of 120 ohms and a gauge factor of about 2.0. These values may vary. The gauge wire is

Fig. 176 Strain gauge testing of a welded warehouse rack. Electric resistance strain gauges are cemented to the frame and wired to the strain indicator shown at the bottom of the rack.

analysis and testing
407

selected from one of the high nickel resistance wire alloys. The gauge is cemented to the work and is aligned carefully in the direction of the specimen strain, supposing the strain to be unidirectional and its direction known. Wire leads are soldered to the gauge terminals. The gauge is then checked for proper resistance and for resistance to ground with a multimeter. If the resistance to ground is less than about 50 megohms the gauge is shorted and cannot be used. The gauge and an identical compensating gauge are then wired to the proper terminals of a suitable strain indicator which reads out strains directly (Fig. 176).

17.5   material defects

Today's routine quality standards were impossible in the materials of 25 years ago. Tomorrow's quality standards will be even higher. Defect inspection thus assumes ever greater importance, and instrumentation for defect disclosure becomes more sophisticated. Defect inspection in many industries calls for 100 percent inspection of all items produced, instead of sampling techniques. Complete inspection of tubing coming off a tube mill at a rate of 250 ft per min obviously calls for rather remarkable inspection devices.

One of the major problems in such inspection procedures as ultrasonic flaw detection, eddy current testing, or radiography, is the interpretation of the defect. This is usually more difficult than merely finding the defect. The nature of the defect must be known in order to determine its seriousness. There is the further possibility that defect-testing equipment may indicate defects where none exist. For example, false marks may be introduced on an X-ray film due to faulty handling in the course of developing the film.

Defects may arise from three general sources:

1. **Material defects,** put into the original raw material during primary processing. An example of a material defect would be an aluminum oxide inclusion in a steel plate resulting from the killing of the steel during pouring operations. A refractory inclusion in the plate may be washed out of the brickwork of the melting furnace. A casting may include a blowhole or a sand inclusion as a result of poor pouring practice.

2. **Processing defects,** which arise from fabrication of the finished part. A slag inclusion in a butt weld is such a defect. So is a grinding crack.

3. **Service defects,** which arise from the use of the material in service, such as fatigue cracks.

A type of defect that arises as a result of many manufacturing operations is a residual stress. A residual stress may be defined as an internal stress condition produced as a result of a manufacturing process on the material. Any of the following processes normally produces parts with such "locked-in" stresses: welding, adhesive-bonding, machining, casting, heat-treating, cold-forming, and rolling. Residual stresses give a permanent stress condition even when external loads are removed from the part and thus reduce the load capacity of the part. They also promote cracking tendencies and brittle fracture. Such stresses are elastic stresses only, and are more serious for materials with high E-values.

Residual stresses can be reduced or relieved by stress-relieving heat treatments. These are performed at temperatures in the range of 1100–1300°F in the case of steels, or just below the transformation temperature. At this temperature level the E-value of the steel and its yield stress are greatly reduced, and the material can yield plastically to remove some of its residual stress.

There is no lack of examples of residual stress conditions. Consider the case of a tool steel die. The die is hardened by quenching. The exterior of the die cools fastest and is held in tension by the hotter interior of the die. Worse still, the exterior transforms to martensite before the interior, and this transformation is accompanied by an increase in volume. If the die is hardened without being tempered, it cracks as a result of residual tension stress at the surface. The usual tempering operation actually serves as a stress-relief treatment.

Residual stress conditions accompany most welding operations. The distortion that follows welding is well known and serves as an indicator of residual stress. To prevent this distortion, the workpiece may be clamped in a restraining fixture; after welding and removal from the fixture, there may be high residual stresses in the part.

Suppose two sheets of aluminum are bonded with an epoxy cement and cured at 250°F. They are then cooled back to room temperature. The epoxy has a higher coefficient of expansion than the aluminum sheet, and shrinks more on cooling. The cement therefore imposes a compression stress on the aluminum sheets, and the latter produce tension stresses in the epoxy joint.

Cold-rolling of metal sheet deforms the surface layers of the sheet, with little deformation of the interior of the sheet. Such rolling leaves a stress condition in the sheet, compression at the surface, and tension in the interior. A cold-rolled sheet therefore is more prone to warping than a hot-rolled sheet.

Residual stresses can be measured with X-ray diffraction methods by noting the change in space lattice dimensions as a result of such stresses.

These stresses may also be investigated by strain gauge techniques. Strain gauges may be cemented to the exterior of a bar or tube to read stresses in the radial and tangential directions. The stresses are read as successively larger holes are bored in the specimen.

17.7 nondestructive testing

A tension test or a Charpy impact test is a destructive test. Such tests are performed on samples, under the assumption that the sample fairly represents the material in the actual fabrication. Only rarely are whole fabrications subjected to destructive tests because of the expense involved. Destructive tests on samples, however, may *not* be fairly representative of the actual fabrication. A sample casting may have no sand inclusions or blowholes, but this slender evidence offers no guarantee that the whole series of castings which it represents contains no such defects.

Methods of testing that can be applied to the completed part are therefore more reliable. Such test methods must not require destruction of the part, that is, they must be nondestructive. Thus radiography of a whole series of castings will reveal conclusively whether or not there are any blowholes: the tests are performed on the actual parts and not on "representative" samples.

The years since World War II have seen remarkable growth in nondestructive testing methods. The growing use of nondestructive testing, or NDT as it is called, has led to increased use of the principle of 100 percent inspection, that is, inspection of all production. It is no longer unusual for 100 percent NDT to be cheaper than spot inspection or sampling.

Three nondestructive testing methods lead in importance:

eddy current testing — usually an automatic method
ultrasonic testing — sometimes used as a production-line method
radiography — rarely used as a production-line method

Other NDT methods in common use include magnetic particle testing, electric resistance measurement, and dye penetrant methods. Other methods are available but have not yet become standard practice.

17.8 dye penetrant inspection

This is one of the simplest NDT methods and does not require extensive skill or experience. It is used for the detection of flaws, cracks, holes, or

Fig. 177 Set of spray cans for dye penetrant flaw detection.

leaks that extend to the surface of the work, and is especially useful for locating grinding cracks, weld cracks, fatigue cracks, and pinholes.

In this method the surface of the work is first cleaned, since surface soil may absorb the penetrant material. The penetrant, a liquid containing a red dye, is then applied by brush, dip, or spray. The penetrant enters any cracks by capillary action. After allowing a short interval for penetration, the penetrant is removed from the surface. A white developer fluid is then applied to the surface. This has a blotting-paper action, drawing penetrant from any cracks so that a red blush appears on the surface to indicate the defect. Figure 177 shows the aerosol spray can of the cleaner, penetrant, and developer.

Fluorescent penetrants may also be employed. Here a fluorescent dye replaces the red dye. The method of application is the same as before. Disclosure of flaws is made by illuminating the surface with a mercury bulb producing ultraviolet "black light" which causes the penetrant dye to fluoresce.

17.9 magnetic particle inspection

This NDT method is restricted to ferromagnetic materials which conduct electricity. The method will disclose surface cracks, and has some capacity also for disclosing subsurface cracks close to the surface. The workpiece is magnetized with a powerful magnetic field. Then a thin layer of magnetic powder is sprinkled on the surface. If there is a small crack, the magnetic field establishes a north pole on one side of the crack and a south pole

Fig. 178 Magnetic particle inspection of an engine block.

on the other. The magnetic powder is attracted to these magnetic poles and marks the crack.

The magnetic field requires a high-current low-voltage transformer, which may be a magnetic particle transformer (Fig. 178) or a welding transformer.

Electric resistance testing uses the principle that a part with a crack or other defect will have a higher resistance than a part without such a defect. The electric resistance method is also used as a check on metallurgical purity, since small amounts of alloying impurities have pronounced effects on specific resistance. Poorly brazed joints, faulty spot welds, laminations in rolled sheet, and other such defects have been checked with electric resistance methods.

17.10 eddy current testing

Most eddy current testing installations are production-line installations for high speed testing of products of uniform cross-section, such as tubing, rod, and nuclear fuel rods, but the method is by no means restricted to production work.

If an alternating-current coil is positioned close to, or around, a workpiece, eddy currents are induced in the workpiece. A search coil, also called a pickup coil, positioned close to the workpiece will have its impedance affected by the induced eddy currents. Any defect in the work-

Fig. 179 (a) Exciting and search coil-layout for eddy current testing.

Fig. 179 (b) Automatic eddy current flaw detection instrumentation, to which the search coil is connected. (Budd Instruments #600 eddy current tester)

piece will distort the induced currents in the workpiece and can be "read" out by the pickup coil into suitable circuitry to a current meter or other device. An arrangement of an eddy current device is shown in Fig. 179.

The induced eddy currents in the specimen will be influenced not only by cracks and other defects, but also by the following:

1. the ends of the workpiece
2. variations in the magnetic permeability of the workpiece
3. variations in diameter of the workpiece
4. variations in the spacing between exciting coil and the workpiece
5. variations in grain size of the workpiece
6. frequency variations of the exciting coil
7. current variations of the exciting coil
8. variations in specific resistance of the workpiece
9. variations in alloy content and segregation in the workpiece
10. variations in hardness of the workpiece (affecting the permeability)
11. variations in the heat treatment of the workpiece (affecting the permeability)

The first problem to be dealt with is the fact that the eddy current instrumentation will tend to examine for all defects and variations, relevant or irrelevant: it will write a complete medical case history instead of concentrating on the disease being investigated. If the workpiece is of mild steel, random variations in the ferromagnetic permeability may be so large as to mask completely the defects sought. Therefore the eddy current instrument coils and the applied frequency must be designed to disclose the defects or variations of interest and to ignore those variations that are not of interest. It may be necessary to decrease the effective permeability of ferrous metals to avoid reading out the large variations in this property; this can be done by magnetic saturation of the workpiece with a d-c coil, so that the ferrous workpiece is presented to the exciting coil as a virtually paramagnetic material with a permeability equal to 1.

The eddy currents induced in the specimen are concentrated near the surface due to the "skin effect" of alternating current. The current decays with depth in the workpiece according to the exponential decay law that governs so many phenomena in the field of mechanical engineering:

$$I = I_0 e^{-kt}$$

where I = current at depth t
I_0 = current at the surface
k = a constant determined by the electrical characteristics of the workpiece.

If surface flaws are to be detected, a high frequency is required to avoid reading out subsurface defects or variations in internal diameter of tubing.

Because of these complications and other considerations, the design of an eddy current testing system may have to fit a specific installation in order to read out only that defect information that is pertinent. The design may have to be tested and calibrated with specimens containing known defects.

Eddy current testers are suited to a surprising range of duties. Among the jobs they are successfully performing are these:

1. detection of defects as shallow as 0.005 in.
2. separation of magnetic from paramagnetic stainless steel
3. measurement of electrical conductivity
4. detection of alloy variations
5. detection of hardness variations
6. separation of the parts of a structure that have been damaged by fire from those that have not
7. detection of grain size variations in metals
8. determination of the thickness of surface coatings on metals
9. detection of carbide precipitation in stainless steels
10. determination of sheet thickness

17.11 ultrasonic flaw detection

Ultrasonics is the science of acoustic energy at or above 20,000 cycles per second. For flaw detection purposes, frequencies between 1 and 10 mega-cycles are employed. The smallest defect that can be discovered is of the same order of magnitude as the length of the acoustic wave used. Hence the use of very short wave acoustic energy, as in the following example.

What is the approximate size of the smallest defect that can be detected in a stainless steel 304 plate by ultrasonic testing at 2.25 megacycles? Assume that this minimum defect has the same length as the acoustic wave. The velocity of sound in stainless steel 304 is 226,000 in. per sec at 70°.

$$\text{Frequency} \times \text{wavelength} = 226,000$$

$$\text{Wavelength} = 0.1 \text{ in.}$$

Actually a defect somewhat smaller than 0.1 inch can readily be discovered under these conditions.

Figure 55 (p. 117) shows the method of ultrasonic flaw detection. A frequency generator produces high frequency alternating voltage, which is impressed across a piezoelectric crystal. The crystal transducer is shown under the hand of the operator. The acoustic beam is produced by the transducer and fired into the workpiece. An echo will be returned to the transducer by any defect. The transducer converts the echo acoustic energy back into electric energy, and the defect is disclosed as a trace on the oscilloscope. The method is therefore a kind of acoustic radar.

Three types of acoustic waves are used in ultrasonic testing: longitudinal waves, shear waves, and surface waves. These are illustrated in Fig. 180. In the case of the longitudinal wave, the acoustic vibrations are axial to the path of the acoustic beam. For a shear wave, the vibrations are at right angles to the axis of the beam. Surface waves must be used

Fig. 180 Longitudinal, shear, and surface wave flaw detection. The piezoelectric transducer can listen for the echo from the flaw, or two transducers may be used, one to transmit and one to receive.

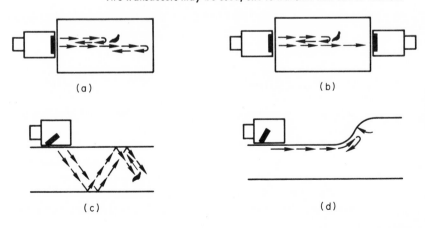

(a)

(b)

(c)

(d)

on thin sheet, and the motion of the vibrating particles is more complex, somewhat like the circular motion of a particle of water in a wavy sea.

Ultrasonic testing requires a degree of skill, particularly in interpreting the echoes that appear on the scope. It is quite easy to get traces on the scope, especially with wrong adjustment of the control knobs of the instrument. In examining a butt weld for defects, there will usually be two traces at least on the scope. The left-hand trace is the reference trace, and is thought of as representing the top surface of the workpiece in contact with the transducer. There will be an echo off the bottom of the welded plate also, and this will appear to the right of the first trace on the scope. The distance between the two traces represents the thickness of the workpiece. A flaw will give a trace between the first two traces, its distance from them indicating the depth of the flaw.

17.12 radiography

Radiography is a photographic method. The X-ray film is a special blue-sensitive photographic film with an emulsion on both sides, since X rays can readily penetrate the film. X-ray film costs far less than camera film and is used in much larger quantities.

The work being examined is irradiated with either an X-ray tube or a radioactive source in a gamma camera. A gamma camera is shown in Fig. 11 (p. 33). The photographic technique depends upon *differences in absorption* of the X rays to disclose defects. The absorptivity of materials for X-radiation improves with lower energy (i.e., longer wavelength, or lower voltage) radiation. Therefore the lowest useful X-ray voltage will be used for best disclosure of defects. For aluminum and other light metals, voltages of 50–100 kv are employed; for steel up to 0.75 in. thick, 150–300 kv or Iridium-192; and for thick steel, Cobalt-60 rather than X rays. The result is a shadowgraph. A blowhole or other porosity will result in less absorption, giving an increased blackening of the film. The photographic negative is always used, but a positive contact print may be taken from it. Figure 17 (p. 42) is a radiograph of an aircraft magnesium casting. The blowholes in the casting and the steel insert in the middle of the casting can be seen.

The exposure for ordinary photography is expressed in seconds. For radiography, exposures are given in milliamp-minutes (mam) or curie-minutes, since the amount of radiation produced is proportional to the product of tube current and time. The inverse square law applies to X-radiation as well as to light; therefore if the tube-to-film distance is doubled, the exposure mam must be quadrupled.

The production of a radiograph does not automatically guarantee that defects will be disclosed. To check that a radiographic technique suitable

Fig. 181 A penetrameter or artificial defect for radiography. The penetrameter is placed on the workpiece to be radiographed and the resulting radiograph must disclose the penetrameter and its three holes. The "FE 50" designates this penetrameter as suited to the radiography of steel 0.50 in. thick.

for disclosure of defects has been employed, an artificial defect is added to the workpiece. This artificial defect is called a penetrameter (Fig. 181). The penetrameter is a small piece of sheet metal, of the same material as the workpiece, but 2 percent of its thickness. If the radiograph shows the penetrameter, then the radiographic technique must disclose any other defects which are as small as 2 percent of the workpiece thickness.

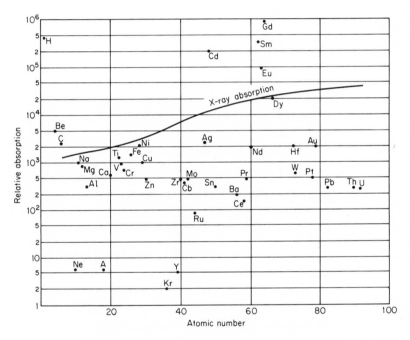

Fig. 182 Relative absorption of X-radiation and of neutrons by elements.

Absorption of X-radiation by elemental materials is almost exactly proportional to atomic number, as indicated by the graph of Fig. 182. The absorption coefficient covers a range of about 50 to 1 for all elements. The X-ray method will differentiate between aluminum and tin but cannot distinguish nickel from copper by absorption. Radiography may also be performed with slow neutrons. Note from Fig. 182 that the absorption of neutrons is highly irregular, and does not seem to follow any immediately apparent rule. Nickel and copper can be distinguished by their differences in neutron absorption (2 to 1 respectively). Also, the light elements H, B, Li, C, Cl absorb neutrons strongly, but have very limited absorption for X rays. Thus X-raying an automobile tire for disclosure of the tire cords is exceedingly difficult, but could be done with slow neutrons. The data in the figure are results for slow neutrons; high energy neutrons show smaller differences in absorptivity, just as do high energy X rays.

Neutrons have little effect on photographic film. Neutron radiography can be carried out with X-ray film by the use of a fluorescent screen behind the film, by allowing the neutrons to activate the phosphor on the screen. The phosphor exposes the film.

PROBLEMS

1 State the electrical characteristics of flames, including the relationship of flame resistance to flame temperature.

2 Why are wet test-tube methods of chemical analysis in general not practical in such primary industries as cement and steel?

3 The K electron level in hafnium corresponds to −65.0 Kev. The Kα and Kβ characteristic emission lines for hafnium correspond to 0.227 A and 0.196 A respectively. Determine the L and M energy levels in this element.

4 The K level in barium corresponds to −37.3 Kev, with Kα and Kβ emissions of 0.39 and 0.34 A respectively. Determine the L and M levels in this element.

5 Explain the principle of operation of the X-ray spectroscope.

6 Could the elastic stress-strain behavior of a metal be determined by X-ray methods?

7 Suppose a metal deforms plastically by slip. Can its plastic deformation be determined by X-ray methods?

8 Strains are being determined with an electric resistance strain gauge wired to a strain indicator. The strain indicator cannot register a strain smaller than 0.000003 in./in. The strain gauge has a nominal resistance of 120.0 ohms and a gauge factor of 2.08. What is the change in resistance for a strain of 0.000003 in./in.?

9 What is a residual stress?

10 The usual production sequence in the making of a forming die is machining, heat-treating, grinding. The ideal method would be heat-treating, machining, grinding. Why is the second sequence preferred?

11 Explain the principle of eddy current, magnetic particle, and dye penetrant inspection.

analysis and testing
418

12 Why is it necessary sometimes to saturate a steel part before subjecting it to eddy current inspection?

13 Why are high acoustic frequencies necessary for ultrasonic flaw detection?

14 What is the purpose of a penetrameter in radiography?

15 What is the principal advantage and disadvantage of neutron radiography as compared with gamma radiography?

18.1 materials and their market

The last group of material characteristics we shall discuss are the economic ones. Although they are placed last for reasons of organization, they are ultimately the most important ones. Indeed, all material characteristics are economic characteristics. The excellent specific resistance of pure copper has only a limited economic value; if copper were to double in price, probably most electrical conductors would be made of aluminum.

It is interesting to note the high value at which the market rates some properties and the low value applied to others. Relatively little economic value is attached to a high modulus of elasticity, for example. The high E-value of tungsten probably has a trivial economic significance to the broad field of engineering generally; the low E-value of the thermoplastics is accepted. A far higher value is given, for example, to surface appearance. Stainless steel costs about ten times as much as painted steel, yet in many products where a painted steel might be acceptable, a stainless steel is substituted, as in the mail receptable of Fig. 183. The attractive appearance of the plastics vastly overweighs their poor dimensional stability. The predominant market importance of appearance is best illustrated by the use of whitewall tires on cars; such tires contribute no useful function whatever to the automobile and have only two characteristics to recommend them: they are more expensive and people buy them. The latter

ECONOMIC CHARACTERISTICS OF MATERIALS

18

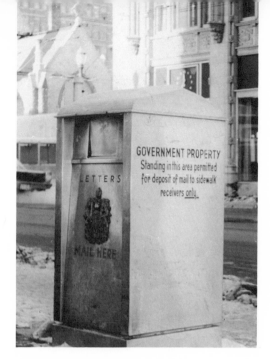

Fig. 183 Mail receptacle made of stainless steel.

characteristic of market acceptance cannot be safely ignored merely because it satisfies no scientific or engineering criteria. Even scientists who feel that marketing considerations are no part of their lofty calling have bought whitewall tires.

Of more immediate economic importance are such processing characteristics as machinability and weldability. Such characteristics, when properly employed, have the effect of reducing processing time, labor and overhead costs. There remain to be considered a few other economic characteristics.

18.2 specific weight

Specific weight means the weight of a material in pounds per cubic foot. Low specific weight is becoming an increasingly desirable characteristic, as illustrated by the following examples: the use of aluminum in transport vehicles and ship superstructures, magnesium in material-handling equipment, beryllium in rocket components, and the substitution of plastics for metals in small machine and equipment housings. The advantages of low specific weight are numerous, including low dead weight, low freight costs, lighter crating, easier material-handling, lighter supporting structures.

A number of interesting analyses have been made of the cost of extra weight in transport vehicles. Mathematical analysis suggests that the financial saving resulting from the removal of each pound of dead weight from an aircraft with a service life of 10 years is $275. This of course assumes that the one-pound weight saving becomes 1 lb of revenue freight carried under average conditions. For highway trucks, calculations indicate a saving of $5.50 per lb. The dramatic case for such weight saving lies in aerospace rockets. On the average it costs about $20,000 to put 1 lb in orbit around the earth.

Miniaturization of components, as extensively practised in the electronics industry, exploits volume rather than weight. Transistors, silicon-controlled rectifiers, and printed circuitry have contributed notably to miniaturization. The industry now talks of microminiaturization of miniaturized components. To a lesser degree, other industries also miniaturize; high strength, low alloy steels are used in the construction industry to reduce structural sections in the pursuit of smaller weight and height of buildings. In the food industry, dehydration of foods performs the same function as electronic miniaturization.

18.3 various economic

characteristics

Corrosion resistance is certainly an economic factor for materials. This characteristic determines both the life and cost of the material and its maintenance costs. The final cost of a steel structure is increased because of the necessity for surface protection by paint, and allowance for regular repainting of such a structure must be made in annual budgets. Perhaps maintenance painting costs account for the use of stainless steel in the receptacle of Fig. 183.

Shelf life refers to the longest safe storage period for perishable materials. For foods, this may be only a few days. Photographic film is always supplied with a terminal date for development printed on the carton. Radioisotopes lose their activity by 50 percent every half-life.

Cost and availability are frequently related. Water is cheap because of its availability. So is iron ore, or clay. But in the case of manufactured articles, it is volume of sales which largely determines cost. Articles made one at a time, such as replacement parts made in a maintenance shop, are very expensive owing to the high labor content. But if the techniques of mass production can be applied to large production runs, the manufacturing cost often can be made astonishingly low. Working against this low production cost is the high marketing cost and advertising cost associated with volume production, for high-volume production with low cost requires a high-volume market to absorb the products.

18.4 fire and explosion hazard

Fire hazard is associated with a great many materials of industry: magnesium and zirconium dust, solvents, paints, fiberglass plastics, fuels, oxygen tanks, paper, molten metals, and others. Fire protection methods often add onerously to the cost of storing, handling, and processing such materials. Explosion-proof electrical systems may be required, which are expensive. Paint booths are expensive; so are large ventilating fans, as are safety-training, and enforcement of safety regulations, proper receptacles, fire equipment, fire insurance, accidents, workmen's compensation assessments, and lawsuits. The rapid development of materials technology continually opens up more possibilities of explosion and fire hazard if proper precautions are not foreseen.

18.5 toxicity

A vast number of materials have toxic potential. An even wider range of materials are toxic to certain individuals or produce allergies in individuals. Even seemingly innocuous materials such as firebrick mortar or machining oils may produce isolated cases of dermatitis.

The range of potentially toxic materials is surprisingly wide. Heated polyvinyl chloride may produce acid fumes. Freons may produce phosgene gas under adverse circumstances. Welders become temporarily ill if they breathe the zinc fumes when welding galvanized metal. Cadmium fumes are even more dangerous, especially since cadmium plating may be mistaken for zinc. Even copper and lead compounds present a possible hazard.

Perhaps the toxic hazards of beryllium and radioisotopes are best known. However, these materials are so dangerous that personnel will make a serious effort to observe safety regulations. In this respect less toxic materials may be more dangerous, for personnel may take chances with them. It should be no surprise that the safest of all industries (statistically) is the radiation industry: about 100,000 times more people are killed by automobiles than by radiation. Perhaps the only dangerous materials are those regarded as safe.

This chapter deals with the various shapes in which metal is supplied to the fabricator for conversion into finished products. Such shapes include metal sheet for forming, cold-drawn bars for machining, and plate for welding.

19.1   sheet and strip

The most useful of all shapes for conversion into products is a sheet or a strip of sheet metal. Sheet too is one of the cheapest shapes to buy since it can be produced continuously on high speed rolling mills. A sheet gives almost unlimited freedom of shape in forming operations, together with least weight, and can often be formed on simple and inexpensive equipment. Because of these advantages, a greater tonnage of metal is rolled into sheet and strip than into any other shape. Consider the variety of commodities that are formed from sheet:

curtain wall panels	hinges
table tops	camping trailers
roof decking	trowels
automobile bodies	band saw blades
automobile frames	nuclear fuel rods
automobile wheels	aircraft windows

SEMIFINISHED
PRODUCTS

19

Fig. 184 Display of electrical hardware formed from sheet metal.

file cabinets	ashtrays
kitchen sinks	domestic can openers
ventilating ducts	flashlight shells
fan blades	electric switch boxes
aircraft	bottle caps
belt conveyors	steel strapping
cigarettes	

Plain carbon steel sheet containing up to 0.30 percent carbon may be formed by drawing. Both hot- and cold-rolled sheet is used for drawing and forming, though hot-rolled sheet, having somewhat better ductility, is somewhat more formable. Hot-rolled sheet is not available in the thinnest gauges. Both rimmed and killed steels are used for sheet. Killed steels have superior drawing quality, but are expected to contain more surface defects than a rimmed steel.

Cold-rolled sheet and strip are available in several "tempers":

No. 1 or Hard Temper — very stiff, hard, and springy. This temper is used for flat work or slight deformation. R_B hardness may be 90 or more.

No. 2 or Half-Hard Temper — this sheet may be bent 90 degrees across the rolling direction to a radius of its own thickness. $R_B = 70$ to 85.

No. 3 or Quarter-Hard Temper — may be bent 180 degrees across the rolling direction to a radius of its own thickness. $R_B = 60$ to 75.

No. 4 or Skin-Rolled Temper — a soft and ductile sheet capable of deep drawing. It can be bent flat on itself. $R_B = 65$ max.

No. 5 or Dead-Soft Temper — this temper is used for the most difficult drawing operations. $R_B = 55$ or less.

Steel decking is made by corrugating steel sheets in 24-in. wide sections which interlock. These are used for roofing and subflooring of buildings.

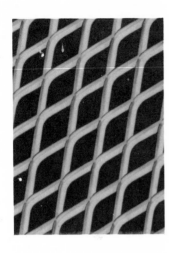

Fig. 185 Expanded metal mesh.

Expanded metal mesh (Fig. 185) has a wide range of uses in tote boxes, nonskid walkways and gratings, storage cabinets, partitions, ventilating screens, lockers, animal cages, etc. The usual method of designating such mesh is with two numbers, sometimes three. The first number is the size of the mesh, that is, the center-to-center distance of the diamond-shaped openings, measured the short way of the diamond. The second number designates the gauge of the metal. Thus $\frac{3}{16}$-22 is a light-weight mesh with small openings, while $1\frac{1}{2}$-12 is a very heavy mesh with $1\frac{1}{2} \times 3$-in. diamond openings.

Stainless steel sheet is available in the several 300 and 400 alloys. Several finishes of stainless sheet are available, designated No. 1 to No. 8. Two are more commonly used than the others:

No. 2B — cold-rolled, annealed, pickled in acid, then given a skin pass on polished rolls to produce a smooth, mildly reflective finish.
No. 4 — belt-ground with 150–180 grit abrasive to produce a polished finish.

The subject of gauge thicknesses is a matter of some confusion, since steel sheet, nonferrous sheet, and wire may use the same gauge numbers but have varying dimensions. Steel sheet uses the United States Standard Gauge (U.S.S.) while nonferrous sheets such as aluminum use the American or Brown and Sharpe gauge system (B & S).

semifinished products
426

Gauge No.	U.S.S. oz/sq ft	Thickness	B & S Thickness
10	5.625	0.1345	0.102
11	5.000	0.1195	0.091
12	4.375	0.1046	0.081
14	3.125	0.0747	0.064
16	2.500	0.0598	0.051
18	2.000	0.0478	0.040
20	1.500	0.0359	0.032
22	1.250	0.0299	0.025
24	1.000	0.0239	0.020
26	0.750	0.0179	0.016

The weights in ounces per square foot in this table are those for mild steel sheet. It will be noted that the U.S.S. system is based on weight of mild steel, not on thickness. The B & S system is based on thickness. Nonferrous sheets of any given gauge will be thinner than mild steel sheet of the same nominal gauge.

19.2 strapping

Nowadays materials are handled either in bulk or in unit loads. A *unit load* is a rigid arrangement of a number of items which can be handled as a single object by mechanized material-handling equipment such as lift trucks. For the unitizing of loads, strapping is often required (Fig. 186). For these and similar purposes various types of strapping are available in both steel and plastic. Some of the more important strapplications are these:

1. reinforcement of boxes and crates
2. closure of containers
3. baling of cloth, paper, and leather
4. securing of loads to wood pallets
5. bundling of rod, wire, and plastic pipe
6. securing of loads in railroad cars
7. tiering and stacking

The use of strapping requires a stretcher to tension the strap, and a sealer to make the joint in the strap with a strap seal.

Steel strap is available in coils, in widths from $\frac{1}{4}$ to $\frac{3}{4}$ in. or wider, in a black finish. Standard gauge thicknesses are not used with material-handling strap, strap thicknesses being 0.010, 0.012, 0.015, up to 0.028 in.

Fig. 186 A unit load of tires being compressed and strapped. (Machine and photo by Signode Corporation)

Such strap has a tensile strength of 100,000 psi and a controlled ductility. If the strap is not sufficiently ductile, it will snap when being pulled or bent around a sharp corner. Standard steel strap has an elongation of 1 percent.

Steel strap is not suitable for unit loads which compress, such as bagged bulk material. Such material will compact under the jolting received in transportation, and a ductility of 1 percent is insufficient to accommodate this shrinkage. For such service nylon or polypropylene strapping is superior. Plastic strap is $\frac{1}{2}$ in. wide, with an elongation of about 10 percent. If the unit load should shrink 5 percent, nylon strap would still confine the load, though not with the original tension set up in the strap. Plastic strap also does not present the housekeeping problem that steel strap does, since it can be incinerated.

19.3 plate

How thick must a sheet become to be called a "plate"? The answer to this question depends on a number of factors, including width of material, but roughly speaking, metal sheet which is $\frac{3}{16}$ in. or thicker over 48 in. wide, or

$\frac{1}{4}$ in. thick over 6 in. wide, is called "plate". Plate thickness may be specified either in fractions or in decimals. At the other extreme, sheet 0.005 in. or thinner is termed "foil".

For purposes of quick estimate, a convenient figure is the following: 1 sq ft of mild steel plate $\frac{1}{4}$ in. thick weighs 10.2 lb. From this information the weight of steel plate of any thickness or area can be quickly determined. The weight of aluminum plate can also be estimated from this figure, since aluminum is one-third the specific weight of steel.

Since about 1900 the standard specification for steel plate and rolled structural shapes has been ASTM Standard A7. In this specification the chemical composition of the steel was not given, except to restrict sulfur and phosphorus to 0.06 percent maximum. Carbon content was assumed to be 0.20 percent, but varied, since the steel mill adjusted the carbon content to obtain the required strength. The manganese content was similarly adjusted for ductility and ease of rolling, but ranged from 0.3 to 0.6 percent. As a result of these variations, the Charpy 15 ft-lb transition temperature varied from $-10°$ to perhaps $+100°F$. Minimum yield strength was 33,000 psi, ultimate strength 60,000 psi or higher, and elongation in 2 in. was 24 percent. Allowable stress for structural work in this steel was 20,000 psi.

Industry has abandoned A7 steel, for reasons of brittle fracture hazard, some difficulties in welding, and its poor strength-to-weight ratio. A7 steel is now superseded by ASTM A36.

A36 steel has the following chemistry: 0.28 percent carbon maximum, 0.05 percent sulfur maximum, 0.04 percent phosphorus maximum. Manganese content is increased in heavier sections to a maximum of 1.20 percent. (While carbon promotes the brittle fracture tendency, manganese improves brittle fracture performance.) Mechanical properties of A36 steel are:

yield strength 36,000 psi minimum
ultimate tensile strength 60,000–80,000 psi
elongation in 2 in., 23%

A36 steel costs about 3 percent more than A7 steel, but offers a yield strength and an allowable strength (22,000 psi) 10 percent greater.

19.4 structurals

Structural shapes are rolled in many standard sizes. In addition, certain mills roll special sizes. The usual shapes are wide flange (WF) beams, channels, angles, tees, zeds, and bulb angles. These shapes are produced by rolling, if made of steel, and by extrusion if made of nonferrous metals such as aluminum. The extrusion process permits much greater latitude in the shapes that can be produced.

The usual method of designating a steel structural shape is by two numbers designating the principal dimension (depth) and the weight per lineal foot. Thus 16WF78 indicates a WF shape approximately 16 in. deep (actually $16\frac{3}{8}$ in.) and 78 lb per lineal foot. It is usual to specify angles by the length of the two legs and the thickness: thus $2 \times 2 \times \frac{1}{8}$, $6 \times 4 \times \frac{1}{2}$, etc.

The largest of the steel shapes is a WF beam 36×300 lb. Larger beams are made by welding plate together into a wide flange section. The largest of the extruded aluminum shapes is a 12-in. I beam 0.437 in. thick weighing 15.44 lb per ft.

19.5 wire, rod, and bar

These three products are similar. In general, wire is considered to be any solid section with no cross-sectional dimension exceeding $\frac{1}{4}$ in. The term "rod" means a circular cross-section. A bar has a noncircular cross-section, such as hexagonal or square. Tube is hollow rod.

For concrete work, reinforcing bar (rebar) sizes are designated by a number which is the number of eighths of an inch in the nominal diameter. Thus a #5 bar has a diameter of $\frac{5}{8}$ in. The range of sizes is from 3 to 11. Either plain rod bars may be used, or deformed bars, the latter having two longitudinal raised beads and also circumferential beads. Three strength grades are used: 55,000, 70,000, and 80,000 psi ultimate strength. The carbon content controls the strength. Structural grade rebar contains about 0.20 percent carbon, intermediate grade 0.30–0.45 percent, and hard grade 0.45–0.60 percent carbon.

Since rebar must frequently be bent to follow the stress contours of reinforced concrete, ductility is a matter of concern. Required elongation is of course much less for the hard grade of bar than for the other two grades.

While 20 ft is the standard length for most bars, pipe, and tubing, bars for machine shop work are furnished in 12-ft lengths. This shorter length is more convenient for feeding through the spindle of an automatic or turret lathe. Machining bars are usually cold-finished to rather close tolerances, the cold-finishing operation making the surface of the bar slightly harder and easier to machine. Stainless steel machining bar is commonly furnished in the HRAP condition, that is, hot-rolled, annealed, and pickled.

Wire for welding filler metal is supplied either in coils for automatic welding or in short straight lengths for manual welding. Rods for the manual arc welding of mild steel have a mild steel composition of approximately 0.1 percent carbon. They are available with different flux coatings to provide different welding characteristics. Thus E6010 and E6011 rods have a flux coating that includes cellulose. The hydrogen in this coating provides an arc which penetrates deeply into the weld area. Hydrogen, being an interstitial element in steels, promotes brittleness. If this embrittling effect is to be avoided, low hydrogen electrodes are used, usually E7018 for mild steels and low alloy structural steels. Low hydrogen electrodes contain a lime or a rutile flux coating. Welding rods for the welding of stainless steels are always of the low hydrogen type.

The American Welding Society and the American Society for Testing and Materials use a four-digit number system for classifying manual arc welding rods. Taking E6011 rods for an example, the letter E signifies a rod for electric arc welding. The first two digits, 60xx, indicate the minimum ultimate tensile strength of the welding wire in thousands of psi, or 60,000 psi minimum. The third digit, xxlx, indicates the welding positions for which the rod is suited. A "1" indicates a fast-freezing rod that may be used in all positions, flat, horizontal, vertical, or overhead. A "2" indicates a rod suited only to flat and horizontal welding. The last digit does not indicate any single item of information, and will not be discussed here because of its complexity.

Hence an E6011 rod will provide 60,000 psi and may be used in any welding position. A 7018 rod has a minimum tensile strength of 70,000 psi and may be used in all positions. A 6024 rod is used for flat or horizontal welding seams, such as horizontal fillet welds.

For production welding, spooled wire is automatically fed into the arc. Wire diameters of 0.030 to 0.062 in. are the usual sizes for factory welding operations, although heavier wire may be used where heavy deposition rates are required on thick plate.

19.7 forged rings

Probably the most reliable type of machine part for conditions of high stress is a forging. In a forging, the direction of the grain can be controlled during the forging operation to suit the stress condition, i.e., the anisotropy can be suited to the stress direction. Further, during the forging operation the material can be homogenized and strengthened by plastic working.

Compared to a forging, a casting is not plastically worked, and the orientation of its grains is determined by the direction of heat flow in the material as it cools. Again, a machined part may be weak if the machined grooves cut across the direction of rolling of the raw material. Such heavily stressed articles as crane hooks, socket wrenches, and crescent wrenches are invariably forged.

Forged seamless rings are used as frames, stiffeners, and other machine parts in a wide range of equipment. For such rings the direction of grain flow must be specified. Three such directions are possible: *circumferential*, *radial*, and *axial*. See Fig. 187. A stiffener ring for a tank, rocket, or submarine would require a circumferential grain to resist hoop stresses. Rings with this grain direction are forged or compressed while being rotated on a supporting mandrel. On the other hand, if the ring is to be machined into a large-toothed gear ring, the grain direction should be parallel to the axis of symmetry of the gear tooth, that is, radial. Such a ring is usually termed a bored biscuit. Finally, the axial grain direction is provided by a bored and sliced multifaced round.

19.8   pipe and tube

It is not easy to differentiate between a pipe and a tube, particularly when both have the same cross-sectional dimensions. The major differences between the two may be rapidly summarized as follows:

1. **Raw material.**   Tubing is formed from coiled strip. Pipe is manufactured from coiled skelp, which is plate rolled to less rigorous specifications than tubing strip.

2. **Tolerances on dimensions.**   Most pipe specifications allow a variation in wall thickness of ± 12.5 percent. Most tubing specifications allow a maxi-

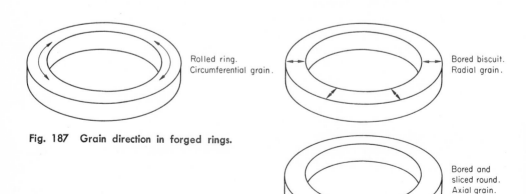

Rolled ring.
Circumferential grain.

Bored biscuit.
Radial grain.

Bored and
sliced round.
Axial grain.

Fig. 187   Grain direction in forged rings.

mum variation of ± 10 percent in wall thickness, and even closer tolerances may be called for.

3. Dimensions. In general, pipe has only one critical dimension: the outside dimension. The outside dimension does not correspond to the nominal diameter, and neither does the inside dimension. All pipe of the same nominal diameter, despite any variations in wall thickness, has the same outside diameter; this allows the use of standard pipe threading equipment, threaded pipe fittings, and standard threaded and welded flanges. Thus all 4-in. pipe measures 4.500 in. in outside diameter. Its inside diameter may be more or less than 4 in.

Tubing on the other hand has two critical dimensions. There are actually three dimensions to a tube: O.D., I.D., and wall thickness, but only two are specified, either O.D. and wall thickness or I.D. and wall thickness. The tolerance error falls on the third and unspecified dimension.

4. Finish. Mill scale is not usually removed from pipe. Tubing is usually furnished in an oiled, bright finish.

5. Method of manufacture. It is hardly possible to differentiate pipe from tubing by the method of manufacture. Most pipe, but not all pipe, is made by hot-forming, using pressure-welding methods for the longitudinal joint. Most tubing is cold-formed and welded by electric welding methods. But both pipe and tubing may be produced also by seamless methods.

Pipe is available in a wide range of materials and in several wall thicknesses. The most commonly used wall thicknesses are Schedule 40 and Schedule 80. Higher schedule numbers indicate heavier wall thickness. Schedule 40 is standard wall; Schedule 80 is about 50 percent thicker. Nominal pipe sizes range from $\frac{1}{8}$ inch to indefinitely large diameters.

SCHEDULE 40 AND 80 PIPE

Schedule 40 Nominal Size	O.D.	I.D.	Wall Thickness	Metal Area, sq in.	Schedule 80 I.D.	Wall Thickness
½	0.840	0.622	0.109	0.25	0.546	0.147
¾	1.050	0.824	0.113	0.33	0.742	0.154
1	1.315	1.049	0.133	0.49	0.957	0.179
1¼	1.660	1.380	0.140	0.67	1.28	0.191
1½	1.900	1.610	0.145	0.80	1.50	0.200
2	2.375	2.067	0.154	1.075	1.94	0.22
3	3.500	3.068	0.216	2.23	2.32	0.276
4	4.500	4.026	0.237	3.17	3.83	0.337
6	6.625	6.065	0.280	5.6	5.76	0.43

Fig. 188 Square tubing used as the frame of a sound control booth for Expo 67, Montreal.

Tubing is made in two principal types: mechanical and pressure tubing. Pressure tubing is used for such purposes as hydraulic cylinders. Mechanical tubing is general-purpose tubing. Both are produced to wall thicknesses ranging from 22-gauge to about 2 in. The weight of carbon steel tubing and pipe can be determined from the formula

$$W = 10.68(D - t)t \text{ pounds per lineal foot}$$

where D = O.D. in inches
t = wall thickness in inches

The versatility of tubing as a semifinished product is suggested by the following list of uses:

bar stock for machining	grease guns
roller bearing races	ink reservoirs for ball
boiler tubing	point pens
conveyor rollers	soldering irons
warehouse racking	chrome furniture
hydraulic cylinders	hypodermic needles
bicycle frames	wrist bars to hold straps
drive shafts	to wrist watches

The uses of tubing in automobiles include exhaust piping, steering column, gas tank filler tube, rear axle housings, tubular front axles, seat frames, drive shaft. This list is not complete.

semifinished products
434

Mild steel tubing is furnished in low carbon grades 1015, 1022, and 1025. Medium-carbon tubing is also available in 1030, 1035, 1040, and 1045 grades. Low alloy grades are used for higher stresses, such as 4140 for aircraft landing gear and engine mounts. The common grades of stainless tubing are used where good corrosion resistance, cleanliness, or appearance of stainless steel is desired. Nonferrous tubing is available in most metals, including the refractory metals tungsten, molybdenum, and tantalum. Finally, tubing is produced in square, hexagonal, oval, and other shapes.

When tubing is used as bar stock for machining operations, either seamless cold-finished or free-machining tubing is preferred. If the tubing is to be chucked to O.D., then O.D. and wall thickness are specified; if chucked to I.D., then I.D. must be specified. The required tube dimensions for machining stock are governed by the machining allowance and the allowances for eccentricity and other tolerances of the tube stock.

19.9 fasteners

Welding, brazing, soldering, and adhesive bonding produce permanent joints between components. Although some types of fasteners such as rivets are intended to produce a permanent joint (just as pressure-sensitive adhesives do not produce a permanent bond), where disassembly is to be expected, fastening devices will be used.

A *fastener* is defined in ASA B18.12-1962 (American Standards Association) as "a mechanical device for holding two or more bodies in definite positions with respect to each other". The number of types of fasteners is of course very large, mainly because many of the types are either developed for special purposes (such as aircraft bolts or track bolts), or are proprietary in their design. Most fasteners are bolts, nuts, washers, lock fasteners, staples, studs, dowels and pins, screws, or rivets.

Details on bolts, bolt heads, nuts, and washers are available from standard hardware catalogues. Special industries use special bolts. *Cap screws* are quality bolts machined all over to closely controlled dimensions. They are used in those applications where special care is required in making the joint. For example, tooling, jigs, and fixtures are made with great care and attention to detail, and socket-head cap screws are ordinarily used in this work. In structural bolting, high strength bolts are employed. These develop very high clamping pressures so that any racking of the joint will be resisted by high friction forces between the mating members. Expansion bolts are used to anchor to concrete. One type contains a lead tube: as a lag screw is screwed in, it forces the lead to deform against the hole drilled in the concrete.

Fig. 189 An air-conditioning unit during erection. This unit uses both welded and bolted joints for its assembly.

Self-locking fasteners are shake-proof, that is, they will not release or relax in service. These use interference fits or other methods of self-locking. One simple but ingenious method is to use a two-component epoxy, one component placed on the bolt thread and the other on the nut threads.

A screw may be almost any kind of externally threaded fastener, other than a bolt. Machine screws and cap screws are used in the same manner and functions as bolts. A set screw is threaded into one part and holds the other mating part by pressure of the end of the set screw against it. A tapping screw is intended to cut its own mating thread in the part or parts to be joined. Self-tapping screws are commonly used for joining sheet metal.

A rivet is a headed fastener on which an opposite head is formed after the rivet is inserted in the aligned holes of the mating parts.

PROBLEMS

1 For what reasons is sheet metal a preferred semifinished product for conversion into manufactured articles?

2 Why is 16-gauge aluminum sheet not the same thickness as 16-gauge steel sheet?

3 Estimate the weight of aluminum plate in a vertical cylindrical tank 30 ft in diameter and 27 ft high, using $\frac{1}{4}$-in. plate. Include bottom plates, roof plates, and wall plates.

4 Why is a forging superior to a casting or a machined part for carrying very high stresses?

5 Why do pipe and tubing of the same nominal size have different outside diameters?

6 Determine the weight of a lineal foot of 2-in. steel tubing with a 16-gauge wall.

7 Assuming that aluminum is one-third the specific weight of steel, determine the weight per lineal foot of a 3-in. O.D. aluminum tube with a $\frac{1}{4}$-in. wall.

20.1 material versus manufacturing cost

The properties of materials are evaluated in terms of their potential use in manufactured articles, finished or semifinished. The selection of a material for a specific product such as a gear wheel requires a compromise between material properties and the economics of using the material.

The cost of converting a material into a product involves two factors: the cost of the material and the cost of converting it. These combine to give the total manufactured cost of the article. This is not the price to the ultimate user of the article. The article must still be marketed, though marketing costs are not of concern here. By and large the methods of mass production are so efficient that the actual manufacturing cost for most common articles is surprisingly low and is quite often exceeded by the marketing costs. Manufacturing costs are low because articles are made many at a time, and marketing costs are necessarily high when most articles are sold one at a time.

The selection of a manufacturing method is a tangle of complex questions. Three of the more important considerations in this selection are the following.

First, the material itself may influence the manufacturing method.

THE CONVERTING
OF
MATERIALS

20

Polyethylene is too soft to machine, tungsten carbide can be machined only by grinding, cast iron cannot be forged, and beryllium cannot be deep-drawn.

Second, the number of parts to be produced determines the manufacturing method. If only 1 is to be made, it may be machined without special tooling. If 1000 are to be made, perhaps the part will be rotary-swaged. The longer the production run, the more complex the tooling and the manufacturing method will be. In mass production methods, tooling is used to replace the manipulative skills of highly trained craftsmen. The manufactured cost of the article is primarily determined by the number of parts in the production run. The cost of a single hole produced by a machinist on a drilling machine may be a dollar; the cost of 1000 holes produced on a punch press may be 100 dollars, or 10 cents a hole. Most of the latter cost is for tooling.

Third, there is no single method of making any article. Grooves may be formed by milling, broaching, slotting, shapering, extrusion, rotary-swaging, grinding, hot-forming, rolling, and other methods. Which is the cheapest method of making a groove? There is no general answer to such a question. The material to be grooved, the number of grooves to be made, the precision required, and other manifold considerations narrow the choice, but even so, two different manufacturing companies might arrive at two different decisions. Presumably both would be correct answers, for in the science of costs there is never a single correct answer.

20.2 manufacturing methods

Here we will be concerned with the secondary manufacturing industries and not the primary industries such as mining or paper-making. There is such a diversity of secondary manufacturing operations that it is impossible to discuss them without first reducing them to general types. While no doubt there are many possible ways to classify them, here we will say that there are only three basic manufacturing operations:

> shaping
> assembling
> finishing

A number of subsidiary operations must complete the manufacturing process, chiefly inspection, material handling, and heat-treating, but few of these add value to the manufactured product.

Each of these three basic operations may be further subdivided into two methods:

1. shaping	{ machining forming
2. assembling	{ welding fastening
3. finishing	{ surface treatment packaging

This chapter will be concerned with the ways that characteristics of materials influence the manufacturing processes. A proper discussion of the manufacturing methods themselves will not be attempted beyond a few clarifying remarks where appropriate. Fastening methods are not especially dependent on material characteristics, and will not be discussed. Surface treatments were discussed in Chapter 15, and will not be dealt with here.

The initial step in manufacturing is to produce the required shape in the several components of the finished article. The first approximation to the final shape is given by the semifinished product selected as raw material. Previous chapters have mentioned the two primary manufacturing methods that produce the initial product shape in metals: ingot casting and powder metallurgy.

Ingot casting is the cheaper method. The shape and size of the ingot will in part be dictated by the shape of the semifinished product into which it will be rolled, but the ingot also must be designed to produce quality metal during solidification, and considerations such as resulting grain size and shrinkage also govern. Those metals which cannot be conveniently melted, such as tungsten, or which do not solidify into suitable ingots, such as beryllium, must be formed by the methods of powder metallurgy. In the powder metallurgy process the metal powder is compressed in a die under heavy pressure, then sintered in a reducing atmosphere.

Secondary manufacturing thus proceeds from an ingot through a semifinished product to the shaping of the final product. Sometimes the final product is a casting, such as a die-cast automobile carburetor, a cast iron machine base, a compression-molded Bakelite part, or a concrete beam. Metal manufacturing would be simpler if all products or their components could be cast to final shape in the primary metal mill. This is not possible for a multitude of reasons, mostly of a technical nature. In Sec. 19.7 the importance of grain direction was mentioned. Castings lack controlled grain direction. They also lack the controlled and fine grain size that only rolling, forging and related operations can supply. Since castings must cool through many hundreds of degrees, there is considerable shrinkage in a casting. This shrinkage will not be uniform in a casting of complex shape, since one part of the casting will restrain the shrinkage of another part. Such restraints also produce warping. Dimensional accuracy in castings cannot be held to the close tolerances required in most articles. Other casting difficulties that call for secondary operations are gas evolution, oxidation, and nonuniform segregation of alloy ingredients. However, powder metallurgy avoids these difficulties and can produce parts to accuracies as close as 0.001 in. Such dimensional consistency is sufficient for a great many manufactured components.

20.3 *machining*

Machining is a sculpturing operation in which the final shape is produced by removing material from the raw stock in the form of chips. Usually a hard tool sharpened to a cutting edge is used for chip-making, as in the operations of milling and grinding, though in electric discharge machining, high-frequency pulses of electric power from an electrode are used to remove metal by spark erosion. Machining is a process suited to either ductile or brittle materials, but preferably the latter type if cutter bits are used. Very soft materials are not machinable by orthodox methods: very hard materials may be machined by sintered carbide or diamond cutters, or by electric discharge machining.

In an ideal economic system, machining would be an inadmissible method of producing a shape. The converting of useful raw material into scrap chips is basically unacceptable, especially if the supply of the raw material is limited. Nevertheless, the extensive machining done in secondary manufacturing operations indicates that in the present state of production technology, machining is a competitive method of shaping. Compared to most forming methods, it is not a complex operation to set up, and the basic machinery is not usually expensive. But as the quality and hence the cost of raw materials increase in the future, and forming operations such as forging receive more attention than they have heretofore, it is to be expected that machining will decline in importance.

Machining has the further limitation that it is often slow. Only so many cubic inches of volume can be shaped per unit of time if material must be reduced to chips. Forming methods are often less restricted in this regard. However, forming methods have limitations in the precision with which they can be executed. The required precision may have to be supplied by a terminal machining operation. Machining has virtually no limitations in its precision, and accuracy of a millionth of an inch is possible.

The enigmatic property of machinability has been discussed earlier, and the free-machining grades of metals have received attention in the chapters on metals. The question of when to use, and when not to use, free-machining bar stock can be a complex problem in financial mathematics. If the bar must be converted entirely into chips, then obviously a free-machining bar would be used. But only a part of the bar is converted

Fig. 190 The Gorton Tapemaster, a numerically controlled, vertical spindle milling machine. The machining cycle is automatically executed in accordance with instructions to the machine punched into paper tape. The control cabinet on the right reads the holes in the punched tape and controls the movements of the machine.

into chips, although the whole bar is free-machining, and bought at free-machining prices. Justification for paying the premium for free-machining quality is based chiefly on two factors: the amount of the bar converted into chips and the length of the production run.

Consider the production of 100,000 hose couplings on a four-spindle automatic lathe. Such a lathe is in effect four lathe spindles mounted on one machine bed, all cutting simultaneously, each doing one-fourth of the machining on each part. Suppose the overhead charge for this lathe is $10.00 per hr. This is very nearly $\frac{1}{4}$ of a cent per sec. Suppose also that by the use of free-machining stock 1 sec can be saved in the machining of each coupling. Then $\frac{1}{4}$ of a cent is saved. If the free-machining premium is $\frac{1}{8}$ of a cent per part, then the use of free-machining bar has saved $50 in overhead charges alone, taken over the production of 100,000 parts.

In machining with cutter bits, the angles to which the bit is sharpened must be suited to the material being machined. The material especially influences the *back rake angle* on lathe cutter bits (Fig. 191). A sharp or positive back rake will tend to pull the tool into the material and will reduce

Fig. 191 Negative and positive back-rake of a lathe tool.

the cutting forces and power involved, thus making for easier machining. A blunt or negative back rake will tend to pull the tool out of the material, and will increase the cutting force and power. The back rake angle is exploited for various purposes in machining. In the machining of brass, a positive back rake may pull the tool too deep into the work in a sudden hogging cut which will ruin the workpiece. A negative rake therefore is used with this material. Particularly with plastics, too great a positive rake will cause the tool to deform the work upward and will produce an undersized part. But a sharp positive rake must be used in machining rubber, because the higher cutting force of a negative rake will cause the rubber to deform elastically and then return to an oversize dimension behind the cutting edge.

The heat generated during machining may be a controlling factor in the machining process. A burnishing tool may be used to produce a smooth finish on steel, but such an operation may melt the surface of a thermoplastic.

Heat generation is a factor in the machining of stainless steels. These alloys have a low thermal conductivity and therefore heat is retained in the region of the tool point. Tool life is then shortened. The austenitic stainless steels are easily work-hardened, and machining operations must limit this tendency. Shallow cuts are avoided. A deep cut will get underneath the work-hardened layer.

It is not possible to produce a hole of an exact diameter by drilling. Since drills cannot be sharpened to absolute accuracy, a drill will produce a hole several thousandths of an inch larger than the diameter of the drill when drilling in metals. In the case of thermoplastics, the hole is likely to be smaller than the drill size, because of elastic recovery of the material after the drilling operation. Accuracy is obtained by first drilling an undersized hole, then opening the hole to the required size either by reaming or boring.

Grinding is a machining operation in which abrasive grains serve as the cutting tools. Since the abrasive grain is very small, the grinding chip is much smaller than a machining chip. Since grinding reduces stock to smaller chips, considerably more power is required to remove a cubic inch of metal by grinding as compared to tool-point machining. Economics dictates that rough machining be done first, leaving grinding for the finishing

the converting of materials

cut. Extremely hard materials, however, are machined only by grinding methods.

Grinding methods permit considerably greater precision and smoothness than tool-point machining. A tolerance of ±0.0005 in. is about the best obtainable in tool-point machining. Grinding methods can obtain ±0.00005 in. or better.

20.4 forming

Forming includes all those shaping methods that use a combination of force and tooling or dies to displace material into the final shape. Most manufactured articles are made by forming methods. The bulk of metal and plastic production goes into sheet: all sheet is formed. A casting is made by using the force of gravity to fill a sand mold with molten metal. A sheet-metal ashtray is formed by shallow-drawing the sheet between matching dies.

Compared to machining, forming methods usually require some elaboration in their tooling and set-up, and only a few forming methods are suited to the making of one of a kind or very short production runs, as machining is. To illustrate, consider the forming of a hexagonal head on a bolt. The cost of a heading die for this purpose is in the hundreds of dollars. If only a few bolts are to be headed, this expense can be circumvented by machining the bolt head and bolt shank out of bar stock. But if bolts are to be produced by the thousands, machining is too slow and expensive, and the heads will be cold-formed (and will be superior in strength).

In the production of threads on a bolt, again machining and forming are in competition. The threads may be machined with a threading die,

Fig. 192 Micrograph showing the grain flow lines produced by cold-heading operation of forming the head of a bolt.

or they may be rolled into the bolt blank. Often thread-rolling is the cheaper method. Smaller diameter stock is used, since the thread-rolling dies roll material out of the valleys to make the hills. Further, the work-hardening effect of the rolling operation produces a stronger bolt thread.

The cup test for formability was discussed in Chapter 9. Cup tests determine the formability of sheet metal for deep-drawing operations. Many types of sheet have insufficient ductility to be drawn, such as 2024 aluminum in hard temper, or beryllium sheet. It would appear that the forming possibilities offered by any material would be determined by its ductility. If this is true, then forming operations are limited to materials of adequate ductility, whereas machining is not thus limited, since any material may be machined. Firebrick, concrete, and cast iron are virtually unformable unless molten. Actually, recent studies suggest that no material is completely unformable, though certain types of forming operations may not be possible on some materials.

At least two methods are available for the forming of brittle materials: extrusion, and high-energy-rate forming.

In the extrusion process, the material, hot or cold, is subjected to high "hydrostatic" pressure (pressure on all surfaces) and forced out through a die aperture of the required shape. In principle at least, any material may be formed by extrusion. It is reported that marble has been extruded in laboratory work. Extrusion is the most suitable forming method for the problem metal beryllium.

In high-energy-rate forming methods, brittle materials are blasted into final shape with intense and instantaneous force. The easiest of such methods to explain is explosive-forming. In explosive-forming the material is positioned over a die, and blasted into the die with an explosive charge. Several other methods are also in use. A homely definition of high-energy-rate forming is "the forming of metal before it knows what happened to it".

The many methods of forming can be grouped into four classifications, according to the type of force applied: compression, tension, shear, and bending.

Compression Forming	Tension Forming	Shear Forming	Bend Forming
forging	wire drawing	shearing	flanging
swaging	tube expanding	notching	drawing
extrusion	flaring	punching	crimping
rolling	stretch forming	stamping	corrugating
coining	(stretching over dies)		folding
die casting			bending
injection molding			spinning

Compression forming methods are especially useful in the shaping of ceramics and plastics. Brick and concrete shapes are made by compression or casting in dies. The compression methods used with plastics include injection molding (thermoplastics), compression molding (thermosets), extrusion (thermoplastics). The blow-molding method of making plastic bottles and containers is a tension method. Air pressure expands the plastic against a die.

Metals may be *hot-formed* or *cold-formed*. Cold-forming reduces ductility and increases strength and hardness through strain-hardening. These effects are usually advantageous. The residual stresses resulting from cold-working are not usually desired, however. Hot-working means the forming of metal at a temperature above the recrystallization temperature for the metal. According to this definition, some low-melting metals may be hot-formed at room temperature. At hot-forming temperatures neither work-hardening nor residual stresses are produced by the operation.

20.5 welding

There are as many definitions of welding as there are people who define it. Here welding will mean the joining of components without the use of fastening devices, while fastening is joining by means of special hardware components. This definition would seem best adapted to more recent developments in the technology of welding and probable future developments. Such a definition must necessarily embrace the mortaring of brick in a wall, the gluing of plywood veneer, brazing, and soldering.

Most welding methods are fusion methods which melt the metal to be joined. Such welding methods are actually casting processes using the material as its own mold. But welding need not be performed by a fusion process; virtually any kind of energy can be used to produce a weld, including ultrasonic energy (ultrasonic welding), electromagnetic radiation (laser welding), friction (friction welding), or the energy in a beam of electrons (electron beam welding). However, in production work two types of welding are principally used, and only these two types will be discussed here: *MIG welding* and *electric resistance welding*. Both are fusion methods. These methods, together with adhesive bonding, constitute the welding methods used in assembling the modern automobile.

Metal-inert gas welding, or *MIG welding*, is an arc welding method, the arc being drawn between the end of a filler wire continuously fed into the arc, and the workpiece. Usually no flux is used, a flow of shielding gas from the welding gun being used to protect the metal from atmospheric gases. Carbon dioxide gas is used for this purpose when welding mild steel, and argon and helium for welding the more reactive metals such as aluminum, magnesium, and titanium. Currents of 100 to 300 amps are usual, with arc voltages of 20 to 30 v.

Fig. 193 Automatic MIG welding. These two photographs show the method of welding a steel plate to the end of a steel tube. The tube is rotated in a vertical position underneath the welding arc while continuous wire is fed from the welding gun. The operator does not operate the gun, its movements being under the control of the automatic cycle.

In the many methods of *electric resistance welding*, the welding heat is provided by passing a current through the workpiece, thus using the workpiece as its own electrical resistance. The commonest and simplest of these resistance welding methods is spot welding. In spot welding, two sheets or plates are lapped. One electrode contacts the surface of the bottom sheet, the other electrode being forced against the top sheet with considerable force in order to forge the weld. A heavy 60-cycle alternating current of 2 to 20 cycles duration passes from one electrode to the other through the overlapped sheets. Since the largest resistance in the path of the current is the contact area between the two sheets, the greatest heat is

the converting of materials
447

Fig. 194 A large resistance welder in an aircraft plant.

developed in this region, this heat concentration fusing the two sheets together in a small nugget of melted metal (Fig. 41 on p. 73). Typical currents for the process are in the range of 10,000 to 50,000 amps. The circuit resistance across the workpiece is of the order of 25 millionths of an ohm.

No production methods are sensitive to as many material properties as the welding methods, and only a few of these considerations will be discussed here.

Arc welding can be considered as a miniature version of the electric arc melting of metals, and has all the problems of this melting method. In the deposition of stainless steel welding wire, chromium has a tendency to oxidize. In arc melting, chromium lost to the slag can be recovered in a double-slagging practice; in arc welding the welding wire is enriched in chromium content to allow for such losses. Despite the speed of the melting operation during welding, carbide precipitation is a serious problem with the austenitic stainless steels. The methods of circumventing precipitation were outlined in Chapter 10. In many respects, however, stainless steels are not difficult to weld; these steels have a low thermal conductivity, which causes heat to be retained in the region of the weld (though this may be a cause of excessive grain growth). The high electrical resistance of the stainless steels makes them easy to spot-weld.

Aluminum is not an easy metal to weld. Its high coefficient of expansion causes it to warp during welding; even the making of a few spot welds will cause warping. The high thermal conductivity of aluminum makes it difficult to retain heat in the weld region and extra welding heat is needed to compensate for this conductive heat loss. This extra heat can be supplied by using helium as a shielding gas rather than argon. Helium produces a voltage drop across the arc that is about 30 percent larger than that for argon. Aluminum is especially difficult to spot-weld. Minute differences in the thickness of its oxide surface cause variations in spot weld strength and quality. Because of the negligible electrical resistance of aluminum and its high thermal conductivity, it can be spot-welded only by short pulses (as little as 2 cycles of 60-cycle power) of very high current, 30,000 amps or more.

Copper is almost an unweldable metal because of its very low electrical resistance and exceedingly high thermal conductivity. It cannot be spot-welded, and even MIG welding with helium gas is difficult.

Around the joint of a fusion weld there is a region where the metal has been brought to a high temperature below the melting point. This heated but unmelted region is referred to as the *heat-affected zone*. Here the metal will be heat-treated, but to no useful purpose. Such adverse effects as grain growth, excessive hardness, and cracking develop in this area. The cracking tendency in the heat-affected zone is measured as weldability, discussed in Sec. 9.18. Still another difficulty in the heat-affected zone is its tendency to collect hydrogen, especially in such metals as the hardenable steels and zirconium.

The problem of *dilution* in fusion welds often calls for special welding procedures. This problem arises because the composition of the filler wire does not usually correspond to the composition of the metal being welded. Each of these two metals therefore dilutes the concentration of alloys in the other to form a new alloy of fusion which does not necessarily contain suitable amounts of alloy ingredients. Dilution is inevitable, for example, if a mild steel sheet must be welded to a stainless 304 sheet with a stainless 308 welding wire. The methods of adhesive bonding, brazing, and soldering, all of which are conducted at temperatures below the melting point of the bonded metal, avoid the problems of dilution, the heat-affected zone, and grain growth.

From this brief discussion of some of the aspects of welding, it should be clear that welding raises problems not of welding technique (virtually any material can be welded), but of proper procedure, proper metallurgy, and metallurgical diagnosis. The present need in welding production is less for welding skill than for welding knowledge.

Fig. 195 Packaging is the last stage of the manufacturing cycle.
This illustration shows an automatic palletizing machine.

20.6 packaging

Most products are sold "FOB factory," and the production process therefore ends when the product is secured in place in the transport vehicle. At this time legal ownership of the manufactured goods is transferred from the manufacturing company to the buyer.

Packaging embraces all the operations of preparing the product for delivery to the buyer. These include the design of unit loads and their protective packaging, their handling, securing in place, and loading into transport vehicles. Even the loading pattern in the vehicle is the subject of elaborate study. Packaging is not necessarily a minor cost component of manufacturing. The cost of the corrugated carton to ship a five-dollar prefabricated chimney section may be a dollar, or 20 percent of the product cost. The value of the container of some types of consumer goods may exceed the value of the goods.

The material properties that govern the design of the packaging system are chiefly the economic ones of size, shape, weight, value, transport hazard, and fragility of the product, the mechanical properties of the packaging material, and the compatibility of the goods and the package. The design of packaging and material-handling systems adopts approaches to material properties that cannot be discussed at sufficient length here. For example, can acids and pineapple juice be safely shipped in paper cartons with plastic liners? (They can.) How high can such containers safely be stacked? Do they require palletization for shipment? The search for answers to such questions as these can be an investigation of surprising complexity, length, and cost. Packaging and material handling have become major engineering specialties within the materials sciences.

As a final comment, we may remark that psychological properties of materials may sometimes influence packaging, especially export packaging. For reasons unknown to the author, imported whisky meets with an undue incidence of accidents at some ports during stevedoring operations. Shipping whisky in steel containers has been tried, but since the oxyacetylene cutting torch has been invented, this turns out to be an unsatisfactory solution. Perhaps firebrick containers might be found suitable. Even in materials science, sometimes the proper study of mankind is man himself.

PROBLEMS

1 Why are shallow cuts avoided when machining austenitic stainless steels?

2 Why is dimensional accuracy better in powder metallurgy than in metal casting processes?

3 Why would a negative back rake angle be avoided in machining a heat-sensitive material?

4 How might thread-rolling provide a superior bolt to one threaded with a cutting tool?

5 Why is it possible to form by extrusion materials which are unformable by other methods?

6 Briefly describe the MIG welding process.

7 Why are the stainless steels easy to spot-weld?

8 What properties in a metal would contribute to ease of spot welding?

9 When is helium substituted for argon in the MIG welding process?

10 What is meant by dilution in fusion welds?

INDEX

WITHDRAWN

No longer the property of the
Boston Public Library.
Sale of this material benefits the Library